SS, JULY 4, 1776.

RATION

TATIVES OF THE

S OF AMERICA,

GRESS ASSEMBLED.

ry for one People to diffolve the Political Bands which have connected them
rth, the feparate and equal Station to which the Laws of Nature and of
ns of Mankind requires that they fhould declare the caufes which impel them

Men are created equal, that they are endowed by their Creator with certain
and the Purfuit of Happinefs—-That to fecure thefe Rights, Governments are
erned, that whenever any Form of Government becomes deftructive of thefe
new Government, laying its Foundation on fuch Principles, and organizing
and Happinefs. Prudence, indeed, will dictate that Governments long ef-
all Experience hath fhewn, that Mankind are more difpofed to fuffer, while
y are accuftomed. But when a long Train of Abufes and Ufurpations, purfu-
efpotifm, it is their Right, it is their Duty, to throw off fuch Government,
Sufferance of thefe Colonies; and fuch is now the Neceffity which conftrains
t King of Great-Britain is a Hiftory of repeated Injuries and Ufurpations, all
To prove this, let Facts be fubmitted to a candid World.
ublic Good.
tance, unlefs fufpended in their Operation till his Affent fhould be obtained;

People, unlefs thofe People would relinquifh the Right of Reprefentation in

diftant from the Depofitory of their public Records, for the fole Purpofe of

irmnefs his Invafions on the Rights of the People.
ected; whereby the Legiflative Powers, incapable of Annihilation, have re-
e expofed to all the Dangers of Invafion from without, and Convulfions within.
bftructing the Laws for Naturalization of Foreigners; refufing to pafs others
tions of Lands.
for eftablifhing Judiciary Powers.
es, and the Amount and Payment of their Salaries.
o harrafs our People, and eat out their Subftance.
fent of our Legiflatures.
Power.

MILESTONES!

200 Years of American Law

MILESTONES!

OXFORD UNIVERSITY PRESS New York/WEST PUBLISHING COMPANY St. Paul, Minn.

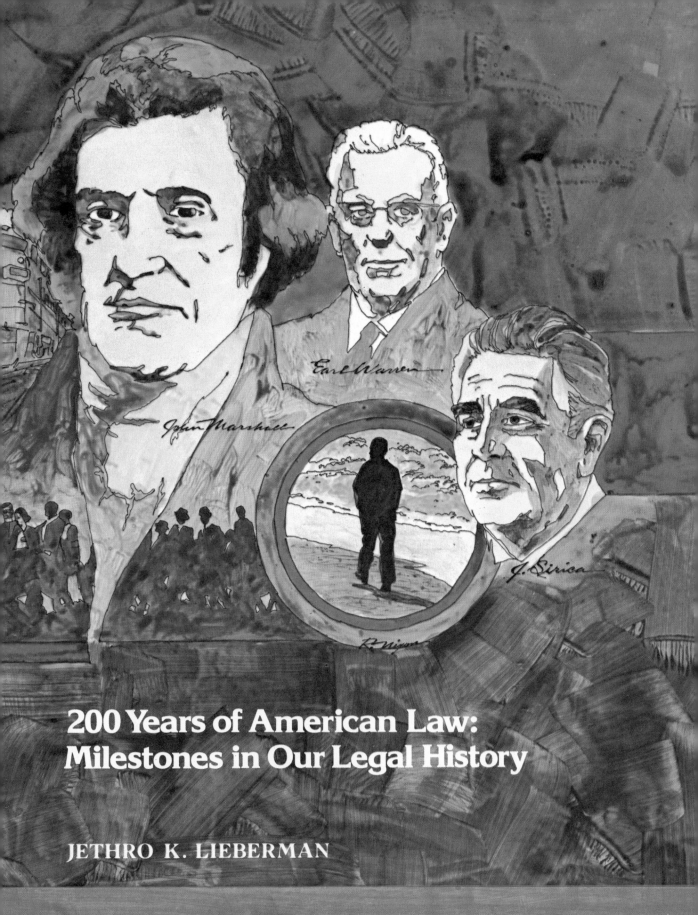

John Marshall

Earl Warren

J. Sirica

R. Nixon

200 Years of American Law: Milestones in Our Legal History

JETHRO K. LIEBERMAN

The "lost" Declaration of Independence is reproduced on the inside front and back end pages of this book. It is a copy of one of the original first printing done the night of July 4, 1776, by printer John Dunlap of Philadelphia. It bears no signatures, as does the more famous second authorized version which was handwritten on parchment and delivered on August 2. This "lost" copy was found in December 1968, in an old wooden box in Leary's Book Store in Philadelphia as it was going out of business after 132 years in the same building. The rare document was put up for bids on May 7, 1969, and Ira Corn, Jr., of Dallas, Texas, representing himself and Joseph P. Driscoll paid $404,000 for it, the highest price ever paid for a printed document. It is the only privately owned Dunlap printing.

Library of Congress Catalog Card Number: 76-5953

ISBN: 0-19-519881-6

Publisher's Foreword

What are the milestone events of the 200 years of American legal history? How did they evolve? What has been their meaning and influence? What about the individuals concerned in these events, the drama inherent in them, the contentiousness that surrounded them?

It would be fatuous to suggest that within the compass of a single book anyone can portray all of the important legal happenings of our history. And, quite naturally, there will be division of opinion, perhaps even emotional disagreement, about what should be included as the truly milestone events.

The publishers decided early that the task of making the determination on what would be surveyed within these pages could be best made by the members of the legal profession. Since members of the bench and bar are daily involved in the making and shaping of the laws of this country, they were the best judges of what this book should include.

Late in 1974, a tear-out ballot was tipped into the pages of the American Bar Association Journal along with an explanatory page inviting voting participation by the readers of that publication. They are lawyers, judges, law professors, and others who are members of the American Bar Association. They make up the bulk of the bench and bar of this nation. Theirs is one of the most respected of all of our national professional organizations.

The ABA members were informed about the plan to publish a book tentatively entitled, "Two Hundred Years of American Law: Milestones in Our Legal History." They were invited to vote on the milestones to be included. It was explained that the book was to be published in commemoration of the U.S. Bicentennial and the 100th anniversary of West Publishing Company as a law book publisher.

It was further stated that the eminence of the Declaration of Independence and the Constitution was conceded, and the voters were instructed not to include them on the ballot.

The milestones examined in the chapters to follow are those that received the highest number of votes in the balloting. There are eighteen and they span almost the entire 200 years of our history. Mr. Lieberman treats them chronologically, but their ranking according to number of votes received, is as follows:

1. Marbury v. Madison
2. Warren and Warren Court
3. U.S. v. Richard Nixon
4. Miranda Case
5. Brown v. Board of Education
6. Dred Scott Decision
7. Social Security Act
8. Dartmouth College Case
9. In Re Gault
10. Schechter Poultry Case
11. Baker v. Carr
12. Marshall and Marshall Court
13. Gideon v. Wainwright
14. Fourteenth Amendment
15. Erie v. Tompkins
16. Mapp v. Ohio
17. McCulloch v. Maryland
18. Roe v. Wade

The milestones which are listed above, and which are treated in the pages to come, were chosen by an eminently qualified constituency.

We thank and commend all who took part in the voting for their interest and cooperation.

Introduction

ALTHOUGH the American Revolution was confirmed by the inevitable bloodshed and sacrifice of war, it was conceived as a matter of legal right and born with lawyers acting as midwives. The Revolution was grounded solidly on claims of rights denied — rights the colonists contended were due them through the usages and customs of English law.

On July 2, 1776, when the Continental Congress adopted a resolution declaring that "these United Colonies are, and of right ought to be, free and independent states," the fateful corner was turned. But for weeks before, Thomas Jefferson, a Virginia lawyer who did not like the practice of law, had been at work on an explanation of the drastic act. An explanation of revolution? Only lawyers, who dominated the Continental Congress, could have considered this essential.

Two days later, on July 4, 1776, Jefferson's explanation, the Declaration of Independence, was adopted. That great document was not merely a renunciation of political allegiance to the crown, but a justification of the deed supported by a catalog of specific grievances. Such a reasoned justification was required, Jefferson wrote, by a "decent respect to the opinions of mankind..."

Lawyers remained a dominant force in the newly independent states and formed the nucleus of the Constitutional Convention of 1787. From then until today lawyers have contributed their talents not only to their profession and to the judicial branch of government, but to aspects of government at all levels — from President and Congress to mayor and city council.

It is altogether fitting, then, that the West Publishing Company, in observance of the nation's bicentennial and its own centennial, should ask American lawyers to select milestones in the first two hundred years of American history. West polled lawyers in 1975, and this book, in which Jethro K. Lieberman has woven the story of those two hundred years of legal history, is the result. It is not surprising, either, that the lawyers' selections center on pivotal cases decided by the United States Supreme Court and on significant periods of the Court's history.

Pre-eminent among the milestones is the Court's decision in 1803 in *Marbury* v. *Madison,* 1 Cranch 137, in which Chief Justice Marshall trenchantly established the doctrine of judicial review — a decision that made the United States Supreme Court a uniquely powerful governmental institution. That case became the bedrock on which the Court was able to stand in shaping the nation's legal history by the other milestones that gained votes in the polling.

As Mr. Lieberman recalls, Alexis de Tocqueville many years ago observed: "There is hardly a political question in the United States which does not sooner or later turn into a judicial one." One can attest the correctness of this comment today. Courts across the land issue orders and decisions binding high government officials to observe constitutions and laws as the courts interpret them, and most of the political thickets into which courts were once loath to enter have been cleared and are inhabited.

This should give all of us pause to consider the important role that lawyers play in the life of this nation and its people. Lawyers construct and conduct the cases that decide major points of law and policy for all citizens. In doing so they must be careful, competent and devoted to a spirit of commonwealth. An appreciation of their responsibility should be especially acute in lawyers themselves, for it is a truism that those to whom influence and power are accorded must account for their use of it.

This story of two hundred years of milestones — of lawyers on the bench and in the pit of litigation — is inspiring, but it should not end here in 1976. It needs to be impressed on future citizens and future lawyers. Our system of government is perhaps inherently no better devised for permanency than many others that have fallen, but it does give us the ability to adapt to change. In preserving and tending to the prosperity of this system, lawyers will play a leading role in creating the milestones that are to come.

Justin A. Stanley
President, American Bar Association, 1976-1977

Contents

Lawyer, working journalist and author of five previous books, Jethro K. Lieberman brings to "Milestones" impressive credentials in interpreting and popularizing the law.

As Legal Affairs Editor of Business Week Magazine, his day-to-day job is to relate and analyze the changing law for hundreds of thousands of business readers. In this responsibility, he follows legislation, court decisions, administrative regulations, and other aspects of law and legal institutions that affect our commercial and personal lives today.

He received a B.A. from Yale and his law degree from Harvard, graduating from both with honors. He has taught at Yale and was awarded a Phi Beta Kappa Bicentennial fellowship for a book, "The Limits of the Public and the Private," also to be published this year.

Previous books include "How the Government Breaks the Law," "The Tyranny of the Experts," "Are Americans Extinct?" and "Understanding Our Constitution."

Prior to becoming a journalist, he spent several years in law practice in a variety of capacities: serving on active duty as a Navy lawyer, practicing antitrust law with a large Washington firm, and working as vice-president and general counsel of a New York publishing house.

He lives in Hastings-on-Hudson, New York, with his wife Susan and two young children.

Jethro K. Lieberman
Photograph c 1976
Jill Krementz

Author's Preface

A torrent of volumes in this bicentennial year will celebrate the difference that is America: will ponder it, analyze it, dissect it, confirm it, praise it, deplore it, deny it, and restate it.

What is this difference?

America, its communicants will remind us, remains what it always was: a land of equality and opportunity, an open society, a melting pot, a home of pioneers brave and free, a people of plenty, a nation of pragmatists, a classless culture, a country of the common man, a friend of free enterprise.

America, its critics will declare, never fulfilled its promise; it is instead a people of paradox: violent, racist, the impoverished left to languish unseen among obscenities of affluence, justice delayed and denied to benefit the privileged, a sprawling center of antiintellectualism, a culture of the lowest common denominator, the quintessential home of the "booboisie":

America, tower of technology, producer of pollution.

America, best hope of the world.

America, its patriots will demand, love it or leave it.

America, its detractors will retort, your "political-economic system [is] the principal obstacle to justice in the modern world."

America, we discern at last: symbol of a thousand meanings, common images, hurled clichés, buffed and polished to a special pitch at this splendid, unending commemoration of the two-hundredth anniversary of autonomy for its citizens.

A search for the unique essence of the America that this independence wrought may seem to lead to an impasse, for America is a land of borrowings. Nothing in America is wholly original, yet what great novelty did the recombinations portend! The uses to which the restless continent has put the customs and traditions of every square inch of the old world—nothing original except for the way it has selected, mingled, and recreated them— have long been recognized.

Still there is one difference that stands out. In that seminal year, 1776, one occurrence distinguishes America from all the nations of the world: America was consciously created and fashioned as a nation. By the very act of independence, the people of America created themselves. This was true not only in the sense that no king granted them municipal liberty, no outsider decreed their autonomy, but also in the sense that the people who rebelled formed a part of a young culture of contradictory currents. Of course, Americans had had a century and a half to develop a sense of themselves, and this is a long time as Americans measure time. But it is the merest speck in the history of all other peoples, for whom social arrangements were formed over long ages and unquestioned because things had always been that way, or at least seemed so.

Unlike the rulers of other peoples, America's rulers were not indigenous and did not evolve to places of power through the slow and tortuous process by which aristocracies have always been formed. And except from the dismal vantage point of the Indians, the only nonimmigrants America has ever known, the government was not imposed through conquest with new governmental forms implanted atop the surface of native custom.

No. America was a collection of colonies, seeds planted in a new world, that sprouted into a flowering social order distinct from the mother country that nurtured them. After a while, colonial rulers were viewed as representatives of a sovereignty that was an ocean away, separate, not of the people in the new world. Americans, or a certain, articulate group of them at any rate, wished to do the impossible: to rule themselves as all true nations did, not subject to the dominance of a foreign power, but at the same time not to be ruled, not to let the civil government itself act as a foreign power in the midst of a community of equal citizens. A domestic despot would be no solution to a foreign tyrant. Americans wished to possess their own government but not to be the slaves of it.

This could only be done through law. A people who wanted a government that would act as a rational instrument for carrying out the expressed purposes of its citizenry could not rely on the political structures and traditions of ancient customs. And the inalienable rights of man could not be preserved for long in the absence of law that would curb governmental power or of courts that would enforce the law against the government itself. To create a political system that would preserve human liberties and at the same time permit a people to respond to changes in their conditions required something new: a written constitution, clear evidence of the compact the people made among themselves, documentation of the fundamental rules of a free society that would not be subverted through generational lapses of memory.

The Constitutional tradition: If rule by law is not the only meaning of America, it is a crucial one. Though the superlative may be disputed, it is not straining to suggest that the tradition of constitutionalism was—and is—the chief legacy of the American experience to the people of the world. The new "united States," as they were captioned in the first state document common to the nation, the Declaration of Independence, would be a society dedicated to freedom and equality. But this would be possible only under law, a law that the people would themselves make. The difference of America was thus the difference of law that applied equally to all.

On the surface this seems a curious claim to be making about America, that the most original contribution America has made to the world is a system of law. It seems curious on three counts. First, Americans did not invent law, of course; it was an import like everything else. And, as we shall shortly see, what they imported they retained, even after they had severed political ties with Britain. Second, it would be naive to assert that equal opportunity under law was the actual state of affairs at the time of independence. We know it was not, and this we shall also explore.

Third, the United States has long been depicted in folklore in every home and in movies around the world as an essentially lawless society. From the cowboys of the wild west and the spirit of the vigilantes to the urban riots of a few years past and the not so punctilious behavior of the CIA and FBI that dominates the headlines as this is being written, other countries are often vexed and occasionally astonished by the level of violence in America. Indeed, lawlessness is even praised, for among the most vaunted traditions of our crazily contradictory culture is the importance of civil disobedience, from the earliest legends, such as the Boston Tea Party and the Revolution itself, to the theory of Thoreau and the modern civil rights movement. How, then, can law be offered not merely as *a* fundamental American development but as *the* fundamental one?

The answer is to be found in how the colonists changed the fundamental law. They adopted a written constitution that placed immense power in the hands of a new institution, the Supreme Court of the United States. This single body was perhaps the most novel structural innovation the Founding Fathers made. As Alexis de Tocqueville was to observe in his prescient account of new world political institutions, *Democracy in America:* "There is hardly a political question in the United States which does not sooner or later turn into a judicial one." This has been true throughout the course of American history, but it has been true only because of the Supreme Court.

The significance of this fact can scarcely be understated. That the great controversies of each age will inevitably come before a bench of nine judges means that passions will be articulated in a legalistic way. This means, in turn, that the solution of pressing social problems must involve lawyers. In America, law permeates the whole. "Law touches every concern of man," Felix Frankfurter once wrote; "Nothing that is human is alien to it." This is not true in many nations, among many peoples, but it is true in America.

That all were not equal when America began its independent course—that all are not equal still—is no rebuke to the promise of law. The American dream is no less real because not everyone has achieved it or can yet achieve it. Similarly the multitudinous evidence of lawlessness does not disprove the claim or denigrate the ideal. Law has been the means by which minorities have won equality over the years—with one searing exception that we will examine in Chapters 7 and 13.

Law that can be made by legislative majorities can of course oppress minorities, and there have been innumerable instances in American history when "the law" has been unjust. But a democratic nation does not stay forever frozen to the tracks of ancient majorities. The constitutional ideal is a potent counterweight to the parochialism of special interests, at least over the long haul. Sometimes, it is true, individuals and groups have had to break the law to publicize their plight and to insure fidelity to the Constitution. When the law is momentarily sluggish because it is rigged or because its interpreters are insensitive to the misery that bad law brings about, it may be necessary to step outside the law. Philosophically, these are treacherous waters; practically, they may be the only way to cross the river. But a nation that respects its fundamental constitutional process will muffle and contain the explosion of civil disobedience and will recognize the merit, where there is merit, of those who appeal by putting themselves in legal risk. This has happened time and again in American history.

This book is an exploration of some of these themes. It is not, however, a history of American law. Useful though that might be, it is a curious fact that Americans have never dwelt on their legal history. Though there have been scores of penetrating historical analyses of particular doctrines, legal policies, statutes, and judicial decisions, the comprehensive history has not yet been written. Indeed, "the first attempt to do anything remotely like a general history, a survey of the development of American law, including some treatment of substance, procedure, and legal institutions" was published in 1973—three years short of the bicentennial we now celebrate. How astonishing! And troublesome: for the surest way the law will lose its force in a democracy is when the people themselves have no understanding of it. Few today would agree with the sentiments of one of Mr. Stanley's predecessors, E. J. Phelps, president of the American Bar Association in 1879, who complained bitterly of public involvement with the Constitution, which, he said, was too sacred an instrument to be "hawked about the country, debated in the newspapers, discussed from the stump, elucidated by pot-house politicians and dunghill editors, or by scholars . . . who have never found leisure for the grace of English grammar or the embillishment of correct spelling."

If the people do not agree that they do not have the right to discuss their law—what right could be more sacred?—they do not always care to do so. And, what is worse, they do not always know how. Perhaps the most encouraging by-product of the constitutional crisis that Richard Nixon threatened to provoke was the reawakening of talk about constitutional law—not merely in the law schools but at the dinner tables and in the streets.

But there is much more to be done. Aside from the lawyers themselves, who constitute something less than one-fifth of one percent of the population, the American public is schooled in law only when one of its members needs to write a will, buy a house, recover from an automobile accident, sue a doctor, or separate from a spouse. This is not sustained, sophisticated, or sensible education.

This book is an attempt to fill a tiny corner of that void. It is a selection of some of the best and worst moments in American legal history. It is written for the general reader, with the assumption that the general reader does not have any knowledge of law, but it is also to be hoped that the lawyer—a specialist in law but not in history—will find something new. The highlights, if you will, of the most significant course of legal history the world has known: milestones of American law, during the first two hundred years.

In CONGRESS, JULY 4, 1776.

Patrick Henry

Give me Liberty or give me Dea

Lexington Green

Paul Revere

PART I: FOUNDATIONS OF AMERICAN LAW

1/ THE DECLARATION OF INDEPENDENCE

American law did not begin with the Declaration of Independence. It came aboard the first ships that flew the flags of King James I and the Virginia Company in 1606. It also came on all the subsequent ships to reach the shores of the New World from the early seventeenth century until the break with Great Britain a century and a half later. For that matter, a truly *American* law did not begin even then; as we shall see, English law has long remained the cornerstone of American jurisprudence.

This is not to say that colonial law and legal procedures were identical to those in England. There were many differences, owing to a variety of factors that distinguished England from the colonies and the colonies from each other. The colonies were founded over the course of 125 years, Virginia first in 1607 and Georgia not until 1733. During that time the law of England had not remained static. Historical differences in the founding of the colonies also played an important part. In Massachusetts and other colonies where Puritans long dominated the social structure, the role of the church in political affairs was much stronger than elsewhere. Similarly the law that emerged from crown colonies was not the same as law in states that began as proprietary colonies. In some colonies, other legal systems had been instituted, and these formed a blend that could not be repeated elsewhere. New York, for example, had to contend with Dutch law, the "Bible codes" of the Puritans, and the English law first introduced there in 1665.

The Common Law

A more fundamental reason for the divergence between English and American law lay in the nature of English law. The colonists did not bring "the law" in bound volumes and set them up in public places throughout the colonies for all to know. This would have been impossible even if they had thought to do so, because English law was not written down at all in the form of a code when the first Virginia ships or the Mayflower set sail.

English law was not, in fact, even one uniform law. In 1628, Sir Edward Coke, who had been lord chief justice of England, published the first of his famous *Institutes,* in which he counted no less than fifteen separate kinds of law. These included admiralty and maritime law—an international law of trade that was distinct from domestic commercial law—and ecclesiastical law, which dealt with such personal concerns as marriage. They also included *equity,* a flexible system of jurisprudence administered by the king's chancellor and designed to get around the baffling rigidities and complexities of the most important system (at least in historical perspective), the *common law.* Each of these systems was distinct. These were not merely different in the sense that our antitrust law is different from real property law; they were not simply separate statutes. They were entirely different systems of law, each with its own distinct forms and procedures, each administered by separate courts, each (theoretically) independent of the other.

The King's Law

The common law was a system that developed as early as the eleventh century. It grew out of the king's royal courts, which were distinct from the manorial courts that noblemen operated on their estates. In those days, every nobleman who was in possession of a landed estate could exercise judicial power over the inhabitants of his properties. He not only promulgated the law for his serfs; he also adjudicated disputes, including those that concerned him. For a variety of reasons, the early kings were intent on broadening the jurisdiction of their own courts—what we would think of today as public courts. Over the years the body of law that developed from the decisions of these courts came to be known as the common law, because it was (again, theoretically) common to the entire realm, not dependent on the particular idiosyncrasies of the landed aristocrats.

But this great body of law was not statutory. That is, it was not an enactment of Parliament, and it was not written down in the form of official-sounding rules. It was known only to the lawyers and judges who read the various judicial decisions that saw their way into print. For several hundred years, judges and lawyers alike deceived themselves into believing that the common law judges were not making law when they decided cases. They believed—or said they believed—that the law, in Justice Oliver Wendell Holmes's striking phrase, was a "brooding omnipresence in the sky." That is, they thought they were "discovering" a law that

George III of England. He was intermittently insane until around 1820, when he became permanently insane. That year also marked his death.

H. Armstrong Roberts

preexisted on some kind of Platonic cloud. In fact, they were making law whenever some case did not fit the pattern of a well-known rule. Also, although the hold of precedent was very strong (the House of Lords, England's highest court, refused to admit until 1966 that it could legitimately overturn a rule announced in a prior decision), they did not refrain from formulating a new rule if it better suited the judges' notions of what was fair in the circumstances.

It is not entirely fair to suggest that the judges were always making law, because the source of common law is custom—the ways of the community. Where these customs are well known and their application is obvious, a judge may simply act as an official maintaining order in the community against a recalcitrant member. But few customs are so simple that their application in a particular case will be immediately apparent to everyone. As matters became more complex with the development of towns, of technology, and of a Parliament disposed to enacting legislation that in turn raised many questions, judges were necessarily in the business of making law. This was not a usurpation of power, as is sometimes charged to courts today; it was the essence of law and the legal process.

The common law dealt with a host of familiar topics: rights in and to land, inheritance, personal property, assaults, trespass, and acts of negligence that harmed another (although this last did not begin to flower until well after England and America had separated). But what was important about common law was that it dealt, until comparatively recently, with the problems of "a tiny group of people" only. "Leaf through the pages of Lord Coke's reports, compiled in the late 16th and early 17th century; here one will find a colorful set of litigants, all drawn from the very top of British society—lords and ladies, landed gentry, high-ranking clergymen, wealthy merchants. Common law was an aristocratic law, for and of the gentry and nobility. The masses were hardly touched by this system and only indirectly under its rule."

This use meant, however, that the common law of England was not entirely suitable for conditions in the New World, where actual aristocracy was even smaller in numbers than at home. Law that had to cope with conflicts among nobles over land in a small country of contiguous estates had very different concerns than law that would order a society that lived on a continent of boundless land worked by relative equals. American law, though rooted in English tradition, necessarily began to diverge from the mainstream as communities grew in size.

Moreover, America could not wait the centuries that it took British common law to develop. It did not have a stable, preexisting body of institutions, such as the monarchy and aristocracy, that was necessary for this kind of system to mature, so colonial assemblies early on began enacting codes governing a variety of common law concerns. These codes included both civil and criminal matters and also set forth how the colonial self-government was to be administered. In the absence of formal, easily ascertainable English law that could be received and quickly assimilated in the New World, the colonists were compelled to forage for themselves. Thus, although the orientation and structure of the law was the same as in England, American law necessarily diverged from the main trunk of common law, just as the mother tongue itself began to deviate from that spoken in its birthplace across the ocean.

Blackstone

Paradoxically, however, English common law came to take on a much greater importance shortly before the Revolution and was in fact destined to play a part in causing the Revolution. This was due to the publication, more than a century and a half after the landing at Jamestown, of the first attempt to summarize the entire corpus of common law, Sir William Blackstone's famous *Commentaries on the Laws of England*. The *Commentaries* were delivered first in lecture form at Oxford in 1753. The four-volume work was published between 1765 and 1769. It exerted an immense influence over the American bar, simply because it was the only handy treatise available.

Until well into the nineteenth century, "Blackstone" was the one basic law book. The American appellate courts did not routinely submit their judicial opinions to publishers to be bound in the never-ending stream of volumes that is characteristic of the law today. Although there were court reporters, their records of decisions were neither complete nor regular, and few lawyers could afford a substantial library. Instead, there was Blackstone. As Daniel J. Boorstin has put it, "In the first century of American independence, the *Commentaries* were not merely an approach to the study of law; for most lawyers they constituted all there was of law."

If in the nineteenth century Blackstone was to be a drag on the progress of law, in the eighteenth century it was an enormously liberating influence. It made the legal system accessible to the entire educated class of the colonies, men who soon would instigate and lead the rebellion.

The common law tradition was a vital part of the growing colonial resentment and alienation that led to the break with England. From the very beginning of the British expeditions to America, the common law of England was made a part of the colonial communities. The Virginia Company's first charter in 1606 granted to the colonists and their descendants "all liberties . . . to all intents and purposes as if they had been abiding and born within this our realm of England." One of the most important facets of British political tradition was the right of commoners to representation in Parliament. The representative principle found early root in America: King James I specifically permitted the Virginia assembly, the House of Burgesses, to continue functioning after Virginia was reorganized as a crown colony in 1624. James not only recognized the assembly, but he also did not interfere with the laws enacted for the governing of the colony. And of course in Massachusetts, the famous Mayflower Compact bound the first settlers of Plymouth Plantation to the laws that they themselves would enact through the government they established.

But the settlers did not have complete freedom. Self-government was a privilege granted by the crown, and it was conditioned by the requirement that the colonies recognize a higher power. The 1629 charter to the Massachusetts Bay colony gave its ruling bodies the power to make "Lawes and Ordinances for the Good and Welfare of the saide Companye, and for the Government and orderings of the saide Landes and Plantation, and the People inhabiting and to inhabite the same." But the laws could not be "contrarie or repugnant to the Lawes and Statutes of this our Realme of England." This was an ambiguous phrase, and its exact meaning never was clarified satisfactorily. It did not mean that the colonies were prohibited from passing codes that might not mirror the common law. They passed many such. But it did reserve power to the British throne, acting through the Privy Council, to nullify laws that were contrary to British interests and British policy. Occasionally the Council did so. It rejected Connecticut's intestacy laws in 1727, for example. Overall, it rejected less than 6 percent of more than eighty-five hundred laws submitted to it.

The legal historian Lawrence M. Friedman has suggested that the smallness of the number does not necessarily mean the Council had little impact: "In ways difficult to measure, the council may have had an important effect on legal behavior. Legislatures debating a bill, litigants pursuing lawsuits, may have been aware of the council's distant shadow; this awareness may have modified their action in real but unknowable ways."

Nevertheless, for more than a century, the overwhelming bulk of colonial legislation and judicial decisions remained untouched by the home government. There can be little doubt that the policy followed by kings and royal governors of allowing the colonies to enact their own local law led to a firm belief that this was the only proper arrangement. When, after 1760, the crown determined to impress its own will on colonial affairs ever more minutely, the stage was set for the rupture embodied in the Declaration of Independence.

Second-Class Subjects

The story of the acts leading to the Revolution is familiar, and nothing will be gained by lengthy detail here. The colonists were first aroused in the early 1760s by the Writs of Assistance, in effect search warrants that gave British agents the right to invade homes to catch customs law violators. Rum smuggling was a profitable enterprise, which the writs threatened. But they also violated individual privacy.

In 1765, Parliament brought on the first colonywide storm: the Stamp Act. It was a direct tax on, among other things, newspapers and legal papers that provoked an outcry from "the most articulate groups—the editors and lawyers." The Stamp Act gave rise to the immortal cry: "no taxation without representation" and to riots and refusals to abide by the act throughout the colonies. In 1766, Parliament repealed the law because the stamp collectors resigned in droves, rendering the law unenforceable. But at the same time Parliament enacted the Declaratory Act, "which asserted the right to legislate for the colonies in 'all cases whatsoever.' "

The Townshend Acts were passed during the next year. These imposed duties on a variety of commodities, including tea, provoking resolutions of defiance from many assemblies and leading to a British order to the colonial governors to dissolve these assemblies. Although this order angered the colonists, more important damage had already been done. The colonies had begun to act in concert against a common enemy.

After several years of relative quiet, Parliament passed the British Tea Act in 1773. The colonies exploded anew. The first colonial reaction, the Boston Tea Party, led to the closing of the Boston port and the attempted restructuring of the Massachusetts government, pursuant to the so-called Coercive Acts. "But, far from intimidating the colonials and isolating the Massachusetts culprits, these caused patriots from one end of the colonies to the other to rally in support of Boston." The ultimate result, stemming from the suggestion of the Massachusetts House of Representatives, was the first meeting of what came to be known as the Continental Congress in Philadelphia in 1774.

Now the fat was in the fire; from here on events proceeded apace, though there were still some attempts to mitigate the coming clash. By 1775, when Patrick Henry declaimed, "Give me liberty, or give me death," and the shot that was heard round the world was fired on April 19 in Lexington, there was no turning back. In the summer of that year, George III proclaimed a rebellion in the colonies. It remained only to the colonists to renounce their last remaining, still-professed loyalty—to the king himself—and to declare their independence from all foreign power.

In January 1776, Thomas Paine published his immortal *Common Sense.* It galvanized the colonies in its sparkling call for swift and complete independence. "A government of our own is a natural right," he declared, and even more boldly cried to his fellow Americans: "O receive the fugitive, and prepare in time an asylum for mankind."

The Fateful Step

The Third Continental Congress convened in Philadelphia in May 1776. On June 11, the Congress appointed five men to draft a declaration of independence: Thomas Jefferson, John Adams, Benjamin Franklin, Roger Sherman, and Robert R. Livingston. These men appointed Jefferson to prepare a rough draft, which was finished by June 28. This rough draft was worked over by the other members of the committee, then edited, tightened, and slightly censored by the Congress as a whole on July 3, one day after a unanimous vote (New York abstaining) in favor of independence. On July 4 the Declaration of Independence was formally proclaimed.

Unlike the only other sacred state document—the Constitution—the Declaration of Independence has no legal authority today. This was intentional. The Declaration was just that—a declaration. It severed all ties with the crown and announced in its very caption a new nation, the United States, but it did not establish a form of government. This was not its purpose. What was remarkable about it—what is remarkable about it still—is its total break with the medieval theory that certain people possessed by right the power to rule over others. Equally remarkable was its ringing affirmation of the social contract theory of government that John Locke had set forth in his *Second Treatise of Government* in 1690, which was foreshadowed even before that by the Mayflower Compact. In

The drafters of the Declaration of Independence.

H. Armstrong Roberts

language that retains its freshness and eloquence at every reading, the fifty-six signers proclaimed:

We hold these truths to be self-evident, that all men are created equal, that they are endowed by their Creator with certain unalienable rights, that among these are life, liberty, and the pursuit of happiness. That to secure these rights, governments are instituted among men, deriving their just powers from the consent of the governed. That whenever any form of government becomes destructive of these ends, it is the right of the people to alter or to abolish it, and to institute new government, laying its foundation on such principles and organizing its powers in such form as to them shall seem most likely to effect their safety and happiness.

Robert Livingston, one of the five men appointed by the Third Continental Congress in May, 1776, to draft a declaration of independence.

Deriving their just powers from the consent of the governed: The government is an instrument of the people, rather than the people for the ultimate benefit of a select group who constituted the government. Here is the vision that has not yet been superseded, of a democratic state. As importantly, the language of the Declaration admitted no qualifications; its phrases were universal. "*All* men are created equal": though the signers themselves did not think so, since most did not consider the slaves to be men, the Declaration spoke to a future that would sweep all within its compass. Equal justice for all—the motto carved on the frieze of the United States Supreme Court—was foreshadowed in the Declaration.

Governments long established should not be changed for light and transient causes, the Declaration affirms, but when a long train of abuses and usurpations, pursuing invariably the same object evinces a design to reduce them under absolute despotism, it is their right, it is their duty, to throw off such government, and to provide new guards for their future security. In proof of this, said the Continental Congress, "let facts be submitted to a candid world." The Declaration lists thirty-odd types of depredations and tyrannous acts that George III committed against the colonists and the colonies, acts that "impel them to the separation." Historians believe that many of these acts of tyranny were "exaggerated." The Declaration concludes:

that these United Colonies are, and of right ought to be Free and Independent States; that they are absolved from all allegiance to the British Crown, and that all political connection between them and the State of Great Britain is and ought to be totally dissolved; and that as Free and Independent States they have full power to levy war, conclude peace, contract alliances, establish commerce, and to do all other acts and things which independent States may of right do. And for the support of this declaration, with a firm reliance on the protection of Divine Providence, we mutually pledge to each other our lives, our fortunes, and our sacred honor.

The King's Law: America's Law?

The Revolution accomplished, the question of what legal system the newly sovereign states would adopt remained. It may seem an anomaly that the former colonies opted for the English law. In fact there was a curious ambivalence concerning the common law, a suspicion of it because it was English yet a desire to adapt it to the conditions of the states. Thomas Paine, as late as 1805, denounced the courts in Pennsylvania because they had "not yet arrived at the dignity of independence." In 1812, Thomas Jefferson denied in a letter to a federal judge "the ordinary doctrine that we brought with us from England the Common Law rights. This narrow notion was a favorite in the first moment of rallying to our rights against Great Britain. The truth is that we brought with us the rights of men." A common toast following the Revolution declared: "The

Thomas Jefferson.

Charles Phelps Cushing from H. Armstrong Roberts

Common Law of England: may wholesome statutes soon root out this engine of oppression from America." Some states, such as New Jersey and Kentucky, actually went so far as to prohibit lawyers and judges from discussing British law postdating the war in the courtroom. Henry Clay was stopped in the middle of an argument in the Kentucky court of appeals in 1808 when he attempted to cite a part of an opinion of the famed British jurist, Lord Ellenborough.

But this was not the universal opinion. The Revolution was not directed against the law itself; it was waged, rather, because the king refused to abide by the law. The colonists rebelled against what they considered lawlessness, not against a law that was itself oppressive. In 1774, the First Continental Congress had declared that the people of America were "entitled to the common law of England," especially the right to trial by jury, the denial of which was explicitly incorporated in the Declaration of Independence as one of the King's acts of tyranny. Moreover, English statutes that "existed at the time of colonization and which [the people] have, by experience, respectively found to be applicable to their several local and other circumstances" were likewise declared to be the common rights of Americans.

Furthermore, it would have been impossible to "root out" the common law from every court and every legislature in the land. The traditions of Americans were necessarily close to those of Englishmen, for they had been English subjects for 175 years. What principles could have replaced the common law? There was some possibility that the civil codes of France might supplant English law, but it was never all that great and it died out by the 1830s. French law could not match the habits of generations and the influence of Blackstone, the only formal legal scholarship that was universally available to lawmakers after the Revolution.

So the newly emancipated states, by legislative enactments, *received* the common law of England. Virginia, in 1776, passed a law providing that the "common law of England, all statutes or acts of Parliament made in aid of the common law prior to the fourth year of the reign of King James the first [1607], and which are of a general nature, not local to that kingdom . . . shall be considered as in full force."

The reception statutes (sometimes they were embodied in the state constitutions) created many perplexing problems. Were acts of Parliament part of the common law? Most supposed they were not, so it was necessary, as in Virginia, to receive some statutory law as well (the famous Statute of Frauds of 1677 was received throughout the Union and is still in force in every state today). But the reception of Parliamentary acts was not consistent; Virginia itself repealed its provision relating to such acts in 1792. (Nevertheless, the Virginia reception statute had far-reaching effects. In 1795, the judges of the Northwest Territory, whom Congress empowered to choose territorial law, adopted the original Virginia ordinance of 1776, in spite of the fact that it was repealed later. From there, the common law of England, plus Parliamentary statutes enacted prior to 1607, made their way into Illinois Territory and later became part of the law of other states also.)

The King's Law in the Commoners' Land

But the larger problem was how to interpret and apply English common law. Were the rules laid down in England to be absorbed lock, stock and barrel into the fabric of state law simply because a reception statute declared in general terms that the common law of England was the common law of the State?

The answer was clear that they were not to be. In *Seeley* v. *Peters,* a case that came before the Illinois Supreme Court in 1848, the question arose whether an owner of cattle was required to fence them in to prevent damage to a neighboring farm. Under the common law the cattle owner had such an obligation and under the Illinois reception statute the common law was to be applied in the state.

Peters sued Seeley because Seeley's hogs trampled Peters's wheat fields. Seeley showed that Peters's property was poorly fenced, but the jury was instructed to disregard that fact, since by the common law Seeley, the hog owner, was required to fence in his animals, and if he did not, he must suffer the consequences of their actions. There was no debate that this was the common law rule, but the Illinois Supreme Court declared that this had never been the custom in Illinois, a territory of boundless land, where, owing to "the scarcity of timber, it must be many years yet before our extensive prairies can be fenced, and their luxuriant growth sufficient for thousands of cattle must be suffered to rot and decay where it grows, unless the settlers upon their borders are permitted to turn their cattle upon them." The conditions in Illinois, in other words, called for the exact opposite of the common law rule, so the Illinois Supreme Court declared: the wheat grower, not the hog farmer, must enclose his fields.

If the American courts were not free to disregard the rules and precedents of English common law, some extremely bizarre circumstances would result. Consider, for example, the situation that faced the Texas Supreme Court as late as 1913. In a case styled *Grigsby* v. *Reib*, the question was, Who inherited the property of Mr. Grigsby, who died in 1906: his sister Mrs. Reib, or a woman who claimed to be his wife and called herself Mrs. Grigsby? The putative Mrs. Grigsby had not married the deceased in a formal ceremony, but she claimed that they had agreed to be man and wife, although they never lived together as such. Would Texas recognize such a marriage, which, under the old ecclesiastical law as accepted by English common law for centuries, was entirely valid?

In 1840, the Republic of Texas enacted a law that was retained when statehood was achieved. The law declared that "the common law of England (so far as it is not inconsistent with the Constitution and laws of this State) shall, together with such Constitution and laws, be the rule of decision and shall continue in force until altered or repealed by the Legislature." The Texas legislature had never altered the rule. But there were two complications. In 1823, Parliament repealed the common law marriage in England; thus, an official ceremony was required. Did this mean that in 1840, when Texas received the common law, there was no common law marriage? Moreover, and here the difficulty became truly baffling, the House of Lords in 1843—three years after Texas adopted the common law—declared that what people had assumed for centuries was proper under common law (marriage by consent without actually living together) was in fact not *and never had been* proper. Legal scholars in England agreed that the House of Lords had made a woefully erroneous judgment, but the judgment nonetheless had been made. So in England the common law could no longer be said to have recognized Mrs. Grigsby's claim.

Was the Texas Supreme Court bound by any of these English actions? No, said the Texas Supreme Court. Neither the 1823 Parliamentary statute nor the 1843 House of Lords decision could alter the common law in Texas as it was generally understood. Texas, said the state supreme court, had long recognized common law marriages, and the 1840 act, therefore, "was not to introduce and put into effect the body of the common law, but to make effective the provisions of the common law so far as they are not inconsistent with the conditions and circumstances of our people." This same reasoning applied to the 1843 House of Lords decision.

How could that august body in 1843 settle for a Texas court in 1913 what the common law of England was in 1840? It did not and could not: reception statutes did not freeze into place the particulars of the common law of England; they accepted the English common law as it had been modified by American traditions. What was received, in other words, was the *process* of the common law—the authority of judges to make judgments by relying on an uncodified body of law (that is, not enacted by the legislature)—not the particular results that English judges had reached.

Thus the problem was solved generally throughout the states and in the federal courts as well. Independence did not mean that American courts would forego the flexible, case-by-case process, but it did mean that American courts would decide these cases in accordance with American principles, customs, and traditions. This principle, after all, was largely what inspired the Revolution: the right of Americans to make the law for themselves. Reception statutes governed the process, but not the substance, of the law.

The Declaration and the American Tradition of Law

What more can be said about the legal effect of the Declaration of Independence? One curious thing—the actual parchment on which the original Declaration was penned has had a meandering career. It went from Philadelphia, to New York, and in 1800 to the new city of Washington. During the War of 1812, it was spirited out of the city, but it soon returned and in 1820 went for storage in the State Department building. In 1841 it was consigned to the Patent Office, and during the Centennial celebration it was sent to Philadelphia.

By this time the ink had faded considerably, and the document was in considerable danger of fading altogether, so in 1894 it was sealed away in a safe. After a committee of experts examined it during World War I, the decision was made that it could be exhibited under conditions that would shield it from sunlight, and in 1921 it was housed in the Library of Congress. During World War II, it was brought for safekeeping to Fort Knox, and in 1944 it was returned to the Library of Congress, where the ministrations of a new generation of experts caused it to be placed in a vacuum-packed glass container adjusted for temperature changes. Finally, in 1952, with the construction of the National Archives, the Declaration of Independence was moved to the place where it rests today along with the Constitution.

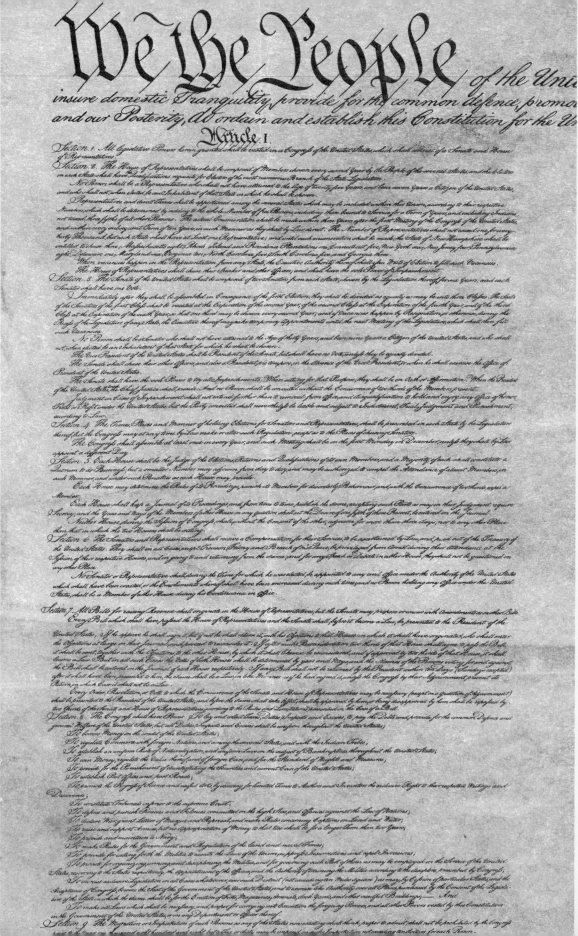

Dumas Malone Describes The
Enshrinement of The Declaration:

On December 13, 1952, in company with the Constitution, it was borne down the steps by guards from all the armed services, transported in a tank which breathed defiance against all foreign and domestic enemies, and escorted by service men and women to the National Archives building. There on December 15, it was again displayed to the public . . . The ceremonies accompanying this event were more elaborate than earlier ones in the Library of Congress. The various states were officially represented and state flags were much in evidence. The Chief Justice presided; the Chairman of the Joint Congressional Committee on the Library unveiled the shrine; and the President of the United States delivered an address.

During the time these eminent and suitable ceremonies were being performed, a lawsuit was wending its way through the courts of Illinois. In 1950, a recent law graduate named George Anastaplo had successfully passed the Illinois Bar examination and was awaiting admission. His parents were Greek immigrants, and he was reared in southern Illinois. At the age of eighteen, he quit school and joined the Air Force in the middle of World War II, flying missions as a navigator. In 1947, receiving an honorable discharge, he went to the University of Chicago, where he took his undergraduate and law degrees. Before being admitted to the bar, he was required, as is customary in most states, to answer questions on a personal history form and to be interviewed by members of a bar committee. One of the instructions on the form was to "state what you consider to be the principles underlying the Constitution of the United States." Anastaplo's response was, in part, as follows:

Another basic principle (and the most important) is that such government is constituted so as to secure certain inalienable rights, those rights to Life, Liberty and the Pursuit of Happiness (and elements of these rights are explicitly set forth in such parts of the Constitution as the Bill of Rights). And, of course, whenever the particular government in power becomes destructive of these ends, it is the right of the people to alter or to abolish it and thereupon to establish a new government. This is how I view the Constitution.

In 1950, these were apparently dangerous words, though they are almost an exact quotation of the Declaration of Independence. Though there was not the slightest reason to suspect Anastaplo's loyalty or his past conduct, the bar interviewers wanted to know what exactly he meant by the right of the people to alter or to abolish government destructive of the just ends of the people. A discussion ensued, and Anastaplo ultimately said that in the event of a too tyrannous government, the people might have no recourse but to rebel. Thereupon an interviewer asked: "Are you a member of any organization that is listed on the Attorney General's list, to your knowledge?" and "Are you a member of the Communist Party?" Sticking to a principle too punctilious for the committee members to follow, Anastaplo insisted that the questions violated his constitutional rights. After dozens of committee hearings and court cases, the Illinois Supreme Court refused to order his admission to the bar. Eleven years later, in 1961, after it had dismissed an earlier appeal, the United States Supreme Court, by a five to four vote, upheld the Illinois court's decision.

Because he affirmed a belief in the Declaration of Independence the bar examiners might reasonably conclude, said the Court, that he was unfit to practice law.

There was never any evidence that Anastaplo believed in violence, that he was subversive, or that he belonged to any prohibited organization, but an openly expressed belief in the principles of the Declaration, too rigid for the taste of the majority of the Court at that time, was sufficient to prevent a man from practicing the law that the Declaration was designed to protect.

The Declaration of Independence is a noble document and deserves to be considered one of the sacred state papers of the United States, but it sets forth only a philosophy, not a code of law. In itself, it exercises no restraints on the actions of government duly instituted in its name. To the document that does, the Constitution of the United States, we must now turn.

2/ THE CONSTITUTION OF THE UNITED STATES

"The American Constitution is the most wonderful work ever struck off at a given time by the brain and purpose of man."

So wrote British Prime Minister William Ewart Gladstone in 1878, and so most Americans are pleased to consider the document that is the fount of their government and their liberties. Gladstone's assessment may very well be true; one would have to ponder for quite some time before hitting upon any other public work that would measure up.

Because it is today the oldest living written constitution in the world and because the American people still live under a political structure that can be seen to flow from its original clauses, the temptation is strong to conclude that the delegates to the Constitutional Convention in Philadelphia in the late spring and summer of 1787 possessed some divine guidance that permitted them to anticipate national problems far into the future. This is not quite accurate. There were men of genius among the delegates: Benjamin Franklin was understood to be by his contemporaries, and history has judged James Madison, principal architect of the Constitution to have been a genius of the first order. At least a score were among the most extraordinary men ever to participate in American public life.

A Grinding Necessity

These men did not put the Constitution together by accident; Madison sent to Jefferson, who was then minister to France, for books "that may throw light on the general constitution and *droit public* of the several confederacies which have existed," and he received more than a hundred volumes, which he gobbled up.

But the delegates also were practical men, and their objective was not to cement an organic law that would carry the nation, whose complete existence was not yet fully perceived, through all crises for all times. Some did not expect the constitution they had just drafted to live out twenty-five years.

The Constitution was a work of brilliant insight, of subtle judgment, to be sure, but it was born of practical necessity ("extorted from the grinding necessity of a reluctant nation" was the way John Quincy Adams later described the situation). It was designed to remedy defects in the national system that had prevailed for a decade under the Articles of Confederation. "There is practically nothing in the constitution," said Max Farrand, the eminent chronicler of the Philadelphia convention, "that did not arise out of the correction of these specific defects of the confederation."

The genius of the Constitution is not only the work of those who labored in the heat for five months; it is also the genius of a people who, as much as the Constitution was adapted to them, adapted to it. The Constitution endures because people wish it to; the same document in other nations might be long forgotten.

The success of any venture depends not only on the foresight of those who propose and launch it but also on the willingness of those who come after to adhere to its values. On this point, history is ambivalent. The Constitution was saved because the Constitution was amended. We have learned to live with it because we have learned to change it. But this is getting ahead of the story.

The Confederation

The Constitution began, in a sense, with the attempt of the newly independent states to live without it. At the time independence was declared, the Continental Congress began to consider a plan of confederation. This was not to be a superstate or new nation but a means by which thirteen separate, sovereign states could jointly carry out common tasks. Two years later, in July 1778, the Continental Congress adopted the Articles of Confederation, subject to ratification by all the states. Though eleven states did so within the next twelve months, Delaware and Maryland delayed, and the formal articles were not declared in effect until March 1781.

In these Articles were the seeds of disaster. The crux of the problem lay in the second Article, which declared: "Each state retains its sovereignty, freedom and independence, and every Power, Jurisdiction and right, which is not by this confederation expressly delegated to the United States, in Congress assembled." The express powers delegated to Congress, dealt principally, and understandably, with foreign affairs, with war and treaty-making, and with certain domestic matters that crossed state boundaries (regulating money, fixing the standard of weights and measures, establishing a post office). But most of the important powers could only be exercised if nine states agreed.

Benjamin Franklin, whose genius was a beacon in the nation's fledgling days.

Charles Phelps Cushing from H. Armstrong Roberts

What the Articles did not contain, moreover, was a portent of difficulties lying ahead. It did not permit Congress to raise taxes to support any of the Confederation's policies; all revenues were to be raised by the states. Congress did not have the power to regulate commerce between the states. Each state was to have one vote, regardless of the differences in populations. There was no provision for a federal executive or court. Congress was the sole governing body, and it was also "the last resort on appeal in all disputes and differences now subsisting or that hereafter may arise between two or more states." Congress had no mechanism to enforce its laws or decisions. The states merely pledged to "abide by the determinations of the united states in congress assembled, on all questions which by this confederation are submitted to them." And, finally, the Articles themselves could not be amended unless every state agreed to the change.

Here was a union of states, not of citizens. Though the Articles gave citizens of any state the right to travel freely through all, the principal loyalty of a person was to his state, not to the Confederation. One was a citizen of Virginia or New York or Massachusetts, and these were members of the united states of America. Congress was not a government of the people but a "congress of states" with no power to compel any common policy, no matter how desperately they might be needed. Congress could not enact laws that would operate directly on the citizens of the states. The states alone were empowered to implement Congressional decisions. Only the states could pass laws directing the citizens to pay taxes or to refrain from doing something on pain of criminal sanction. In 1786, James Madison noted the difficulties in his *Vices of the Political System of the United States:* "A Sanction is essential to the idea of law, as coercion is to that of Government. The federal system, being destitute of both, wants the great vital principles of a political constitution. Under form of such a constitution, it is in fact nothing more than a treaty of amity and of alliance between independent and sovereign states."

In 1781, even before final ratification, Congress was in serious need of funds, so it proposed an amendment to the Articles to permit a tax on imports and on goods from ships seized at sea. Twelve states assented, but Rhode Island balked, so money could not be raised. Two years later, Congress tried again with another amendment, this time seeking the power for twenty-five years to raise $1.5 million annually. By 1786—three years after Congress proposed this plan—only nine states had consented, and though special appeals prompted three more states to agree to the amendment by the end of the year, New York held out, so the plan was wrecked.

In the meantime, problems of internal commerce began to grow. States with special advantages for trade, such as good harbors and waterways, used these to the disadvantage of their neighbors. Some states, James Madison said, "having no convenient ports for foreign commerce, were subject to be taxed by their neighbors, through whose ports their commerce was carried on. New Jersey, placed between Philadelphia and New York, was likened to a cask tapped at both ends; and North Carolina, between Virginia and South Carolina, to a patient bleeding at both arms." But Congress had no power to intervene.

Besides being unable to tax and to prevent onerous state trading monopolies, the Confederation could not come to the aid of beleaguered state governments. This became markedly apparent during the so-called Shays' rebellion in Massachusetts. Economic conditions and state taxing policies combined to depress the financial condition of farmers, small shopkeepers, and labor. Court judgments threatened to strip the farmers of their land. Debtors were being slapped into prison. Many of these people reacted to the situation as the colonists had done a decade before: they massed in front of courts to prevent them from sitting and began agitating for change. "This was a grim joke on the leaders of the American Revolution who were now running the state government. Samuel Adams, now a respectable member of the state council, proposed to hang anyone who used the methods he had employed in 1774."

In September 1786, the governor of Massachusetts forbade assemblies of people he deemed agitators, and he called out the militia to enforce his order. In January 1787, Daniel Shays led eleven hundred men in an attack on Springfield to prevent the state supreme court from sitting. Within two weeks, the state militia had routed the rebels. But the state's appeal to the Confederation for aid was useless because Congress had no authority to lend assistance. And if it was useless to Massachusetts, how could Congress support the states against the very real possibility of attack by England in the north or Spain in the south?

Addressing the Problems of Living Without the Constitution

It chanced that a meeting to resolve trade problems was scheduled at the time that the disorders in Massachusetts occurred.

Virginia and Maryland had entered a pact to regulate the navigation and fishing in the Chesapeake and wished Pennsylvania and Delaware to cooperate with them. To further these ends, Virginia proposed that the commissioners of all the states meet in Annapolis in September 1786. The meeting was "to take into consideration the trade of the United States," but only five states were represented.

The delegates failed to reach a substantive agreement on trade, but they made a fateful recommendation to their respective legislatures. They asserted that since "important defects in the System of the Fœderal (sic) Government . . . of a nature so serious as, . . . to render the situation of the United States, delicate and critical," it was imperative that a convention of delegates from all the states meet to try to remedy those defects. The Annapolis delegates recommended that the convention undertake its work in Philadelphia the following May. Virginia quickly appointed its representatives to the forthcoming convention, and other states soon followed suit. In February 1787, a scant three weeks after the back of Shays' rebellion had been broken, Congress approved the recommendation made five months earlier in Annapolis.

On the twenty-fifth day of May, 1787, the convention that was called to revise the Articles of Confederation finally had a quorum of delegates from seven states. Eleven days after the convention was to have begun, it officially convened. Spring rains had made roads to Philadelphia impassable with mud, and while they waited for their colleagues, the delegates from Virginia and Pennsylvania laid the groundwork for what was to become the Constitution. Fifty-five delegates (thirty-four of them lawyers) from twelve states, Rhode Island refusing to participate, ultimately attended what later became known as the Constitutional Convention. The leaders of the Revolution met again to complete peacefully what had begun in violence slightly more than a decade before. Of all the political leaders in America, only two of the most eminent were conspicuously absent: Jefferson, who as has been remarked, was in Paris, and John Adams, who was minister in London. (Some others, such as Patrick Henry, refused to attend.)

The delegates chose George Washington as their presiding officer, and they adopted a rule of secrecy so that their proceedings would not become daily topics of discourse among the residents of Philadelphia, thereby avoiding being subjected to pressures other than those, fierce enough, that swirled around them daily within the State House. There would be time enough for public sentiment.

Francis Hopkinson, a signer of the Declaration, noted in a letter to Jefferson: "Their deliberations are kept inviolably secret, so that they set without censure or remark, but no sooner will the chicken be hatch'd but everyone will be for plucking a feather."

The Heart of the Matter

From the very first, there was a fundamental tension between the large states and small. Edmund Randolph, governor of Virginia, began the Convention's principal business by submitting the Virginia plan: a national government would be established and divided into three parts (legislative, executive, and judicial), and each state would be represented in the legislative body according to the size of its population. Under the Virginia plan, there would be two houses in the national legislature: a lower house, elected popularly in each state, and an upper house, which would be selected by the lower house from a list of people compiled by the state legislatures. Each house would contain state delegations in proportion to the size of the populations they represented.

The small states feared that this plan would destroy their sovereignty, for three states alone—Virginia, Pennsylvania and Massachusetts—contained nearly half of the entire population of all thirteen states. So William Paterson, from New Jersey, proposed that each state have an equal voice in the national legislature.

This so-called New Jersey plan threatened to wreck the entire Convention. It unmasked the deep division between the large states and the small ones, between the desire to create a new form of government and the desire merely to patch up the old. "We shall be charged by our constituents with usurpation," Paterson declaimed. "We are met here as the deputies of thirteen independent, sovereign states, for federal purposes. Can we consolidate their sovereignty and form one nation, and annihilate the sovereignties of our states who have sent us here for other purposes? . . . The people of America are sharpsighted and not to be deceived. The idea of a national government as contradistinguished from a federal one never entered into the mind of any of them . . . We have no power to go beyond the federal scheme, and if we had, the people are not ripe for it."

To this speech, James Wilson, Madison's colleague from Pennsylvania, replied, "Shall New Jersey have the same right or council in the nation with Pennsylvania? I say no! It is unjust . . . If no state will part with any of its sovereignty it is in vain to talk of a national government."

William Paterson, constitutional authority and a Supreme Court justice from 1793 until his death in 1806. He was author of the New Jersey plan favoring the small states at the Constitutional Convention; the plan was rejected.

The Great Compromise

The solution that saved the Convention and the Constitution was embodied in the Great Compromise, proposed by Roger Sherman of Connecticut (hence it is sometimes known as the Connecticut or Sherman Compromise). He made the simple suggestion, which he had been advocating since 1776, that the states have it both ways. The lower house would be elected popularly, each state having representatives proportional to the size of its population. The upper house would consist of an equal number of representatives from each state. For one month the debate raged; "the fate of America was suspended by a hair," Gouverneur Morris later said.

In the end, of course, the Sherman Compromise, the plan that has ever since been the core of the American federal system, was accepted. Each state contributes two members to the United States Senate; states with large populations send more members to the House of Representatives than smaller states do. The Senate is the states' legislative chamber; the House of Representatives was the people's. On July 16, 1787, the Great Compromise was accepted, and the Convention turned to dozens of other questions raised by the various proposals that formed the Virginia and New Jersey plans.

Several alternatives were considered in a debate that was too lengthy to detail here. But one example of the complex issues the delegates wrestled with is the all-important question of the national executive. The Articles of Confederation provided, as we have seen, for no such office; the legislative power was supreme. Should there be an executive? The delegates agreed early on that there should be one—even before the New Jersey plan was put forth. But the Convention was by no means certain of anything else. Should the national executive be single, that is, composed of one person, or should it be plural, a council of officers, perhaps one from the North, one from the South, and one from the middle states? Should the executive be elected by the people or by the legislature or by some other means? How long should his term of office run: three, four, seven, fifteen years? Should he serve for life: might he even be a king? This seems to be a strange thought, but it was debated. Should he be paid? Franklin thought not. Should he be eligible for reelection? Delegates were of many minds. Should he be permitted to strike down legislation? What should he be called? John Adams later suggested that it be "His Highness, the President of the United States and Protector of their Liberties," but the Convention and later Congress rejected such appellations. So the questions went on and on; it took sixty ballots alone to decide on the method of electing the president.

Before examining the Constitution as it was finally adopted, it is important to reiterate that the Philadelphia Convention did not merely amend a treaty that would help the states live together more harmoniously. They produced a Constitution that created a new political consciousness and a new political unity. True, "there is practically nothing in the constitution that did not arise out of the correction" of defects in the Articles of Confederation. As James Madison argued in the *Federalist Papers:* "The truth is, that the great principles of the Constitution proposed by the convention may be considered less as absolutely new, than as the expansion of principles which are found in the Articles of Confederation . . . If the new Constitution be examined with accuracy and candor, it will be found that the change which it proposes consists much less in the addition of *New Powers* to the *Union,* than in the invigoration of its *Original Powers.*"

But the defects were so many and the invigoration so mighty that something altogether new was created. "It is possible to say that every provision of the federal constitution can be accounted for in American experience between 1776 and 1787," Farrand wrote. That experience showed that a free people could not live easily or well together on a continent divided into a host of petty principalities, with the prospect of still more to be fashioned. A new nation, a whole people, was necessary. And this is what the Constitution created.

This sense of national unity can be seen most significantly in the Preamble. A committee of the Convention tried to begin: "We the People of the States of New Hampshire, Massachusetts," etc., following the Articles of Confederation, which was an agreement among the states. But there were stylistic and political difficulties in this approach. So in the end, the Convention agreed to: "We, the People of the United States"—a people of a new nation, transcending the colonial boundaries that were their birthright.

The Constitution and the American Form of Government

What, then, is this Constitution? It is both a structure of government and a set of principles, a method of making law and a law itself. But of all the principles in this seven-thousand-word document, the single most important is that the government is one of delegated powers. The government does not preexist the people; it is not superior to them; its powers come only from them. This is fundamentally different from the contemporary European conception that kings ruled, if not by divine right, then by right of their birth.

The Constitution is too well known and explored to require any exegesis here. But no book on the milestones of American law can omit discussion of at least the larger matters of substance that the Constitution contains. Thus, what follows is a synopsis of major concepts in the articles.

Article One: This first of seven articles (only six of which are operative today) deals with the most pressing problem that the nation faced in 1787 and one of the most obviously important matters for a people who govern themselves: the legislature. Article One declares that "all legislative Powers herein granted shall be vested in a Congress of the United States." The Constitution does not define "legislative powers," but this phrase reflects the concept of the *separation of powers*—that all the functions of government cannot be entrusted to the same agency.

A legislature may pass laws, but it must not have the power to enforce them or to interpret them in a particular case. This splintering of power prevents the amassing of power in the hands of one person or a small group of persons, and it militates against the tendency of any government toward dictatorship or oligarchy. So Congress, and no other body, possessed the legislative power, the people's power to enact law through their representatives.

This article contains the Great Compromise. Congress comprises two chambers, a Senate and House of Representatives, each to act as a check against the other. Members of the Senate were to be chosen by the legislatures of each state. Each state has two senators, and each senator has one vote. The Philadelphia delegates considered this provision to be so important that they fought to make it the one provision that could not be amended. Article Five, which spells out the amendment procedure, declares "that no State, without its Consent, shall be deprived of its equal Suffrage in the Senate." The provision regarding the election of senators was amended, however, in 1913 by the Seventeenth Amendment, which provided for the popular election of senators in each state.

Since membership in the House is based on state populations, Article One requires a decennial census to apportion the House seats.

Article One says that there can be no more than one Representative for every thirty thousand people; today each member of the House represents some half million people. Apportionment raises problems we will explore in Chapter 15.

Under this article, impeachment—the only provision in the Constitution, according to Farrand, that was not written to deal with a problem of the Confederation—is given to Congress. The House has the "sole Power of Impeachment." This means, contrary to a misapprehension that was quite current until the impeachment debate concerning President Nixon, that the House has the power to issue a formal accusation, something like a grand jury indictment. Impeachment is not equivalent to removal from office; that happens only upon a trial in the Senate, which has the "sole Power to try all Impeachments." By a majority vote, the House can impeach any officer of the government: the president, other executive officials, and members of the judiciary. A two-thirds vote in the Senate is necessary for conviction and removal. These provisions were necessary, it was felt, because the Constitution created two branches of government that did not exist under the Confederation: an executive and a judiciary.

Members of each House are paid a salary out of funds in the Treasury of the United States. They are not dependent on the states for their pay. Each House determines its own rules of procedure and conduct and publishes a journal, now called the *Congressional Record,* containing discussion, debate, and a record of the members' votes.

Laws of the United States may originate in either house in the form of bills. The only exception to this procedure is that only the House of Representatives may first consider "bills for raising revenue." The cry "No Taxation without Representation" was still strong; only the popular body, the house representing the people, was given the power to initiate taxes.

All bills must clear three hurdles before they can become laws. They must first pass each house in identical form. Then they must meet the approval of the president. This was an entirely new provision, and it excited much suspicion. The power of kings and royal governors to negate the acts of legislatures had long been used to extort benefits for the rulers, such as exemption from taxation. "No good law whatever could be passed without a private bargain with him," Benjamin Franklin argued, citing the experience of Pennsylvania when it was a proprietary colony ruled by the Penn family. "An increase of his salary or some donation was always made a condition; till at last it became the regular practice to have orders in his favor on the Treasury presented along with the bills to be signed, so that he might actually receive the former before he should sign the latter."

On the other hand, there could be as great a danger arising from a too hasty enactment of the legislature: mob action by the representatives against the wishes of the people. So the issue was resolved in another ingenious compromise: the president would have the power to veto, but Congress in turn could override that veto if each house, by a two-thirds vote, chose to do so.

Section Eight of Article One is the central, substantive change in the power of the federal Congress. Specific powers are granted to Congress so that it may enact legislation. The original powers of Congress enumerated in the Articles of Confederation, such as coining money and establishing post offices, are brought forward, but new, all-important ones are added. These are:

☐ the power to lay and collect taxes
☐ the power to borrow money on the credit of the United States
☐ the power to regulate international and interstate commerce
☐ the power to naturalize foreign-born citizens
☐ the power to enact a uniform bankruptcy law
☐ the power to raise and govern the military forces
☐ the power to declare war

In what has come down to posterity as the "elastic clause," Congress also was given the power "to make all Laws which shall be necessary and proper for carrying into Execution the foregoing Powers, and all other Powers vested by this Constitution in the Government of the United States, or in any Department or Officer thereof." No group of constitution-makers can possibly spell out in precise detail what is within or without a specific power, what act is in furtherance of the power to borrow money on the credit of the United States, and what is not. A constitution that was miserly in the amount of power it granted could cripple a government by causing it to be apprehensive about using legislation in any of its legitimate spheres to extend its power beyond the proper limits.

Thus Congress was granted an enormous potential reserve of power to do what was "necessary and proper" to legislate for the nation. We will examine this particular clause more closely in Chapter 6. What is important to note here is that through all its powers, the new Congress could do for the first time what the old

Congress could not: enact legislation that directly affected the people themselves. The federal government no longer had to ask the states for permission to carry out national policies. Hence-forth its own law would bind the people.

Article Two: The presidency was created to carry out the laws; to have a commander in chief of the military forces; to carry out the foreign policy of the nation, including entering into treaties with other nations and to appoint the various ambassadors, judges, and officials necessary to the functioning of the government. The president is a single person, not a ruling council, chosen neither by the people nor by the states, but through an intricate procedure that has been changed by constitutional amendments on three occasions.

The provision for choosing the president is one of the few structures established in the Constitution that has not stood the test of time. However, the current method is still modeled on the original scheme and on the Twelfth Amendment that modified it only fifteen years after the Constitution was adopted.

The president is chosen by "electors," who in turn are selected according to procedures that may vary from state to state. Each state is entitled to a number of electors that equals its number of senators and representatives in Congress. The person who receives the majority of votes in this so-called electoral college that meets once every four years becomes president. If there are more than two candidates, and none receives a majority, the election is thrown into the House of Representatives, where each state is entitled to one vote.

This procedure of electing the president is weighted toward the states. The people alone, acting as a single mass electorate, were not entrusted with the power to pick their president, and they still are not. As a practical matter, presidential electors are chosen in each state by statewide referendum, but the quadrennial presidential election is still greatly influenced by the desire of the states to function as units in determining the national executive. Not only do small states get votes out of proportion to their population, but also by state law and custom, all the electoral votes of each state go to the candidate who receives the most votes in the state. This means that it is possible for a person to be elected president without receiving a majority of the popular votes. How? If the battle is close in the most populous states, the winner by a razor-thin margin may garner enough electoral votes to be elected even though all the popular vote in the other states is against him. Many people are uncomfortable with this possibility (in 1888, Grover Cleveland won the popular vote, but lost the presidency in the electoral college).

From time to time proposals have been advanced to amend the provisions governing the election of the president by abolishing the electoral college. So far Congress has refused to authorize this change.

As a check against the fears that Franklin and others expressed, and also as a check against a vindictive Congress, the Constitution prohibits the president from receiving an increase or decrease in his salary during his term of office. It also prohibits him from receiving any other emolument from the federal or state governments (a provision that was invoked during the impeachment debate in 1974).

Also as a check against the president's power to act unilaterally, many of his most significant actions are subject to the consent of the Senate, which means, again, that the states may play a direct role in national policy (a larger role when the state legislatures chose their senators than today, when members of the upper house are popularly elected). Treaties require a two-thirds vote; judges and appointed executive officials are confirmed by a majority vote.

Aside from the specific roles that he is required to play, such as commander in chief, and the specific powers that he is given— the power to appoint—the Constitution does not attempt to sketch out the day-to-day activities of the president. He must report to Congress from time to time on the state of the Union, and he may recommend laws that he thinks Congress should enact. But his most important duty is phrased, as is characteristic of many of the Constitution's provisions, in only the most general way: "he shall take Care that the Laws be faithfully executed."

The Constitution vests "the executive Power" in the president, but it does not spell out what this power is. Of course the Constitution was not written in a vacuum, and England and the states had departments or offices that carried out the functions of governments—for instance, the office of the attorney general, who as chief law enforcement officer of the realm has the power to file lawsuits to enforce the laws. The existence of these departments, and their mechanics, were left to Congress to legislate. The president's duty is to see to it that whatever departments and offices and policies Congress establishes and declares are properly supervised and carried out. This provision, too, was critical in the 1974 impeachment debate.

Article Three: The third article rounds out the structure of the national government by vesting "the judicial Power of the United States" in a Supreme Court. Congress is empowered to create inferior courts. The lower federal courts were first created in 1789. The judges of the federal courts are appointed by the president, but they hold office for life (subject to the power of Congress to impeach them). These courts did not exist during the Confederation. Interpretation and declaration of the law rested with the states rather than an agency of the national government. Without these courts it had been impossible for Congress to enforce its laws.

This article spells out the kinds of cases that may be considered in federal courts, including all cases "arising under this Constitution, the Laws of the United States, and Treaties," maritime matters, cases involving ambassadors, states themselves, citizens of different states (a provision creating a problem explored in Chapter 11), and certain other categories. Congress is given the authority to regulate the dockets of the courts by deciding what kinds of cases the Supreme Court may hear on appeal and, because it may create inferior courts as it pleases, what kinds of cases these lower courts may entertain. Congress has made some of these categories exclusive to the federal courts—for instance, cases arising under federal law may be heard only in federal courts. Other categories, such as the power to hear cases between citizens of different states, may be brought either in state or in federal courts.

The power of Congress to regulate the jurisdiction of the courts is another illustration of the structure of the government. The United States is not only structured according to a principle of separating the powers of government, but it also is a system in which each branch of government is given significant power to affect the others. Congress enacts laws, but the president may veto them, and the courts may interpret them. The president appoints, but the Senate must concur, and Congress may override a presidential veto. Courts may, as we will see in Chapter 4, void enactments of Congress, but the legislature may restrict the power of the courts to do this by limiting their jurisdiction to hear cases.

This power has been sparingly but tellingly used. In 1869 a southern newspaper editor was taken into custody in Mississippi by military authorities. He sued for his release, challenging the validity of the Reconstruction Act that permitted his detainment. The Supreme Court had already heard arguments on the case when

Congress, nervous at the prospect of having the Reconstruction laws (or part of them, at any rate) overturned, simply voted to take away the jurisdiction of the Supreme Court to hear the appeal. The Court bowed and dismissed the appeal.

The power of the federal courts and the novelty of the third article rest largely on a provision not even contained in it. This is the famous supremacy clause, the second section of the sixth article; it reads as follows:

This Constitution, and the Laws of the United States which shall be made in Pursuance thereof; and all Treaties made, or which shall be made, under the Authority of the United States, shall be the supreme Law of the Land; and the Judges in every State shall be bound thereby, any Thing in the Constitution or Laws of any State to the Contrary notwithstanding.

Under Article One, Congress has the power to make laws governing the use of the armed forces "to execute the Laws of the Union," but what would these laws be to sovereign states? Here, in a stroke, was the solution to the problem of dual sovereignty. It was denied. In matters over which the Constitution grants the federal government authority, the states must bow.

This clause did not subjugate the states, however, because the power of the federal government was thought to be relatively limited. But within its proper sphere, its law had to be dominant, and by this provision the Constitution declared itself the supreme law of the land. "Not a treaty, nor an agreement between sovereign states, but a law. It was a law enacted by the highest of all law-making bodies, the people; and in its enforcement the government backed by all the armed power of the nation; but the significance is that it was a law, and as such was enforceable in the courts." This clause thus established the supremacy of federal law, but it was to do something else of momentous significance: it was to permit the Supreme Court to become the ultimate body deciding whether laws and actions of the government circumvent the Constitution itself and to invalidate them if they do so. (This power and its logic is explored in Chapter 4).

Article Four: This article contains a variety of miscellaneous provisions, some taken over from the Articles of Confederation, that further spell out the nature of the federal union being created. It makes court judgments of one state binding in other states ("full faith and credit" clause) and declares that "the Citizens of each State shall be entitled to all Privileges and Immunities of Citizens in the several States," an ambiguous clause at least four meanings of which have been discovered. Today this clause is taken to mean that a state cannot discriminate against nonresidents in favor of its own citizens (although there are many exceptions even to this seemingly simple statement of the rule).

The article also deals with criminal extradition, formation of new states, and the power of Congress to govern in territorial lands that are not yet states. This last provision played an important part in the *Dred Scott* case, as we will see in Chapter 7. Finally, the article guarantees a "Republican Form of Government" to every state, but courts have been loathe to interfere with the internal structure of state government because the power to decide whether a particular state government is republican in form or not rests with Congress and the president. Presumably, however, if a state were to decide to elect a governor for life, Congress would have the power to overturn such a law.

Article Five: This article prescribes the methods by which the Constitution itself may be amended. After a two-thirds vote in each house of Congress, a constitutional amendment is submitted to the states for ratification. Three-fourths of the states (which now means thirty-eight states) must approve any such change, or, the legislatures of two-thirds of the states (thirty-four states) may call for a constitutional convention. Amendments emerging from such a convention then must be submitted to the states as before. However, all twenty-six amendments to the Constitution have been proposed first by Congress: there has never been a second constitutional convention (although close to two-thirds of the states asked for one during the 1960s as a result of unhappiness over the Supreme Court's reapportionment decisions (Chapter 15), among others).

Article Six: Aside from the supremacy clause discussed above, this article affirms that the debts of the United States under the new Constitution remain valid if contracted before its adoption. It also requires the allegiance of every federal *and state* official to the Constitution, further underscoring its supremacy as the law of the land. Though it requires officials to take an oath to this effect, it prohibits any religious test as a qualification for holding federal office. (In 1961, the Supreme Court extended this principle to state office).

Clearing the Air: The Great Debate

Except for certain prohibitions against governmental action (which we will shortly examine), the foregoing is the substance of the Constitution that was finally adopted in Philadelphia on September 17, 1787. Objections to it, both in minute detail and in general purpose, continued to the last—and even beyond. Only thirty-nine of the fifty-five delegates to the Constitutional Convention signed the final instrument, and the fight in the states over ratification was sharp and fierce. Nine states were required to assent before the Constitution could have legal existence; only after considerable doubt about the outcome did New Hampshire become the ninth state to ratify it on June 21, 1788. Four days later it was affirmed by a close margin in Virginia.

But the enormous, widespread, and vituperative debate that attended ratification in each state was cleansing. "Upon the whole," George Washington wrote, "I doubt whether the opposition to the Constitution will not ultimately be productive of more good than evil; it has called forth, in its defence, abilities which would not perhaps have been otherwise exerted that have thrown new light upon the science of Government, they have given the rights of man a full and fair discussion, and explained them in so clear and forcible a manner, as cannot fail to make a lasting impression."

One of the notable by-products of the debate was that matchless series of essays by Hamilton, Madison, and Jay. Almost immediately collected under the title *Federalist Papers,* they are indispensable reading to anyone who undertakes to discover the intellectual origins and meaning of the Constitution.

In the end, those who made the difference agreed with Benjamin Franklin, whose speech to the Convention on its final day called for adoption because nothing better was likely to emerge: "I confess that there are several parts of this constitution which I do not at present approve," he said. "But I am not sure I shall never approve them. For having lived long, I have experienced many instances of being obliged by better information or fuller consideration, to change opinions even on important subjects, which I once thought right, but found to be otherwise . . . I consent, Sir, to this Constitution because I expect no better and because I am not sure that it is not the best."

The Price of Ratification: The Bill of Rights

The largest outcry against the Constitution arose because it lacked a bill of rights. The omission was not due to the novelty: eight states had such bills in their constitutions. It was due, rather, to the prevailing belief among the delegates in Philadelphia that a formal declaration of rights was unnecessary because the government created was one of limited powers only. In other words, the Constitution by its terms did not grant Congress or the other branches the power to interfere with the fundamental liberties of the citizens. Five days before the end of the Convention, by a vote of ten to none, Elbridge Gerry's motion that a bill of rights be included was defeated.

The omission was the focus of debate over ratification. Those who had opposed such a bill argued strenuously on behalf of their position. "Why declare that things shall not be done which there is no power (in Congress) to do?" asked Hamilton. Roger Sherman said that "no bill of rights ever yet bound the supreme power longer than the honeymoon of a new married couple, unless the rulers were interested in preserving the rights; and in that case they have always been ready enough to declare the rights, and to preserve them when they were declared." And Noah Webster, not a delegate to the Convention, contributed his sarcastic best in suggesting that the bill of rights might contain a clause "that everybody shall, in good weather, hunt on his own land, and catch fish in rivers that are public property . . . and that Congress shall never restrain any inhabitant of America from eating and drinking, at seasonable times, or prevent his lying on his left side, in a long winter's night, or even on his back, when he is fatigued by lying on his right."

Alexander Hamilton, who defined in The Federalist *what he believed to be the proper role of the Supreme Court in interpreting the Constitution as fundamental law of the land.*

But all such expressions of opinion—plain and flowery, simple and clever—were far of the mark. The Constitution created a government with power over people; it was no mere treaty among states. Within its sphere, it was supreme. Eight states felt the necessity of restraining their governments by declaring the rights of man. Why should the federal government be immune to such restraint? Why would a federal government be insensible to the passions that move those who rule to abrogate what the plain people consider their rights? Did not the Constitution itself grant Congress the power to do what was necessary and proper to carry out its delegated powers? Who would say that an invasion of individual rights might not be justified as a necessity, as an appropriate

response to a situation that none had foreseen?

More to the point, the Constitution did contain several provisions that imposed direct restraints on the power of Congress and the states to act. Section Nine of Article One forbade the suspension of the writ of habeas corpus, by which a person who is imprisoned may come before a court to plead that he has been unlawfully detained, "unless when in Cases of Rebellion or Invasion the public Safety may require it." More absolute were the prohibitions of bills of attainder and ex post facto laws. Parliament had used these devices to punish those whose actions it disliked, though they had done nothing unlawful at the time they acted. Also Congress could not grant a title of nobility. Likewise, by Section Ten of Article One, the states were forbidden from taking these same actions and also from "impairing the Obligation of Contracts," a clause that as we will see in Chapter 5 had, for a time, a certain bite.

But why did these protections stop there? On this fundamental question of a bill of rights, it must be conceded that the framers of the Constitution were obtuse (and also exhausted from the hot, summer-long debate). It may well be that they omitted to protect the liberties they had fought a war to preserve because they, the Founding Fathers, knew what they were about. *They* knew that the government of the United States was not being established in order to impose a national religion, to shackle the press, to abolish the jury system, to confiscate the private property of the citizenry, to invade their homes, to quarter soldiers there. They also knew that George Washington, who sat silent for four months as presiding officer in Philadelphia, would be the first president, and they knew he would not have such designs on his countrymen. But what of those who would come after? How could it be supposed that the separate branches of government would not all agree with one another about the necessity of violating the rights of the people? To these questions there simply were no reasonable answers.

As a result of popular demand in state after state, many of which attached to their ratifications a demand or statement of expectation that the new Congress would prepare a bill of rights (New York, a holdout, finally ratified with the notation that it was doing so "in full confidence" that amendments would "receive an early consideration"), a bill of rights came up for consideration. It was introduced by James Madison, then a congressman, in June of 1789. After a heated debate, the House sent seventeen amendments over to the Senate in the fourth week of August. The Senate

Opposite page:

James Madison, who, like Franklin, was gifted with genius; principal architect of the Constitution.

Charles Phelps Cushing
from H. Armstrong Roberts

pared the list to fourteen. Members of both houses, including Madison, then sat down to iron out their differences. On September 25, just a week more than two years following the conclusion of the Constitutional Convention, Congress sent twelve amendments to President Washington for transmittal to the states, which would have to ratify them. Of these twelve, ten were adopted. They constitute our present Bill of Rights.

Ironically, two states that had been the most persistent advocates of enshrining civil liberties in the Constitution, were among the last to ratify: Virginia was the eleventh and last state necessary to make the amendments operative (in December 1791). But Massachusetts, which for a time had threatened not to ratify the Constitution until a bill of rights was adopted, did not get around to giving its consent until 1941, one hundred fifty years later.

In briefest compass, the Bill of Rights contains the following provisions:

The First Amendment embraces a cluster of liberties that relate to the individuality of each person: the freedoms of thought, belief, and speech. So fundamental are these freedoms that there is something of a double meaning in their having come to be known as "First Amendment rights." The amendment is worth quoting here in full: "Congress shall make no law respecting an establishment of religion, or prohibiting the free exercise thereof; or abridging the freedom of speech, or of the press; or the right of the people peaceably to assemble, and to petition the Government for a redress of grievances."

The amendment applies only to the federal government. Madison wanted these restrictions to apply equally to the states, and the House proposed language to accomplish this in its version of the amendment. However, the Senate deleted it, and it was not restored. Today, however, by virtue of the Fourteenth Amendment, these restrictions have come to be applicable to the states as well.

The Second Amendment preserves the right of the people "to keep and bear Arms," but the courts have said that this is not an absolute right. Laws prohibiting private paramilitary associations and the carrying of concealed weapons have been upheld. The Third Amendment prohibits the government from quartering soldiers in private homes in peacetime without the owner's consent. This amendment has the distinction of being the only provision of the Constitution that the government has never attempted to violate.

The Fourth Amendment is concerned with privacy, though

not so broadly as many proponents of the right of privacy today would like. It prevents the government from searching a person, his home, or his personal possessions or from seizing them, unless the government has "probable cause" to believe that a crime has been committed, and only then if it has obtained a search warrant issued by a judge in which "the place to be searched and the persons or things to be seized" are described in detail. (This capsule description is necessarily loose: the police need not obtain warrants for every arrest or for every search. In the past fifteen years there has been an enormous volume of litigation over the precise limits of this amendment.)

The Fifth Amendment lays down a number of strictures. A person cannot be tried for a felony without a grand jury indictment. The amendment also prohibits double jeopardy, which means that a person who has been acquitted by a jury of a crime may not be retried for the same offense. It prohibits the government from forcing a person to testify against himself, hence the expression "pleading the Fifth." It also contains the famous due process clause: "nor shall any person . . . be deprived of life, liberty, or property, without due process of law." It also requires the owner of private property taken for public use to be justly compensated.

The Sixth Amendment sets forth the elements of a fair trial that the government may not refuse. The trial must be convened speedily (the accused may not be compelled to languish in prison), and it must be open to the public. The accused is entitled to an impartial jury in the community where the crime occurred, and he must be advised of the crimes the government is charging him with. He must be permitted to cross-examine witnesses who testify against him, and he must be able to compel witnesses who will testify in his favor to come to court. He has the right to be represented by a lawyer.

The Seventh Amendment preserves the right to trial by jury in common law cases "where the value in controversy shall exceed twenty dollars." This is one of the few clauses in the Constitution that refers to a figure that has lost meaning in a later age. By law today, federal courts cannot hear cases where the value in controversy is less than ten thousand dollars unless the case involves federal law. The amendment also forbids courts to reexamine facts found by juries, except as the common law permits.

The Eighth Amendment prohibits excessive bail and excessive

fines. It also bars cruel and unusual punishment.

The Ninth Amendment reads as follows: "The enumeration in the Constitution of certain rights, shall not be construed to deny or disparage others retained by the people." This amendment was added to answer the objections of those who thought that naming some rights but not all might result in the government's claiming the power to prevent a person, in Webster's words, from "lying on his left side on a long winter's night."

The Tenth Amendment further underscores the intent of the framers. "The powers not delegated to the United States by the Constitution, nor prohibited by it to the States, are reserved to the States respectively, or to the people." This amendment establishes no rights, nor takes any away; it serves to remind that the government is for the people, and not the reverse.

The Constitution as Organic Law

So the Constitution and the Bill of Rights were brought into being. But they were not, thereby, finished works. To the contrary. George M. Dallas, President Polk's vice-president, wrote in the middle of the last century that "the Constitution in its words is plain and intelligible, and it is meant for the homebred, unsophisticated understandings of our fellow citizens." He was wrong. The Constitution and its amendments are written in vague, general terms. Who can define with precision what "legislative power" means and where the line is between it and the "judicial power"? Who can spell out what is Due Process, which punishments are "cruel and unusual," and what is an interference with the "free exercise" of religion?

The very construction of the Constitution and the creation of a system of government, which gives each branch power and motive to check the others, inevitably means that great issues will become legal ones—that is, constitutional ones—and brought into court. That is inescapable because any action of government may be fitted to one of the constitutional prohibitions and found wanting. There is always some way to challenge the government, and a society whose traditions are deeply rooted in the concept of control over government will not lack for people who will try. So American society has become a litigious society in which virtually no law that passes in Congress and is signed by the president is ever really secure until the courts dismiss the inevitable suits that challenge it and test its limitations.

One final point should be made here. The Constitution has the distinction of being an almost timeless document but for one grievous flaw. It did not abolish slavery. Despite the enlightened rhetoric of the Declaration of Independence and the freedoms nobly guaranteed in the Constitution, one class of citizens was completely outside the law. Many members of the Constitutional Convention did want to eradicate slavery once and for all, including members from the South as well as the North.

Feeling was too high, and the Convention sought first and foremost to preserve the Union. So a series of compromises were woven throughout the Constitution.

For purposes of apportioning seats in the House of Representatives, slaves were counted as three-fifths of a person. This led some to dissent. Since slaves were property, why should not the Northern states, which forbade slavery, be permitted to count three-fifths of their horses or pigs. A special provision in Article One prohibited Congress from restricting the "migration or importation of such persons as any of the states . . . shall think proper to admit" for twenty years or until 1808. A slave who escaped to a free state could not thereby be declared free; the second state had to deliver the slave back to his owners in the first state—all this despite the command that the United States guarantee a republican form of government in the states.

Those who detested slavery reconciled themselves to this grievous and glaring flaw that contradicted the Declaration of Independence at its most solemn point—that all men are created equal—by assuming that slavery would in time vanish naturally. But it would not go away so easily. The compromise that saved the Union could not be peacefully eliminated, and the amendments that would make the Constitution true to itself could come about only after the bloodiest war in American history.

NEW-YORK HEI

No. 129.   SATURDAY, MARCH 26, 1803.

MANDAMUS.

Opinion of the Supreme Court, delivered by
Chief Justice Marshall, Feb. 24, 1803.

William Marbury   } On a motion for a
        vs.   }   Mandamus.
The Secretary of State,

McCulloch vs. Maryland

PART II:
BRINGING THE
SYSTEM TO LIFE

3/ JOHN MARSHALL AND
THE MARSHALL COURT

I f one were to play the game of guessing who the most important people in American history were, one correct answer would be John Marshall. He surely ranks in the list of the top ten, and it would be difficult to dispute that he ranks in the top five, perhaps even the top three. Indeed, there might be a case for naming him *the* most important person, except that such a game is silly. It obviously is impossible to single out one person because a democratic society depends upon too many others.

Yet for all his importance, John Marshall is curiously unknown to the descendants of his countrymen. That is because he sat on the bench of that most unknown of American institutions, the Supreme Court. Today, even from the educated classes, the judicial process is remote and mysterious. For all its notoriety, the Supreme Court is barely understood. Its decisions are rarely read, except by practicing lawyers, judges, and an occasional law professor. This is not to say that Americans are unmindful of the thunderbolts that seem regularly to be cast from the nine justices; the Supreme Court has been in the headlines for years, and not infrequently. More and more newspapers and the broadcast industry are hiring lawyers as journalists. But most of the nuances go unexplored and unappreciated, unlike the torrents of commentary that probe hidden meanings and chart new turns of policy in every pedestrian speech that the presidents make.

This was much less true in Marshall's time. What the Court said and how it ruled generated excitement as well as long and passionate commentary in the press and elsewhere. Newspapers printed the full text of several rather lengthy decisions, a practice totally abandoned today. (Of course there are services available at a steep price that deliver full texts to lawyers and libraries, but they do not find their way into the homes or offices of the nonlegal, literate world).

There are several reasons for this difference. One is that the literate population at the turn of the nineteenth century was far smaller and more homogeneous than it is today. For another, the opinion leaders, when Marshall began his tenure in office and for several years thereafter, had been participants in the Revolution and the Constitutional Convention and its ratification aftermath. These were no bystanders or descendants raised on theory. These were practical men who fought for the law, who made it, decreed it, persuaded others of the need for it, and were now arguing before the Supreme Court for their interpretations of it.

Also, the slate was cleaner, and the issues were far more basic, because while many knew the local law of everyday life, they did not know the constitutional law of the nation. There was an impressive body of commentary on the common law in the opinions of English judges, in the opinions of colonial and, later, in the opinions of state courts, and in Blackstone. These could serve as precedents, to be followed or not as the needs of the time dictated. But there was no such body of law interpreting the Constitution, no guide to its application in concrete cases. The ratification in 1788 was a profound rupture of the law on the constitutional plane. Majestic phrases conjured up a government, but how it all was supposed to work was, in 1787 and for long afterward, yet to be determined.

The Supreme Court did not have its beginnings in 1801, when the "great Chief Justice" was confirmed and took his seat. A Court existed since 1789, when President Washington appointed a chief justice (John Jay) and four associate justices, but it did not begin to play its role as a powerful and oracular tribunal until John Marshall consolidated its power and wrote masterful, enduring opinions for the ages to come. The pre-Marshall Court ruled on two constitutional questions, one of which—that the states may be hauled into federal court by citizens of another state—so provoked fear in the states, though it was undoubtedly a correct decision, that they pushed through the Eleventh Amendment, denying jurisdiction to federal courts in such cases. It remained to the Marshall Court to scale down the extravagant claims made for the Eleventh Amendment so that a practical, orderly, and lawful system of government could result.

The other constitutional case settled the meaning of the ex post facto clause; in *Calder* v. *Bull,* the Court ruled that only retroactive penal laws were prohibited. Congress (and the states), that is, cannot pass a law subjecting someone to fine or imprisonment for an act that was not unlawful when it was undertaken, but laws that do not directly have such an effect are permissible. Thus a law changing the rules of evidence, allowing evidence against a defendant that would not have been admissible at the time the crime

John Jay, the first Chief Justice. He resigned from the Supreme Court in 1795 to become Governor of New York.

was committed, is entirely constitutional. This distinction—between penal and nonpenal laws—has pretty much stood the test of time, though the Court has occasionally made some fishy rulings (one example is the approval of a law deporting a person for having joined the Communist Party, though membership was not unlawful until after he had resigned).

But little else is remembered from those early days. So insignificant did the Court seem, in fact, that when the federal government moved to the new capital city, Washington, in 1800, a place for the justices to meet was entirely omitted from the otherwise splendid—some said extravagant—architectural arrangements being made for Congress and the president. Space was made available only two weeks before the Court's term was to commence. Then the justices were given only "a small and undignified chamber" on the main floor of the North or Senate side of the Capitol building. And the Court did not move into its own quarters, the Supreme Court building north of the Library of Congress and east of the Capitol, until 1935.

It was this seeming insignificance, plus the onerous requirement that the justices "ride circuit" throughout the country in between sessions of the Supreme Court, that caused John Jay to decline reappointment as chief justice by President Adams in 1801, when Oliver Ellsworth, then in ill health, resigned. Jay had resigned in June, 1795, though he had left the Court fourteen months earlier to serve as Washington's special envoy to London. He then served two three-year terms as governor of New York but had been ousted in the Jeffersonian sweep of 1800. As was customary for a time in those years, Adams reappointed him without bothering first to check to see whether Jay would accept. Then fifty-four, he cited health as his primary reason for declining the appointment, which the Senate had already confirmed. But his refusal also was motivated by the belief that the job would never amount to much. "I left the Bench perfectly convinced," he wrote Adams, "that under a system so defective, [the Court] would not obtain the energy, weight and dignity which are essential to its affording due support to the National Government, nor acquire the public confidence and respect which, as the last resort of the justice of the nation, it should possess."

Leading politicians then assumed that associate justice William Paterson would be named chief justice, and they pressured Adams to do so. Marshall himself had recommended Paterson's appointment, but Adams had eliminated Paterson in his mind even before the Jay nomination. For one thing, naming Paterson would have insulted the senior associate justice, William Cushing, who was almost sixty-nine and considered too old to be appointed chief. Moreover, Paterson, then fifty-five, was identified with Hamilton, who had fallen out with Adams in a major party split that cost Adams his reelection.

Finally, a bill called the Judiciary Act of 1801, whose passage Adams had pushed, was pending. The intent of this bill (it would be enacted in the near future) was to reduce the number of Supreme Court judges from six to five. Consequently, he had to hurry with his nomination to avoid being stuck with a five-man bench. He had but a short time to insure a sixth Federalist on the Court for life. So, on January 20, 1801, he forwarded to the Senate the name of his forty-five-year-old secretary of state.

Marshall later recounted the moment that Adams reported this decision to him (in his 1827 autobiography). "When I waited on the President with Mr. Jay's letter declining appointment, he said thoughtfully, 'Who shall I nominate now?' I replied that I could not tell . . . After a few moments hesitation he said, 'I believe I must nominate you.' I had never before heard myself named for the office and had not even thought of it. I was pleased as well as surprised, and bowed in silence."

Though Marshall was destined to imprint the Federalist philosophy on our constitutional law, the Federalists were at first shocked and upset at the nomination. It was not that Marshall was unknown. The secretary of state could scarcely be invisible, and he had gained reknown in 1798 as one of the three American commissioners to France who had stood up to the solicitations of bribery by Talleyrand's agents in the XYZ affair. Moreover, he was unquestionably one of the three or four leading members of the Richmond (Virginia) bar. But he had stood apart from the Federalists by condemning the Alien and Sedition Acts, and one party leader feared that "he will think much of the State of Virginia, and is too much disposed to govern the world according to rules of logic; he will read and expound the Constitution as if it were a penal statute, and will sometimes be embarrassed with doubts, of which his friends will not perceive the importance." In retrospect, this was a colossal misjudgment, but it was widely shared at the time. The Senate held off his confirmation for a week in the hope that Adams could be persuaded to change his mind and nominate Paterson. When it was clear that Adams would not budge, the Senate capitulated and confirmed Marshall on January 27, 1801.

Marshall was born in 1755, in the village of Germantown, in Fauquier County, Virginia. His father, Thomas Marshall, grew up as a neighbor and friend of George Washington. Thomas was a farmer, surveyor, and commercial agent for Lord Fairfax, and in 1767 he was appointed sheriff of Fauquier County. John Marshall was educated at home until the age of fourteen. Then he went a hundred miles away to a modest boarding school for one year; one of his classmates there was James Monroe. The following year Thomas imported a Scottish tutor for his children; from him Marshall learned Latin and the classics. At the age of twenty John joined the Continental Army and fought in several battles. He was with Washington during that terrible winter of 1777 at Valley Forge and remained with the army and in the war until 1779.

Over the course of the next year he spent some three months at William and Mary, taking courses in law from George Wythe, the nation's first professor of law. On August 28, 1780, after producing a formal document from Governor Thomas Jefferson attesting to his fitness, he became a member of the Fauquier bar.

During the Confederation and for a time thereafter, Marshall sat in the Virginia House of Delegates, and for two years he was a member of the Virginia Executive Council of State. During the 1780s he was judge in a court with jurisdiction over small claims and minor crimes. Except for the council position, the other posts were elective, and Marshall's popularity gained him frequent re-election. In 1788, at the age of thirty-four, he was a delegate to the Virginia Convention to ratify the Constitution; his three speeches in favor of ratification helped consolidate the narrow majority that ultimately voted for the Constitution.

But none of these activities took a large amount of time from his law practice. With his marriage in 1783 to his beloved Polly Ambler, Marshall determined to put his burgeoning family on a sound financial footing. His Richmond practice grew, and, it has been suggested, he was becoming an "embryonic" political boss in the 1790s. He declined Washington's offer in 1789 to make him the first U.S. attorney for Virginia, and he declined several other offers of both Washington and Adams. In 1793 he entered into negotiations with a syndicate to purchase a vast tract of land from the successors to Lord Fairfax's claim in Virginia. He was not to be finished worrying over the due dates of the notes taken out to finance the deal until 1806. His involvement in this land speculation caused some criticism of him when he wrote the opinion in *Fletcher* v. *Peck*, and he was unable to participate in other Court cases later, notably *Martin* v. *Hunter's Lessee*, because of it.

In 1797, however, he acceded to Adams' request that he go to France to try to preserve the fragile peace. He hoped for a reward

from Congress, and he was not disappointed, though a large financial grant came as a result of his standing up to Talleyrand's agents rather than through any successful negotiation. Somewhat relieved of his financial burdens, he served his only term in Congress, 1799-1800, at the former president's urging and then accepted Adams' invitation to serve the collapsing administration as secretary of state. In 1798 he declined Adams' offer of the Supreme Court seat vacated by James Wilson's death. The salary of a justice was then only $3500, and Marshall was not financially secure enough to accept a position that would preclude him from carrying on his lucrative law practice.

Whatever his own partisans' doubts about his political leanings or his statesmanship, there was little doubt about his ability as a lawyer. "This gentleman, when aroused," said one Virginian, "has strong reasoning powers, they are indeed almost unequalled." Another said of his performances in court: "He possesses neither the energy of expression nor the sublimity of imagination of Innes [James Innes, Virginia's attorney general], but he is superior to every other orator at the Bar of Virginia, in closeness of argument, in his most surprising talent of placing his case in that point of view suited to the purpose he aims at, throwing a blaze of light upon it, and of keeping the attention of his hearers fixed upon the object to which he originally directed it. He speaks like a man of plain common sense, while he delights and informs the acute. In a less captivating line of oratory than that which signalizes Innes, he is equally great and equally successful. The jury obeys Innes from inclination, Marshall from duty."

Even Jefferson, who detested from the start what he called the "spirit of Marshallism," paid him a backhanded compliment. According to Justice Story, Jefferson once said, "When conversing with Marshall, I never admit anything. So sure as you admit any position to be good, no matter how remote from the conclusion he seeks to establish, you are gone. So great is his sophistry you must never give him an affirmative answer or you will be forced to grant his conclusion. Why, if he were to ask me if it were daylight or not, I'd reply, 'Sir, I don't know, I can't tell.' "

It is customary to separate the Court's history into periods denoted by the names of the chief justices. Thus the current bench is commonly referred to as the "Burger Court." Usually this is a mistaken practice, because the chief justice has but limited formal power to persuade his fellow justices (all of whom are senior in service at the time of his appointment) to follow his views. The only time that there is any logic in calling the Court by its chief's

Opposite page:

John Adams, who as President moved John Marshall from Secretary of State to Chief Justice of the Supreme Court.

Charles Phelps Cushing
from H. Armstrong Roberts

name is when a single president appoints several justices who share a common philosophy. Then there actually might be more logic to call it by the president's name, as is sometimes done today, for instance, the "Nixon Court."

In fact, the force of the custom springs from history and the precedent Marshall set, not from logic. Against the odds at the time, Marshall forged the Court into a powerful pronationalist weapon, though after a few years most of the other justices were at least nominally Republican, not Federalist. Marshall created the "Marshall Court" by making a basic change in the way it conducted its business as an institution. Under Jay and Ellsworth, the justices were in the habit of each pronouncing an opinion on the case at hand. Rather than a court speaking, there were several justices speaking. Marshall changed this procedure to one whereby a single justice voiced the *opinion of the Court*. This gave much greater power and dignity to the opinion. It also gave much influence to Marshall, because as chief justice he took upon himself the task of announcing them. It has been estimated that Marshall delivered in his name for the Court about half of the opinions the Court issued between 1801 and 1835.

It would be unwarranted to conclude that Marshall succeeded in changing the character of the Court because of the weakness or unimaginativeness of his brethren. In 1955, on the bicentennial of Marshall's birth, Justice Felix Frankfurter spoke to this point. He said:

It is not to be assumed that what Marshall wrote was wholly the product of his own brain, freed from infusion of his brethren's thinking. In his day there was the closest intimacy among the judges. It is inconceivable that they did not discuss their cases in their common boardinghouse. A man of Marshall's charm and power was bound to make himself deeply felt among his brethren. But the assumption that he dominated his colleagues leaves out of reckoning the strong personalities among them. Story had the deepest devotion to Marshall, but he also had views and vanity. Johnson's opinions reveal tough-mindedness, abounding intellectual energy, and a downright character. Likewise, we may be sure that Bushrod Washington was no mere echo. And so one may be confident in inferring that the novelty of the issues, the close social relations of the Justices, the ample opportunities they had for discussion among themselves, precluded Marshall's pathbreaking opinions from being exclusively solo performances. Then as now, constitutional decisions were the outcome of the deliberative process, and as such, more or less composite products. But their expression is individual. The voice of the Court cannot avoid imparting the distinction of its own accent to a Court opinion. In the leading constitutional cases Marshall spoke for the Court. But he

*spoke. The prestige of his office, the esteem which he personally aroused,
the deference he evoked, enabled Marshall to formulate in his own way
an agreement collectively reached.*

The length of Marshall's tenure is another reason for his decisive place in American history. If he had proclaimed the decision
in *Marbury* v. *Madison* only, and made it stick, there would still
need to be a biography of the man. But he also decided *Fletcher* v.
Peck, Dartmouth College v. *Woodward, McCulloch* v. *Maryland,
Cohens* v. *Virginia, Gibbons* v. *Ogden,* and *Osborn* v. *Bank of the
United States.* These seven decisions made the Union that the Civil
War preserved. It was a breathtaking, prodigious achievement. The
majestic sweep of his opinions gave flesh and blood to the Constitutional skeleton. His writing style, said Justice Benjamin N.
Cardozo (himself no mean stylist) in his essay on *Law and Literature,* was of the highest order; Cardozo called it "magisterial." So
penetrating and forceful were these opinions that one of his bitterest
opponents, John Randolph of Roanoke, was reduced to saying of
them: "All wrong, all wrong, but no man in the United States can
tell why or wherein." And during his entire tenure on the bench,
Marshall dissented in only one constitutional case. This was *Ogden*
v. *Saunders.*

Owing to his relative youth when appointed and his long life—
until three months short of his eightieth birthday—his influence was
immense. (It is said that his life was prolonged, unwittingly, by the
Jeffersonians in 1802, when they abolished the summer term of the
Court, to delay Marbury's case, thus releasing the justices from the
oppressive tropical Augusts of Washington.) Marshall sat on the
Court longer than any but two other justices (Stephen B. Field,
1863-1897, and William O. Douglas, 1939-1975). During his thirty-
four years on the bench, Marshall served with fifteen other justices,
appointed by every president from Washington through Jackson.
The tenure of those who labored with Marshall stretches seventy-
eight years, from an original appointment in 1789 (William Cushing, who served until his death in 1810) to 1867 (James M. Wayne,
appointed a few months before Marshall's death). Considering that
there have been exactly a hundred justices as of the beginning of
the bicentennial year, and that until 1837 there were only six
justices on the Court (compared with nine since then), the Marshall
Court comprises a noteworthy 15 percent of the Court's entire
membership. (By contrast, Field served with twenty-one other
justices, whose tenure ranged from 1835 to 1911, or seventy-six
years. Douglas served with twenty-nine justices, the earliest of
whom was appointed in 1914, sixty-one years).

To the end of his life, Marshall was known as a decent, unassuming, even humble man, never one to flaunt his position or put on airs. His dress was always at least slightly disheveled, and the stories about his kindnesses in Richmond are legendary, despite the hostility with which his opinions were received by a large number of influential Virginia citizens. His ideas may have been detested, but the man was venerated. This was true wherever he went. In 1833 Marshall went to the theater one evening with Joseph Story, "and on the Chief Justice's entrance into the box," Story later reported, "he was cheered in a marked manner. He behaved as he always does, with extreme modesty, and seemed not to know that the compliment was designed for him." Marshall died on July 6, 1835, and his death was mourned throughout the nation.

It is not possible in a book of this scope to take more than a cursory look at some of Marshall's colleagues. But some of the more eminent of these justices deserve at least brief mention.

Joseph Story: At age thirty-two, the youngest man ever appointed to the Court (in 1811), Story is generally considered to have been the greatest legal scholar ever to sit on the Supreme Court and "one of the great jurists of the western world." His service was almost as lengthy as Marshall's; he died in 1845, two months short of his thirty-fourth year on the bench. Story was born in 1779 in Marblehead, Massachusetts, the oldest of eleven children. He qualified for Harvard largely through self-tutoring and graduated in 1798. He decided to be a poet but became a lawyer instead, as some poets still do, because there are few opportunities to employ the muse. He was admitted to the bar in 1801, the same year Marshall became chief justice.

In 1805 a work of poetry and his first book on law were published; he married and was elected to the state legislature, a rush of happy events before the storm. Only a few months after his marriage, his wife and then his father died, and he turned his full attention to the law to escape his grief. He came to national attention as the successful lawyer in *Fletcher* v. *Peck* in 1810, having been elected to the House of Representatives in a special election to fill an unexpired term in 1808. His waffling stand on Jefferson's embargo on foreign trade (he began by supporting Jefferson, a dangerous position in Adams' Federalist Massachusetts) cost him renomination. He returned to Massachusetts and became speaker of the state house.

In 1810, Justice Cushing died. Had Jefferson still been president, he certainly would not have named Story. As it was, Madison almost did not, though he knew and admired Story. But three nominations ran into trouble. Levi Lincoln, his first choice, as well as his third, John Quincy Adams, turned down the job, though the Senate had confirmed both. The second choice, Alexander Wolcott, was rejected.

Though appointed as a Republican, Story quickly assumed an expansive, nationalist philosophy. He was largely responsible for a broad reading of Congressional power over inland waterways, a significant step in view of the vast commerce carried on the rivers before the advent of the railroads. He wrote the opinion in *Martin v. Hunter's Lessee,* joined Marshall in *McCulloch,* and issued a lengthy and scholarly concurring opinion in the *Dartmouth* case.

Joseph Story, at age 32 appointed to the Supreme Court in 1811. Intimate friend of Marshall, he was regarded as one of the finest legal scholars ever to serve on the high bench.

In 1829 he accepted the position of Dane Professor of Law at Harvard, teaching and judging simultaneously until his death. At Harvard he wrote nine immensely influential commentaries on various fields of law, "an outburst virtually unrivalled in the history of legal writings." Among the most famous were those dealing with the Constitution, equity, and conflicts of laws. But his scholarship was not devoted to treatises. He injected deep, weighty learning into most of his opinions on the Court; the scope and detail of his knowledge was so vast and he held his beliefs so tenaciously that Andrew Jackson reportedly called him "the most dangerous man in America."

Besides his activity as judge and professor, he also devoted time to activities that would today be frowned on as inconsistent with judicial duties. He participated in the drafting of several statutes, including the federal criminal code, made necessary by the Court's ruling in *United States* v. *Hudson and Goodwin* in 1812 that the federal courts could not define and punish federal crimes in the absence of a Congressional statute. In the field of criminal law, in other words, there could be no common law. Story dissented from this position, and he wrote the opinion in *Swift* v. *Tyson* (see Chapter 11), which for nearly a hundred years enabled the federal courts to develop a federal common law in civil disputes. He was also president of the Merchants Bank of Salem from 1815 to 1838 and a vice-president of the Salem Institute for Savings, which gave him practical experience and judicial interest in the law of negotiable instruments and bankruptcy. He was a keen advocate of federal bankruptcy law. And in the year before his death, Story was president of the American Unitarian Association.

In the 1840s, Story decided to resign from the bench, if he could do so in the expectation that a president would appoint a congenial successor. This was not to be: in 1845 he planned to retire upon completion of his work but died while engaged in preparing circuit court opinions.

Bushrod Washington: The inheritor of his uncle's Mount Vernon estate, Bushrod Washington was the first of Adams' three appointments to the Supreme Court, where he served from 1798 to 1829, largely eclipsed by his old classmate and friend, John Marshall. Born in 1762, Washington graduated from William and Mary College in 1778 and thereafter studied law with John Marshall in George Wythe's classes at the college. For about a year, in 1780, he served in the American army in Virginia at the close of the war. He then studied in the Philadelphia law office of James Wilson, who was one of President Washington's first appointments to the Court and to whose seat he succeeded. In 1792, after having practiced elsewhere, he moved to Richmond, where he continued his private practice until assuming his duties on the Court.

Like his more eminent friend and colleague, Washington was a thoroughgoing Federalist; he and Marshall took separate positions in only three cases before the Court during their twenty-eight years of joint service. Though not insensitive to human suffering and human rights, he reneged on his uncle's promise to emancipate the Mount Vernon slaves upon Martha Washington's death. He was the first president, in 1816, of the American Colonization Society, whose purpose was to settle freed slaves in Africa. On his death, Story said in his eulogy:

His mind was solid, rather than brilliant; sagacious and searching, rather than quick or eager; slow, but not torpid; steady, but not unyielding; comprehensive, and at the same time cautious; patient in inquiry, forcible in conception; clear in reasoning. He was, by original temperament, mild, conciliating and candid; and yet was remarkable for an uncompromising firmness. Of him, it may be truly said, that the fear of man never fell upon him; it never entered into his thoughts, much less was it seen in his actions. In him the love of justice was the ruling passion—it was the master-spring of all his conduct.

William Johnson: Jefferson's first appointment to the Court in 1804, Johnson was the first great dissenter. Born in Charleston, South Carolina, in 1771, he graduated from Princeton in 1790 at the top of his class and went on to study law under the direction of Charles Cotesworth Pinckney. Admitted to the bar in 1793 and married the following year, he quickly made his way in politics, rising to the speakership of the state House of Representatives by

1798. The next year he was elected to the highest state court, at the still tender age of twenty-eight. Vouchsafed to Jefferson as a man of strong Republican principles, Johnson became the second-youngest appointee at the age of thirty-two, only slightly older than Story would be when he was appointed seven years later.

Johnson wrote the opinion that denied the existence of a federal common law of crimes: "The legislative authority of the Union must first make an act a crime, affix a punishment to it, and declare the Court that shall have jurisdiction of the offense." But he was not able to curb Story's broad interpretation of federal maritime law. He dissented in *Osborn* v. *Bank of the United States*, which granted the right to the federally chartered bank to sue state officers in federal court. He would not buy Story's view that the Constitution vested all judicial power automatically in the federal courts, and Johnson's view—that Congress could control the jurisdiction of the courts—ultimately won out. But he was not an obstructionist, and he did not serve as a catalyst to the other Republicans, who a short time after his appointment outnumbered the Federalists on the Court five to two. He agreed with the decisions in *McCulloch* and *Gibbons*.

Nevertheless, he did attempt to institute one reform that Jefferson continually harped about, namely, a way to overcome Marshall's practice of speaking for the entire court. Writing to Jefferson in 1822, he said of his experience on the Court thus far: "At length I found I must either submit to circumstances or become such a cypher in our consultations as to effect no good at all. I therefore bent to the current, and persevered until I got them to adopt the course they now pursue, which is to appoint someone to deliver the opinion of the majority, but leave it to the discretion of the rest of the judges to record their opinions or not *ad libitum*." Johnson gave thirty-four of the seventy-four dissenting opinions issued during his thirty years on the Court and twenty-one of the thirty-five concurring opinions. The precedent he set established for individual justices the respectability of speaking their minds when they did not agree with the majority.

In many of his later dissents, after 1823, he struck out at the Court's voiding of state laws atempting to regulate chaotic commercial conditions within their borders, though he upheld, in even broader terms than Marshall, Congressional power to regulate interstate commerce. But he was dedicated to the Union throughout and in his last years denounced the Nullification Movement that was agitating in his home state. He died one month after Marshall.

4/ THE SURPREME COURT HAS THE LAST WORD—ALMOST: MARBURY v. MADISON

In a noted epigram, Justice Robert H. Jackson once concisely described the power and role of the Supreme Court: "We are not final because we are infallible," he said, "but we are infallible only because we are final."

This power of pronouncing the last word on constitutional questions distinguished the American legal system in its earliest days from every other system of law throughout the world, including England's. And to this day the Supreme Court remains unique among the courts of the world, as it regularly pronounces on the most delicate and difficult questions of public policy. Though it has often been embroiled in controversy, some of it extremely heated, the history of the United States is remarkable for the attitude of its people—individual citizens and governmental officials alike—in generally respecting and accepting the decisions that this tribunal renders. Yet its most important single power—the power to declare a federal or state law or activity unconstitutional—is nowhere spelled out in the Constitution.

Why Such Power?

How did so astonishing a power arise? Why should a court—a collection of judges, after all, who are not elected by the people and who are privileged to serve for life—be empowered to dictate to Congress and the president (both more representative of the people than the judiciary) what the government may do or what it may not do? And what does this power entail? How far may the Court go in ruling on constitutional questions? When may it act?

Many of these questions have no fixed or definite answer; many indeed are still being answered as every term of the Supreme Court commences each October in Washington. Most of the milestones of law considered in this book involve these very issues: the extent of the Court's power to act and the necessity of doing so.

But the basic power, the fundamental, overriding power of passing on constitutional questions, was decided very early on by the Supreme Court itself (less than fourteen years after General Washington was first inaugurated as president). To some, the fact that the Supreme Court proclaimed that it possessed such extraordinary power has always seemed at least a little self-serving. Yet it is scarcely credible that a mere usurpation of power would have long been tolerated—as it still is, one hundred seventy-three years after it was first firmly declared—especially in the face of a strong opposing power. This doctrine of judicial supremacy, next to the Constitution itself perhaps the most important milestone of law in our history, was announced in a single brilliant decision of Chief Justice Marshall, which, if he had not remained on the Court for thirty-one more years, would still have entitled him to be placed in the ranks of our foremost jurists. The case was *Marbury* v. *Madison*, and to it we must now turn our full attention.

The Judiciary Act of 1801

From the earliest proposals of the Virginia delegates to the Constitutional Convention, the dominant political philosophy in the United States had been the creation of a national government. Those who espoused this philosophy and succeeded in making it the very tissue of our political institutions came to be known as Federalists. Although not elected as the leader of any party in the modern sense, George Washington was clearly a leading member of that group that would shortly coalesce into the Federalist party, and his successor, John Adams, along with Alexander Hamilton, was clearly identified as the chief exponent of Federalist ideals: a strong national government, prescribing rules for governing all the states in common, in large part to promote and enhance a thriving interstate commerce. Those who opposed what they feared would become a dangerously powerful central government were first known simply as anti-Federalists. Later they were called Republicans (though they were the ancestors of the modern Republican party's traditional antagonist, the Democratic party). The Founding Fathers did not perceive the growth of parties as institutions destined to play an integral role in the political system. Madison denounced them and saw in the structure created by the Constitution a means of keeping them in check. In-this he was only partially correct; a two-party system kept extremists in check, but this tendency to mute the worst excesses came about only because the parties had in fact emerged.

In any event, by 1800 the Federalist party could no longer maintain its hold over the presidency or Congress. John Adams was

defeated in his bid for reelection, and after a protracted battle in
the House of Representatives where the election had been thrown,
Jefferson won. (Jefferson and Aaron Burr received an equal number
of electoral votes. This situation would not occur again because the
Twelfth Amendment, which was ratified before the next election,
changed the electoral system.) The Republicans were at last to take
charge, and the dominant political philosophy was in imminent
danger, or so it seemed, of extinction.

In those days, owing to the difficulties of communication and
transportation over the large areas of the United States, there
was a considerable lag between the election and the commencement
of the new administration. Elections were held in early November,
but the new president did not assume office until March 4 (the date
was finally changed to January 20 by the Twentieth Amendment
after the 1932 elections). During this "lame duck" period, the Federalists had the opportunity to take action consolidating their control over the one branch of government that the Republicans had
not captured in the election: the judiciary.

On February 17, four days before Jefferson finally received a
majority of the votes in the House of Representatives, the Federalist
Congress passed the Circuit Court Act of 1801, generally known as
the Judiciary Act of 1801. This was not a sudden creation. Various
proposals had been put forward for several years to reform the
judicial system created by the Judiciary Act of 1789. The chief
defect was the provision that required Supreme Court justices to
ride circuit, a practice with distant roots in English legal history.
The practice worked this way. Federal trial courts, called district
courts, were located in each state; appeals from their decisions
were to be made to the circuit courts. These courts were not really
distinct bodies in the sense that different judges were appointed to
them. Instead the circuit court consisted of district court judges
plus a Supreme Court justice specifically assigned to the circuit in
which the court sat.

In retrospect, this system seems peculiar, though it endured
for nearly a century, for it meant that lower court judges could
sit in and decide appeals of their own decisions. The Supreme Court
might later be involved in appeals from these courts, which would
require one justice to review his own decision in the lower court.
Despite this structural anomaly, the greatest complaint was from
the justices, who were required to go out on horseback across great
distances to hold court at least twice a year.

As difficult as this prospect was for a young man in his twenties, it was prodigious work for men who tended to be in their fifties and sixties—who were older and in poor physical condition. This indeed was the principal reason that John Jay declined his second appointment to the Court as Chief Justice. Although Jay doubted that the Court would ever amount to much as an independent branch of government, he might have been persuaded to resume his judicial duties if Congress would have acted on the numerous suggestions for reform, including those of Washington himself. "Independent of other considerations," Jay wrote of his decision against Adams's offer of reappointment, "the state of my health removes every doubt, it being clearly and decidedly incompetent to the fatigues incident to the office."

In 1799, Adams proposed that Congress revise the law requiring the justices to ride about the country, and after a false start and some maneuvering, the House enacted a bill on January 20, 1801. The onerous burden was removed. The bill also created six circuit courts and sixteen new and separate judgeships. Three weeks later, the Senate passed the bill, and Adams quickly signed it into law.

In view of the fact that, although Jefferson had not yet been elected, there was no doubt that neither Adams nor any other Federalist would be, the Republicans reacted bitterly and savagely. They argued that the law enabled the Federalists to widen their penetration of the judicial branch. A leading Republican newspaper, shortly before passage, branded it "one of the most expensive and extravagant, the most insidious and unnecessary schemes that has been conceived by the Federal party . . . now before Congress under the name of the Judiciary bill, but which might with greater propriety be called a bill for providing sinecure places and pensions for thoroughgoing Federal partisans." A constituent wrote to Kentucky Senator John Breckenridge that "it is a law which may be considered as the last effort of the most wicked, insidious and turbulent faction that ever disgraced our political annals, the *ne plus ultra* of an expiring faction to enthral the measures likely to be pursued by the new Administration, and to serve as one of the principal cogs in the wheel of consolidation."

It was, in fact, a sensible reform. It established in broad outlines the federal judicial system we know today. But in the heated, partisan atmosphere of the day, exacerbated by certain decisions that Federalist judges had recently made, it could reasonably be interpreted as a threat to the Jeffersonians. The threat was made credible, moreover, by the hasty actions of Adams and the outgoing Federalist Congress. When the Judiciary Act became law, Adams had remaining only eighteen days as president. In less than two weeks, he submitted his nominations for the new judgeships to the Senate. By March 2, two days before Jefferson was to become president, the Senate had approved each of the appointments, most of whom were Federalists.

The Midnight Judges

Not all of the judges ascended the circuit court bench. Just five days before Jefferson took the oath of office, Congress enacted another law giving Adams the opportunity to appoint more judges. This was the basic law for the District of Columbia. It established, among other things, the position of justice of the peace to be appointed by the president for a five-year term. On March 2, after the Senate had approved Adams's choices for the circuit courts, he submitted forty-two names for confirmation as justices of the peace, and the Senate obliged him the following day, March 3, Adams's last day in office.

To make their appointments formal, it was necessary to draw up formal documents, known as commissions, for the new justices of the peace. These papers were prepared by the secretary of state, who was then John Marshall (though he had been sworn in as chief justice a month before). There is nothing in the Constitution to prevent a member of the judiciary from holding executive office, though if widely practiced, such double assignments would surely be dangerous to a system dedicated to checks and balances. Chief justices in the past had taken on special duties for the president, and though the practice is rare, it has happened in recent times as well. Chief Justice Earl Warren, for example, chaired the official investigation of the assassination of President Kennedy. In Marshall's case, the assignment was obviously temporary (though, interestingly, Jefferson asked him to remain for one day, March 4, as his secretary of state as well).

So, during the day and into the night of March 3, the commissions of the new justices of the peace were prepared in Marshall's office, sent to the president for his signature, and returned to Marshall's clerks, where the seal of the United States was placed on each. (This at any rate is the official version; a Republican Congressman the following December told a somewhat different story: "The commissions had been made out in blank, and subscribed by Mr. Adams before the nominations were made to the Senate. The Senate, however, agreed to the nominations, but the third of March was not long enough to allow the commissions to be entered on record in the

office of the Secretary of State or to be forwarded to the nominees.")

Whatever the exact sequence, what is not in dispute is the fact that at least four of the commissions were not delivered by midnight, the final moment of Adam's term of office. John Marshall, as secretary of state, was charged with the responsibility of seeing that the commissions were sent out. The entire task would have been completed "but for the extreme hurry of the time and the absence of Mr. Wagner (his chief clerk) who had been called on by the President to act as his private secretary," Marshall wrote in a letter to his brother two weeks later. But he was not perturbed that last evening: "I entertained no suspicion" that the commissions would not ultimately be delivered.

The following day, however, Jefferson later recounted, "I found them on the table of the department of State, on my entrance into office, and I forbade their delivery." Jefferson resolved to treat the appointments as "mere nullities" and to take upon himself the power to designate those who could hold the newly created offices. (This Jefferson did without the benefit of Congressional legislation. His justification was that the office of justice of the peace for the District of Columbia was different from that of circuit court judge. "This outrage on decency," he said of the midnight appointments, "should not have its effect, except on the life appointments which are irrevocable." To remove these Federalist circuit judges, Jefferson would seek specific legislation, as we will shortly see.)

Notwithstanding his contempt for Adams' act in appointing the "midnight judges," as they came to be called, Jefferson showed political moderation by reappointing most of Adams' men to the same positions. But four he did not reappoint: William Marbury of Washington, and Dennis Ramsey, Robert R. Hooe, and William Harper, all of Alexandria, which was then a separate county within the District of Columbia. Marbury resolved to test the validity of the new administration's refusal to tender his commission, and at the next term of Court, the following December, he, along with the others, filed the most significant lawsuit in American history.

Marbury sought a writ of mandamus, which is an order from a court to a government official, requiring that official to take a specific action. If, for example, the state department of motor vehicles improperly refused to give someone a driver's license, he could seek to compel the proper official to do so by asking a court to mandamus him. So Marbury and the others wanted the Supreme Court to mandamus Jefferson's secretary of state, James Madison, to turn over the withheld commissions.

Opposite page:

John Marshall. Giant in American legal history.

National Portrait Gallery— Smithsonian Institution

On December 21, at the request of Marbury's attorney, Charles Lee (who had been Adams' attorney general), the Court granted what is known as a motion to show cause, directed against Madison. This simply meant that those who opposed Marbury's position would be permitted to come forward to contest the issue. The Court postponed hearing the case until its next term, the following June.

In essence, nothing much happened that December day in Court, but the order to show cause excited the fears of leading Republicans. Senator Breckenridge wrote to James Monroe, then governor of Virginia: "I think it the most daring attack which the annals of Federalism have yet exhibited." The order also hardened Jefferson's resolve to repeal the Judiciary Act of 1801, enacted only ten months before. Several questions concerning the attempt to repeal the law arose, but the most significant was whether the Constitution permitted such an action. Could new federal courts be abolished after judges who, by virtue of the Constitution, held lifetime positions were already appointed according to the law that created those courts? The Jeffersonians had no doubts, so on March 31, 1802, the one-year-old act was repealed. The circuit courts were abolished, and the appointments of the judges who sat on them were terminated. A subsequent law again required the justices of the Supreme Court to attend judicial hearings in courts away from Washington.

Exulting in this legislative triumph, Congress passed another law that prevented the Court from even considering Marbury's case, at least for a time. They did this by abolishing the Court's June and December terms, declaring that the next term of court would not be before February 1803. This blatant interference with the judicial calendar was undertaken largely to prevent the justices from meeting in session of the Supreme Court to debate the repeal of the Judiciary Act.

Marshall wrote to each of the justices to determine whether any resistance to the new law changing the Court's calendar was warranted. Only Samuel Chase avowed the necessity of doing so. The rest, Marshall certainly included, decided there was little to be gained from themselves taking an action that would be viewed as a personal decision to break the law. (Though they might declare unconstitutional the law requiring them to ride circuit, it would be impossible to convince the public at large, much less the Jeffersonians, of their disinterest in the case.) So Marbury's case was put off until February 1803, and the justices heard appeals in the circuit courts until then.

Opposite page:

The New York Herald reports the Marbury decision in the journalistic fashion of the day.

NEW-YORK HE

No. 129.   SATURDAY, MARCH 26, 1803.

MANDAMUS.

Opinion of the Supreme Court, delivered by Chief Justice Marshall, Feb. 24, 1803.

William Marbury
vs.   } On a motion for a
The Secretary of State.   Mandamus.

At the last term on the affidavits then read and filed with the clerk, a rule was granted in this case, requiring the Secretary of State to shew cause why a Mandamus should not issue, directing him to deliver to William Marbury his commission as a justice of peace for the County of Washington, in the District of Columbia.

No cause has been shewn, and the present motion is for a Mandamus. The peculiar delicacy of this case, the novelty of some of its circumstances, and the real difficulty attending the points which occur in it, require a complete exposition of the principles, on which the opinion to be given by the court, is founded.

These principles have been, on the side of the applicant, very ably argued at the bar. In rendering the opinion of the court, there will be some departure in form, though not in substance, from the points stated in that argument.

In the order in which the court has viewed this subject, the following questions have been considered and decided.

1st. Has the applicant a right to the commission he demands?

2d. If he has a right, and that right has been violated, do the laws of his country afford him a remedy?

3d. If they do afford him a remedy, is it a Mandamus issuing from this court?

The first object of enquiry is,

1st. Has the applicant a right to the commission he demands.

His right originates in an act of Congress passed in Feb. 1801, concerning the district of Columbia.

After dividing the district into two counties, the 11th section of this law, enacts, 'that there shall be appointed in and for each of the said counties, such number of discreet persons to be justices of the peace, as the President of the United States shall, from time to time, think expedient to continue in office for five years.'

It appears, from the affidavits, that in compliance with this law, a commission for William Marbury, as a justice of peace for the county of Washington, was signed by John Adams, then President of the United States; after which the seal of the United States was affixed to it; but the commission has never reached the person for whom it was made out.

In order to determine whether he is intitled to this commission, it becomes necessary to enquire whether he has been appointed to the office. For if he has been appointed, the law continues him in office for five years; and he is entitled to the possession of those evidences of office, which, being completed, became his property.

The 2d section of the 2d article of the Constitution declares, that 'the President shall nominate, and, by and with the advice and consent of the Senate, shall appoint ambassadors, other public ministers and consuls, and all other officers of the United States, whose appointments are not otherwise provided for.'

The 3d section declares, that 'he shall commission all the officers of the United States.'

An act of Congress directs the Secretary of State to keep the seal of the United States.

mission, the performance of such public act would create the officer, and if he was not removeable at the will of the President, would either give him a right to his commission or enable him to perform the duties without it.

These observations are premised solely for the purpose of rendering more intelligible those which apply more directly to the particular case under consideration.

This is an appointment made by the President, by and with the advice and consent of the Senate, and is evidenced by no act but the commission itself. In such a case, therefore, the commission and the appointment seem inseparable; it being almost impossible to show an appointment otherwise than by proving the existence of a commission; still the commission is not necessarily the appointment, though conclusive evidence of it.

But at what stage does it amount to this conclusive evidence?

The answer to this question seems an obvious one. The appointment being the sole act of the President, must be completely evidenced, when it is shewn that he has done every thing to be performed by him.

Should the commission, instead of being evidence of an appointment, even be considered as constituting the appointment itself; still it would be made when the last act to be done by the President was performed, or, at farthest, when the commission was complete.

The last act to be done by the President, is the signature of the commission. He has then acted on the advice and consent of the Senate to his own nomination. The time for deliberation was then passed. He has decided. His judgment, on the advice, and consent of the Senate concurring with his nomination, has been made and the officer is appointed. This appointment is evidenced by an open, unequivocal act; and being the last act required from the person making it, necessarily excludes the idea of its being, so far as respects the appointment, an inchoate and incomplete transaction.

Some point of time must be taken when the power of the executive over an officer, not removeable at his will, must cease. That point of time must be when the constitutional power of appointment has been exercised. And this power has been exercised when the last act, required from the person possessing the power, has been performed---This last act is the signature of the commission.

This idea seems to have prevailed with the legislature, when the act passed converting the department of foreign affairs into the department of State. By that act it is enacted, that the Secretary of State, shall keep the seal of the United States, 'and shall make out and record, and shall affix the said seal to all civil commissions, to officers of the U. States, to be appointed by the President:' 'Provided that the said seal shall not be affixed to any commission, before the same shall have been signed by the President of the U. States; nor to any other instrument or act, without the special warrant of the President therefor.'

The signature is a warrant for affixing the great seal to the commission; and the great seal is only to be affixed to an instrument which is complete. It attests, by an act supposed to be of public notoriety, the verity of the President's signature.

It is never to be affixed till the commission is signed, because the signature, which gives force and effect to the commission, is conclusive evidence that the appointment is made.

The commission being signed, the subsequent duty of the Secretary of State is prescribed by law, and not to be guided by the will of the

to give validity to the commission, it has been delivered when executed and given to the Secretary for the purpose of being sealed, recorded and transmitted to the party.

But in all cases of letters patent, certain solemnities are required by law, which solemnities are the evidences of the validity of the instrument. A formal delivery to the person is not among them, in cases of commissions the sign manual of the President, and the seal of the United States, are those solemnities. This objection therefore does not touch the case.

It has also occurred as possible, and barely possible, that the transmission of the commission, and the acceptance thereof, might be deemed necessary to complete the right of the plaintiff.

The transmission of the commission, is a practice directed by convenience, but not by law. It cannot therefore be necessary to constitute the appointment which must precede it, and which is the mere act of the President. If the executive required that every person appointed to an office, should himself take means to procure his commission, the appointment would not be less valid on that account. The appointment is the sole act of the president; the transmission of the commission is the sole act of the officer to whom that duty is assigned, and may be accelerated or retarded by circumstances which can have no influence on the appointment. A commission is transmitted to a person already appointed; not to a person to be appointed or not, as the letter inclosing the commission should happen to get into the post-office and reach him in safety, or to miscarry.

It may have some tendency to elucidate this point, to enquire, whether the possession of the *original*, commission be indispensably necessary to authorise a person, appointed to any office to perform the duties of that office. If it was necessary, then a loss of the commission would lose the office. Not only negligence, but accident or fraud, fire or theft, might deprive an individual of his office. In such a case, I presume it could not be doubted, but that a copy, from a record of the office of the Secretary of State, would be, to every intent and purpose, equal to the original. The act of Congress has expressly made it so. To give that copy validity, it would not be necessary to prove that the original had been transmitted and afterwards lost. The copy would be complete evidence that the original had existed and that the appointment had been made, but, not that the original had been mislaid in the office of State, that circumstance would not affect the operation of the copy. When all the requisites have been performed which authorize a recording officer to record any instrument whatever, and the order for that purpose has been given, the instrument is, in law, considered as recorded, although the manual labour of inserting it in a book kept for that purpose may not have been performed.

In the case of Commissions, the law orders the Secretary of State to record them. When therefore they are signed and sealed, the order for their being recorded is given; and whether inserted in the book or not, they are in law recorded.

A copy of this record is declared equal to the original, and the fees, to be paid by a person requiring a copy, are ascertained by law. Can a keeper of a public record, erase therefrom a commission which has been recorded? Or can he refuse a copy thereof to a person demanding it on the terms prescribed by law?

Such a copy would, equally with the original, authorize the justice of peace to proceed in the

2dly been ford h

The consis claim receiv gover Great respec fails t court.

In the Blacks dy is a

'In and t legal suit o invade

And he say 'as ar mon l 'only 'sove 'tical, 'for th 'the co 'settle 'Engla 'must 'prope

been e laws, a to dese furnish legal ri

If this dence o culiar c

It be be in shall ex clude th pursuin present ged wit the des loss wit

This conside conside of hono of peac office; and gui that att created been se rity to t lessness party ca

Is it t act of d to be co ing to th perform ced by t tive, an the inju

That question governi be admi

By th June, 1

Marbury's Case

On February 9, 1803, the hearing in Marbury's case began, amid peculiar circumstances. Since this was an original proceeding in the Supreme Court—that is, the justices were not reviewing the decision of a lower court but actually inquiring into the particular facts themselves—it was necessary to produce the commissions, or at least witnesses who knew something about them, to prove that there was a basis for the suit. This should not have been difficult; indeed, it would have been extremely easy had not the one person who was intimately involved in the actual mechanics of the preparation of the commissions been sitting in judgment as chief justice.

Marshall obviously knew firsthand that the commissions existed, but he could not testify. So it became necessary to call Levi Lincoln, his immediate successor as secretary of state. By the time the suit was filed, Lincoln had become attorney general, and Madison, who was secretary of state when the suit was filed, and still was in that position, refused to have anything to do with it. He did not appear in court and was not represented by counsel at court. There then ensued what we would today call a runaround: Marshall's former chief clerk, Wagner, and one of his assistants at first refused to answer questions, as did Lincoln, who insisted that the Court's questions be put in writing so that he could decide whether he ought to answer them or not. None supposed at first that they ought to reveal information that came to them while in the employ of the executive. The Court recessed until the following day, and when Lincoln took the stand, he said, in terms that would become famous one hundred seventy-one years later at the Watergate hearings, that although he remembered that there were some commissions, he did not "recollect" whether they belonged to Marbury or the others. Proof finally arrived in the form of affidavits of a state department clerk.

The Court Decides

On February 24, 1803, with the country enflamed at the prospect of going to war with France, John Marshall announced the decision in *Marbury* v. *Madison*. Significantly, he announced it as the "opinion of the court," not merely as his own opinion; there were no dissents and no separate opinions, as had been the custom.

Marshall began by noting that three questions had been raised in the proceeding, and each had been considered and would be answered. They were as follows:

1st.   Has the applicant a right to the commission he demands?
2nd.   If he has a right and that right has been violated, do the laws of
his country afford him a remedy?
3rd.   If they do afford him a remedy, is it by a mandamus issuing from
this Court?

Marshall took eight pages in the official reports to discuss in an exhaustive fashion the law relating to the vesting of public office. The question was whether Marbury was entitled to assume the duties of justice of the peace (and receive the federal salary that the office paid) because the president had signed the commission or whether it was necessary for the secretary of state or one of his agents in fact to have delivered the actual piece of paper to him.

Marshall reasoned that, under the Constitution and a federal law establishing the duties of the secretary of state, there were three distinct acts required to make someone an officer of the United States. First, the president must nominate him. This is exclusively the prerogative of the president; no one may require him to nominate one person rather than another. Second, the Senate must confirm the choice; again, this is the prerogative of the Senate, and no one may question its decision to do so. Third, the president must "commission" the officer, which means he must sign an official document. This is the "last act" required of the president. "Some point of time must be taken when the power of the executive over an officer, not removable at his will, must cease. That point of time must be when the constitutional power of appointment has been exercised. And this power has been exercised when the last act, required from the person possessing the power, has been performed. This last act is the signature of the commission."

Once the commission is signed, Marshall said, the secretary of state has no discretion to withhold the commission because his duties of affixing the seal and recording the act in an official log are prescribed by law. This proceeding, Marshall declared in words whose eloquence remain undimmed, "is a precise course accurately marked out by law, and is to be strictly pursued. It is the duty of the secretary of state to conform to the law, and in this he is an officer of the United States, bound to obey the laws. He acts, in this respect, . . . under the authority of law, and not by the instructions of the president. It is a ministerial act which the law enjoins on a particular officer for a particular purpose."

But it might be objected that the last act to be performed is not the president's signature, but the actual delivery of the commission, much as title to property does not pass from the seller to the buyer unless the written deed is transferred from the one to the other. Marshall said that even if this were true, it has never been the case that presidents have personally delivered the commissions to the officeholder. Then to whom? To the secretary of state for sealing and recording, and this was in fact done.

Still another objection: perhaps the nominee must actually possess the presidential parchment before he can be considered to hold his office. But if this were true, Marshall replied, then the appointee must take his chances, in the first instance, that the post office actually gets it to him, an undertaking in that time even more chancy than today. Moreover, if possession of the document were critical, "then a loss of the commission would lose the office. Not only negligence, but accident or fraud, fire or theft, might deprive an individual of his office." No government could operate on such a basis.

Everything considered, therefore, the failure of the secretary of state to tender Marbury his commission was a violation of Marbury's vested legal right.

That concluded, the second question must then be answered: do the laws of the United States afford Marbury a remedy? "The very essence of civil liberty certainly consists in the right of every individual to claim the protection of the laws, whenever he receives an injury." On what grounds could the law not provide relief for the violation of a right? Might it be that the Constitution places "entire confidence" in the "supreme executive" so that a court may not question what he does?

Marshall considers some examples of acts that the executive clearly has no discretion to refuse to undertake. Under a law providing pensions for disabled veterans, Marshall noted, the secretary of war is required to place on a pension list the names of all those whose disabilities had been previously reported to Congress. If the secretary "should refuse to do so, would the wounded veteran be without remedy? Is it to be contended that where the law in precise terms, directs the performance of an act, in which an individual is interested, the law is incapable of securing obedience to its mandate? Is it on account of the character of the person against whom the complaint is made? Is it to be contended that the heads of departments are not amenable to the laws of their country?" Marshall asked rhetorically.

Surely not; and if Marshall's reasoning seems to be less an argument from premise to conclusion than the acceptance of an assumption, it is because Marshall is really defining in this discussion what it means to say that the nation is governed by law and not by men. If the Constitution gives the president discretion to act in a certain manner—to conduct the foreign affairs of the nation, for example—then a court may certainly not examine his conduct. All the more this is true when one of the president's ministers— the secretary of state—carries out the president's will in the exercise of those powers. But when the legislature precisely spells out certain duties that the secretary must undertake and when the rights of an individual depend on the secretary's faithfully carrying out these duties, then it cannot be said that a court may not inquire whether the officer did in fact carry them out or order him to do so if he has not. "Where the heads of departments are the political or confidential agents of the executive, merely to execute the will of the President, or rather to act in cases in which the executive possesses a constitutional or legal discretion, nothing can be more perfectly clear than that their acts are only politically examinable. But where a specific duty is assigned by law, and individual rights depend upon the performance of that duty, it seems equally clear that the individual who considers himself injured, has a right to resort to the laws of his country for a remedy."

Stripped to their essentials, the two points thus decided are really mirror images: a vested right must mean one that a person has a means of enforcing. The law spelling out that the secretary must record and deliver the commission is at once the source of Marbury's right and the source of Madison's duty.

So far, Marbury has prevailed. He has a right to his commission, and he may enforce that right in court. But a third question remains to be answered: Is "he entitled to the remedy for which he applies?" At this point Marshall delivered his master stroke.

What remedy was being applied for? It appeared clearly to be a writ of mandamus, an order directing Madison to carry out his ministerial duties. Henry Lee, Marbury's counsel, discoursed at great length on the origins, powers, and appropriateness of this ancient writ. There was little dispute—indeed, no dispute, since the government did not contest the case—that a court may mandamus other courts or executive officials in the appropriate case. Marshall agreed and substantially repeats the point he had already made, that whether mandamus is proper depends on whether it is directed toward a ministerial or discretionary act. Here he took the opportunity to disclaim any suggestion that the court was attempting to interfere with the executive and, at the same time, to lecture the administration on its responsibilities. Commenting obliquely on the sensational political charges that had been raised in the press about what the Court might do, Marshall spoke as follows:

The intimate political relation subsisting between the President of the United States and the heads of departments, necessarily renders any legal investigation of the acts of one of those high officers peculiarly irksome, as well as delicate; and excites some hesitation with respect to the propriety of entering into such investigation. Impressions are often received without much reflection or examination, and it is not wonderful that in such a case as this the assertion, by an individual, of his legal claims in a court of justice, to which claims it is the duty of that court to attend, should at first view be considered by some, as an attempt to intrude into the cabinet, and to intermeddle with the prerogatives of the executive.

It is scarcely necessary for the court to disclaim all pretensions to such jurisdiction. An extravagance, so absurd and excessive, could not have been entertained for a moment. The province of the court is, solely, to decide the rights of individuals, not to inquire how the executive, or executive officers, perform duties in which they have a discretion.

Since Marshall had already concluded that the secretary of state had no discretion to withhold the commission, he concluded that "this, then, is a plain case for a mandamus."

But there is one problem. The remedy Marbury applied for—the third question Marshall is now considering—was not merely a mandamus; it was a mandamus *to be issued by the Supreme Court itself*. On this latter point, Marbury is to lose his case.

What gives the Supreme Court the power to issue a writ of mandamus? The power arises from the Judiciary Act of 1789, by which Congress created the lower federal courts and laid out the types of cases that they and the Supreme Court can hear. This law authorized the Court "to issue writs of mandamus in cases warranted by the principals and usages of law, to any courts appointed, or persons holding office, under the authority of the United States." Doesn't this conclude the case? Having already decided that Marbury is entitled to his commission and that mandamus is the proper remedy, here is a law that authorizes the Supreme Court to go ahead and issue it. Marshall could see only one difficulty: "If this court is not authorized to issue a writ of mandamus to such an officer (as the secretary of state), it must be because the law is unconstitutional, and therefore absolutely incapable of conferring the authority, and assigning the duties which its words purport to confer and assign."

This was an astonishing turn of events. The public excitement over the case had had nothing to do with a possible constitutional defect in the technical statute that gave jurisdiction—that is, authority to hear the case—to the Supreme Court. This question had scarcely been confronted during the oral argument. It had not been pressed in the newspapers. It came up, as it were, out of thin air; one of those questions that moves a discussion onto an entirely different plane, like a disquisition on the refractive powers of the atmosphere that proceeds from a poetic remark about the beauty of sunsets.

What was the problem? It involved the constitutional provision assigning judicial power to the Supreme Court. Article Three spelled out certain types of cases that the Supreme Court and other Federal courts may hear (for example, cases involving ambassadors, cases to which the United States is a party, cases involving federal law), but it did not distribute the power equally to the Supreme Court and the lower courts. Except for a few restricted types of cases (involving ambassadors and the states themselves), the Supreme Court was given *appellate* jurisdiction only. That means that it may hear appeals of cases tried in lower courts, but it may not sit as a trial court and determine facts. This it could do only in cases involving ambassadors and the states. Lower federal courts, by contrast, could (Congress permitting) exercise *original* jurisdiction; that is, try the cases initially. (In fact, of course, Congress had created two types of lower courts: the district courts, with original jurisdiction only; and circuit courts, which initially had both original and appellate jurisdiction.) The problem was thus whether the Congress could confer upon the Court the power to mandamus an executive official in a case that did not involve an ambassador or a dispute between two or more states and that was not on appeal. Marshall concluded that it could not and that the provision of the Judiciary Act of 1789 that purported to do so was unconstitutional.

Henry Lee had argued, without much thought, that this was a crucial point: since the Constitution did not say that Congress could not expand the Court's original jurisdiction—that is, extend to it other types of cases that it might hear as a trial court—there was nothing to prevent it from giving the Court the power to issue a mandamus in a case like Marbury's. Marshall replied that if this were so, then the Constitutional provision in Article Three would make no sense. The second paragraph of the second section of that article says:

In all Cases affecting Ambassadors, other public Ministers and Consuls, and those in which a State shall be Party, the Supreme Court shall have original Jurisdiction. In all the other Cases before mentioned, the Supreme Court shall have appellate Jurisdiction . . .

"If Congress," Marshall declared, "remains at liberty to give this court appellate jurisdiction, where the constitution has declared their jurisdiction shall be original; and original jurisdiction where the constitution has declared it shall be appellate; the distribution of jurisdiction, made in the constitution, is form without substance." This, Marshall said, cannot be admitted: "It cannot be presumed that any clause in the constitution is intended to be without effect."

John Marshall

Therefore, it must be shown that the court would be acting as an appellate court if it issued the mandamus. But it was not acting as an appellate court in Marbury's case. For to be an appellate court means that a decision from a lower court is being reviewed. There was no lower court decision in this case; the first and only court Marbury had come to was the Supreme Court. So the law giving the Court the authority to issue a mandamus as though it were a trial court violates the Constitution.

The final question remains. Should an act of Congress that violates the Constitution be followed or struck down as null and void? "Happily," said Marshall, this question is "not of an intricacy proportional to its interest." There are two ways for the people to organize a government, Marshall explained. They can create departments and assign powers to them, leaving them free to act as they please—or they can establish limits to what these departments of government may do. The people of the United States, said Marshall, opted for the second form and established limits through the Constitution. What else can be implied by the existence of a written constitution that by its own terms is the supreme law of the land than that it, and not some legislative act, must bind a court when the two conflict? The doctrine that the courts must close their eyes to the Constitution when a conflicting law is cited "would subvert the very foundation of all written constitutions . . . It is prescribing limits, and declaring that those limits may be passed at pleasure."

Moreover, there are many other provisions in the Constitution that make this conclusion inescapable, he said. The Constitution declares "that no bill of attainder or ex post facto law shall be passed." Marshall asks: "If, however, such a bill should be passed, and a person should be prosecuted under it, must the court condemn to death those victims whom the constitution endeavours to protect?" And to what end are judges required to take an oath to support the Constitution if they are not to read it or heed its terms when sitting in court? The Constitution is not a "solemn mockery" or worse. It means what it says: it is the supreme law of the land.

Congress cannot, therefore, give the Court the power to mandamus the secretary of state in an original proceeding, and the Court may not exercise such a power on behalf of a fellow like Marbury, even though he has been wronged. If Marbury is to have his remedy, he must go to a lower court and file his suit there.

The Reaction

Marshall's great opinion was coldly received by Jefferson. It was, said the president, "an attempt in subversion of the independence of the Executive." But what rankled Jefferson (and continued to do so throughout his life) was not the principle for which the case is so centrally prized today (a principle that Marshall's biographer has said is "America's original contribution to the science of law")—namely, that the Court sits to enforce the commands of the Constitution as it sees them and may strike down acts of Congress that run contrary to supreme law. No, what irritated Jefferson was the lecture that Marshall read him, loudly stating that Jefferson had violated the law in refusing to turn over the commissions. His irritation was all the greater because of Marshall's adroit twist in making the opinion irresistible: since Marshall ultimately sided with Jefferson, in refusing to order Madison to turn over the commissions, there was nothing to do but accept the decision and try to denounce the barbs that Jefferson saw aimed at him. The point that Jefferson made (as other commentators did, both then and later) was that Marshall had gone farther than necessary in his opinion; having decided the law under which the case was brought was in fact invalid, the Court had no jurisdiction to consider the question of executive propriety. "Three questions are reported to have been decided," said one critic. "The last decision was that the Court had no jurisdiction to decide the other two, which they nevertheless decided." This, he said, is itself a violation of the law.

How fair is this criticism? Why did Marshall decide all three questions, instead of only the last one? The answer, though it was not spelled out at the time, must surely be that the Court should not lightly overturn laws of Congress. If the Court had decided that Marbury was not entitled to his commission or that mandamus was not a possible remedy against an executive official, then it would not have had to reach the constitutional question. Only because the first two questions were answered in Marbury's favor did the final question have to be faced. The critics were simply wrong: the Court did not decide that it had no jurisdiction to consider the case; only that it had no jurisdiction to issue the mandamus.

Now the reader may have reflected during the discussion of Marshall's reasoning that much of the opinion was redundant; that the Chief Justice spent a lot of time on propositions that seem self-evident. Why? The answer is not merely that the Supreme Court had not squarely faced the question before, though this is part of the reason. A more important reason is the nature of the public debate that had been raging for more than a year over whether the Court had the power to declare laws unconstitutional. The whole issue was alive because of Jefferson's successful push to repeal the Judiciary Act of 1801 that had allowed Adams to put in all his life-tenured Federalist judges. The Republicans were afraid that the Supreme Court might thwart the repeal by striking it down as unconstitutional, so they argued that the Court did not have the power to do so. *Marbury* v. *Madison,* therefore, is Marshall's answer to this debate.

Those who argued the Court had no such power were never on very firm ground. Indeed, they were very much inconsistent, for during the 1790s, the anti-Federalists had publicly looked to the courts to strike down federal legislation that encroached on the sovereignty of the states, and many had condemned the Alien and Sedition Acts of 1798 as unconstitutional and complained vociferously that the courts had not struck them down (they never reached the Supreme Court). Arguments that the Court usurped the power to review Congressional acts (occasionally heard even to this day) simply overlooked the overwhelming weight of history. State courts had voided state laws as unconstitutional prior to the adoption of the federal Constitution, and these cases and the reasons that supported them were well known to the framers. The principle of judicial review was not expressly included in the Constitution because it was simply assumed that the federal judicial power included it. At the Constitutional Convention, Edmund Randolph of Virginia had proposed a "Council of Revision," to be composed of the president and federal judges, who would be empowered to review every act of Congress. This idea was rejected, the power of veto ultimately being placed exclusively with the president (with provision for Congress to override it). Eldridge Gerry, in arguing against the Council of Revision, said (as recorded by Madison) that the judiciary "will have a sufficient check against encroachments on their own department by their exposition of the laws, which involved a power of deciding on their Constitutionality. In some States the Judges had actually set aside laws as being against the Constitution. This was done too with general approbation."

Several others made unequivocal statements affirming the power of the courts to set aside unconstitutional legislation: a large majority of the Convention took it for granted—and for good reason. Jefferson, as we noted earlier, thought one of the significant defects in the original Constitution was its lack of a bill of rights to restrain Congress from violating fundamental human rights. But who would stop Congress from violating the Bill of Rights itself, if not the courts? The principle and its reasons were fully laid out in the *Federalist Papers,* where Hamilton (No. 78), wrote as follows:

Limitations [on Congressional power] *can be preserved in practice no other way than through the medium of courts of justice, whose duty it must be to declare all acts contrary to the manifest tenor of the Constitution void. Without this, all the reservations of particular rights or privileges would amount to nothing. . . . There is no position which depends on clearer principles than that every act of a delegated authority, contrary to the tenor of the commission under which it is exercised, is void. No legislative act, therefore, contrary to the Constitution, can be valid. To deny this would be to affirm that the deputy is greater than his principal; that the servant is above his master; that the representatives of the people are superior to the people themselves; that men acting by virtue of powers may do not only what their powers do not authorize, but what they forbid . . . The interpretation of the laws is the proper and peculiar province of the courts. A constitution is, in fact, and must be regarded by the judges as, a fundamental law. It therefore belongs to them to ascertain its meaning as well as the meaning of any particular act proceeding from the legislative body. If there should happen to be an irreconcilable variance between the two, that which has the superior obligation and validity ought, of course, to be preferred; or, in other words, the Constitution ought to be preferred to the statute, the intention of the people to the intention of their agents.*

Though Hamilton was an ardent Federalist, there was no outcry against this clearly stated position. As the historian of the Supreme Court, Charles Warren, has argued, the years between 1789 and 1802 witnessed intense political debate: "At no period in American history were political questions more generally, more thoroughly, and more hotly discussed in print than during the first fifteen years after the formation of the Constitution. Every political, social or legal doctrine upheld by either the Federalists or the anti-Federalists was debated and denounced by their opponents, in editorials, in letters to the newspapers, and in privately published pamphlets." Yet during that entire period, "there was almost no opposition to the exercise of the power of the Court to pass upon the validity of statutes."

Though the decision in *Marbury* v. *Madison* further provoked the debate that had begun the year before, it was destined to carry the day, for two reasons. First, the decision itself was in Jefferson's favor. Second, several days later, the Court ruled that the law that repealed the Judiciary Act (which had given the impetus to the debate initially because of Republican fears that the Court would strike it down) was in fact constitutional. Again Jefferson was sustained: the new circuit courts were dissolved, and the justices of the Supreme Court went back to riding circuit. In ruling against their own private interests, they showed themselves willing to abide by the law.

The Position of the Court Since Marbury

Since that time, the power and duty of the Supreme Court to pass on constitutional questions has never been successfully challenged, although it took several subsequent decisions to flesh out the meaning of that power. For instance, the power to pass on laws of Congress did not necessarily imply, proponents of states rights thought, the power to pass on the laws of the state legislatures or the decisions of state courts. During the next two decades, the Court, with Marshall leading the way, determined that this was precisely a power it did have and must exercise. Thus, a state's attempt to impair a contract, in violation of Article One of the Constitution, was reviewable by the Court (as we will see in the next chapter) as was the attempt of a state to tax a bank chartered by the federal government (as we will see in Chapter 6).

In 1816, in *Martin* v. *Hunter's Lessee*, the Court ruled that state courts must abide by decisions of the Supreme Court. In 1821, in a case of great importance, the Court further buttressed its power. That case concerned the conviction of a man charged with violating a state anti-lottery law that was allegedly contrary to a federal lottery law. The Virginia legislature enacted a law preventing its state supreme court from hearing an appeal and thus, it was argued, the Supreme Court could not hear an appeal either. In *Cohens* v. *Virginia,* the Court rejected the state's contention, ruling that an Act of Congress superseded a state law and that Section 25 of the Judiciary Act constitutionally empowered the Supreme Court to review any conviction where it is claimed that the federal law makes the conviction void. Having thus determined its power, the Chief Justice went on to hold that the state law was not in fact contrary to the federal law, and he let the conviction stand.

Until late in the nineteenth century, the Supreme Court's use of its power to construe the Constitution was almost exclusively devoted to reviewing state laws, in fact. "I do not think the United States would come to an end if we lost our power to declare an Act of Congress void," Justice Oliver Wendell Holmes wrote in 1913, but he added, "I do think the Union would be imperilled if we could not make that declaration as to the laws of the several states."

As great and decisive a principle as judicial review is, it suffers from one very real and practical difficulty: What is to stop the Court from usurping its own power, from striking down a law that is in fact not unconstitutional? Recall Justice Jackson's words: the Court is not final because it is infallible, but it is infallible only because it is final. There is only half an answer or, rather, an answer with only half an assurance.

The Supreme Court is not a legislative body; it cannot look about and hand down decisions whenever there is some law or some executive act of which it disapproves. This power was denied it when the Constitutional Convention rejected the idea of a Council of Revision. The Court must wait, instead, for cases to come before it, and only in the context of a particular dispute, when one or both of the parties question the constitutionality of a law that affects the case, may the Court legitimately pass its judgment. In the course of its development, the Court has devised an internal policy of not deciding a constitutional question if there is some other ground on which to make a ruling, a policy that is usually, though not always, adhered to. (The Court may also be controlled in another manner: as we saw (pp. 39f), Congress may restrict the Court's jurisdiction, in effect prohibiting it from hearing cases that will raise constitutional questions. But this power has been sparingly used).

But these "controls" are, however, no guarantee against judicial mistake, judicial blindness, even judicial malice, when a case is properly before the Court. A government of law ultimately must depend upon the skill and wisdom of those who apply the law. There can be no government of law that is not also a government of people, and they may err. In *Marbury* v. *Madison* the Court established a great and mighty principle, the power of judicial review itself. But on the very next occasion that the Court exercised this power to strike down an Act of Congress, its decision contributed directly to the most awful war the country has ever known (Chapter 7).

In the end, therefore, protection even from the excesses of the Court lies in the people themselves, as the framers intended. The Court has the last word—almost. The Court's decisions remain only as long as they are convincing; when they no longer persuade, they may be reversed. On four occasions, the Court was reversed by constitutional amendment: the Eleventh Amendment (1798), the Fourteenth Amendment (1868), the Sixteenth Amendment (1913) and the Twenty-sixth Amendment (1971) were explicitly designed to overturn prior decisions of the Supreme Court. On many more occasions, the Court has reversed itself, either because new justices have seen constitutional questions in a different light or because the same justices become persuaded that they were wrong, as happened in 1937 when the Court finally began to reprove an economic doctrine it had embodied in scores of decisions that during the preceding half century had struck down state and federal laws designed to protect workers, consumers, and citizens from economic

Marshall's letter of resignation from the U.S. Congress upon his appointment as Secretary of State.

Original in the Archives Division, Virginia State Library

distress. In the famous words of Mr. Dooley, "th' Supreme Court follows th' 'illiction returns."

Marbury v. *Madison* guarantees no results; it could not. Its permanent greatness lies in securing to the Supreme Court its intended role as a lawful and peaceful check against the excesses of the other branches of government.

As for William Marbury, the Court's decision was of surprisingly little help. Marshall had affirmed his right to the commission and even gone out of his way to say that Marbury had a legal remedy. But that remedy could be invoked only if Congress actually invested the lower courts with the power to mandamus. Whether such power was in fact given was doubtful; in 1813 the Court ruled that the circuit courts had no jurisdiction under the Judiciary Act to issue mandamus against the government. Curiously, though it did Marbury no good at all, three years after he died, the Court ruled that circuit courts in Washington, D. C., as opposed to all other federal courts, *did* have such jurisdiction. But the likelihood of such a ruling must have seemed remote to Marbury in 1803, with nearly half his five-year statutory term already passed. Moreover, not until Congress established the Court of Claims in 1855 could anyone sue the United States for money claims, so Marbury would have found it probably impossible to recover any back salary that might have been owed. All in all, the chances of winning any lawsuits must have seemed too remote to take the trouble to bring them. So Marbury let his claim to office lapse. In 1814 he became the president of a bank in Georgetown, and in 1835, the same year as Marshall, he died.

5/ THE SANCTITY OF CONTRACTS: DARTMOUTH COLLEGE v. WOODWARD

The first clause of Section Ten of the First Article of the Constitution declares that "no state shall . . . pass any law . . . impairing the obligation of contracts." But as with its other important phrases, the Constitution does not provide a definition of the words in those phrases. And there is not a very ready reference in other phrases and clauses against which the meaning of the Contract Clause can be determined.

Nevertheless, its purpose was clear to the Philadelphia delegates: it was to prevent the states from enacting bankruptcy legislation that would prevent creditors from recovering debts owed to them. Massachusetts, for example, had passed a law prohibiting creditors from collecting in court what was owed them, at least temporarily, to prevent farmers and others from becoming completely destitute. The law also permitted debtors to pay off in goods or paper money, rather than gold, contrary to their original undertakings. Such laws, which might be radically different from state to state, might seriously distort commercial relationships and hamper the incentive of those who were in a position to lend desperately needed money. At the Convention, there was almost no discussion of the merits of this prohibition, the clause itself having been first suggested by the Committee on Style toward the end of the proceedings.

This did not mean that the framers did not recognize the importance of a bankruptcy law that would protect those who could never hope to pay off their debts from being impressed into perpetual serfdom or from being clapped into jail, perhaps for life. But they did not want this power to reside within each state legislature. Congress was given the power to enact uniform bankruptcy legislation to apply to the entire country, and this power was buttressed by the refusal of the Convention to write into the Constitution a Contract Clause for the federal government. Elbridge Gerry of Massachusetts recommended that the national government also be prohibited from impairing the obligation of contracts, but his motion did not carry.

Since so much of American history is interwoven with the ability of entrepreneurs to make deals and on the ability of the courts to enforce them, the clause should seem unremarkable. The fact that there was little debate is not surprising. But it is important to note that the clause does not specifically say that the states cannot pass laws that might make it difficult to enter into contracts. It simply says that contracts (implying, presumably, those already made) cannot be impaired. This is an important distinction, for an industrial nation must be no less concerned with the ability to enter into contracts than to see that they are lived up to once made. And because the Contract Clause does not speak to the former concern, it ultimately became pretty much (though not completely) a dead letter. The due process clauses of the Fifth and Fourteenth Amendments were found to be far more powerful weapons to protect the contractual society.

The Inviolability of Contracts

Despite its ultimate demise, the Contract Clause played an important role in helping to shape the industrial age. It engaged the attention of the Supreme Court for decades, and several of the decisions it rendered in connection with the clause had a profound affect on the future of the country. Of these, the most famous was the *Dartmouth College* case, which set the stage for the development of the private corporation during the first half of the nineteenth century, though it has little practical importance today.

The story begins in 1795, when the Georgia legislature sold twenty million acres along the Yazoo River (comprising most of what is now Alabama and Mississippi) to four land companies for half a million dollars, or two and one-half cents an acre. (It later turned out that thirty-five million acres had been included in the deal). Although the land was not particularly valuable at the time, situated as it was near Indian and Spanish territory, the sale price was so low that it could be accounted for only by corruption. So it was. Bribery, fraud, and conflict of interest were rampant in that session of the legislature. Those legislators who were not bribed directly were either purchasers themselves or had holdings in the companies that profited from the grant. The public was outraged and voted the legislators out in 1796. Their successors repealed the land grant law; so intense was the feeling, in fact, that the paper on which the 1795 law was written was committed to a public fire.

After the sale but before the law repealing it was enacted, however, one of the land companies resold much of its acreage to the New England Mississippi Company, which in turn sold to individual speculators in the North. Georgia claimed that the land belonged once again to the state; the investors insisted that the 1796 law could have no such effect. In 1802 the state transferred its claim to the federal government, where the question was debated until 1809. Then, unable to secure a settlement, a case was brought that eventually wound up in the Supreme Court. In that case, one Fletcher had bought fifteen thousand acres of the disputed land for $3,000 from Peck, who had bought it in turn from an earlier purchaser of the land. Fletcher sought to recover his money from Peck on the ground that his title to the land was clouded because the Georgia legislature had corruptly granted the land. In other words, he said, he had contracted to buy land that Peck had the legal right to convey, but because of the events in Georgia, Peck might not have had good and lawful title.

In 1810, the chief justice, in *Fletcher* v. *Peck,* ruled for Peck (whose counsel before the Court had been Joseph Story): the land title was good. The original grant of land was a contract, said Marshall, and those who were not party to the corruption, but who purchased in good faith, were entitled to keep what they paid for. In passing the 1796 law that purported to take back the land, Georgia had acted unconstitutionally. The repeal act was an attempt to impair the obligations of the contract that it had entered into the year before.

This was the first time that the Court struck down a state law as unconstitutional, and the decision was roundly criticized by states' rights advocates, who had not supposed that the Supreme Court could do to state legislation that Marshall in *Marbury* had said the Court could do to federal law. The decision also has been criticized as having been issued in a case that everyone knew to be collusive, staged by those who could scarcely have been innocent purchasers, to secure a ruling from the Court. This may have been true: surely no one who had the slightest sophistication was unaware of the scandal, and those who purchased from the original four land companies were scarcely ignorant of the corruption or of the pledge of the new Georgia legislature to repeal the 1975 grant.

In a fascinating diatribe against the Supreme Court published in 1912, Gustavus Myers condemned Marshall for failing to probe the question of corruption: "But what devious tack did Marshall take," Myers asked, "so as to evade the settled principle of law that fraud vitiated every contract? With unsurpassed audacity, he proceeded upon the complacent assumption that the bribery of legislators was merely a fanciful story, and waved the facts lightly aside." Myers argued that the Contract Clause had been inserted in the Constitution at the suggestion of James Wilson, later an associate justice of the Supreme Court, who in the 1780s had been a director of the Bank of North America, chartered in Pennsylvania. When the state passed a law repealing the bank's charter, Wilson was among those who strenuously argued that the original charter was a contract and that the repeal was an impairment of the contract. Moreover, Myers charged, Wilson was one of a number of "noted politicians (who) bribed" the Yazoo grant through the Georgia legislature.

But the thrust of this argument supports rather than refutes Marshall's reasoning. If the Contract Clause was placed in the Constitution by those with landed and corporate interests who sought to preserve them against state interference, then Marshall was faithful to the meaning of the clause. Moreover, if Marshall had accepted the argument that the Court should have annulled the land grant because the legislature had voted it fraudulently, the Court would have been left with even more power, the existence of which would have threatened the stability of every legislative grant. "Nothing could more certainly bring the Court into violent conflict with the Legislative branch of the Government than any such judicial attempt to investigate its motives, and to set aside a statute, upon a judicial finding of corruption." Should a legislative act be subject to attack in the courts if it can be construed as granting someone a right through corrupt motives? How many legislators must be corrupted before the act can be struck down? One? Several? A majority? It is, of course, possible to imagine a government in which legislative enactments are scrutinized for sincerity, but the resulting system would give far more power to the courts than that which Marshall claimed in *Fletcher* v. *Peck*.

Two years later, in 1812, the Court had its second constitutional contract case. In 1758, New Jersey granted land to the Delaware Indians in return for a pledge that they would not claim any other territory within the state. By the terms of the legislation approving the grant, the state agreed not to tax the land, and the Indians agreed not to dispose of it. In 1801, desirous of moving to New York, the Indians persuaded the legislature to permit them to sell their land. Three years later, after the sale was consummated, New Jersey decided to tax the land once more. Marshall voided the tax as an impairment of the new owners' contractual rights. The state could have restored the tax when it voted to permit the Indians to sell, Marshall said, but the state did not do so, and it could not do so after others became legal owners of land which they assumed to be untaxable.

In 1815 the Supreme Court heard two other impairment cases. In one, Justice Story refused to permit Virginia to take back lands it had granted decades before to the Episcopal Church when that body was the official state church. So far the Court had only dealt with grants of land in its contract cases. One important question remained: Did the Contract Clause protect corporate charters in a similar manner? To the attentive reader of Justice Story's opinion in the Episcopal case, there could be little doubt how the Court was leaning. The following year, in 1816, events in New Hampshire led conclusively to a ringing declaration in behalf of the sanctity of corporate charters in the famous case of *Trustees of Dartmouth College* v. *Woodward*.

A Journey Back

To understand the case, we must journey back to 1754, when the Reverend Eleazar Wheelock used his own funds to establish Moor's Charity School in Connecticut for the education and Christianization of American Indians. Wanting to expand the school, Wheelock sought funds in England, incorporation in America, and a college for himself. His plan, which he referred to often as "ye affair," required complicated maneuvering among supporters in America, the royal governor of New Hampshire, John Wentworth, and contributors in England, chief of whom was the Earl of Dartmouth.

The difficulties were great. The English backers were interested only in Wheelock's carrying on his missionary work among the Indians. For this reason they wanted the power to appoint Wheelock's successor when he died. They also wanted to refuse payment of any bills chargeable to the English trust, which had been set up to channel money into Wheelock's school. Wheelock wanted control himself, wanted the power to name his successor, and wanted any power beyond that to remain with American trustees. More than that, he desired to found a school for the education of American ministers, not merely a charity school for Indians but a college for the colonists.

To accomplish these purposes, Wheelock needed a charter to incorporate his school. In 1765 William Smith, who drafted the first charter of the College of New Jersey (Princeton) two decades before, strongly advised this course: "Incorporation," he wrote, "sets up ye scheme as an Object of Notoriety. Donors knowing ye name of ye body corporate give *with legal certainty* by last will or otherwise, & with great *Ease and confidence* than by searching out private friends who after all may not be thought to be fit to be trusted." Moreover, "an incorporated Body will not only acquire Rights maintainable by Law in the Courts of Justice, but command the favour of the officers of the Government, who, without this sanction, may at such distances from the Crown, oppress the undertaking in a thousand ways, and utterly destroy it."

But there were many obstacles to incorporation. Connecticut, itself a chartered colony, refused to grant a charter on its own because the law did not permit one corporation to incorporate another. Other colonies faced the same prohibition. Several attempts to secure a charter directly from the English authorities were fruitless. But New Hampshire presented many possibilities. It contained a good supply of Indians, who were fast being lost to Wheelock through denominational squabbling. As a royal colony, New Hampshire could legally grant a charter, and since it had no colleges of its own, it might be willing to grant Wheelock his fondest wish. And the citizens were eager. Many of its most prominent had contributed to his school already and were anxious to see it moved permanently to their community and were willing to donate land.

In 1768 Wheelock began a round of intensive and shrewd politicking. By April of the following year, Governor Wentworth had agreed to grant a charter for the charity school. His own motives were not exactly pristine. He believed in bringing the Gospel to the Indians, and also believed he could advance his political career. If the Indians in his colony were civilized, settlers would be attracted to New Hampshire and the region would be at peace. By insisting on members of the Church of England as trustees, Wentworth could cement his relationship to that important institution at home.

After much bargaining and compromising, Wheelock got essentially the charter he desired. The school was to be maintained "for the education & instruction of Youth of the Indian Tribes in this Land in reading, writing & all parts of Learning which shall appear necessary and expedient for civilizing & christianizing Children of Pagans as well as in all liberal Arts and Sciences; and also of English Youth and any others." This last phrase—"English Youth and any others"—was Wheelock's artful way of permitting the school to function also as a college for colonists. Believing that the English trustees understood that the Indian charity school would be merged into a school with larger purposes, Governor Wentworth agreed to Wheelock's suggestion that the school be referred to as a college and that the charter expressly permit it to grant degrees. Moreover, it was the governor who countered Wheel-ock's suggestion that the school be named Wentworth College by pro-posing that it bear the name it carries to this day. So, on December 13, 1769, the royal charter was granted, in the name of King George III, to Dartmouth College, to be settled in Hanover, New Hampshire, along the Connecticut River. By the terms of the charter, Wheelock retained tight control over the institution, including the power to appoint his successor. The charter permitted the trustees to hold land in the corporate name, to acquire and sell property, to hire and pay faculty and administrators, to provide replacements for them-selves, and otherwise to govern the college, so long as their rules were not contrary to English or New Hampshire law. The number of trustees was set at twelve "forever."

Shortly thereafter, Wheelock received word from Lord Dart-mouth of the extreme displeasure with which the English trustees viewed the incorporated college. Their understanding had been betrayed, they felt, since they had expressly stated that their con-tributions were to be given exclusively for the education of Indians. They wanted no part of any college. "It is not difficult to imagine the consternation which this communication must have caused Wheelock," wrote Richard W. Morin, Dartmouth College librarian emeritus and historian of the case. "But he had before bent with the wind in pursuit of his great design, and he was prepared to do so again to retain access to the English funds. He restored to life by legerdemain Moor's Charity School as an institution separate and apart from the College. Only after his assurance to the Earl of Dartmouth that the English money would be used exclusively in support of Moor's School did the English Trust continue to remit to Wheelock."

In 1779 Wheelock's son John became the college's second presi-dent at the age of twenty-five. For a quarter of a century, his administration was relatively placid. But beginning in 1804, there arose a series of conflicts with the trustees (many of the original ones had died), which led, ten years later, to a move by a group of eight trustees, known thereafter as the Octagon, to dismiss him from his teaching duties. John Wheelock retaliated with an inflam-matory anonymous pamphlet accusing the trustees of having abused the powers of their office, forsaken the principles of the college, and plotted to alter the government of the state. He appealed to the state legislature to intercede.

The legislature appointed a committee to investigate the accusa-tions, which ultimately boiled down to charges of diverting funds improperly, interfering with the local church, and interfering with the proper performance of Wheelock's duties. The evidence was weak. The trustees retaliated by investigating the authorship of the pamphlet. After charging Wheelock himself with five counts of abuse (including authorship of the pamphlet) and receiving no relevant response, the Octagon dismissed him from the presidency of the college and elected the Reverend Francis Brown of Maine as his replacement.

Rather than quiet the affair down, their actions stirred matters up considerably. Wheelock refused to concede his ouster and required those who rented facilities from the college to turn their payments over to him, thus crippling the college. The affair was not contained within the Hanover community. It excited comment throughout the state, due in part to Wheelock's exertions during the 1816 elections, which resulted in a smashing Republican victory and a repudiation of the Federalist trustees.

Events now moved rapidly. In his first message to the new Republican legislature, the newly elected governor, William Plumer, declared that the Dartmouth charter "emanated from royalty" and "contained . . . principles congenial to monarchy"; he declared that the provision for a self-perpetuating board was "hostile to the spirit and genius of a free government." He called for legislation to amend the charter.

The legislature promptly granted his request. The new law enlarged the number of trustees from twelve to twenty-one, gave the governor the power to appoint the additional trustees, and created a board of overseers, also to be filled by the state. This board was given supervisory authority over the trustees. In essence, the law converted the college from a private institution into a public one. The name of the school was changed from "Trustees of Dartmouth College" to "Trustees of Dartmouth University" ("university" had been frequently used interchangeably with "college" before 1816).

The Issue

The necessity of testing this law in the courts was apparent, all the more so because of a later law, known as the "penal act." This law subjected any trustees who defied the state takeover and continued to act on behalf of the college to large and continual fines. A New Hampshire merchant, John Wheeler, gave $1,000, an enormous gift in those days, to contest the laws. The trustees filed suit. Various types of suits were possible; the law of pleading was ex-

John Wheelock.
Second President of
Dartmouth around
whom controversy
swirled.

Courtesy of the Trustees
of Dartmouth College

tremely technical and troublesome. In February 1817, they chose to sue the secretary-treasurer of the college, William H. Woodward, who defected to the state's trustees, for the return of the books, records, and the seal of the college that he had taken with him. (Since Woodward was also a judge of the state's trial court, the suit was transferred to the state's highest court.)

The contest for control was understood to be something more than a local dispute. Universities throughout the nation were alarmed. ("Harvard College [has no] surer title than Dartmouth College," Daniel Webster would argue to the Supreme Court. "It may, to-day, have more friends; but to-morrow it may have more enemies. Its legal rights are the same. So also of Yale College, and indeed of all the others.") The stakes were equally clear on the other side. Jefferson, in retirement, wrote to Plumer before the litigation commenced:

Opposite page:

Daniel Webster: age 35; junior counsel for the Dartmouth trustees.

National Portrait Gallery—
Smithsonian Institution

The idea that institutions established for the use of the Nation cannot be touched nor modified, even to make them answer their end, because of rights gratuitously supposed in those employed to manage them in trust for the public, may, perhaps, be a salutary provision against the abuses of a monarch, but it is most absurd against the Nation itself. Yet our lawyers and priests generally inculcate this doctrine; and suppose that preceding generations held the earth more freely than we do; had a right to impose laws on us, unalterable by ourselves; and that we, in like manner, can make laws, and impose burdens on future generations, which they will have no right to alter; in fine, that the earth belongs to the dead, and not to the living.

Jefferson's observation, surely true in its general outline, nevertheless avoided or evaded the issue in the *Dartmouth* case. The question was not whether the present generation could make laws for itself but whether certain kinds of laws were prohibited because they invaded the rights of others. As an early proponent of the Bill of Rights, Jefferson could scarcely have quarreled with this (again, abstract) proposition. The Constitution, together with the Bill of Rights, is the preeminent reminder that the past does continually exert control on the future. But if the Founding Fathers thus imposed laws on their descendants, they did not preclude any succeeding generation from changing those laws. Rather, they prescribed the manner in which the change could be made. If Dartmouth's charter was not a contract, protected by the Contract Clause in the Constitution, then the New Hampshire legislature could alter it at will. But if it was a contract, which meant that altering it would constitute the impairment of its obligations, then

the change could be made only if the Constitution itself were amended. So the question the Court had squarely to face was whether a corporate charter is a contract and, if it is, whether the legislative enactment impaired its obligations.

The college engaged the state's two foremost lawyers, Jeremiah Smith, who had served as a congressman, governor, and chief justice of the state, and Jeremiah Mason, who had been the state's attorney general, senator, and in 1816 had declined appointment as the state's chief justice. As their junior counsel, the trustees retained Daniel Webster, an alumnus of the college. Webster, then thirty-five years old, was a congressman from New Hampshire. While still a congressman, Webster moved to Boston in 1816. Because he had just relocated in Boston, his participation in the case before the state court was minimal. (He left the House in 1818 but was reelected, this time from Massachusetts, in 1823.)

The argument before the state court turned on whether the college was a private institution. The state attorney general, who argued on behalf of the university, asserted that the college was "a public corporation, created expressly—created exclusively for the public interest." The charter itself proved this, he said, in its own words. One section called for "the best means of education [to] be established in our Province of New Hampshire for the benefit of said Province." But even if it were to be held a private institution, the legislature could certainly alter the charter's provisions "when the public good requires it." The charter was not a contract, and even if it was, it was not the kind that the constitutional provision was intended to protect. Smith and Mason launched an elaborate counterargument, expressing in great style their contention that the legislature had violated both state and federal constitutions.

Since Governor Plumer had appointed the entire bench, the state court's decision was not unexpected: "A corporation, all of whose franchises are exercised for public purposes, is a public corporation. A gift to a corporation created for public purposes is . . . a gift to the public." The Contract Clause was "obviously intended to protect private rights" and is not to be understood "to limit the power of the states in relation to . . . public officers . . . or . . . civil institutions." But the court recognized, contrary to the beliefs of many Virginians, that the constitutional point could be appealed to the United States Supreme Court.

The state court handed down its decision against the college in November. By Christmas Day, 1817, the appeal papers were readied, Webster having been chosen to represent the trustees in the argument in Washington. On November 15, he had written to President Brown, asking whether his services were sought: "I am aware," he wrote,

that there must be great difficulty in obtaining funds on this occasion. I wish you therefore to write me very plainly what can be done and what cannot, and I will give you my advice as plainly in return. I think I would undertake for a thousand dollars to go to Washington and argue the cause and get Mr. Hopkinson's assistance also. I doubt whether I could do it for a much less sum. Mr. Hopkinson will be very competent to argue it alone and probably would do so for something less, though no counsel of the first rank would undertake this cause at Washington probably under six or seven hundred dollars.

. . . There is no cost of any consequence in carrying the cause to W. except counsels fees.

Hopkinson, forty-eight, a noted Pennsylvania lawyer, was then a Federalist congressman from that state; he agreed to assist Webster in the case. Webster wanted payment by January 15. The college, with almost no money, at first looked to Yale and then Harvard to help finance the suit, but to no avail. Finally, Brown journeyed to Boston to meet with well-heeled alumni, who provided the money.

The university forces, for its part, were sluggish. Having won a judicial victory, they assumed at first that their troubles were ended. Governor Plumer even doubted that the college trustees would appeal. When it became apparent that they would take their argument to Washington, the state trustees chose John Holmes to represent them. Holmes, forty-five, was a congressman from Maine. He was regarded as a second-rate lawyer. Moreover, he had little time to prepare because he was not selected until December 31. Alarmed by their own tardiness and the possible deficiencies of their counsel, the university trustees, after prodding from Washington, chose William Wirt, forty-six, who was attorney general of the United States, as cocounsel. He was considered one of the foremost lawyers of the day, but through ignorance and confusion, the trustees provided little assistance to either Wirt or Holmes.

The Case Before the Supreme Court

On March 10, 1818, Webster began his argument before the Supreme Court. He spoke before a large audience for most of the day. There have been several accounts of his lengthy argument in addition to the one printed in the official reports of the Court. Although they were written many years after the debate, they agree on at least one point: Webster's impact on the Court. Except for some moments of dramatic emphasis, he spoke "in the calm tone of easy and dignified conversation," Chauncy A. Goodrich wrote in 1853. (Goodrich, a professor of oratory at Yale, had been sent to the trial to gain any information the university in New Haven might need someday.) "His matter," Goodrich wrote, "was so completely at his command that he scarcely looked at his brief, but went on for more than four hours with a statement so luminous and a chain of reasoning so easy to be understood and yet approaching so nearly to absolute demonstration, that he seemed to carry with him every man of his audience without in the slightest effort or weariness on either side." After giving an extremely detailed explanation of the college's legal position, he said:

The case before the court is not of ordinary importance, nor of everyday occurrence. It affects not this college only, but every college, and all the literary institutions of the country. They have flourished, hitherto, and have become in a high degree respectable and useful to the community. They have all a common principle of existence—the inviolability of their charters. It will be a dangerous, a most dangerous experiment, to hold

A painting (1962) by Robert Burns depicts Webster presenting his argument before the U.S. Supreme Court. Clockwise from the standing Webster are Joseph Hopkinson, counsel representing the College; Justices Thomas Todd, Henry Brockholst Livingston, Bushrod Washington, John Marshall, Joseph Story and William Johnson; and the counsels representing the University, John Holmes, Maine Congressman, and William Wirt, U.S. Attorney General.

Courtesy of the Trustees of Dartmouth College

"THIS, SIR, IS MY CASE! IT IS THE CASE NO[T] LY OF THAT HUMBLE INSTITUTION, IT IS TH[E] OF EVERY COLLEGE IN OUR LAND!...IT IS, [AS] I HAVE SAID, A SMALL COLLEGE. AND YE[T] *these institutions subject to the rise and fall of popular parties, and the fluctuations of political opinions. If the franchise may be at any time taken away, or impaired, the property also may be taken away, or its use perverted. Benefactors will have no certainty of effecting the object of their bounty; and learned men will be deterred from devoting themselves to the service of such institutions, from the precarious title of their officers. Colleges and halls will be deserted by all better spirits, and become a theatre for the contention of politics. Party and faction will be cherished in the places consecrated to piety and learning. These consequences are neither remote nor possible only. They are certain and immediate.*

The official version of Webster's remarks omits the conclusion for which he became famous and for which the case is largely remembered. But according to Goodrich, he came to the end of his argument and addressed the chief justice as follows:

Sir, you may destroy this little institution; it is weak; it is in your hands! I know it is one of the lesser lights in the literary horizon of our country. You may put it out! But if you do so, you must carry through your work! You must extinguish, one after another, all these great lights of science which for more than a century have thrown their radiance over our land!

It is, Sir, as I have said, a small college. And yet there are those who love it!

As Webster finished, according to an 1830 account, "there was a painful anxiety towards the close. The whole audience had been wrought up to the highest excitement; many were dissolved in tears; many betrayed the most agitating mental struggles; many were sinking under exhausting efforts to conceal their own emotion. When Mr. Webster ceased to speak, it was some minutes before anyone seemed inclined to break the silence. The whole seemed but an agonizing dream, from which the audience was slowly and almost unconsciously awakening."

Extralegal Tactics

The oral arguments took two more days to complete, and on the following day the Court adjourned for the year without handing down a decision. But during the ten months the litigants had to wait for start of the new Court term, there was much activity. Webster believed that he would prevail, but he wished, nevertheless, that separate lawsuits be started in the lower federal courts to permit questions other than the constitutional one he had so far argued to come up on appeal (he could not raise the state issues in the appeal from the state court). Three such suits were initiated, and they came before Justice Story in the circuit court. Story heard argument in September, and further proceedings, including an appeal, were expected for the following year.

Other, more subtle, tactics were employed as well. Webster arranged for his oral argument to be printed and circulated discreetly to influential citizens, lawyers, and even judges. Chancellor James Kent of New York, for example, was a close friend of Justice Johnson, and his reading of Webster's argument, he said, made him favorably disposed to the college's case (against his earlier opinion). Kent thereupon convinced Johnson (who had dissented in *Fletcher* v. *Peck* on the ground that a land grant is not a contract) to side with the college. Dartmouth's sister institutions also pitched in, cheaply. Princeton and Harvard both chose the spring of 1818 to bestow the LL.D. degree on Livingston and Johnson (who were both Princeton alumni). Story was elected to the Harvard board of overseers (he had been named a trustee of Dartmouth University after its creation in 1816, but he failed to attend any meetings and was dropped from the roster).

The college's opponents were also busy. They became uneasy because the Court had not immediately decided in their favor. Their apprehension was compounded by the realization that their counsel had been woefully unprepared: a thorough search of the original Wheelock files revealed the true sequence of events that had led up to the founding of Dartmouth. Webster had told the Court that the English contributors had given moral and financial support to the College and hence that it consisted entirely of private donations. His adversaries did not know enough to challenge this proposition. But the search of the files showed that this story was a legend that had grown up around the charter's deliberate ambiguities and Wheelock's success in obscuring the facts. The English trust funds were given solely for the support of the charity school, not the college. The English trustees had not wanted the Indian school to be converted into a college. (As already noted, they almost withdrew from the project, and Wheelock was forced to maintain two separate entities.)

The Corporate Person

Instead, it appeared that despite the statement in the charter (a point heavily relied on at the argument before the Court), Wheelock was not the founder of the college: Wentworth was, by virtue of his issuing the charter. Moreover, the initial gifts to the college (as distinguished from the charity school) came from the crown and from the province of New Hampshire. This put matters in an entirely new light, or so the university's advocates hoped. They decided to hire William Pinkney, Baltimore attorney and U.S. attorney general under President Madison, to ask for a rehearing in view of these "new facts."

These efforts came to naught, however, because the Court, during its ten-month recess, had reached a decision by a five-to-one vote, and Marshall delivered it on the second day of the new term (one justice did not vote, and the others broke from the tradition Marshall had inspired for each to keep his thoughts to himself: Justices Story and Washington filed lengthy concurring opinions, Justice Livingston announced that he concurred with all three, Justice Johnson that he concurred only with Marshall, and Justice Duvall dissented).

Marshall's recital of the facts led him to conclude that "it is apparent that the funds of the college consisted entirely of private donations. . . . Dartmouth College is really endowed by private individuals, who have bestowed their funds for the propagation of the Christian religion among the Indians, and for the promotion of piety and learning generally. . . . It is, then, an eleemosynary, and, as far as respects its funds, a private corporation." From these facts, it followed that Dartmouth was a private institution insofar as its source of funds and the uses to which they were put were concerned. Also, said Marshall, the college does not assume a public character from the act of incorporation alone.

At this point Marshall drew out the meaning of a corporation: "A corporation is an artificial being, invisible, intangible, and existing only in contemplation of law. Being the mere creature of law, it possesses only those properties which the charter of its creation confers upon it." What are these properties? "They enable a corporation to manage its own affairs, and to hold property without the perplexing intricacies, the hazardous and endless necessity of perpetual conveyances for the purpose of transmitting it from hand to hand. It is chiefly for the purpose of clothing bodies of men, in succession, with these qualities and capacities, that corporations were invented and are in use." But, said Marshall—and this is the critical point—the grant of corporate status does not automatically convert the corporation into a public body. It merely gives the object of the incorporation—in this case, the school—a means by which it can more efficiently carry out its business. The grant of corporate status, like the grants of land in the earlier contract cases, becomes the property of those who receive the grants. If individuals are carrying out private functions, their newly acquired corporate powers do not make them a public institution. Only if the corporate body were created specifically to perform a public purpose would it be a public body and subject to control by the legislature.

The weak point in Marshall's argument turned on the question of the object of Wheelock's enterprise. Was it public or private? Isn't it the purpose of the college to provide education for members of the public? Even so, Marshall declared, the people of New Hampshire have no right to the property of the college. The charter secured a benefit to the people of New Hampshire by giving an incentive to the proprietors of the college to move it there. This benefit would be lost if the state were permitted to interfere with the government of the school because future donors would know that they could not establish charitable institutions for the purpose of education with the assurance that their purposes would forever be carried out.

It requires no very critical examination of the human mind to enable us to determine that one great inducement to [the making of] *these gifts is the conviction felt by the giver, that the disposition he makes of them is immutable. It is probable that no man ever was, and that no man ever will be, the founder of a college, believing at the time that an act of incorporation constitutes no security for the institution; believing that it is immediately to be deemed a public institution, whose funds are to be governed and applied, not by the will of the donor, but by the will of the legislature.*

This statement sounds curiously speculative to a twentieth-century reader, but its concern about the motives of people who establish schools is understandable in its historical context. The social standing of schools was much less clear than it is today. People did not assume that government, or government-related institutions, automatically acted in the public interest. Colleges were questionable institutions; there were few of them. And we know from our own experience that there is a point to "withdrawing them from the influence of legislative bodies, whose fluctuating policy, and repeated interferences, [produce] the most perplexing and injurious embarrassments." There ought to be some assurance, guaranteed by the Constitution, of academic freedom, of the right of private individuals to set up a school and run it as they please. This is sound reasoning, but it masks a difficulty that became apparent half a century later in connection with corporations of another character: business corporations. The same arguments are applicable to commercial companies, yet there could be little doubt of their potential for taking actions injurious to the public. We will return to this point shortly.

This assurance of academic freedom—that is, exclusive power of the trustees to govern the college—could only be found in the Contract Clause. But was the charter of incorporation a contract? Marshall had no doubts: "This is plainly a contract to which the donors, the trustees, and the crown (to whose rights and obligations New Hampshire succeeds), were the original parties. It is a contract made on a valuable consideration. It is a contract for the security and disposition of property. It is a contract, on the faith of which real and personal estate has been conveyed to the corporation." Finally, Marshall ruled, there can be no doubt that the New Hampshire legislation impaired the obligations of the charter.

The whole power of governing the college is transferred from trustees appointed according to the will of the founder, expressed in the charter, to the executive of New Hampshire. . . . The will of the state is substituted for the will of the donors. . . . This is not an immaterial change. The founders of the college contracted, not merely for the perpetual application of the funds which they gave, to the objects for which those funds were given; they contracted also . . . for a system which should, as far as human foresight can provide, retain forever the government of the literary institution they had formed, in the hands of persons approved by themselves. This system is totally changed. The character of 1769 exists no longer. . . . This may be for the advantage of this college in particular, and may be for the advantage of literature in general, but it is not according to the will of the donors, and is subversive of that contract, on the faith of which their property was given.

The Court clearly had moved a long way from its ruling in *Fletcher* v. *Peck*. This was not simply a matter of limiting the states' power to control the negotiation of debts owed by one person to another. The charter was not a contract in this sense. It was not even a contract in the sense of land cases, in which parties dealing at arms length entered into an agreement that the state sought to change at a later date. The parties asked the state for the power to conduct their business expeditiously through a corporate form, and the entire case rested on the proposition that once the state gives such power to private parties, it cannot change its mind later.

This does not mean that there was no warrant in the law of the time for considering the grant a contract. Story showed in a long and intricate opinion that there was. But the thrust of the opinion went beyond the notion of contracts, at least as we consider them today, to embrace the idea of property. A corporate grant is property, and property, the Court said, cannot be taken away from the people it was given to. Story made it abundantly clear that the case was not limited to private, charitable institutions, which psychologically provided a more appealing case for the application of the doctrine. Story said the case stood for any corporation: "It is perfectly clear," he wrote, "that any act of a legislature which takes away any powers or franchises vested by its charter in a private corporation or its corporate officers, or which restrains or controls the legitimate exercise of them, or transfers them to other persons, without its assent, is a violation of the obligations of that charter."

That is strong language, and it is perhaps ironic that in the very next sentence Story provided the rationale by which the case could be avoided in the future. "If the legislature mean to claim such an authority (to take away any of the powers it granted the corporation), it must be reserved in the grant." In other words, the legislature must keep hands off a private corporation unless in the act incorporating the business or other institution, it specifically says that in the future the legislature may lay its hands on it.

But for Dartmouth College, the future was secure. In a matter of months, after the pending federal circuit court cases were laid to rest, the university faction capitulated and returned complete control of the college to the rightful trustees. Sadly, the health of Francis Brown, president of the college, was shattered by the strain of his three-year ordeal, and he died five months after his victory, at the age of thirty-six.

Though the *Dartmouth case* stirred the people of New Hampshire immediately, its greater significance was not immediately understood. This was partly because it was obscured by the announcement of a decision two weeks later that had a far more pressing effect on national concerns. In *Sturges* v. *Crowninshield,* one of the trio of great cases that the Court decided in 1819 (the third, *McCulloch* v. *Maryland,* will be discussed in the next chapter), the Court declared that a state bankruptcy law that discharged debtors who had contracted their debts before the law was passed was an unconstitutional impairment of the contract between the debtor and creditor. Initial reports of the decision led to much confusion, and its effects greatly troubled many individuals and institutions because Congress, which had the power to enact a bankruptcy law, had failed to do so, and did not do so until 1841. *Dartmouth* was lost in the confusion created by *Sturges.*

But Story understood its deep import. Writing to Chancellor Kent, he said, "Unless I am very much mistaken, these principles will be found to apply, with an extensive reach, to all the great concerns of the people, and will check any undue encroachments upon civil rights, which the passions or the popular doctrines of the day may stimulate our State Legislatures to adopt." This was remarkably prescient. In 1800 the total number of corporations throughout the United States was only 213, most of which were for banks, turnpikes, and canals. There were only a handful of manufacturing concerns. But following the end of the War of 1812, manufacturing and industry began to grow, and the *Dartmouth* case was tailor-made for them (as Story knew).

The importance of the *Dartmouth* case to the growth of the American economy is, in light of these statistics, incalculable. It provided the assurance that businessmen needed to invest their capital in companies that would grow into enormous entities. Without this assurance, some kinds of enterprises might have been forestalled or taken much longer to develop; the railroads, for example, required enormous capital and large-scale operations to have any reason for being.

Yet for all its greatness, the *Dartmouth College* case continues to have validity today primarily for Dartmouth College (and for other private schools similarly situated) rather than business. What happened can be told briefly.

First, as noted, the decision itself allowed an escape valve, at least as concerned future corporations. The legislature, in granting a corporate charter, could always reserve the right to amend it. Although legislatures did not use this power until late in the nineteenth century, when general incorporation statutes became the rule (before then, investors had to apply specifically to the legislature for a charter), today the power is all but universal.

Second, the rule announced eighteen years later in the famous case *Charles River Bridge* v. *Warren Bridge* limited the importance of the *Dartmouth* case to business. Massachusetts chartered a company to construct a toll bridge across a river. It subsequently chartered another company to construct a free, parallel bridge. The question was whether the state impaired the charter rights of the first company. The Court, now led by Chief Justice Roger B. Taney, held that it did not. There were no words in the charter that granted the first company an exclusive (monopoly) right to build a bridge, and in the absence of such words the Court would not infer them. Story was despondent; "the old constitutional doctrines are fast fading away," he wrote. And Chancellor Kent, writing to Story, agreed: "I have re-perused the *Charles River Bridge Case,* and with increased disgust. It abandons, or overthrows, a great principal of constitutional morality, and I think goes to destroy the security and value of legislative franchises. It injures the moral sense of the community, and destroys the sanctity of contracts."

In this view they were mistaken, luckily for the nation. The *Charles River Bridge* case did not overthrow the existing company or subject it to different management. It restored to the states a measure of power to govern in the public interest. If Story's view (that the monopoly should have been implied in the state's first charter—how else would the company be secure?) had been accepted, the old dangers of *Fletcher* v. *Peck* might have created a disastrous situation. An investor or group of investors might have been able to bribe a legislature to grant monopolies that were contrary to the public good for all time to come. Whatever this system might have been, it would not have been the competitive capitalism that developed. Those who decry the power of private corporations might well ponder how things would be if companies could spend their money to bribe existing legislatures and thus bind all successors.

Third, in a series of cases more than a half century after *Dartmouth,* the Supreme Court ruled that the state possesses an inherent "police power" that it can use to protect the health, safety, and morals of its citizens against the claim of a corporation that its corporate rights may not be diminished.

In essence, the thrust of the cases upholding the police power is that the states have no constitutional right to bargain this power away. This doctrine, which comprises an enormous part of our more recent constitutional history, is very sweeping. In 1933, in the depths of the Depression, Minnesota passed the Mortgage Moratorium Law, which postponed the foreclosure of mortgages for two years. The purpose of the law was to protect those who would have lost their homes or farms because of the economic crisis. The law did not cancel the mortgage debt, but it did increase the amount of time that banks and other lenders had to wait for payment. The following year, the Supreme Court upheld the law. Thus, the Contract Clause, which was placed in the Constitution to prevent states from interfering with the payment of debts, and by degrees in its early years was extended to protect public grants of land, then to freedom from taxation, and then to corporate charters, at last was held to be no bar to at least temporary postponement of debt.

Fourth, and most important, another constitutional provision was discovered to have far greater potential to protect private prop-

Dartmouth College

erty rights. It was not discussed in Marshall's and Story's day because the Due Process Clause of the Fourteenth Amendment had not yet been written. It entered our constitutional history after the Civil War in 1868. Its sweeping command that no state shall "deprive any person of life, liberty, or property, without due process of law" provided a powerful buffer against state interference for some fifty years. It was far more flexible than the Contract Clause.

Fifth, the Contract Clause is a prohibition only against the states. This clause does not bar the federal government from regulating corporate affairs and practices. Congress's power to enact bankruptcy legislation was always understood to permit the federal government to do what the states could not do under the Contract Clause. Similarly, the Congress's power to regulate interstate commerce later provided the federal government the means to circumvent the Court's prohibitions against state regulations. Through its power to regulate commerce the federal government can enact a great variety of regulations to govern activities that affect interstate commerce—from the creation of banks to civil rights laws.

In the early years of the nation, few corporations conducted business across state lines. But the growth of large-scale enterprise meant that the federal government would inevitably come to center stage as the primary regulator. When it did so, the Contract Clause was destined to fade away, at least with respect to corporations. Today the issuance of securities, competitive practices, safety conditions, and employment patterns within companies are all subject to federal regulation. Opponents of those who today advocate federal chartering of corporations, whereby state charters of existing corporations would be abolished and replaced with federal charters that strictly control internal corporate practices, will not find the *Dartmouth* case any constitutional support for their position.

Still, it is not entirely accurate to say that "the clause is of negligible importance, and might well be stricken from the Constitution," as some scholars have contended. Thus, in 1973, a federal court in Florida overturned a state law that permitted counties to purchase public land that had already been leased to private parties with an option to buy. There still are purely local situations where states occasionally may attempt to deprive a person, deliberately or otherwise, of what by contract he has a right to have. But these cases do not usually make headlines. In late 1975, however, with a grave fiscal crisis facing the City of New York, the state legislature attempted to ameliorate the situation by enacting a law under which the courts could, in the event of default on the city's municipal bonds, stay claims of the city's creditors while working out a "repay-ment plan." But many lawyers thought that the state could not thereby unilaterally wriggle out of its obligations—for any such plan to be effective, they thought, the creditors would all have to agree. Why? Because to forego their consent, the state would be impairing the obligation of contracts—its own. This proposition is not entirely free from doubt, in view of the 1934 Minnesota Mort-gage Moratorium Case, but it does seem reasonably clear that the state could not, by enacting bankruptcy legislation, avoid paying its debts altogether. Such debts can only be avoided under the federal bankruptcy law. But for most important clashes between private rights and public authority, the Contract Clause has become a matter of historical importance only.

6/ THE POWER AND SUPREMACY OF THE FEDERAL GOVERNMENT: McCULLOCH v. MARYLAND

The formation of a national government in 1789 was something more than an act of faith, but not much more. The people—at least that narrow segment of them who could then vote—selected ratifying conventions in each of the states, and the debate over the merits and demerits of the proposed constitutional scheme certainly sparked intense interest throughout the land. Thus, both the people and their politicians and intellectual leaders at least knew the outlines of the new form of government that was created: a new and higher government was the stated purpose and result of the ratification. But the Constitution was, after all, written rather broadly and its terms were rather vague, so it was reasonable to hope that the federal government would play a rather limited role in the affairs of Americans. At least the advocates of state sovereignty hoped this was what would happen. Things might have developed this way if it had not been for the Marshall Court.

The Historical Issue

This precise question—the extent to which the federal government could act and dominate the states—was what divided Americans into two great camps, Federalist and Republican. The Hamiltonian vision of a strong central government actively engaged in aiding the commercial enterprises of the people opposed the Jeffersonian ideal of the agricultural society in which the federal government functioned mainly to preserve harmony among the states and to protect them all from foreign invasion. This division touched virtually every issue and policy that was debated during the first three decades under the Constitution. But the most divisive and important one was the Bank of the United States.

In December, 1790, Alexander Hamilton, Washington's secretary of the treasury, submitted a plan for Congressional incorporation of a national bank. This was one of a series of proposals that made up Hamilton's comprehensive financial and economic policy. To put the credit of the United States on a firm basis, he saw to it that the federal government assumed the debts of the states (contracted during the Revolution and afterward). Through the Tariff Act of 1789, he devised a federal tax on imports so that the government could pay off the debt, which then amounted to some $77 million. The bank had a variety of functions: it could accept deposits, make loans to individuals, states, or the federal government, issue notes, and make disbursements for the federal treasury.

The First Bank of the United States

Congress passed the bill creating the Bank of the United States in 1791. By the terms of its charter it was to expire automatically in twenty years unless Congress renewed it. Since some questions concerning its constitutionality were raised, Washington sought the opinion of his attorney general, Edmund Randolph. Taking a strict constructionist view of the Constitution, Randolph concluded that the law was unconstitutional because it did not grant Congress the power, in so many words, to incorporate banks or anything else. That was a power, Randolph said, reserved to the states. Washington questioned Hamilton, whose lengthy answer convinced the president to sign the bill establishing the bank.

At the Constitutional Convention, the delegates discussed giving Congress the specific power to establish corporations generally, a joint recommendation of James Madison and Charles Pinckney, Franklin, reporting the deliberations of the committee on style concerning this recommendation, apparently made a formal motion giving Congress the power to cut canals (the record of the debate is not clear). Some delegates apparently thought that the form of his motion would permit Congress to charter banks and other commercial enterprises. While some wanted to give this power to Congress, others opposed it strongly, so Franklin's motion (the exact nature of which has not been recorded) was voted down.

Hamilton faced the argument that the action of the Convention (not explicitly giving Congress the power to establish corporations) showed that Congress could not constitutionally enact a law establishing a national bank. Though this was only four years after the Convention, Hamilton replied that there were conflicting recollections over this debate, and he noted that there were no authentic documents concerning it. In any event, quarrelling over the reason for the Convention's refusal to spell out such a power did not matter, he reasoned, because other language was adequate authority for such legislation.

He was referring to Paragraph Eighteen of Section Eight of Article One, which says that Congress shall have the power "to make all laws which shall be necessary and proper for carrying into execution the foregoing powers, and all other powers vested by this Constitution in the Government of the United States, or in any department or officer thereof." This provision was not debated at the Convention. It was routinely presented and adopted, but, Hamilton argued, its meaning was clear. It meant that Congress has "a right to employ all the *means* . . . fairly applicable to the attainment of the *ends* of [powers specifically granted], and which are not precluded by . . . exceptions specified in the Constitution, or not immoral, or not contrary to the *essential ends* of political society."

What were these ends toward which the bank would be an appropriate means? Hamilton cited a host of specific provisions: the power to collect taxes, to borrow money, to raise and support an army and navy, to regulate commerce between the states. Washington sided with Hamilton and signed the bill, thus creating the first bank.

The Republicans were not convinced. Jefferson had urged Washington to veto the bank bill. Congress should be strictly confined to its enumerated powers, he believed, and he continued to profess this belief throughout his life, though he did not always act consistently with it (most notably when he approved the negotiations over the Louisiana Purchase with Napoleon and signed the treaty in 1803, against the objection that the power to acquire territory by treaty had never been granted to the federal government). Nevertheless, as to federal chartering of private corporations, Jefferson was implacable. In 1800 he wrote:

The H. of R. sent us yesterday a bill for incorporating a company to work Roosevelt's copper mines in New Jersey. I do not know whether it is understood that the Legislature of Jersey was incompetent to do this, or merely that we have concurrent legislation under the sweeping clause [Paragraph Eighteen of Section Eight, which is today called the "elastic" clause]. *Congress are authorized to defend the nation. Ships are necessary for defence; copper is necessary for ships; mines, necessary for copper; a company necessary to work the mines; and who can doubt this reasoning who has ever played at 'This is the House that Jack Built'? Under such a process of filiation of necessities the sweeping clause makes clean work.*

The bank performed useful services for the nation, but when its charter came up for renewal in 1811, its Republican opponents had been in office for a decade and had sufficient strength to prevent the renewal of the bank's charter, though by a narrow margin (65-64 in the House).

This was a serious mistake as it turned out. With war breaking out the next year, the state banks were unable to meet the credit demands of the United States. At war's end the country was afflicted with recession and, simultaneously, inflation as state banks issued notes willy-nilly, without regard to deposits that backed them up. The federal government was hard pressed to raise any cash at all; the monetary system was in chaos because the notes of state banks could not be redeemed except by the banks that issued them. As a result the federal government had difficulty even transferring its deposits from one part of the country to the other. After six attempts in Congress to establish a new bank and a veto by President Madison of one bill that cleared Congress (he vetoed it because of technical problems), the Republicans overcame whatever constitutional scruples they might have had and finally created the Second Bank of the United States in 1816 (also with a twenty-year charter). It opened its door, and those of its several branches throughout the states, in January 1817.

The Infamous Second Bank

If the First Bank had been maintained and its charter had never been allowed to lapse, even more serious difficulties might have been averted. It had performed its functions in an orderly manner, and its directors had been honest. Not so at the new bank. In an effort to stabilize the currency, it made several serious mistakes, the most critical of which was allowing notes of any one of its branches to be redeemed at any other branch. This meant that the sound branches in Boston and New York paid out hard currency for notes from western and southwestern branches that were backed by speculative mortgages and questionable loans. As long as their notes were honored, these branches had no incentive to curtail their irresponsible lending practices, and currency was drained away from the financial centers. When the parent directors finally decided to put an end to this mischief, the solution only aggravated the calamity: they called for payments in specie, in other words, hard cash, against the loans. This action forced depositors to withdraw cash from state banks, which caused several of them to fail.

Moreover, in certain branches (Pennsylvania, Virginia, and Maryland) dishonesty in the form of loans to the branch's own officers and imprudently large loans to friends was rampant. At the Maryland branch, the president, some of his associates, and the cashier, James W. McCulloch, were involved in a long-run fraud that caused that branch to lose $1.7 million. In the face of all this, foes placed the blame for the financial and business woe besetting the nation squarely on the national bank, that "monster of fraud and corruption without parallel."

The states directed stern reprisals against the bank. The 1818 Illinois constitution forbade banks not chartered by the state from opening there. Tennessee put a $50,000 tax on nonstate banks within its borders. Georgia, North Carolina, and Kentucky rushed forward with similar legislation. The latter state placed a tax of $60,000 on each branch of a bank chartered elsewhere. In February 1818 Maryland began a course of action that would put the entire matter before the Supreme Court.

Maryland's law imposed a stiff stamp tax on notes issued by any bank that was not chartered in the state. The law provided that this tax could be waived if the bank paid a $15,000 annual fee. The Maryland branch of the Bank of the United States did not pay this fee, and in May 1818 the state treasurer, John James, sued the branch cashier, James McCulloch (his larceny had not yet been uncovered) to collect a $100 penalty because McCulloch had issued a bank note without attaching the stamp.

The case was rushed quickly through the state courts, in favor of Maryland, state and federal officials cooperating in order to get it to the Supreme Court as a test case. One month after the suit was first filed, the highest court of Maryland affirmed the constitutionality of the tax law, and the case was readied for its final appeal, which began in February 1819 in Washington, three weeks after Chief Justice Marshall announced the *Dartmouth College* decision.

The Questions and the Participants

Two questions were at the heart of the case. First, could Congress constitutionally create the bank? Second, did the states have the constitutional power to tax a corporation chartered by the federal government? The greatest lawyers in the nation argued the cause. Daniel Webster for the bank, along with his previous adversary, Attorney General Wirt, and William Pinkney, formerly attor-

The Philadelphia branch of the Second Bank of the United States, which was accused by its foes of fraud and corruption. This was one of the branches involved in dishonesty in the form of loans to its own officers and in imprudent loans to friends.

ney general of the United States and the U.S. senator from Maryland (the bank had retained him as its private attorney). For the state appeared Luther Martin, attorney general of Maryland, Joseph Hopkinson, Webster's ally the previous year, and Walter Jones of Washington. The argument consumed nine days, and the rhetorical talents of the six were employed to the utmost. Of Pinkney's argument, which itself lasted three full days, Justice Story wrote on its concluding day:

I never, in my whole life, heard a greater speech; it was worth a journey from Salem to hear it; his elocution was excessively vehement, but his eloquence was overwhelming. His language, his style, his figures, his arguments were most brilliant and sparkling. He spoke like a great statesman and patriot, and a sound consitutional lawyer. All the cobwebs of sophistry and metaphysics about State rights and State sovereignty he brushed away with a mighty besom [broom]. We have had a crowded audience of ladies and gentlemen; the hall was full almost to suffocation.

William Pinkney. He pleaded brilliantly on behalf of the Bank of the United States.

During the very time of the Supreme Court argument, political debate over the bank's future raged. Congress was debating a bill to repeal the bank's charter. "Justice hides her face," said one congressman; "she wishes not to look at the black catalogue of iniquities which this institution presents; humanity would gladly drop the tear of oblivion on the sickening scene." Although the main thrust of the case favoring the bank was that the abuse of some of its directors and the incompetence of its presidents did not disprove the necessity of a central bank, some went further and asserted the principle of the recently announced *Dartmouth* case. This was, of course, a misreading of that case, since the constitutional provision invoked in favor of the college was no prohibition against the federal government.

The debate was particularly virulent because it was widely assumed that the Supreme Court would rule in the bank's favor. Marshall's views were well known; he had expressed them in an opinion in 1805, in which he said: "Congress must possess the choice of means, and must be empowered to use any means which are in fact conducive to the exercise of a power granted by the Constitution." The earlier case had excited little comment, but the issues in the bank case were of partisan interest. This meant that the Court's decision on the underlying constitutional questions would be hailed or condemned because it would either permit the bank to continue or allow it to be taxed out of existence. "It was highly unfortunate," wrote Charles Warren, "that the decision of a point of constitutional law of so vital importance should have become necessary, in connection with a subject on which the American people were even more excitedly divided—namely the existence of the Bank of the United States. Had the legal question been presented in a case involving a topic less obnoxious than the Bank, unquestionably the doctrines which the court enounced in *McCulloch* v. *Maryland* would have aroused far less antagonism."

On February 24, as Wirt began his argument in the Court, the House turned down the first of a series of attempts to repeal the Bank's charter. This was significant because repeal before the Court's decision might have led to a dismissal of the case without opinion on the ground that the controversy was moot. But Congress refused to do away with the bank. So, on Saturday, March 6, only three days after the closing argument (leading some to suspect that Marshall had written his opinion during the preceding summer) and five weeks after the *Dartmouth* case, Marshall announced the unanimous decision of the Court in favor of the bank.

The Decision

As often in his opinions of great importance, Marshall began with a nod to the gravity of the case and the judicial humility required. "The Constitution of our country, in its most interesting and vital parts, is to be considered; the conflicting powers of the government of the Union and of its members, as marked in that constitution, are to be discussed; and an opinion given, which may essentially influence the great operations of the government. No tribunal can approach such a question without a deep sense of its importance, and of the awful responsibility involved in its decision. But it must be decided peacefully, or remain a source of hostile legislation, perhaps of hostility of a still more serious nature; and if it is to be so decided, by this tribunal alone can the decision be made."

The first question he considered was whether Congress has the power to incorporate a bank. He began by noting that Congress had assumed such power very early in the nation's history, after full debate, and had acted accordingly for nearly thirty years. If it were clear that Congress had usurped a power not given it, then the fact that it had continued "a bold and daring" usurpation would not be enough to save it. But where there is considerable doubt about the claim of usurpation, then the practice of history should be looked at closely. That is, in construing a provision of the Constitution susceptible to a variety of interpretations, such as the phrase "necessary and proper," it is not improper to consider how Congress itself has considered it. In view of the bank's legislative history the charge of usurpation was on shaky ground. A "short experience of the embarrassments to which the refusal to revive it exposed the government" convinced "those who were most prejudiced against the measure of its necessity" to reestablish it. As a result, "it would require no ordinary share of intrepidity to assert that a measure adopted under these circumstances was a bold and plain usurpation, to which the constitution gave no countenance." But this is not the only reason to suppose the bank was created constitutionally.

The attorneys for Maryland took the position that the Constitution emanated from the states, not the people, and that the federal government cannot, therefore, encroach upon the sovereignty of the states. Marshall effectively demolished this argument by establishing for all time the principle that the federal government is supreme in the areas of its undertaking. How else, Marshall wondered, could these matters be understood? It can scarcely matter that the Constitution was ratified on a state-by-state basis. "No political dreamer was ever wild enough to think of breaking down the lines which separate the states, and of compounding the American people into one common mass. Of consequence, when they act, they act in their states. But the measures they adopt do not, on that account, cease to be the measures of the people themselves, or become the measures of the state governments." Indeed, it would not make sense to suppose that the government of the United States was established by the states as sovereign entities. The states received their power from the people. Only the people—certainly not the states themselves—could grant the power necessary to create a government superior to the states. To change the loose alliance of states embodied in the Confederation "into an effective government, possessing great and sovereign powers, and acting directly on the people, the necessity of referring it to the people, and of deriving its powers directly from them, was felt and acknowledged by all."

This does not mean that the federal government can do whatever it wants. Everyone agrees that it can exercise only those powers that are actually granted to it; "that principle is now universally admitted." But the important problem, "the extent of the powers actually granted, is perpetually arising, and will probably continue

to arise, as long as our system shall exist." Yet, if it is decided
that a particular power belongs to the federal government, the
states cannot claim that their sovereignty prohibits the exercise of
that power by the federal government. "If any one proposition could
command the universal assent of mankind, we might expect it would
be this—that the government of the Union, though limited in its
powers, is supreme within its sphere of action."

Nothing in the Constitution says that Congress may not take
actions incidental to its specific powers. Indeed, the Constitution
omits the stringent requirement in the Articles of Confederation
that limited the old Congress to only those actions that were "expressly" conferred upon it. Simply stated, it would be impossible
to spell out every action that Congress might legitimately take. If
the Constitution were to attempt to do so, it would be enormously
long and could scarcely be embraced by the human mind. It would
probably never be understood by the public." The framers of the
Constitution did not write a detailed legislative statement; by its
nature, "only its great outlines should be marked, its important objects designated, and the minor ingredients which compose those
objects be deduced from the nature of the objects themselves." In
determining what powers Congress possesses under this great instrument, Marshall said, in perhaps the single most famous sentence
ever uttered by the Supreme Court, "we must never forget that
it is a constitution we are expounding." A mean and narrow construction of the supreme law would be scarcely consistent with the
aims of the framers.

The Constitution gives Congress far-reaching powers: "The
sword and the purse, all the external relations, and no inconsider-
able portion of the industry of the nation, are entrusted to its government. . . . A government, entrusted with such ample powers,
on the due execution of which the happiness and prosperity of the
nation so vitally depends, must also be entrusted with ample means
for their execution."

But the bank's opponents argued that the power to incorporate
an institution is a fundamental one, like raising taxes and declaring
war. Unless granted specifically, it is reserved to the states. Marshall quickly demolished the argument. Incorporation

*is never the end for which other powers are exercised, but a means by
which other objects are accomplished. No contributions are made to charity for the sake of an incorporation, but a corporation is created to ad-*

minister the charity; no seminary of learning is instituted in order to be incorporated, but the corporate character is conferred to subserve the purposes of education. No city was ever built with the sole object of being incorporated, but is incorporated as affording the best means of being well governed. The power of creating a corporation is never used for its own sake, but for the purpose of effecting something else.

Finally, of course, Congress is given the power to make all laws which shall be "necessary and proper" to carry out its functions. Lawyers for Maryland tried ingeniously to wriggle out of the clause's import. First, they argued, the clause simply gives Congress authority to carry out its powers by making laws. That is, without such a clause, it might have been contended that Congress would not have been able to "exercise its powers in the form of legislation." Marshall's response was that this is a splendid example of the sophistry to which the legal mind is sometimes sincerely prey. Congress was created to exercise legislative power; what more did the necessary and proper clause add to that? "Could it be necessary to say that a legislature should exercise legislative powers in the shape of legislation?"

Second, argued Maryland's lawyers, what is necessary and proper means only what is "absolutely necessary," only what is indispensable to the carrying out of Congress's primary powers. Again, Marshall showed that this is not a very persuasive objection to the creation of the national bank. The work "necessary" can have various meanings: "A thing may be necessary, very necessary, absolutely or indispensably necessary. To no mind would the same idea be conveyed by these several phrases." An inspection of the Constitution shows that if the framers had meant "absolutely" they would have said so, as they did in Section Ten of Article One, which prohibits any state from taxing imports or exports, "except what may be absolutely necessary for executing its inspection laws."

"Necessary and proper" should not, and cannot, be given a narrow meaning. "This provision is made in a constitution intended to endure for ages to come, and, consequently, to be adapted to the various crises of human affairs. To have prescribed the means by which government should, in all future time, execute its powers, would have been to change, entirely, the character of the instrument, and give it the properties of a legal code. It would have been an unwise attempt to provide, by immutable rules, for exigencies which, if foreseen at all, must have been seen dimly, and which can be best provided for as they occur. To have declared that the best means shall not be used, but those alone without which the power given would be nugatory, would have been to deprive the legislature of the capacity to avail itself of experience, to exercise its reason, and to accommodate its legislation to circumstances."

These observations are amply confirmed in practice. Congress enacted a code of criminal laws (declared penalties for violation of federal laws) although this power is not specifically granted in the Constitution. Congress provided for the carrying of mail from place to place, but the Constitution says only that Congress may "establish post-offices and post-roads." To follow such a logic, to deny Congress the power, for instance, to regulate the carrying of mail and to provide punishments for those who rob it, would be to create an impotent and trivial government.

Finally, considering where the "necessary and proper" clause is placed, it seems unreasonable to give it a narrow interpretation. It was placed among the list of Congressional powers, not among the limitations on those powers. by its own terms it purports to enlarge, not diminish, the powers of Congress. "If no other motive for its insertion can be suggested, a sufficient one is found in the desire to remove all doubts respecting the right to legislate on that vast mass of incidental powers which must be involved in the constitution, if that instrument be not a splendid bauble."

Congress must, therefore, be accorded a broad discretion, "Let the end be legitimate, let it be within the scope of the constitution, and all means which are appropriate, which are plainly adapted to that end, which are not prohibited, but consist with the letter and spirit of the constitution, are constitutional." Because incorporation is a means only, and not an end of government, it was not listed as a power of Congress. It is an appropriate measure that Congress may undertake in the performance of its duties. The Court, Marshall declared, will not undertake to examine how necessary something like a bank is. If it is useful in accomplishing a matter entrusted to Congress, then it is within the unquestioned discretion of congress to establish it.

Having upheld the constitutionality of the act creating the Second Bank of the United States, Marshall then confronted the contention of Maryland that it could impose a tax on this federally chartered corporation. His conclusion was that Maryland could not tax the federal bank because of the constitutional provision that the federal government is supreme within its sphere of action. The power of taxation is an attribute of sovereignty, but that does not mean that states can tax whatever is physically within their borders. They can tax only those things over which their sovereignty extends. Can it extend over the national bank? No; "the power to tax involves the power to destroy," and the power of Congress to create the bank necessarily implies a power to preserve it against encroachments that may tend to destroy it. "That the power to destroy may defeat and render useless the power to create; that there is a plain repugnance, in conferring on one government a power to control the constitutional measures of another, which other, with respect to those very measures, is declared to be supreme over that which exerts the control, are propositions not to be denied."

Maryland's attorneys argued that this was presuming too much. Taxation does not inevitably destroy; a state government is entitled to the confidence that it would not do so. This was, like many of their other arguments, disingenuous, for the express purpose of the state's tax law was to prevent the bank from operating within state borders and thus, ultimately, to destroy it. Moreover, to accept Maryland's position would have required the Court to continually hear cases challenging whether a state tax law went too far; motives of the legislature, as *Fletcher* v. *Peck* showed, are not proper subjects of judicial inquiry.

Marshall never reached this problem, however, because the Maryland contention could be disposed of on plainer grounds. To apply Maryland's principle to the Constitution, he declared, would result in

changing totally the character of that instrument. . . . The American people have declared their constitution, and the laws made in pursuance thereof, to be supreme; but this principle would transfer the supremacy, in fact, to the states.

If the states may tax one instrument, employed by the government in the execution of its powers, they may tax any and every other instrument. They may tax the mail; they may tax the mint; they may tax patent-rights; they may tax the papers of the customhouse; they may tax judicial process; they may tax all the means employed by the government, to an excess which would defeat all the ends of government. This was not intended by the American people. They did not design to make their government dependent on the states. . . .

When a state taxes the operations of the government of the United States, it acts upon institutions created, not by their own constituents, but by people over whom they claim no control. It acts upon the measures of a government created by others as well as themselves, for the benefit of others in common with themselves. The difference is that which always exists, and always must exist, between the action of the whole on a part, and the action of a part on the whole—between the laws of government declared to be supreme, and those of a government which, when in opposition to those laws, is not supreme.

So the tax on the operations of the bank could not stand. The states remained free to tax the land the bank owned within their borders and to tax the stock that individuals held in it in the same way that they taxed stock held in other corporations. But the states could not hinder the bank, by tax or otherwise, from carrying out the functions assigned to it by Congress.

The Consequences of the Decision

This bold and confident declaration, this expansive reading of the Constitution, was recognized throughout the land for what it was—and was praised (in the North and East) or condemned (in the South and West) according to the popularity of or hatred for the bank. Great as it was, *McCulloch* v. *Maryland* settled only the legal question of federal supremacy; it did not settle the matter politically. The question of states rights versus national rights remained central to American politics until it was settled conclusively in the Civil War. (Even today, however, the question arises on occasion; in 1958, for example, the governor of Arkansas refused to carry out a desegregation order of the Supreme Court, asserting that he and the state were not bound thereby, a position the Court immediately repudiated and that has no legal standing.)

In fact, in 1819, *McCulloch* v. *Maryland* did not even settle the specific issue of the bank's freedom from state interference. After losing the battle in the Court and in Congress, the determined minority that despised the bank and feared the power of Congress simply disregarded the Court's decision on the simplistic ground that it applied only to Maryland.

Ohio took the lead. The state's economic condition was the worst in the country, and hatred for the bank was especially virulent. Only one month before *McCulloch* was decided, the state enacted a harsh tax—$50,000 on each branch of the bank located in Ohio. The decision would not deter state officials from enforcing the law, declared state officials. Four days before the tax was due, in September 1819, the bank sued the state auditor, Ralph Osborn, and the federal court temporarily enjoined him from levying the tax. But Osborn said that the notice of the injunction had not been properly served on him, and he instructed an assistant, John L. Harper, to seek payment of the tax.

Upon refusal of the bank's officers to meet his demand for payment on September 17, Harper went into the vaults and carried off $120,475 in specie and notes (under authority of the Ohio law). The bank then renewed its service of the injunction on Osborn and served it on Harper also. But Harper disregarded it and took the money to the state treasury in Columbus. This action was generally condemned, even by strong states' rights advocates, but Ohio was determined to press its case, believing that *McCulloch* had been rigged. "In her controversy with the association of Pawn-brokers, nicknamed the Bank of the United States, the State of Ohio has succeeded in placing the dispute upon the proper ground," one Ohio newspaper said. This sentiment was widely, though not universally, shared; Ohio Governor Ethan Allen Brown looked with foreboding on the events in his state: "I view the transaction in the most odious light, and from my very soul I detest it," he said. "I am ashamed it has happened in Ohio."

The denouement was slow in arriving. In 1821 the federal circuit court ordered the state officials to return the money and blocked Ohio from collecting the tax. The state treasurer balked, and he was held in contempt and clapped in prison. Federal officials marched into the state treasury to take back the money. The state challenged the legality of the bank's lawsuit in federal court; under the Eleventh amendment, it was claimed, a state could not be sued against its will. The state also passed a number of different laws that to varying degrees purported to outlaw the bank or subject it to state control.

For a variety of reasons, including a series of attacks in Georgia against the bank that affected the argument in the Ohio case, the Supreme Court did not reach a decision on appeal until 1824, by which time the intensity of the controversy had died down. Again the Supreme Court upheld the bank. In *Osborn* v. *Bank of the United States,* the court went one step further than it had in *McCulloch.* It denied Ohio's contention that states could not be sued in federal court. The Eleventh Amendment, Marshall ruled, does not prevent a suit against a state official who is alleged to be violating the federal constitution (by following a state law allegedly contrary to it). This was a critically important decision. If it had gone the other way, state officials could have violated federal law whenever they pleased without fear of prosecution.

The bank was saved, and in the twelve years that remained in its charter it performed tolerably well. But in the 1830s, a new set of enemies arose. In 1832, Andrew Jackson vetoed a bill to extend its life, and in 1836 it expired forever. Not until 1913, with the creation of the Federal Reserve, did the country once again have a national banking system.

PART III:
SLAVERY AND
ITS AFTERMATH

7/ PEOPLE AS PROPERTY: DRED SCOTT v. SANDFORD*

In the annals of the Supreme Court and our constitutional history, the *Dred Scott* case is unique. No other case paved the path to war. No other case established a new political party by so dividing the country that the traditional parties were doomed to lose the presidency. No other case was so monumentally wrong and error-ridden not only because it denied the essence of humanity to the black population but also because at least its worst features could so easily have been avoided. No other case so weakened the position of the Supreme Court in the national government—a "self-inflicted wound," in the classic phrase of Chief Justice Charles Evans Hughes, that required more than ten years to heal. No other case that set out to settle so much in fact settled so little. The decision that the judges, the president, many politicians, and a considerable part of the population thought would definitively resolve the slavery question instead split the country apart. No case before or since has caused such an outpouring of commentary, commentary that goes on to this day.

Slave or Free: The Unanswered Question

The Constitution did not decide the question of slavery; the Constitution avoided it. For years this issue lay dormant, sleeping amidst more important matters that consumed the attention of the nation. When the question did arise, as it did from time to time when new states were proposed for admission to the Union, timely compromises permitted passions to cool. But the compromises were just that: equivocations that never confronted the moral issue.

The history of slavery's territorial advance, in brief, was as follows. During the 1780s slavery was dead or dying in the Northern states, either by constitutional provision or judicial decision. In 1787 the Congress of the Confederation enacted the Northwest Ordinance, which banned slavery in the vast tracts of

* *The name* Sanford *was misspelled in the official court report.*

land that now comprise Ohio, Indiana, Illinois, Michigan, and Wisconsin. At the time the Constitution was ratified, the population of the Northern free states roughly equaled that of the slaveholding Southern states. The division between the two—scrupulously maintained, though by tacit understanding, not by law—was the Mason-Dixon line and the Ohio River, which separated Pennsylvania from Maryland and Virginia, and Ohio, Indiana, and Illinois from Virginia and Kentucky. Slave states and free states were admitted to the Union alternately, thus preserving the balance.

The Missouri Compromise

This worked well until 1819, when the question of Missouri's admission to the Union arose. The Missouri Territory was part of the Louisiana Purchase, where slavery had existed prior to Napoleon's sale to Jefferson and continued afterward. Slavery was a thriving institution, and the proposed state constitution expressly permitted it. A New York Congressman proposed, however, that slavery be gradually abolished there as a condition of Missouri's entrance into the Union.

An enormous debate ensued. The state was almost entirely

north of the line that separated freedom from slavery. Moreover, there was a growing dissatisfaction with the Constitutional provision that allotted Congressional representation of the states on the basis of voters plus three-fifths of the slaves. This gave the South a swollen representation in Congress, many Northerners felt, and the admission of Missouri as a slave state upset the balance. The South, on the other hand, resented the North's threat to infringe on the right of slave-holders to move their property across the Mississippi and to maintain it there in established communities.

Threats of secession rang throughout many states, but in 1820 a compromise was reached, and this potentially explosive issue was defused. Missouri was admitted as a slave state, but slavery in all territory north of its southern boundary was forbidden. To balance Missouri, Maine was admitted as a free state. The Compromise, said Samuel Eliot Morison, "put the question of slavery extension at rest for almost a generation. It was a fair solution. The South obtained her immediate object, with the prospect of Arkansas and Florida entering as slave states in the near future; the North secured the greater expanse of unsettled territory, and maintained the principle of 1787, that Congress could keep slavery out of the Territories if

The shame of a nation.

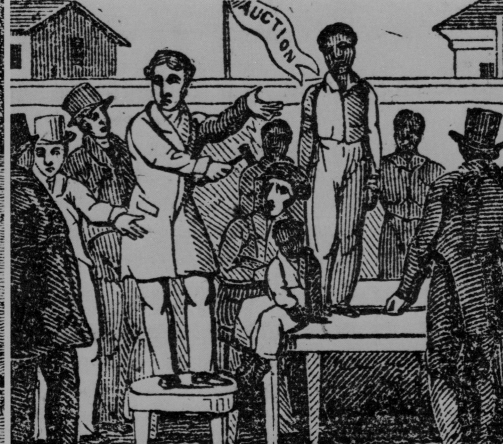

it chose."

But the Missouri Compromise could preserve the peace only so long as the population remained in balance and no large new chunks of territory pressed for statehood. Some farsighted observers saw this at the time. "I take it for granted," John Quincy Adams wrote in his diary, "that the present question is a mere preamble—a title-page to a great, tragic volume."

If the Compromise settled the question officially, it did not prevent the moral issues from being debated, and it did not keep private individuals from taking action. In the North the famous underground railway was organized, bringing thousands of slaves to freedom. In the South, occasional slave revolts bred terror that mounted year by year, resulting in increasingly repressive laws against free blacks and white relations with them, stiffer slave codes, and great agitation. The Fugitive Slave Law, enacted under a constitutional clause providing that any slave who escaped to a free state could not be discharged from "his service or labour, but shall be delivered up on claim of the party to whom such service or labour may be due," caused many frictions because it required Northern officials to cooperate (when they were all too anxious, and able, to refuse) and permitted Southern slaveowners, in effect, to kidnap black people.

In the 1840s, the slavery question again assumed major political importance. During that decade, the United States acquired major new territories: Oregon, Texas (as a slave state), and the spoils of the Mexican War, which, in addition to Texas included California, Nevada, Utah, Arizona, New Mexico, and parts of Colorado and Wyoming. Would this immense territory be slave or free?

In 1846 a Pennsylvania Congressman named Wilmot proposed that since the Mexican territory had no tradition of slavery, any states carved out of it should be free. In his famous Wilmot Proviso, he put forward the principle from the Northwest Ordinance that "neither slavery nor involuntary servitude shall ever exist" in the Mexican territory. This opened up a furious and prolonged debate. The North endorsed the Proviso and the House of Representatives even enacted Wilmot's bill, but the South, through John C. Calhoun, bitterly protested and suggested instead that Congress had no power to prevent slavery in the new territory. Calhoun wished for a constitutional amendment that would have secured the South's right to maintain slaves as property throughout the Union.

Two years later, Senator Clayton of Maine proposed a compromise that, although not accepted in the form he put forward, eventually was embodied in the Compromise of 1850. His idea was to balance the various claims for and against slavery as follows. Oregon would remain free; its laws would prohibit slavery. California and New Mexico would become territories without any power to legislate on the question, one way or the other. Instead, the problem would be left to the territorial judges, "with a right to appeal to the Supreme Court of the United States." The Clayton Compromise was not Calhoun's solution, and it did not pass.

But something had to be done. The South, especially, believed that its very existence was at stake. "This was her last chance," the historian Herbert Agar has written. "The North was far more wealthy than the South and far more populous. [In 1850, of twenty-three million Americans, a little more than seven million lived in the eleven states that became the Confederacy.] In a few years the railways would have built a new Northwest, tied to the Northeast by lines of commerce and by a common aversion to the 'peculiar institution' of slavery. When that happened, the North would win final control of the government at Washington and would reinstate all the Hamiltonian policies, meanwhile interfering in every possible way with the slave system. To Calhoun this meant the doom of Southern agriculture and Southern life. If Southerners waited for secession until all this had happened, they would find themselves too weak, and would be constrained to remain in the Union under Northern domination. Now was the time to force a decision. If Union sentiment in the North was strong enough to secure a constitutional amendment protecting the South forever against exploitation, so much the better. That was the one compromise the South could afford to accept."

Calhoun was wrong. The South and North were persuaded by Henry Clay and Daniel Webster to accept Clay's Great Compromise of 1850. California was admitted as a free state, and slavery was extinguished in the District of Columbia. To these Northern concessions were added two Southern ones. First, the New Mexico territory, embracing four future states and parts of two others, would be organized without regard to slavery. "It is inexpedient," Clay said, "for Congress to provide by law either for [slavery's] introduction into, or exclusion from, any part of the said territory; and . . . appropriate territorial governments ought to be established by Congress in all of the said territory . . . without the adoption of any restriction or condition on the subject of slavery."

For this reason the territorial acts in the Compromise provided for liberal judicial review, including review by the Supreme Court. Clayton's Compromise was resurrected. It made the issue of slavery a legal one to be resolved in the courts instead of a political one to be resolved by Congress. The debates in Congress were quite explicit on this point. "How if we were to attempt to settle this question could it be settled?" Henry Clay wondered. "In the first place we can not settle it, because of the great diversity of opinion which exists; and yet the Senator will ask those who differ with him in opinion to surrender their opinion, and, after they have made this sacrifice of opinion, can they declare what the law is? When the question comes up before the Supreme Court of the United States, that tribunal will declare what the law is."

The North's second concession was a stringent fugitive slave law. For the first time the federal government was given responsibility for the capture and return of slaves. This was bitter medicine for the North. In 1842, the Supreme Court in *Prigg* v. *Pennsylvania* had ruled that it was unconstitutional to enforce federal law through state officials. In the same decision, the Court struck down all state fugitive slave laws, many states having enacted restrictive legislation that drastically interfered with the rather liberal methods embodied in the federal law for recapturing runaway slaves.

The 1850 Fugitive Slave Act, on the other hand, established a new set of federal officials to assist in recapture. And they were given rather large incentives to fight off any attempts to resist their official duties. If a federal marshal lost his prisoner, he was liable to large fines. Bystanders who refused aid to the marshals could be tried for treason. The worst feature was that the word of the person making a claim that a particular black person was his slave was the only evidence the federal marshals needed. The alleged fugitive was not entitled to dispute the claim and could not file a lawsuit to protect his freedom. Hiding a runaway slave could result in a $2,000 fine and six months in prison.

The net result was conflagration throughout the land: freedmen were kidnapped, and attempts to recapture them met riots and murder. But this was the price the South exacted for the admission of free California. So the Compromise was made.

Eroding the Spirit of Compromise: The Kansas-Nebraska Act

In 1854, partly to ensure that the transcontinental railroad, then being built, would go through the center of the country rather than through the South, Illinois Senator Stephen A. Douglas proposed the organization of the Nebraska Territory. Similar measures had been defeated by Southern votes in the past, but Douglas had a different strategy. He proposed that Congress take no position on slavery in this territory, even though it lay above the line prescribed in the Missouri Compromise of 1820 as free soil. Instead, Douglas pointed to the principle of the 1850 Compromise: the people of the territory could decide for themselves whether to allow slavery or not. He called this principle "popular sovereignty" (also known as "squatter's sovereignty").

After a sharp, intense debate, during which it was agreed that the territory be divided in two, the Kansas-Nebraska Act of 1854 was passed and signed into law. It explicitly repealed the Missouri Compromise of 1820 by allowing slavery north of the time-honored line if the residents of the territory wanted it.

The act also incorporated the Clayton Compromise already embodied in the 1850 Compromise. The ultimate question of the extension of slavery was to be left to the courts. Despite attempts by Northern legislators to "clarify" the power of the territorial legislatures to ban slavery, it was agreed that Congress would simply delegate its regulatory power to the territorial legislatures. The extent of that power was not defined. This crucial section, Section Fourteen, of the Kansas-Nebraska Act read: "[It is] the true intent and meaning of this act not to legislate slavery into any territory or State, nor to exclude it therefrom, but to leave the people thereof perfectly free to form and regulate their domestic institutions in their own way, subject only to the Constitution of the United States."

The Court in the Midst of the Turmoil

During the 1840s, the Court reached the zenith of popular esteem. "While there were extremists and radicals in both parties, in the North as in the South, who inveighed against it and its decisions, yet the general mass of the public and the Bar had faith in its impartiality and its ability," Charles Warren has written. But the direct intrusion of the federal government after 1850 into the culture of slave-catching forced the Court into a posture that could not be accepted in the North. It was obliged to uphold federal law, and federal law decreed that human property—that is, property in humans—could be regained by barbarous, unjust acts.

Resistance spread. What had once been a philosophy confined to the South now became a byword in the North, as Nullification raced upward across the Mason-Dixon line. State after state passed laws declaring the federal process void: state courts in the North began to defy the law permitting appeals to the Supreme Court.

The most famous involving such incidents was the Booth case in Wisconsin. Booth, an abolitionist editor, had rescued a fugitive slave in violation of the federal law. Held under arrest by a federal marshal, he was freed by an order of a state supreme court justice. While this order was being appealed, Booth was convicted in federal court, again to be released by the state supreme court, which ruled that the federal law was unconstitutional. Although the Court did not rule against Wisconsin's interference with federal law until 1859, it stirred a debate that, together with decisions of lower federal courts in similar proceedings, largely negated the good feeling that had prevailed in the North toward the Supreme Court.

In a remarkable switch, the South thus became chief defender of the Court's virtues; the North was launched on a campaign of vilification. For years, Northern leaders in Congress blasted the Court as a bastion of Southern slaveholding interests. Into such a maelstrom of distrust and hatred was plunged the strange case of the slave Dred Scott.

The Circumstances of the Dred Scott Case

Too little is known of Dred Scott to write a biography. Too little probably was there of the man himself—the ultimate cost of the peculiar institution. Dred Scott was not the prime mover in his own case. He wanted to be free. He had even offered once to purchase his freedom, the historical record confirms, but he did not have the means of realizing his great dream, just as he lacked the means of fulfilling his less ambitious dreams. Scott was the central figure in his own case only in name; the case that was to shatter beyond repair the fragile unity of the nation used his name as his owners had used his life. The *Dred Scott* case was a manufactured cause; his owners, who sincerely wanted him to be free, did not emancipate him at once, an act that was within their power. Instead they cooked up a lawsuit to test a burning constitutional question: Could slavery be extended into the vast territory of the West?

Scott was born the property of Peter Blow of Virginia at the close of the eighteenth century. In his early years, he was known simply as Sam. During his thirtieth year, in 1827, Sam moved with the Blow family to St. Louis. Following the death of Peter Blow

Dred Scott.

The New York Historical Society

in 1832, the slave who became known as Dred Scott was sold for five hundred dollars to Dr. John Emerson, who shortly before had been commissioned an assistant surgeon in the Army. Scott evidently did not like his new condition. He ran away, but he was quickly recaptured and restored to his purchaser.

In 1834, Dr. Emerson began a series of fateful travels. He was ordered to duty at Fort Armstrong in Rock Island, Illinois (Illinois was a free state). Two years later, the Army left Fort Armstrong, and Dr. Emerson was transferred to Fort Snelling, along the Mississippi River. The fort was in the Wisconsin Territory (in what later became the state of Minnesota). The Missouri Compromise had prohibited slavery in this territory.

Scott and his family remained on free soil for five years. In 1837, his health failing, Dr. Emerson left Fort Snelling, to commence a series of moves to Louisiana, back to Fort Snelling, and elsewhere, apparently unaccompanied by the Scotts. They departed Fort Snelling six months after their master. Although the historical record is not clear, they probably were sent back to the St. Louis vicinity and hired out, a common practice at the time. In 1843, two

days before the new year, Dr. Emerson died, and his property, including his slaves, passed to his widow, Mrs. Irene Sanford Emerson.

Two years later, in 1846, the year of the Mexican War and the Wilmot Proviso, Dred Scott filed suit in a Missouri state court against Dr. Emerson's estate. His claim was simple: he had become free when he accompanied his late master into Illinois and Minnesota, and this status could not be reversed by his return to Missouri. During the course of this lawsuit, Mrs. Emerson had moved to New York and left Scott in the care of two sons of Scott's original master, Peter Blow.

Pressing the Case

The state case dragged on. In 1850, the year of the Great Compromise, Scott won a jury verdict in his favor, but the case was appealed, and in 1852 the Missouri Supreme Court held, overruling a precedent clearly to the contrary, that regardless of the law in Illinois and the Minnesota territory, by the law of Missouri Scott remained or became a slave when again he reentered the state.

Scott and his family, which accompanied him on his travels to and from free soil.

The New York Historical Society

Slavery was a question for each state to determine. This decision was not appealable to the Supreme Court and should have resolved the question of Scott's status, but for a change in Mrs. Emerson's life and the ingenuity of several lawyers interested not only in Scott's fate but also and more importantly in putting the entire question of slavery in the territories to the Supreme Court.

In 1850, Mrs. Emerson married an antislavery Massachusetts Congressman, Calvin Clifford Chaffee, at which time she moved to Springfield, Mass. The administration of her father's estate, of which Dred Scott was a part, passed to her brother, John F. A. Sanford of New York, under a rule that declared a married woman ineligible to administer trust property in Missouri. Because Sanford was not a citizen of Missouri, Scott's lawyers cooked up a new and fateful suit and filed it in the U.S. Circuit Court in St. Louis in November 1853.

Scott Charges Assault

Scott's complaint alleged that Sanford had assaulted him, his wife, and two children on a visit to St. Louis. He asked for damages in the amount of $9,000. Arguing that Scott was a citizen of Missouri, his lawyers pressed the court to accept the case on the basis of its "diversity jurisdiction."

The Constitution says Congress may permit federal courts to hear cases between citizens of different states. From the very start Congress had conferred such jurisdiction on the lower federal courts. But was a man born into slavery, claiming freedom because he had traveled and lived in free territory though having returned to a slave state, capable of being a citizen for purposes of this suit? The circuit court ruled that he was, thus sustaining its jurisdiction.

Sanford then answered Scott's complaint, arguing in his defense that he had only "gently laid his hands on them, as [he] had a right to do," since Scott and his family were Sanford's slaves. The circuit court, in May 1854, upheld Sanford's defense. Fifteen days later, Congress repealed the Missouri Compromise (with respect to Kansas and Nebraska) by enacting the Kansas-Nebraska Act, which gave to the territorial legislatures the sole power to decide for or against slavery within their boundaries, regardless of whether the land was situated north or south of the time-honored line. Scott's appeal was readied for the Supreme Court.

The composition of the Court was very different now. Except for John McLean of Ohio (appointed in 1829) and James M. Wayne of Georgia (1835) none of the justices were from the Marshall

Court. Roger Brooke Taney of Maryland had become chief justice. An old ally of Andrew Jackson, who appointed him to the Court when Marshall died, Taney had been a leading Federalist politician in the state. Jackson first appointed him attorney general, and Taney led the fight for Jackson against the Second Bank of the United States, urging Jackson's famous 1832 veto. He was then appointed secretary of the treasury, but the Senate rejected him (it also rejected his nomination as associate justice a few months before Marshall's death to fill another seat.) He and four other justices were from slaveholding states (in addition to Wayne, John Catron of Tennessee, Peter V. Daniel of Virginia, and John A. Campbell of Alabama). They were all Democrats, as the party of Jefferson was now called, and so were two others, Samuel Nelson of New York and Robert C. Grier of Pennsylvania. Justice McLean was a Republican, and during the 1850s he was an unannounced but obvious candidate for the presidency (on at least two occasions he made unseemly use of his position on the Court to advance his cause). The ninth justice, Benjamin R. Curtis, was a Massachusetts Whig; his brother, George T. Curtis, would be one of the lawyers arguing in Scott's behalf before the Supreme Court.

The Court in a "Compromising" Position

Before its appearance on the Supreme Court docket, the *Dred Scott* case excited little attention. But by the time it came up for argument, in February 1856, its enormous potential was apparent. During the winter and spring there was constant speculation in the newspapers as to the probable outcome of the case. But the Court could not reach a conclusion over the threshold question: Was the case properly before the bench; in other words was Scott a citizen?

Four justices supposed the case could be heard; four believed it could not. Justice Nelson, though leaning in favor of hearing the case, thought that the best course was to hear a reargument, a position the Court decided on in May 1856. The next argument was not to be heard until the following December, after the presidential election that pitted the successful Democratic candidate, James M. Buchanan, against the first candidate of the new Republican party, John C. Fremont, and the ex-president, Millard Fillmore, running on the Know-Nothing ticket. This turn of events was a disappointment to Justice McLean, who hoped that, by writing a stinging dissent to the Court's presumed upholding of slavery, he could take the Republican nomination for himself.

In mid-December the Court heard four days of reargument. By

Chief Justice Taney. He wrote the opinion that, it has been said, elevated Abraham Lincoln to the presidency.

now the entire nation was aware of the implications of the case. The Court could confirm Douglas's concept of popular sovereignty, it could refuse to consider the issue, or it could, as was hoped in the South, declare the Missouri Compromise of 1820 unconstitutional, a ruling which would permit slaveholders to take slaves into the territories without fear of losing their property and make it possible to increase the number of slave states in the Union.

The Court did not meet to discuss the case until mid-February. There had been difficulties for some of the justices. "Our aged Chief Justice, who will be eighty years old in a few days and who grows more feeble in body, but retains his alacrity and force of mind wonderfully," Justice Curtis wrote to his brother George, "is not able to write much. Justice Wayne has been ill much of the winter. Poor Justice Daniel has been prostrated for months by what was a sufficient cause; for his young and interesting wife was burned to death by her clothes accidentally taking fire, almost in his presence."

The initial intention of the justices was to bypass the main issues concerning the legality of slavery and the relative power of the federal government and the states. It was agreed that the Court would issue an opinion based on the authority of an 1851 case, *Strader* v. *Graham*. Then the Court unanimously ruled that, whatever the effect of the Northwest Ordinance or a free state's laws on a slave who actually comes into the territory, a slave's status must be determined by reference to the state law if he returns to a slave state. This would mean that the question of Dred Scott's status depended on Missouri law, as interpreted by its highest court. Of course, in 1852 the Missouri supreme court had ruled that Scott remained a slave. This meant that Scott could not be a citizen and could not maintain a suit in federal court under the diversity jurisdiction of those courts. The case would have to be dismissed. Had the Court followed this course, the *Dred Scott* case would have been relatively unimportant, for such was already the law of the land, and it allowed the people of each territory to decide on the question of slavery for themselves.

But this course proved impossible. Justices McLean and Curtis could not accept the conclusion nor remain silent. They determined to write dissenting opinions that upheld the constitutionality of the Missouri Compromise of 1820. The strategy of the Court majority then changed. Justice Wayne convinced himself that the Court could end the national debate by forthrightly holding that Congress had no power to outlaw slavery in the territories. He persuaded the chief justice and three others of his views, and Taney began to prepare an opinion of the Court.

On February 19, one of the justices, John Catron of Tennessee, an old friend of James Buchanan, took the highly unorthodox step of writing to the president-elect for his discreet help in settling the case. This came about as follows: Buchanan was anxious to know what he might say in his inaugural address about the decisive issue of the day. If the Court ruled before March 4, the day his term of office was to begin, the national situation could change radically, depending on the Court's decision. Buchanan hoped that the Court would settle the issue one way or the other and thus remove a sore burden from his hands. On February 6, in response to an inquiry from Buchanan, Catron wrote to him that the case had not yet been discussed but that he would endeavor to find out when it would be. On February 10 he wrote again saying that it would be the subject of the Court's February 15 conference. He added that nothing the Court did would be of any use to Buchanan, since it seemed clear that only the narrow point would be decided.

On February 19, however, after Taney was persuaded that he had to write a majority opinion covering all the points, Catron again wrote Buchanan and this time asked him to intercede with Justice Grier, Buchanan's fellow Pennsylvanian, who continued to resist the plan to decide the full constitutional question. Catron was anxious that as many justices as possible join the majority opinion. So Catron asked Buchanan to "drop Grier a line, saying how necessary it is, and how good the opportunity is, to settle the agitation by an affirmative decision of the Supreme Court, the one way or the other."

Justice Catron did not tell Buchanan which way the Court was leaning, although the inference was not difficult, and he suggested that the president-elect could "safely say in your Inaugural: 'That the question involving the constitutionality of the Missouri Compromise line is presented to the appropriate tribunal to decide: to wit, to the Supreme Court of the United States. It is due to its high and independent character to suppose that it will decide and settle a controversy which has so long and seriously agitated the country, and which *must* ultimately be decided by the Supreme Court. And until the case is disposed of, I would deem it improper to express any opinion on the subject.'"

If it smacks of impropriety for a justice to recommend a line in a president's inaugural address concerning a pending case,

Justice Grier's response to Buchanan's letter was an even greater breach of the separation between the two branches of government. Grier told Buchanan how the case was going to be decided, having consulted first with Taney and Wayne. In part, he wrote: "A majority including all the Justices south of Mason and Dixon's line agreeing in the result, but not in their reasons,—as the question will be thus forced upon us, I am anxious that it should not appear that the line of latitude should mark the line of division in the Court. I feel also that the opinion of the majority will fail of much of its effect if founded on clashing and inconsistent arguments. On conversation with the Chief Justice, I have agreed to concur with him. Brother Wayne and myself will also use our endeavors to get brothers Daniel and Campbell and Catron to do the same. So that if the question must be met, there will be an opinion of the Court upon it, if possible, without the contradictory views which would weaken its force. But I fear some rather extreme views may be thrown out by some of our southern brethren. There will therefore be six, if not seven (perhaps Nelson will remain neutral) who will decide the Compromise law of 1820 to be of *non-effect*."

With such assurances, the naive Buchanan addressed the nation on inaugural day, March 4, 1857, delivering himself of the opinion that the differences of opinion throughout the country on the question of slavery in the territories were "happily a matter of but little practical importance. Besides, it is a judicial question which legitimately belongs to the Supreme Court of the United States before whom it is now pending, and will, it is understood, be speedily and finally settled. To their decision, in common with all good citizens, I shall cheerfully submit, whatever this may be." He could not have been more mistaken in his belief that the decision would finally settle the vexing question.

The Decision: The Confusion and Controversy

Two days later, on Friday, March 6, Taney read what was termed the opinion of the Court, but which was more clearly his opinion alone. Contrary to Justice Catron's hopes, all nine justices filed separate opinions, and together they take up more than 250 pages in the official reports. The diverse and conflicting opinions make it difficult to state with any precision what exactly the Court did hold—or, more accurately, why it held as it did—for *Dred Scott v. Sandford* denied Scott his freedom and declared that the Missouri Compromise of 1820 was unconstitutional. Despite the confusion, it is revealing to consider a summary of Taney's discussion.

The question before the Court, Taney began, was whether the Circuit Court in St. Louis had jurisdiction to hear and determine the case between Scott and Sanford. The issue rested on whether Scott was in fact a citizen of the United States or not. "The question," said Taney, "is simply this: Can a negro, whose ancestors were imported into this country, and sold as slaves, become a member of the political community formed and brought into existence by the Constitution of the United States, and as such become entitled to all the rights, and privileges, and immunities, guarantied by that instrument to the citizen? One of which rights is the privilege of suing in a court of the United States in the cases specified in the Constitution."

His answer, boldly stated, was that blacks were not and could not be considered citizens; in other words, they were not the "people of the United States." At the time the Constitution was adopted, he said, these unfortunate people were "considered as a subordinate and inferior class of beings, who had been subjugated by the dominant race, and, whether emancipated or not, yet remained subject to their authority, and had no rights or privileges but such as those who held the power and the Government might choose to grant them."

This was an important point, because it was clear that state laws did not condemn blacks to perpetual servitude. In the North, of course, blacks were free; in the South, they could be emancipated. If Scott were a free man by virtue of Missouri law, would he be a citizen of the United States, entitled to the privilege of suing in federal court? No, said Taney; "no State can, by any act or law of its own, passed since the adoption of the Constitution, introduce a new member into the political community created by the Constitution of the United States. It cannot make him a member of this community by making him a member of its own." In other words, what a state does cannot control or determine the composition of a group—the "people of the United States"—named in the Constitution.

On what ground could it be said that blacks were not citizens of the United States in 1787? Taney wrote:

In the opinion of the court the legislation and histories of the times, and the language used in the Declaration of Independence, show, that neither the class of persons who had been imported as slaves, nor their descendants, whether they had become free or not, were then acknowledged as a part of the people, nor intended to be included in the general words used in that memorable instrument. . . .

They had for more than a century before been regarded as beings of an inferior order, and altogether unfit to associate with the white race, either in social or political relations; and so far inferior, that they had no rights which the white man was bound to respect; and that the negro might justly and lawfully be reduced to slavery for his benefit. He was bought and sold, and treated as an ordinary article of merchandise and traffic, whenever a profit could be made by it. This opinion was at that time fixed and universal in the civilized portion of the white race. It was regarded as an axiom in morals as well as in politics, which no one thought of disputing, or supposed to be open to dispute; and men in every grade and position in society daily and habitually acted upon it in their private pursuits, as well as in matters of public concern, without doubting for a moment the correctness of this opinion.

Taney has long been criticized for this and other similar passages. It is only fair to point out that he did not endorse the view that he supposed his forebears held (Taney was born the year of the Constitutional Convention). He was taking a "strict constructionist" view of the Constitution: what it meant when it was adopted was what it meant in 1857.

The chief justice also pointed to two specific clauses in the Constitution that further supported his position. One permitted the states to import slaves free from Congressional regulation until 1808. The other required each state to hand over slaves who escaped from bondage to their rightful owners. These provisions, he said, "show clearly that [the Negro race] were not regarded as a portion of the people or citizens of the Government then formed." Of course this logic is more than a little suspect: at most, the Constitution's provisions show only that those individuals actually held as slaves were not citizens, not that there were not free blacks.

Taney thus concluded that even if Missouri law made Scott a citizen, he could not be a citizen of the United States entitled to sue in federal courts, because a black, whether born to slaves or freed men descended from slaves, cannot become a United States citizen.

Taney did not stop there, although he could have. The ruling that Scott was not and could not be a citizen meant that he could not maintain his lawsuit, that the federal court had no jurisdiction, and that the case had to be dismissed. Taney went on, instead, to consider an alternative question that also showed the want of jurisdiction. For proceeding to this alternate route, which required showing that the Missouri Compromise was unconstitutional, Taney and the Court have been vilified ever since.

Taney began this second part of the decision by noting straight-forwardly that there could be no jurisdiction if Scott was still a slave, for "no one supposes that a slave is a citizen of the State or of the United States." This was also, of course, the principal question in the suit—whether Scott should have his freedom or not. But Taney was discussing it only because the answer would determine the jurisdiction of the Court. He was converting the substantive question left open in the 1850 Compromise and the Kansas-Nebraska Act—the legality of prohibiting slavery in the territories—into a procedural issue. Neither act was before the Court, but Taney's answer would determine their fate nonetheless.

If Scott was not a slave, it was for one of two reasons. He was released from slavery either because he had lived in territory governed by the Missouri Compromise or because he had lived in a free state (Illinois, as part of the Northwest Territory, had forever forbidden slavery).

Taney dismissed the first possibility—when Scott had lived in Minnesota—by carefully construing a provision of the Constitution that gives Congress power "to dispose of and make all needful rules and regulations respecting the territory or other property belonging to the United States." That provision was irrelevant, he ruled, because

the power there given, whatever it may be, is confined and was intended to be confined, to the territory which at that time belonged to, or was claimed by, the United States, and was within their boundaries as settled by the treaty with Great Britain, and can have no influence upon a territory afterwards acquired from a foreign government. It was a special provision for a known and particular territory, and to meet a present emergency, and nothing more. . . . [The provision] does not speak of any territory, nor of Territories. . . . The power is given in relation only to the territory of the United States—that is, to a territory then in existence, and then known or claimed as the territory of the United States.

This does not mean, however, that Congress does not have the power to acquire territory. Because Congress may admit new states, it must clearly have the power to acquire territory from which the new states will be formed. "But no power is given to acquire a Territory to be held and governed permanently in that character. . . . It is acquired to become a State, and not to be held as a colony and governed by Congress with absolute authority." The federal government has no existence separate from the states; its powers are delegated to it and though supreme within its sphere it acts for the states. Whatever the federal government acquires, "it acquires for the benefit of the people of the several States who created it. It is their trustee acting for them, and charged with the duty of promoting the interests of the whole people of the Union in the exercise of the powers specifically granted."

Taney went on to comment on the need for some form of government in the territories. Otherwise no one would dare enter and settle them. "The power to acquire necessarily carries with it the power to preserve." But Congress could not simply create any form of government. Congress is bound by the Constitution, and it could not legitimately establish an inferior government that is not so bound.

Turning to the Fifth Amendment, which provides that no person shall be deprived of life, liberty, or property without due process, Taney then delivered the coup de grace: "And an act of Congress which deprives a citizen of the United States of his liberty or property, merely because he came himself or brought his property into a particular Territory of the United States, and who had committed no offence against the laws, could hardly be dignified with the name of due process of law." Moreover: "If Congress itself cannot do this—if it is beyond the powers conferred on the Federal Government—it will be admitted, we presume, that it could not authorize a Territorial Government to exercise them. It could confer no power on any local Government, established by its authority, to violate the provisions of the Constitution."

With these words, the Missouri Compromise of 1820 was overturned, and the great accommodation by which slave states and free states were maintained in a rough balance was dead. Both the Congress and the territories were prohibited from interfering with slavery by barring to a settler the use of slaves whom he owned in his state of previous residence. Even if a majority of the inhabitants of a territory wished to ban slavery, they could not constitutionally do so until they became a state. The South had won: popular sovereignty was moribund.

Finally, Taney ruled that Scott's residence in Illinois was not sufficient to free him. Scott's contention in this regard was rather easier to dispose of. The conclusion followed from the Court's earlier ruling in *Strader* v. *Graham* that the status of slavery depends on the law of the state in which the slave is ultimately found, not on the law of the state in which the slave might once have lived. "As Scott was a slave when taken into the State of Illinois by his owner, and was there held as such, and brought back in that character, his status, as free or slave, depended on the laws of Missouri, and not of Illinois."

Criticism of Taney's Opinion

The other justices did not agree with all of Taney's points, though they upheld the substance of his opinion. The largest group —six Southern justices and Justice Nelson of New York—were willing to call Scott a slave because Missouri did so. Two other justices besides Taney were willing to go further, however, and declare that no black could ever be an American citizen. This point was not, therefore, accepted by a majority of the Court. Six justices also agreed that the Missouri Compromise was unconstitutional: five Southern justices and this time Justice Grier of Pennsylvania. Only two—Justices McLean and Curtis—dissented from the entire opinion.

Was the *Dred Scott* case sound law, if only on its own terms, considering the existence of slavery and the undoubted right of the Southern states to maintain it? Putting aside the argument that only the Court is the final interpreter of the Constitution and therefore no other standard can be invoked against it, Taney's opinion, as well as the opinions of the majority of justices, was considerably flawed.

The reasoning that a black of slave ancestry could never be a citizen was particularly tortured. The few number of adherents to the proposition is a good indication. As a purely historical matter, Taney was simply wrong, an error Justice Curtis was quick to point out in dissent. "At the time of the ratification of the Articles of Confederation (1781)," he said, "all free native-born inhabitants of the States of New Hampshire, Massachusetts, New York, New Jersey, and North Carolina, though descended from African slaves, were not only citizens of those States, but such of them as had the other necessary qualifications [e.g., sufficient property] possessed the franchise of electors, on equal terms with other citizens." In other words, when the Constitution was ratified, there were blacks who, though descended from slaves, were part of the "people of the United States."

More importantly, why, except in the most arbitrary way, must the "people of the United States" inevitably be limited to those classes of people who existed in 1787? Congress has the power to enact a uniform law of naturalization. So it is clear that Missouri by itself could not declare a foreigner (from England or France or elsewhere) to be a citizen of the United States. But Dred Scott was not a foreigner; he was born in Virginia. It might equally or better be supposed that the citizens of the United States were any persons born on American soil whom a state itself considered citizens. The slaves were born in America, and they were not the subjects of any sovereign except their private masters. So Justice Curtis concluded:

I can find nothing in the Constitution which, proprio vigore [by its inherent meaning], *deprives of their citizenship any class of persons who were citizens of the United States at the time of its adoption, or who should be native-born citizens of any State after its adoption; nor any power enabling Congress to disfranchise persons born on the soil of any State, and entitled to citizenship of such State by its Constitution and laws. And my opinion is, that, under the Constitution of the United States, every free person born on the soil of a State, who is a citizen of that State by force of its Constitution or laws, is also a citizen of the United States.*

As to the Missouri Compromise, Taney's opinion is fraught with the greatest difficulties and ironies. If, as Taney declares, the inhabitants of the territories are not to be treated as mere colonists, his own opinion denies them the power to determine for themselves the most explosive of all issues, the right to hold slaves. Even though all the people in the territory oppose slaveholding, they suffer without remedy until Congress in its own good time admits the territory to the Union as a state, at which time the residents may adopt a constitution that finally abolishes it.

But the greatest perplexity arises from the inherent tension that existed in a nation that permitted slavery in some states and not in others. There was no rule that required the free states to respect the property right of a slaveholder if he moved north to a free state. Taney found such a rule, however, for the territories in the form of a constitutional prohibition against the federal government: the Due Process Clause of the Fifth Amendment. For the first time, that clause was held to prevent a law that "took property away" rather than merely to prevent the deprivation of property in the absence of legislation or a fair trial. This was an immensely significant step. Although it became moot in regard to slaves after the Civil War, its extension to the states through the Fourteenth Amendment greatly affected the future course of American law, especially as the definition of "property" expanded from a rather narrow class of things, like land and personal possessions, to a far broader concept, including the right to put productive capacity to use.

Taney's interpretation of the Due Process Clause was not envisioned when the Constitution was written. Justice Curtis again vigorously disagreed, at least with respect to slaves. For there is no "property right" in a slave, he asserted, in the absence of specific legislation permitting such a status to exist. This means that the property right in the slave exists only under the law of the particular state in which the slave is held. How—under what provision of the Constitution—are the purely local laws of Missouri to be extended into the vast territories of the United States that Congress has declared to be forever free? How can Missouri create slavery in the territory of Minnesota when there is no law there establishing it? Surely Missouri itself cannot legislate for that territory.

The Due Process Clause, a prohibition against legislation, cannot so easily be transformed into an unwitting creator of legislation, Justice Curtis seemed to conclude. How odd, Curtis said of Taney's reasoning, "that the Constitution has conferred the right on every citizen to become a resident on the territory of the United States with his slaves, and there to hold them as such, but has neither made nor provided for any municipal regulations which are essential to the existence of slavery?" Yet this is the sum and substance of Taney's double-barreled conclusion that Congress has no power to govern the territories except what is related to its power to admit them into statehood and that the Fifth Amendment prohibits Congress from interfering with the settlers' property rights. Justice Curtis then drove his point home: Taney's decision meant that Congress could not enact laws that established slavery in the territories, which was the only way slavery itself could be considered a property right, but at the same time Congress could not prohibit slavery in the territories—a nice paradox.

"Is it not more rational to conclude," Curtis asked, "that they who framed and adopted the Constitution were aware the persons held to service under the laws of a State are property only to the extent and under the conditions fixed by those laws; that they must cease to be available as property, when their owners voluntarily place them permanently within another jurisdiction, where no municipal laws on the subject of slavery exist; and that, being aware of these principles, and having said nothing to interfere with or displace them, or to compel Congress to legislate in any particular manner on the subject, and having empowered Congress to make all needful rules and regulations respecting the territory of the United States, it was their intention to leave to the discretion of Congress what regulations, if any, should be made concerning slavery therein?"

The Consequences of Dred Scott

In any event, as stated earlier, the Court could simply have rested on its earlier *Strader* v. *Graham* decision as to both the period of residence in the territory and that in Illinois. As an initial proposition *Strader* can be disputed. There were sound reasons for declaring that a man who wishes to maintain his slaves must keep them in a state that permits it but that if he ventures outside that state, to travel or to live, the slave is emancipated, regardless of whether he returns to the home state or not. The Court had not reached this conclusion, however, and so Dred Scott, even under the best possible circumstances (barring a reversal by the Court of its earlier decision), was doomed to remain a slave. For he had indisputably returned to Missouri to resume his old status.

For Dred Scott the Court's final disposition of his case actually resulted in leaving him better off than he had been. Sanford had died before the case was announced, and shortly after the March 6 ruling Mrs. Emerson and her husband Dr. Chaffee transferred their rights in Scott to Taylor Blow, the son of his original owner, in St. Louis. This was done so that Blow could emancipate Scott

according to the laws of Missouri. In May Scott became a free man. Of the suit, a newspaper at the time quoted him as saying that it had brought him a "heap o' trouble" and that he would never have begun it if he had known it would last so long. He became a porter in a St. Louis hotel. Fifteen months later, on September 17, 1858, he died of tuberculosis.

For the nation at large, however, the Court's decision was an unmitigated catastrophe. A principle that had been settled for a generation was not merely reopened; it was positively turned inside out. What had been accepted law was reexamined, reversed, and then closed again. This was the effect of a constitutional ruling by the Supreme Court. The decision could be changed only by a constitutional amendment (an impossibility given Southern opposition), by the Court's reversing itself (not possible unless the majority of the bench was replaced with good Northerners, also an impossibility for years to come), or by force.

From that day forward, the drums of war began to beat. This is not to say that the *Dred Scott* case "caused" the Civil War in some direct way. It was probably impossible to avoid an armed con-

test over the right of states to secede, but the case was enormously important in the timing of the war. It acted as a catalyst of public opinion and imposed legal constraints on those who might otherwise have still been able to find some compromise.

The case, Taney's opinion especially, enflamed the North; newspapers were awash with hysterical commentary suggesting that the next step was to require slavery in the free states (not at all an implication of the case). This fear was given added credence during the 1858 Illinois Senate debates, when Abraham Lincoln said, in reviewing the case: "Put this and that together, and we have another nice little niche, which we may, ere long, see filled with another Supreme Court decision, declaring that the Constitution of the United States does not permit a *State* to exclude slavery from its limits."

Buchanan was savaged; he played out his term, so bright at its inception in the belief that the slavery issue would be "finally and speedily settled" by the Court. He was powerless to curb or control the forces that were tearing the country apart. The Court was similarly despised. Despite a stirring and convincing opinion by Taney in the *Booth* cases in 1859 that the states (Wisconsin in the particular case) could not repudiate the lawful proceedings of federal officials, could not cancel a federal court decision, could not release a federal prisoner, could not ignore the direct decision of a federal appellate court, the states showed their contempt for the Court. Wisconsin defied the Court's own decision, entirely correct, that Booth was a federal prisoner. As late as 1860, the Wisconsin courts were nullifying Booth's arrest by a federal marshal.

As important as its effect was on public opinion, the *Dred Scott* case was more important in splitting up the Democratic party. What had been thought to have been solved in the Kansas-Nebraska Act of 1854—that the people of the territories could decide for themselves whether to have slavery or not—had now been declared unconstitutional.

This had been the final compromise. No other compromise was possible. Stephen Douglas had gone as far as he could go in bargaining away the North's position for the sake of the continued viability of the Union and of his own presidential candidacy. Now the Northern and Southern wings of the party were hopelessly apart. The North could never agree to the South's demands for protection of slavery rights in the territories. Douglas insisted on his concept of popular sovereignty; his opponents taunted him with

Taney's works in *Dred Scott.*

This decision, Edward S. Corwin has said, "cannot be, with accuracy, written down as usurpation, but it can and must be written down as a gross abuse of trust by the body which rendered it." From 1857 to 1860 the political course of this abuse was inexorable. "It may fairly be said," Charles Warren wrote, "that Chief Justice Taney elected Abraham Lincoln to the Presidency."

The *Dred Scott* decision, as we will explore in the next section of this book, was formally overturned by the Thirteenth and Fourteenth Amendments to the Constitution, which were ratified in 1865 and 1868, respectively.

8/ BETWEEN THEN AND NOW: THE FOURTEENTH AMENDMENT

The straw poll that determined the milestones included in this volume omitted any case or statute between 1857 and 1935, a rather remarkable void of seventy-eight years. The ground rules specifically asked those who participated in the balloting to assume that the Constitution was preeminent. The Fourteenth Amendment, although strictly speaking a part of the Constitution, did receive a sufficient number of votes to single it out as a milestone, and it will be treated as such here. Certainly it was a seminal event in the history of American law. It was nothing short of a constitutional revolution, though it took a while for it to be recognized as such. To provide a context for the milestones that follow, it is imperative to consider, at least briefly, the course of this critical amendment.

The Abolition of Slavery

On December 13, 1863, an amendment to abolish slavery was first introduced in the form of a resolution in Congress. The major thrust of the debate was over whether Congress itself should have power to take action against any who resisted the abolition of slavery. Should Congress, for example, be given the power to enact a general criminal law punishing anyone who attempted to continue to hold someone in slavery or peonage? Supporters of such federal power eventually prevailed, and several months after President Lincoln was assassinated, the Thirteenth Amendment was officially ratified (on December 18, 1865). "Neither slavery nor involuntary servitude," it declares, "shall exist within the United States, or any place subject to their jurisdiction." And, by Section Two, "Congress shall have power to enforce this article by appropriate legislation."

Extending the Power of the Federal Government

This was the first new grant of power to Congress since the original Constitution was ratified in 1789. It meant that Congress could enact legislation that superseded any state legislation that otherwise might stand in its way. Less than two years later, Congress used this power to enact the first national civil rights act, the Civil Rights Act of 1866, captioned "An Act to protect all persons in the United States in their Civil Rights, and furnish the means of their vindication." It was enacted over President Johnson's veto.

In declaring that all persons born in the United States were to be considered citizens, the act voided the *Dred Scott* case. But it was a response to more than that decision. The South was full of the so-called Black Codes, which seriously hindered blacks from exercising rights freely enjoyed by whites. So the 1866 act also declared that all citizens "shall have the same right, in every State and Territory in the United States, to make and enforce contracts, to sue, be parties, and give evidence, to inherit, purchase, lease, sell, hold, and convey real and personal property, and to full and equal benefit of all laws and proceedings for the security of person and property, as is enjoyed by white citizens, and shall be subject to like punishment, pains, and penalties, and to none other." (The act went on to establish penalties for violations of the act and means for its enforcement by federal officials.)

Johnson had vetoed it because he thought it interfered excessively with the sovereign powers of the states; unconstitutional, he called it. To be freed from slavery was one thing, but did the abolition of slavery imply equal rights? If former slaves were not given equal rights, did it mean that slavery had not really been abolished?

The Northern abolitionists thought so. "What is Liberty without Equality?" Charles Sumner asked rhetorically. He answered his question by declaring that "one is the complement of the other. . . . They are the two vital principles of republican government." To the Radical Republicans, one could not truly be free unless one possessed rights equal to those of any other class. The Black Codes, which among other things prevented blacks from owning property, clearly imposed "incidents of slavery" that Congress had every power to eliminate. So went their argument.

But doubts persisted. To decree a penalty for anyone still attempting to hold a person in bondage surely was within the power granted to Congress under the Thirteenth Amendment. But the Thirteenth Amendment does not give Congress indiscriminate power to enact legislation to alleviate problems of inequality, whether they are caused either by specific, state-directed discrimination or by the private actions of individuals. So to overcome these doubts, the Republicans pushed a new amendment—the Fourteenth —through Congress in 1866. The Southern states were coerced into accepting it, and the required three-fourths of the states ratified it within two years.

There was good reason for the Southern states to suspect and fear the amendment. It augured a radical restructuring of the federal arrangement. Its first sentence merely ratified what the Civil Rights Act of 1866 had declared concerning citizenship. This was the final, formal reversal of the *Dred Scott* decision. "All persons born or naturalized in the United States and subject to the jurisdiction thereof, are citizens of the United States and of the State wherein they reside." The war had already settled the issue, and it was implicit in the Thirteenth Amendment.

What follows, however, was new: specific limitations placed on the states. The second and critical sentence of the Fourteenth Amendment reads as follows:

No State shall make or enforce any law which shall abridge the privileges or immunities of citizens of the United States; nor shall any State deprive any person of life, liberty, or property, without due process of law; nor deny to any person within its jurisdiction the equal protection of the law.

There are three limitations placed on the states. First, they may not abridge the privileges and immunities of citizens. Second, they may not deprive anyone of life, liberty, or property without due process. Third, they may not treat people unequally. By the fifth section of the Amendment, Congress was given power, as in the Thirteenth Amendment, to enforce its various provisions. For the first time the federal government was given an enormous amount of power to intervene in state affairs on behalf of the liberties of the people. How the states treat their citizens became, in 1868, a concern of the federal government for the first time. This was a significant constitutional revolution: the states had become less sovereign, the national government more all-embracing. Most of the significant constitutional confrontations since 1868 have involved these three clauses in the second sentence of the Fourteenth Amendment.

The Central Issues

Although the existence of the Fourteenth Amendment has raised many questions over the years, two of the most fundamental ones were raised early and are still being fought over today. They are, first, whether the Fourteenth Amendment makes the Bill of Rights applicable to the states and, second, whether it permits courts to judge the reasonableness of legislation. In view of the purpose of the framers of this amendment, its later judicial history is rather surprising. Only five years after the Fourteenth Amendment was ratified, the Supreme Court rendered the first clause of the second sentence—the Privileges and Immunities Clause—virtually meaningless. The result was a century's worth of tortured litigation, leading into our own times and still going on.

The problem, which some thought the Fourteenth Amendment had solved, stemmed from an 1833 Marshall opinion. In the 1830s, the city of Baltimore had diverted water in its harbor in order to pave public streets. Because of its engineering activities, gravel and sand were deposited along a channel that had previously led ships to Barron's Wharf. As a result the owner was unable to continue his profitable business because the ships had to dock elsewhere. In a suit against the city, Barron charged that his property had been taken for public use without just compensation, an act expressly forbidden by the Fifth Amendment.

Speaking for the Court, Marshall ruled that the Bill of Rights applied only to the federal government. The Constitution, he said, "was ordained and established by the people of the United States for themselves, for their own government, and not for the government of the individual states." Although the constitution places some restraints on how the states may act, the first ten amendments were clearly intended to impose limits only on the national government. These restraints were like those that the bills of rights in state constitutions placed on the operation of state governments. The First Amendment, for example, begins its description of the limitations of government by saying: "*Congress* shall make no law . . ." Unless the state constitutions reserved rights to the people, and unless state courts were willing to uphold them, therefore, citizens actually had no judicial protection at all.

But the Fourteenth Amendment changed this. It specifically says that "no state shall make or enforce any law which shall abridge the privileges or immunities of citizens of the United States." Did this mean that the federal Bill of Rights now applied to the states, that the privileges and immunities that citizens of the United States had—that is, to be free from governmental action and interference as specifically spelled out in the eight amendments —were now also to be their privileges and immunities as against the state governments?

It is impossible to answer this question with any degree of certainty. The issue has become enmeshed and entangled in a larger historical debate. If we could start on a clean slate, examining the most current information available, we probably would conclude that the drafters of the Fourteenth Amendment did indeed intend the federal Bill of Rights to be enforced in the states. When he spoke for his amendment on the floor of the House of Representatives, John A. Bingham of Ohio, the drafter of the Privileges and Immunities Clause (together with Rep. Thaddeus Stevens of Pennsylvania and Senators Jacob Howard of Michigan and Lyman Trumbull of Illinois, the leaders of the fight for the Fourteenth Amendment), specifically said that he intended to overturn the precedent set by *Barron* v. *Baltimore*.

Senator Howard, in discussing the rights embodied in the first eight amendments, said: "[T]hese are secured to citizens solely as citizens of the United States, . . . they do not operate in the slightest degree as restraints or prohibitions upon state legislation. . . . The great object of the first section of this amendment is, therefore, to restrain the power of the states and compel them at all times to respect these fundamental rights."

The Erosion of the Privileges and Immunities Clause

Although it has been said that "there remains no genuine doubt that the framers of Amendment Fourteen intended it as a lever for the application of the Bill of Rights to the several states of the Union," it was not clear in 1872, when the Supreme Court examined this section for the first time. In the famous *Slaughterhouse Cases* the Supreme Court delivered the Privileges and Immunities Clause a roundhouse blow that rendered it virtually useless for all time to come. Even today it remains a shriveled appendage to the Constitution as a result of the Court's handiwork (because of the amendment's built-in redundancy later Courts—three-quarters of a century later—began to put its original purpose into effect).

The *Slaughterhouse Cases* arose from what Alexander Bickel has termed "a more than ordinarily corrupt enactment of the Louisiana legislature" in 1869. The legislation gave the Crescent City Live-Stock Landing & Slaughter-House Company a monopoly of the slaughtering business in New Orleans. About a thousand butchers were forbidden from performing the actual slaughtering of animals on their own premises. Instead, all such business had to be done by and on the premises of the Crescent City company.

The butchers retained an eminent attorney, John A. Campbell, who had resigned from the Supreme Court when Louisiana seceded in 1861. He was one of the leading members of the Supreme Court bar, and he argued that the Fourteenth Amendment barred the state from depriving the butchers of their right to earn their living. Surely, he stated, the Louisiana law deprived these butchers—citizens of the United States—from exercising several of their privileges now guaranteed by the Fourteenth Amendment: the right "to cultivate the ground, or to purchase products, or to carry on trade, or to maintain himself and his family by free industry."

Not so, said Justice Samuel F. Miller for the five to four majority that dismissed the butchers' case. The Fourteenth Amendment was intended to overrule *Dred Scott,* make the Negro a citizen, and guarantee rights to the emancipated slaves. It did not transfer the rights of national citizenship to citizens of a state.

Then they interpreted the purpose of the Privileges and Immunities Clause. It prohibited the states from interfering with the rights of national citizenship. These included the right of a citizen

". . . without due process of law"

to come to the seat of government to assert any claim he may have upon that government, to transact any business he may have with it, to seek its protection, to share its offices, to engage in administering its functions . . . of free access to its seaports . . . to the subtreasuries, land offices, and courts of justice in the several states . . . to demand the care and protection of the Federal government over his life, liberty, and property when on the high seas or within the jurisdiction of a foreign government . . . the writ of habeas corpus . . . to use the navigable waters of the United States, however they may penetrate the territory of the several States.

These were not new rights, Miller wrote, that citizens could now claim by virtue of the Fourteenth Amendment. These were rights that citizens had always had. The Supremacy Clause of Article Six of the Constitution supported federal law and federal rights over state laws and rights when the two conflicted. So the practical effect of the decision in the *Slaughterhouse Cases* was to reduce the Privileges and Immunities Clause to a tautology, a "practical nullity." The states were commanded, said Justice Miller, not to interfere with what even they had no power to interfere with before the Amendment was written.

Its framers had expected the Privileges and Immunities Clause to be the major instrument in federalizing state government. But the postwar Supreme Court was not willing to see the traditional federal-state relationship altered by any constitutional amendment, at least not if the justices could help it. Through a subtle reinterpretation of the framers' intent, they in effect amended the Privileges and Immunities Clause out of the Fourteenth Amendment. Only those privileges "which owe their existence to the Federal Government, its National character, its Constitution or its laws" are privileges of national citizenship, Justice Miller ruled. Carrying on a butchering business obviously was not one of these. So the case was dismissed.

The majority opinion in the *Slaughterhouse Cases* was a sweeping one, designed in its own terms to prevent an interpretation that would "constitute this Court a perpetual censor upon all legislation of the States on the civil rights of their own citizens." The result of the case, by current constitutional standards, was undoubtedly correct, but the reasons for reaching that result were unnecessarily broad. The Court could simply have said that regardless of whether the Bill of Rights was to be applied against the states because of the Privileges and Immunities Clause, there was nothing in the Bill of Rights to prevent Louisiana from creating a business monopoly. This kind of limited statement would then have preserved the more general question for another day, when a state was acting more clearly in a way contrary to the Bill of Rights.

The dissenters made two points. First, the Court's interpretation of privileges and immunities made it "a vain and idle enactment which accomplished nothing, and most unnecessarily excited Congress and the people on its passage." But it is not a sound rule of judicial construction to presume that those who draft a law or a constitutional amendment intend nothing by their words. The Court should have resolved any doubts about the application of the clause by asserting that it did bind the states. "By the Constitution, as it stood before the War," Justice Swayne said in dissent, "ample protection was given against oppression by the Union, but little was given against wrong and oppression by the States. That want was intended to be supplied by this Amendment. Against the former this Court had been called upon more than once to interpose. Authority of the same amplitude was intended to be conferred as to the latter. But this arm of our jurisdiction is, in these cases, stricken down by the judgment just given."

The second point, made most strongly by Justice Stephen A.

Field, was that the Constitution forbade a state from depriving a person of the right to carry on a lawful business. The Court eventually accepted this position, at least for a period of some fifty years, but it based its rulings on the second great phrase of that second sentence of the Fourteenth Amendment: the Due Process Clause. In 1873, however, this was a minority position, and its realization was two decades away. (Eleven years later, after a new state legislature repealed the law that gave Crescent City its monopoly, the Supreme Court denied Crescent City's appeal to reinstate its monopoly. The monopoly claimed that it was deprived of its "right" to an exclusive slaughtering business without due process of law. Justice Miller denied the claim, this time for a unanimous Court.)

Due Process: The Granger Cases

For a time it seemed unlikely that the Court would eventually accept Justice Field's conception of due process. It seemed even less likely that the chief force of the Fourteenth Amendment would be to protect corporations and private economic enterprise rather than the civil rights of minorities. Yet precisely this happened by the turn of the century, and for the greater part of its history, the Fourteenth Amendment did not bear out the hopes of its framers. How this came to pass we shall briefly sketch.

The concept of the Due Process Clause as a restraint against unreasonable legislation did not originate with Justice Field. It was the explicit holding of the *Dred Scott* case. Chief Justice Taney had declared that the Fifth Amendment's Due Process Clause made any attempt by the federal government (against which the Fifth Amendment applies) to restrict or eliminate the property rights of slaveholders in the territories unconstitutional. The Due Process Clause traditionally had been considered protection only against procedural unfairness. The government could not sentence a person to jail, for example, or impose a fine on him, unless he had first been tried in court by a jury.

Taney's interdiction of legislative interference with slavery sounded a little like the traditional theory. The crux of the matter seemed to be that the right to hold slaves was not taken away after a trial. It was taken away simply because a person moved into a certain territory. Yet Taney's ruling was profoundly different from the procedural interpretation, for he was saying that there are some kinds of regulation that, no matter how sincere the motive of the legislature and no matter how conducive they may be to the public welfare, nevertheless are confiscatory. They deprive a person of his

THE GRANGER DECISION.

Decision of the United States Supreme Court that Elevators and Railroads Are Subject to Legislative Regulation of their Tariffs.

And the Legislature the Sole Judge of What Are Reasonable Charges for Transporting Freight or Persons.

For Protection Against Abuses by Legislatures the People Must Resort to the Polls, Not to the Courts.

These Doctrines Affirmed in a Chicago Elevator Case vs. the People of the State of Illinois.

The Supreme Court of the United States, March 1, decided the so-called granger cases, the first one being that of Ira Y. Munn and George L. Scott plaintiffs in error, vs. The People of the State of Illinois, in error to the Supreme Court of the State of Illinois.

Mr. Justice Waite delivered the opinion of the Court, Judge Field alone dissenting:

The question to be determined in this case is whether the General Assembly of Illinois can, under the limitations upon the legislative power of the States imposed by the constitution of the United States, fix by law the maximum of charges for the storage of grain in warehouses in Chicago and other places in the State having not less than 100,000 inhabitants, in which grain is stored in bulk, and in which the grain of different owners is mixed together, or in which grain is stored in such a manner that the identity of the different lots or parcels cannot be accurately preserved. It is claimed that such a law is repugnant—

First—To that part of section eight, article one, of the constitution of the United States which confers upon Congress the power "to regulate commerce with foreign nations and among the several States."

Second—To that part of section nine of the same article, which provides that "no preference shall be given by any regulation of commerce or revenue to the ports of one State over those of another."

Third—To that part of the fourteenth amendment which ordains that no State shall "deprive any person of life, liberty or property without due process of law; nor deny to any person within its jurisdiction the equal protection of the laws."

We will consider the last of these objections first. Every statute is presumed to be constitutional. The courts ought not to declare one to be unconstitutional unless it is clearly so. If there is doubt the expressed will of the Legislature should be sustained. The constitution contains no definition of the word "deprive" as used in the fourteenth amendment.

To determine its significance, therefore, it is necessary to ascertain the effect which usage has given it when employed in the same or a like connection. While this provision of the amendment is new in the constitution of the United States as a limitation upon the powers of the States, it is old as a principle of civilized government. It is found in Magna Charta and, in substance, if not in form, in nearly or quite all the constitutions that have been from time to time adopted by the several States of the Union. By the fifth amendment it was introduced into the constitution of the United States as a limitation upon the powers of the national government, and by the fourteenth as a guaranty against any encroachment upon an acknowledged right of citizenship by the legislatures of the States.

When one becomes a member of society, he necessarily parts with some rights or privileges which, as an individual not affected by his relations to others, he might retain. "A body politic," as aptly defined in the preamble of the constitution of Massachusetts, "is a social compact by which the whole people covenants with each citizen, and each citizen with the whole people, that all shall be governed by certain laws for the common good." This does not confer power upon the whole people to control rights which are purely and exclusively private, but it does authorize the establishment of laws requiring each citizen to so conduct himself, and so use his own property, as not unnecessarily to injure another. This is the very essence of government, and has found expression in the maxim sic utere tuo ut alienum non lædas. From this source come the police powers, which, as was said by Mr. Chief Justice Taney in the License Cases, "are nothing more or less than the powers of government inherent in every sovereignty, that is to say, the power to govern men and things." Under these powers the government regulates the conduct of its citizens one towards another, and the manner in which each shall use his own property, when such regulation becomes necessary for the public good. In their exercise it has been customary in England from time immemorial, and in this country from its first colonization, to regulate ferries, common carriers, hackmen, bakers, millers, wharfingers, innkeepers, &c., and in so doing to fix a maximum of charge to be made for services rendered, accommodations furnished, and articles sold. To this day, statutes are to be found in many of the States upon some or all these subjects, and we think it has never yet been successfully contended that such legislation came within any of the constitutional prohibitions against interference with private property. With the fifth amendment in force, Congress in 1820 conferred power upon the city of Washington "to regulate . . . the rates of wharfage at private wharves, . . . the sweeping of chimneys, and to fix the rates of fees therefor, . . . and the weight and quality of bread," and, in 1848, "to make all necessary regulations respecting hackney carriages and the rates of fare of the same, and the rates of hauling by cartmen, wagoners, carmen, and draymen, and the rates of commission of auctioneers."

From this it is apparent that, down to the time of the adoption of the fourteenth amendment, it was not supposed that statutes regulating the use, or even the price of the use, of private property necessarily deprived an owner of his property without due process of law. Under some circumstances they may, but not under all. The amendment does not change the law in this particular; it simply prevents the States from doing that which will operate as such a deprivation.

This brings us to inquire as to the principles upon which this power of regulation rests, in order that we may determine what is within and what without its operative effect. Looking then to the common law, from whence came the right which the constitution protects, we find that when private property is "affected with a public interest, it ceases to be juris privati only." This was said by Lord Chief Justice Hale more than two hundred years ago, in his treatise De Portibus Maris, and has been accepted without objection as an essential element in the law of property ever since. Property does become clothed with a public interest when used in a manner to make it of public consequence and affect the community at large. When, therefore, one devotes his property to a use in which the public has an interest, he in effect grants to the public an interest in that use, and must submit to be controlled by the public for the common good, to the extent of the interest he has thus created. He may withdraw his grant by discontinuing the use, but so long as he maintains the use he must submit to the control.

After quoting Lord Hale as to ferries, wharves and wharfingers, and the decision of the Supreme Court of Alabama, because the Court thought they found in them the principle which supports the legislation they were examining, the opinion continues as follows:

Enough has already been said to show that when private property is devoted to public use it is subject to public regulation. It remains only to ascertain whether the warehouses of these plaintiffs in error and the business which is carried on there come within the operation of this principle. For this purpose we accept as true the statements of fact contained in the elaborate brief of one of the counsel or the plaintiffs in error.

From these it appears that the great producing region of the West and Northwest sends its grain by water and rail to Chicago, where the greater part of it is shipped by vessel for transportation to the seaboard by the great lakes, and some of it is forwarded by railway to the Eastern ports. * * * Vessels to some extent are loaded in the Chicago harbor and sailed through the St. Lawrence directly to Europe. * * * The quantity (of grain) received in Chicago has made it the greatest grain market in the world. This business has created a demand for means by which the immense quantity of grain can be handled or stored, and these have been found in grain warehouses which are generally called elevators because the grain is elevated from the boat or car by machinery, operated by steam, into the bins prepared for its reception, and elevated from the bins by a like process into the vessel or car which is to carry it on. * * * In this way the largest traffic between the citizens of the country north and west of Chicago and the citizens of the country lying on the Atlantic coast north of Washington is in grain which passes through the elevators of Chicago. In this way the trade in grain is carried on by the inhabitants of seven or eight of the great States of the West with four or five of the States lying on the seashore, and forms the largest part of inter-state commerce in these States. The grain elevators or warehouses in Chicago are immense structures, holding from 300,000 to 1,000,000 bushels at one time, according to size. They are divided into bins of large capacity and great strength. * * * They are located with the river harbor on one side and the railway track on the other, and the grain is run through them from car to vessel or boat to car, as may be demanded in the course of business. It has been found impossible to preserve the owners' grain separate, and thus has given rise to a system of inspection and grading by which the grain of different owners is mixed and receipts issued for the number of bushels which are negotiable and redeemable if like kind upon demand. This mode of conducting the business was inaugurated more than twenty years ago, and has grown to immense proportions. The railroads have found it impracticable to own such elevators, and public policy forbids the transaction of such business by the carrier. The ownership has, therefore, been by private individuals, who have embarked their capital and devoted their industry to such business as a private pursuit. In this connection it must also be borne in mind that, although in 1874 there were in Chicago fourteen warehouses adapted to this particular business and owned by about thirty persons, nine business firms controlled them, and that the prices charged and received for storage were such as have been from year to year agreed upon and established by the different elevators or warehouses in the city of Chicago, and which rates have been annually published in one or more newspapers printed in said city in the month of January in each year, as the established rates for the year next ensuing such publication. Thus it is apparent that all the elevating facilities through which these vast productions of seven or eight great States of the West pass on the way to four or five of the States on the seashore may be a virtual monopoly. Under such circumstances it is difficult to see why, if the common carrier or the miller or the ferryman or the inn-keeper or the wharfinger or the hackney coachman pursues a public employment and exercises a sort of public office, these plaintiffs in error do not. They stand, to use again the language of their counsel, in the very "gateways of commerce," and take toll from all who pass. Their business "tends to a common charge and is becoming a thing of public interest and use." Every bushel of grain for its passage "pays a toll, which is a common charge," and therefore, according to Lord Hale, every such warehouseman "ought to be under public regulation, viz., that he . . . take but reasonable toll." Certainly, if any business can be clothed "with a public interest, and cease to be juris privati only," this has been. It may not be made so by the operation of the constitution of Illinois or this statute, but it is by the facts.

We also are not permitted to overlook the fact that, for some reason, the people of Illinois, when they revised their constitution in 1870, saw fit to make it the duty of the general assembly to pass laws "for the protection of producers, shippers, and receivers of grain and produce," (art. 13, sec. 7,) and by sec. 5 of the same article, to require all railroad companies receiving and transporting grain in bulk or otherwise to deliver the same at any elevator to which it might be consigned, that could be reached by any track that was or could be used by such company, and that all railroad companies should permit connections to be made with their tracks, so that any public warehouse, &c., might be reached by the cars on their railroads. This indicates very clearly that during the twenty years in which this peculiar business had been assuming its present "immense proportions," something had occurred which led the whole body of the people to suppose that remedies such as are usually employed to prevent abuses by virtual monopolies might not be inappropriate here. For our purposes we must assume that, if a state of facts could exist that would justify such legislation, it actually did exist when the statute now under consideration was passed. For us the question is one of power, not of expediency. If no state of circumstances could exist to justify such a statute, then we may declare this one void because in excess of the legislative power of the State. But if it could, we must presume it did. Of the propriety of legislative interference within the scope of legislative power, the legislature is the exclusive judge.

Neither is it a matter of any moment that no precedent can be found for a statute precisely like this. It is conceded that the business is one of recent origin, that its growth has been rapid, and that it is already of great importance. And it must also be conceded that it is a business in which the whole public has a direct and positive interest. It presents, therefore, a case for the application of a long-known and well-established principle in social science, and this statute simply extends the law so as to meet this new development of commercial progress. There is no attempt to compel these owners to grant the public an interest in their property, but to declare their obligations if they use it in this particular manner.

It matters not in this case that these plaintiffs in error had built their warehouses and established their business before the regulations complained of were adopted. What they did was from the beginning subject to the power of the body politic to require them to conform to such regulations as might be established by the proper authorities for the common good. They entered upon their business and provided themselves with the means to carry it on subject to this condition. If they did not wish to submit themselves to such interference they should not have clothed the public with an interest in their concerns. The same principle applies to them that does to the proprietor of a hackney carriage, and as to him it has never been supposed that he was exempt from regulating statutes or ordinances because he had purchased his horses and carriage and established his business before the statute or the ordinance was adopted.

It is insisted, however, that the owner of property is entitled to a reasonable compensation for its use, even though it be clothed with a public interest, and that what is reasonable is a judicial and not a legislative question.

As has already been shown, the practice has been otherwise. In countries where the common law prevails, it has been customary from time immemorial for the legislature to declare what shall be a reasonable compensation under such circumstances, or, perhaps more properly speaking, to fix a maximum beyond which any charge made would be unreasonable. Undoubtedly, in mere private contracts, relating to matters in which the public has no interest, what is reasonable must be ascertained judicially. But this is because the legislature has no control over such a contract. So, too, in matters which do affect the public interest, and as to which legislative control may be exercised, if there are no statutory regulations upon the subject, the courts must determine what is reasonable. The controlling fact is the power to regulate at all. If that exists, the right to establish the maximum of charge, as one of the means of regulation, is implied. In fact, the common-law rule, which requires the charge to be reasonable, is itself a regulation as to price. Without it the owner could make his rates at will, and compel the public to yield to his terms or forego the use. But a mere common-law regulation of trade or business may be changed by statute. A person has no property, no vested interest in any rule of the common law. That is only one of the forms of municipal law, and is no more sacred than any other. Rights of property which have been created by the common law cannot be taken away without due process; but the law itself, as a rule of conduct, may be changed at the will, or even at the whim, of the Legislature, unless prevented by constitutional limitations. Indeed, the great office of statutes is to remedy defects in the common law as they are developed, and to adapt it to the changes of time and circumstances. To limit the rate of charge for services rendered in a public employment, or for the use of property in which the public has an interest, is only changing a regulation which existed before. It establishes no new principle in the law, but only gives a new effect to an old one. We know that this is a power which may be abused, but that is no argument against its existence. For protection against abuses by Legislatures the people must resort to the polls, not to the courts. After what has already been said it is unnecessary to refer at length to the effect of the other provision of the fourteenth amendment, which is relied upon—viz: that no State shall "deny to any person within its jurisdiction the equal protection of the laws." Certainly it cannot be claimed that this prevents the State from regulating the fares of hackmen or the charges of draymen in Chicago, unless it does the same thing in every other place within its jurisdiction. But, as has been seen, the power to regulate the business of warehouses depends upon the same principle as the power to regulate hackmen and draymen, and what cannot be done in one case in this particular cannot be done in the other.

We come now to consider the effect upon this statute of the power of Congress to regulate commerce. It was very properly said in the case of the State tax on railway gross receipts (15 Wall, 293) that "It is not everything that affects commerce that amounts to a regulation of it within the meaning of the constitution." The warehouses of these plaintiffs in error are situated and their business carried on exclusively within the limits of the State of Illinois. They are used as instruments by those engaged in State as well as those engaged in inter-State commerce, but they are no more necessarily a part of commerce itself than the dray or the cart by which, but for them, grain would be transferred from one railroad station to another. Incidentally they may become connected with an inter-State commerce, but not necessarily so. Their regulation is a thing of domestic concern, and certainly until Congress acts in reference to their inter-State relations the State may exercise all the powers of government over them, even though in so doing it may indirectly operate upon commerce outside its immediate jurisdiction. We do not say that a case may not arise in which it will be found that a State, under the form of regulating its own affairs, has encroached upon the exclusive domain of Congress in respect to inter-State commerce, but we do say that upon the facts as they are represented to us in this record this has not been done.

The remaining objection—to wit, that the statute in its present form is repugnant to section 9, article 1, of the constitution of the United States, because it gives preference to the ports of one State over those of another—may be disposed of by the single remark that this provision operates only as a limitation of the powers of Congress, and in no respect affects the States in the regulation of their domestic affairs. We conclude, therefore, that the statute in question is not repugnant to the constitution of the United States and that there is no error in the judgment.

In passing upon this case we have not been unmindful of the vast importance of the questions involved. This and cases of a kindred character were argued before us more than a year ago by the most eminent counsel and in a manner worthy of their well earned reputations. We have kept the case long under advisement in order that the decision might be the result of our mature deliberations.

The judgment is affirmed.

A SORGHUM CROP.

Can be Raised without Difficulty in Spite of the Locusts—They will Not Eat the Cane—Correspondence.

The following correspondence has been sent to the PIONEER-PRESS with request to publish for the benefit of farmers. It fully explains

---

---

tional. The courts ought not to declare one to be unconstitutional unless it is clearly so. If there is doubt the expressed will of the Legislature should be sustained. The constitution contains no definition of the word "deprive" as used in the fourteenth amendment.

To determine its significance, therefore, it is necessary to ascertain the effect which usage has given it when employed in the same or a like connection. While this provision of the amendment is new in property unfairly, arbitrarily, unreasonably.

This reading of the Due Process Clause—known as "substantive due process" because it deals with the substance of the laws, not with how regularly and fairly they are being enforced—was announced one year before *Dred Scott* by the New York Court of Appeals, the highest court of that state. The New York legislature passed a prohibition law, forbidding the use of alcohol except for medicinal purposes, and requiring the immediate destruction of all liquor aside from that maintained as medicine. The Court of Appeals voided the law because it deprived the owners of alcohol of their property when the law took effect.

The Supreme Court was cautious about extending such novel doctrines, especially given the sorry station to which it fell after it announced the *Dred Scott* decision. During the 1870's in fact, the Court turned its face staunchly against the doctrine, despite the optimistic belief of the nation's leading businessmen that state regulation of some of their practices was unconstitutional.

The test came in the so-called *Granger Cases*. The major one was the famed *Munn* v. *Illinois*. During the early 1870s, the Grange movement succeeded in pushing through several midwestern state legislatures laws fixing the rates railroads could charge. In Illinois, the regulatory laws also fixed the rates of the giant grain elevators that stored the wheat being sold on the Chicago Board of Trade. This was an important business, for the elevators could store up to a million bushels, and the receipts for grain they held were used in commerce, almost like money.

A system such as this, which interlocked with huge daily shipments from farms hundreds of miles away and with the commodities buyers, had to be honest. Unhappily, it was not. Five large firms, including Munn & Scott, dominated the Chicago storage business and developed many techniques for manipulating the market. They rigged storage prices, diverted shipments, diluted the quality of grain by mixing inferior grains with the highest quality crop, issued receipts for grain that did not exist, and caused the price of grain receipts to fall below their value by spreading false rumors.

In 1871, the state created a Railroad and Warehouse Commission to enforce a variety of regulations aimed at curbing discriminatory and monopolistic practices. Munn & Scott resisted the law, was fined, and appealed. Similar proceedings involved several of the railroads. Despite the *Slaughterhouse Cases* and the *Charles River Bridge* case, they remained confident of a judicial victory.

They contended that the Granger laws violated their rights to set prices as they wished, guaranteed by their charters under the *Dartmouth College* case. The laws also infringed on Congressional power to regulate interstate commerce, and, they concluded, they were deprived of property without due process of law.

In 1875 and 1876 the various cases were argued before the Court, though Munn & Scott had gone bankrupt in the meantime, victim of its own greed in trying to corner the market in wheat (successor companies continued the lawsuit). Finally, on March 1, 1877, to the dismay of the railroads and warehousemen, the Court threw out all their arguments. The *Dartmouth College* case was no bar to state regulation. The Contract Clause preserved the charters, not the state of the law as it existed when the charter was issued. Similarly the Constitution's grant of power to Congress to regulate interstate commerce did not prevent the states from enacting their own legislation. Earlier cases had made it clear that unless Congress did act, the states were free to enact regulations to promote the welfare of their citizenry.

As to the due process claim, Chief Justice Morrison R. Waite announced a striking doctrine that barred its invocation. The grain storage business was, he said, affected by a public interest, and this permitted it to be regulated. "Property does become clothed with a public interest when used in a manner to make it of public conse-quence, and affect the community at large. When, therefore, one devotes his property to a use in which the public has an interest, he, in effect, grants to the public an interest in that use, and must submit to be controlled by the public for the common good, to the extent of the interest he has thus created." Because the states might abuse this power is not a sufficient argument for its limitation, Waite ruled. "For protection against abuses by Legislatures, the people must resort to the polls, not to the Courts."

Only Justice Field dissented. He said that the decision was "subversive of the rights of private property" and warned: "If the power can be exercised as to one article, it may as to all articles, and the prices of everything, from a calico gown to a city mansion, may be the subject of legislative direction." In this prediction he was ultimately correct. The wage and price freeze President Nixon imposed (under Congressional legislation) in 1971 controlled large portions of the economy.

For a period of forty years, from around 1895 until 1934, the Supreme Court backtracked. It mainly limited those industries that traditionally had been regulated as monopolies, such as transportation and utilities. In 1934 the Supreme Court upheld New York State milk price regulations in a decision that gave wide latitude to industries that may be thought to affect the public interest: "A state is free to adopt whatever economic policy may reasonably be deemed to promote the public welfare, and to enforce that policy by legislation adapted to its purpose," said the Court, returning to the doctrine first enunciated in *Munn* v. *Illinois*.

The Expansion of the Fourteenth Amendment

The 1877 Granger decisions generally pleased the popular press in the several midwestern states whose laws were upheld. "The decisions in the Granger cases have not been made too soon," the Chicago Tribune editorialized. "They are the preliminary steps to the uprooting of the doctrine that temporary Legislatures may enact irrepealable or unalterable laws to bind peoples and States indefinitely. These decisions indicate that the reign of chartered monopolies has reached its end, and that we are approaching a recognition of the inalienability of the political or governmental powers of the States. The sooner this recognition is made, the better for the corporations and for the Government. It will cheapen special franchises; it will take from Governments the corrupting inducement to grant perpetual privileges."

At the same time, the ultimate implications of the decisions that Justice Field warned against were also recognized. The *St. Paul Pioneer Press* urged an amendment to the Minnesota Constitution so that railroads would always be allowed reasonable compensation. And the *New York Times* said that "the objection properly held is, that if each State may decide for itself what rates are reasonable, the holders of railroad stocks and bonds can have no guarantee against the application of a measure which might practically amount to confiscation, . . . and great properties may be placed at the mercy of a power which is essentially capricious."

During the 1880s, these ideas were percolating, as many railroad cases came up to the Supreme Court, in a variety of contexts. The original notion, that the Fourteenth Amendment solely protected the liberties of blacks, was giving way. In 1883, as we will explore in greater detail in Chapter 13, the Supreme Court struck down the Civil Rights Acts of 1875, which among other things had barred discrimination against and segregation of blacks.

By 1886, two seminal notions, having nothing to do with race relations, came to be implanted in the Fourteenth Amendment. One was that corporations were "persons" entitled to the shield of the Equal Protection Clause. This question was briefed in the case of *Santa Clara County* v. *Southern Pacific Railroad,* which involved the power of the state to discriminate in taxation between natural persons and corporations. At the outset of the oral argument, Chief Justice Waite cut off any debate on this one point. He said: "The Court does not wish to hear argument on the question whether the provision in the Fourteenth Amendment to the Constitution, which forbids a State to deny to any person within its jurisdiction the equal protection of the laws, applies to these corporations. We are all of the opinion that it does."

To some, this result seemed inevitable. Roscoe Conkling, one of the Senate drafters of the Fourteenth Amendment, argued to the Court in 1885 that the drafters had chosen the word person to include corporations so that they would be protected from discriminatory tax laws. Later historians, however, have rejected his contention as wishful thinking at best. But from 1886 on, there has never been any serious challenge to the conclusion the Court then reached.

The second seminal event in that year was the application of the Due Process Clause, which also protects "persons", to corporate affairs. In *Stone* v. *Farmers Loan & Trust Co.,* the Court upheld a Mississippi railroad regulatory scheme. But it gave notice that the state's powers were not without limits: "From what has thus been said it is not to be inferred that this power of limitation or regulation is itself without limit. This power to regulate is not a power to destroy, and limitation is not the equivalent of confiscation. Under pretense of regulating fares and freights, the State cannot require a railroad corporation to carry persons or property without reward; neither can it do that which in law amounts to a taking of private property for public use without just compensation, or without due process of law."

This was a significant retreat from *Munn* v. *Illinois,* at least in language, for the Court had not actually caught a state in the act of imposing unreasonable regulations. There are two important points in this case. First, the Court stretched the definition of "property" beyond the original interpretation. The concept of property was no longer restricted to land or concrete personal possessions, or even to claims to specific tangible property, such as commercial paper. It was increasingly understood, in the words of the economist John R. Commons, as "exchange value," the capacity of a productive enterprise to extract profits from its customers.

A regulation that unreasonably interfered with the capacity of a private concern was, on that view, a deprivation of property. This theory is easier to "feel" than to articulate, since presumably even a reasonable restriction (which, being reasonable, would be constitutional) would nevertheless deprive the private company of property in some degree. How was the reasonable deprivation to be distinguished from the unreasonable? And on what basis does the Constitution preclude legislative enactment that is unreasonable as against a law that is reasonable? Where, that is, does the Constitution say that "a little bit of taking" is permissible but that "a lot" is not?

The answer is that, except for this interpretation of the Due Process Clause there is no such provision. This raises the second point. The Court reinterpreted the words "nor shall any state deprive any person of life, liberty, or property without due process of law" to mean that property may be taken only in reasonable amounts and by reasonable methods, as determined by the judiciary. As Edward S. Corwin put it, "The term 'due process of law,' in short, simply drops out of the clause, which comes to read 'no person shall be deprived of property,' period."

This technique provided even more potent and dramatic interpretation of the word "liberty" in the Due Process Clause. State laws that infringed on a person's right to do something were viewed as violations of this clause. This interpretation received especially strong support if a statute kept a person from entering into a relationship that could be described as contractual. In 1885 the New York Court of Appeals, again leading the way as it had twenty-nine years before in the prohibition case, declared that a state law aimed at ending sweatshop factory conditions in the cigar industry —where workers made cigars in their cramped tenements—violated the workers' right to contract for their services. The law, which banned cigar making on any apartment floor housing more than three families, "arbitrarily [deprived the worker] of his property and of some portion of his personal liberty."

Several state courts followed the tenement precedent, and in 1897, twenty years after *Munn,* the Supreme Court followed suit, voiding a law that prohibited Louisiana residents from contracting for insurance on their property with an out-of-state company. This was followed by the famous case *Lochner* v. *New York* in 1905.

No state shall make or enforce any law which shall abridge the privileges or immunities of citizens of the United States; nor shall any state deprive any person of life, liberty, or property without due process of law; nor deny to any person within its jurisdiction the equal protection of the law.

This decision threw out a state law that limited bakers to ten hours of work a day. The legal reason, the Court said, was that such a law was an arbitrary interference with the baker's right to contract to work longer hours if he pleased. And this right outweighed the state's power to police working conditions in the industry.

These decisions transformed the Fourteenth Amendment from a constitutional provision intended to secure the rights of minorities —particularly the blacks—to a charter of economic laissez faire that corporations could use to have courts void unfavorable legislation.

The statistics tell the story. Between 1873 and 1888, the Supreme Court considered less than seventy Fourteenth Amendment Due Process cases. In 1878, when less than twenty had come before the Court, Justice Miller expressed surprise at these and lectured the bar on the futility of raising such a claim. He said:

It is not a little remarkable that while this provision [the Due Process Clause] *has been in the Constitution of the United States, as a restraint upon the authority of the Federal Government, for nearly a century, and while, during all that time, the manner in which the powers of that Government have been exercised has been watched with jealousy, and subjected to the most rigid criticism in all its branches, this special limitation upon its powers has rarely been invoked in the judicial forum or the more enlarged theater of public discussion. But while it has been a part of the Constitution, as a restraint upon the power of the States, only a very few years, the docket of this Court is crowded with cases in which we are asked to hold that State Courts and State Legislatures have deprived their own citizens of life, liberty or property without due process of law. There is here abundant evidence that there exists some strange misconception of the scope of this provision as found in the Fourteenth Amendment. In fact, it would seem, from the character of many of the cases before us, and the arguments made in them, that the clause under consideration is looked upon as a means of bringing to the test of the decision of this Court the abstract opinions of every unsuccessful litigant in a State Court of the justice of the decision against him, and of the merits of the legislation on which such a decision may be founded.*

That was in 1878. But from 1888 to 1918, a period less than twice as long as the previous period in which some seventy cases were brought, the Court considered some 725 Fourteenth Amendment due process cases.

The Court was now truly a partner of Congress and the state legislatures. And it was rarely a silent partner. It struck down, without much rhyme or reason, whatever laws in the social and economic sphere it disapproved of. In unleashing the Supreme Court, the Fourteenth Amendment had truly wrought a fundamental revolution but scarcely one that its framers, the Radical Republicans, had imagined in 1866. The only class of laws that the Court almost never struck down were those that discriminated against the former slaves. The world of the Fourteenth Amendment was topsy-turvy, and not until the last forty years would it be put aright.

GREAT DEPRESSION

NORMAL

1935   194

SLE
20
O

APPLES
FOR SALE

Franklin D. Roosevelt

PART IV:
THE NEW DEAL YEARS

9/ THE UNCERTAIN CACKLE OF THE SICK CHICKEN: A.L.A. SCHECHTER POULTRY CORP. v. UNITED STATES

History probably will record the National Industrial Recovery Act as the most important and far-reaching legislation ever enacted by the American Congress," Franklin D. Roosevelt said on June 16, 1933, when he signed the bill establishing the National Recovery Administration, symbolized for a brief two years by the Blue Eagle. And on May 31, 1935, just four days after the Supreme Court unanimously voided the act as unconstitutional on two counts, he told a throng of 200 reporters at a White House Press conference that "the implications of this decision are much more important than any decision probably since the *Dred Scott* case."

If the importance of a Supreme Court decision is to be measured by the beliefs and predictions made at the time of its rendering, then President Roosevelt was undoubtedly correct. Yet just as the National Industrial Recovery Act (NIRA) had begun to disappoint many sponsors during its brief heyday, so its demise proved to have far less serious consequences for the nation than the self-inflicted wound had seventy-eight years earlier. The difference between the ultimate effect of the two cases is that in the latter instance, the Supreme Court was given the opportunity to reverse itself, a course it soon chose to follow.

The National Industrial Recovery Act came, of course, in the midst of the greatest economic depression the nation—and the world—has ever known. For more than three years before the law was passed, industry, employment, prices, wages, and productivity had been steadily falling. In 1929, the Federal Reserve Board index of manufacturing production stood at 110. In 1932 it had fallen to 57. Private construction, which before the Crash had been running at $7.5 billion annually, stood at less than $1.5 billion. It was obvious that one national imperative was to start industry ticking again.

Business and Government: NIRA

Although the plan of the NIRA emerged quickly (FDR proposed it formally to Congress less than a month before Congress enacted it, and the informal drafting work outside Congress had begun only a month before that, in April 1933), its roots really went back to World War I. During the war a variety of trade associations were formed to help with the war effort by establishing codes of fair practice within their industries. The idea spread during the 1920s; from 1926 to 1933 some 150 "codes of fair competition" were promulgated in scores of industries. (In 1922, Roosevelt himself served as the president of the American Construction Council.) These codes were voluntary efforts that on more than one occasion ran afoul of the antitrust laws.

These associations and their codes fit in with a line of thinking that more and more businessmen were coming to accept. Only a business government partnership could end the chaos prevailing throughout American industry. Long working hours and cutthroat competition were proving disastrous to workers and management alike. Stabilization of working conditions and competitive practices were desperately needed, but voluntary codes had not worked.

With the wage rates falling drastically (in many places to a few dollars a week) and working hours increasing radically (in some states as much as seventy hours), one trade association resolved to alleviate one aspect of its members' workers' plight. The Cotton Textile Institute decided against making women work at night, but 15 percent of its member-manufacturers rejected the arrangement. It thus became economically impossible for the other 85 percent to go along with this restriction. Capitalists were experiencing similar difficulties in holding production cartels together. The oil industry, for example, struggled with private deals and then arrangements with individual states to allocate production among the various companies in order to cut back on an excess of oil that was driving the price down to insupportable levels, but to no avail. They wanted it done on a national level.

During the spring of 1933, many different administration groups were thinking about plans to effect industrial recovery. Some of these wanted to create a mechanism for bringing about the business-government partnership. Others wanted a large public works program. The Senate had passed a thirty-hour work bill (prohibiting shipment of any goods in interstate commerce made by people who worked a longer workweek) and sentiment there also was increasing for public works. In this atmosphere Roosevelt directed his counselors to cook up a comprehensive bill to accomplish these purposes.

The result was the National Industrial Recovery Act. It was in two parts, the second establishing a $3.3 billion public works program. But the heart of the act, which the Supreme Court would later cut out, was in Title I. This title permitted the president to establish codes of fair competition for any trade or industry.

The general theory was that the industries themselves would propose such codes, which the president would approve if they met certain conditions specified by Congress. But he was also given the power to create them "upon his own motion." The act had several conditions. The associations proposing the codes could not inequitably restrict membership and had to be truly representative of the trades or industries for which the codes were proposed. The codes could not be "designed to promote monopolies or to eliminate or oppress small enterprises" or discriminate against them. The act also empowered the president to establish administrative agencies for carrying out its purposes. President Roosevelt quickly appointed an administrator and several deputy administrators of the National Recovery Administration (NRA), as well as member of three advisory boards, for industry, labor, and consumers. By its terms, the act would expire within two years unless renewed by Congress.

The initial reception for the NRA was enthusiastic. Business no less than labor, many Republicans no less than Democrats, backed it. One of its chief supporters was the president of the U.S. Chamber of Commerce, following a tradition that went back twenty years to Theodore Roosevelt, who had opposed the Federal Trade Commission in favor of national agencies that would regulate prices and practices of all industry.

In its first days and with its first codes, the NRA relied on public sentiment for enforcement. "If a retailer did not comply with the President's Re-employment Agreement [an interim code promulgated by Roosevelt that banned child labor, fixed the workweek at thirty-five to forty hours and set a minimum wage of thirty to forty cents an hour] after receiving a warning, he received a telegram that sternly ordered him to return his Blue Eagle poster and other NRA paraphernalia to the nearest post offiice. Presumably, consumers would then boycott the offender's establishment."

The Love Affair Turns Sour

But it quickly became obvious that the NIRA would spawn a maze of regulations far beyond what had been contemplated when the law was being drafted. The administration thought that codes would be drawn up for the largest industries only. Instead, scores of industries, some of them tiny, rushed to cover themselves with codes of fair competition. "In the course of its short life from August, 1933, to February, 1935, the Administration formulated and approved 546 codes and 185 supplemental codes filling 18 volumes and 13,000 pages; 685 amendments and modifications to these codes. It issued over 11,000 administrative orders interpreting, granting exemptions from, and establishing classifications under the provisions of individual codes; 139 administrative orders bearing generally upon administrative procedure."

The content of the codes varied enormously, as one would expect, since they encompassed such diverse industries as steel, coal, and automobiles as well as "mopstick, corn-cob pipe, and powder puff industries . . . . burlesque theaters, investment banking houses, and pecan shellers." One code that governed the retail trade embraced some 3.5 million workers; others covered as few as 45 workers. Most codes had minimum wage and hour provisions; some had minimum pricing rules, requiring companies to sell above a certain base price; others dealt with advertising, sales techniques, discounts, and production quantities. Altogether, more than 130 trade practices were covered.

Like a stone dropped into a small pond, the codes rippled to the very edges of the NRA, straining its enforcement powers to the limit. Critics began to assert that the codes were mere covers for price-fixing and monopolistic practices. In March 1934 the National Recovery Review Board was created to investigate such problems on a code-by-code basis; its chairman was Clarence Darrow. The board issued reports which, though confusing, seemed to confirm that the codes tended to support monopolies.

Mr. Roosevelt and a Hostile Court

To these difficulties was added a more ominous problem: the specter of unconstitutionality. Since the 1890s, the Court had pursued an erratic course concerning the scope of Congressional power under the Commerce Clause. Chief Justice Marshall had declared expansively in 1824 in *Gibbons* v. *Ogden* that "commerce is undoubtedly traffic (i.e., buying and selling), but it is something more—

it is intercourse." This definition was capable of sustaining the power of Congress to enact legislation dealing with far more than the mere transportation of goods from one state to another.

But in 1934-35 there were serious questions as to how far this extended. In 1895 the Court had dismissed an antitrust case against the Sugar Trust, which held more than 98 percent of the nation's refined sugar manufacturing capacity, on the ground that the manufacture of sugar as such was not commerce. Ten years later, the Court reversed itself and moved toward Marshall's position. It ruled that Congress could legitimately regulate practices that, though local, bore on the flow of commerce between the states. But then in 1918, the Court ruled that Congress could not ban child labor by barring goods made by children from being transported across state lines. And in 1923 it struck down a minimum wage law for women in the District of Columbia.

Though in the early 1930s the Court did sustain some state statutes that seemed consonant with the spirit of the New Deal (the *Minnesota Mortgage Moratorium Case* and a New York milk price regulation case), as well as uphold the Administration's position in the Gold Clause cases (in February 1935), the majority in all these cases was a thin one, and there were plenty of signs that a number of New Deal measures would be put to strict tests.

The first clear sign—so clear that it foretold the ultimate fate of NRA—was the so-called Hot Oil case decided in January 1935. The petroleum industry was one of the first to draw up a code under the NRA. The principal problem it faced was overproduction. Wholesale prices were as low as two and a half cents a gallon, less even than the production cost. The industry itself was, of course, huge (third largest in the nation), and it spread out across eighteen states in which there were more than 325,000 wells. More than one million people were employed in oil production. Most oil was shipped across state lines for sale in some 300,000 gas stations. Without oil transportation and industry everywhere would come to a complete standstill. Independent producers were close to destruction in the face of cutthroat competition waged by twenty giant integrated companies. If ever there was an industry that clearly involved and affected interstate commerce, this was it.

The NRA code set quotas for production in each state, but it left the allocation of production among the several companies to state authorities. In addition, Section 9(c) of the NIRA dealt specifically with the oil industry; it said: "The President is authorized to prohibit the transportation in interstate and foreign commerce of petroleum and the products thereof produced or withdrawn from storage in excess of the amount permitted to be produced or withdrawn from storage by any state law or valid regulation or order prescribed thereunder, by any board, commission, officers, or other duly authorized agency of a State." In other words, if a state lawfully restricted oil production or withdrawal from storage, the president could assist the state policy by preventing the oil company or pipeline from effectively using or selling the oil.

Both the Petroleum Code and Section 9(c) were hauled before the Court by oil producers who chafed under the restrictions. The Court never reached the question of the validity of the code itself, however, because of the sloppy practice by which the administration had promulgated official regulations.

It was the practice, dating back well before the Roosevelt administration, to file executive orders with the secretary of state and publish them annually along with statutes enacted by Congress. But many administrative regulations were not so filed, and even executive orders (which the NRA codes were) were not always sent across town to Foggy Bottom. Sometimes the White House thought it just as well that its orders not be put on public display. Sometimes it did not retain the original orders at all but shipped them over to the NRA, where some of them lay in officials' desk drawers. This was not a safe practice, because mistakes in the executive orders were not likely to be caught and rectified until it was too late.

That is what happened in the petroleum case. Certain producers had violated both the code and Section 9(c) in shipping oil above their quotas across state lines. Under NIRA, violators of the codes were subject to criminal penalties. This was what everyone thought, because the copies of the code distributed by the Interior Department said so. A meticulous lawyer found otherwise. In drafting his brief, he decided to check the punctuation in several quotations against the original executive order promulgating the code. To his horror he discovered that the criminal penalty provision had been technically but inadvertently amended out of existence by a later executive order. The amending order said "Section 4 is amended to read as follows." What followed was only one paragraph.

Unfortunately, the original Section 4 had contained another paragraph, which declared production quota violations unlawful. In omitting to restate it, there was in effect no law against violating the quotas. What the amending order should have said was: "*the first paragraph of* Section 4 is amended to read as follows." The omission of these four words meant there could be no prosecution because the code had not been violated.

The government freely admitted the error and announced that it would not prosecute any violations that occurred before the four words were restored, a step the president quickly took. The Court, as it had to, dismissed the case against the oil producers for violating the Petroleum Code. There could therefore be no test of the code's legality.

Several justices took an almost malicious delight in haranguing the government attorneys for the government's failure to publish executive orders and all amendments. Congress quickly remedied the general problem by enacting the Federal Register Act, providing for publication of all executive orders, rules, and regulations in the daily Federal Register.

But the government had another peg on which to hang the quota violators: Section 9(c) of the NIRA. It was this that the Court struck down, ruling that Congress had unconstitutionally delegated its legislative power. This was an unexpected blow. No act of Congress had ever been declared unconstitutional for such a reason, and the government devoted only 13 perfunctory pages in its 427-page brief to the question.

The principle that the Court invoked was this: the Constitution granted "all legislative power" to Congress, and Congress could not simply delegate this power away to the president. Of course it is impossible to operate a government without prescribing duties for the executive and delegating to him and his assistants the power to carry them out. Since 1789 Congress had delegated a wide measure of power to the president and to regulatory agencies. However, the Court thought, none before had given the executive so much discretion in exercising it. If, for instance, Congress passed a law giving the president the authority to create any antitrust law whenever he thought it proper to do so, this would clearly be going too far. Congress would be telling the president in effect, "You make the law, because we can't figure out what should be in it." To be sustained, a delegation of legislative power must have a standard that confines the president's discretion.

Had Congress gone too far in Section 9(c)? Eight justices thought so, because the NIRA did not tell the president when he should exercise his power to prohibit interstate oil shipments. In the light of history, this was exceedingly disingenuous. As Justice Cardozo argued in dissent, Congress had clearly spelled out the standard under which the president could act. He had no power to prohibit shipments whenever he liked. He could prohibit them only if a producer violated a state law or another·valid order. "There is no fear," he wrote, "that the nation will drift from its ancient moorings as the result of the narrow delegation of power permitted by this section. What can be done under cover of that permission is closely and clearly circumscribed both as to subject matter and occasion. The statute was framed in the shadow of a national disaster. A host of unforeseen contingencies would have to be faced from day to day, and faced with a fullness of understanding unattainable by any one except the man upon the scene. The President was chosen to meet the instant need."

Amid growing discontent with the administration of the NRA codes, it now became clear that the very existence of the government's central mechanism for coping with industrial productions was at stake. Some argued that the best course would be to let the NIRA lapse in June, as it was due to, and then re-enact it with more explicit standards. This would avoid a risky Supreme Court test, which, if it went against the law, might doom the administration's chances of getting a remodeled bill through Congress.

But it became impossible to wait. A federal district judge in Alabama declared the NIRA unconstitutional in a case involving the Lumber Code. The Justice Department could appeal this case, but the risk was high, since this particular code contained production quotas, which were central to the petroleum debacle. Other problems as well convinced the Solicitor General, Stanley Reed, not to appeal. The result was twofold. The Lumber Code went unenforced, since the lower court ruling stood, and morale at the NRA fell. And the administration was pilloried in the press for refusing to allow the law to be tested in the Supreme Court. Moreover, as Arthur Schlesinger has put it, "people in general wondered why they should obey a law which the government was unwilling to test in the courts."

NRA on the Block

Just at this moment the U.S. Court of Appeals for the Second Circuit in New York handed the government a partial victory in a case involving the Live Poultry Code. When the defendants asked the Supreme Court to review their case, the Justice Department could hardly refuse to meet the challenge. So the stage was set.

The importance of the code to the nation as a whole was slight. It applied only to the New York metropolitan area, and it existed solely to police an industry devoted to selling kosher chickens to Orthodox Jews. Chickens are shipped into the metropolitan area and bought by jobbers for resale to slaughterhouse operators. Because the orthodox dietary laws require that the birds be killed according to a particular ritual presided over by religious functionaries known as *shochtim,* they must be received live. After slaughtering, they are resold to retail kosher butchers. Ninety-six percent of all the live chickens thus sold in the New York metropolitan market (which besides New York City included the New York counties of Rockland, Westchester, Nassau and Suffolk, Hudson and Bergen counties in New Jersey, and Fairfield County in Connecticut) came from other states. Three-quarters of these were unloaded in Manhattan.

The live poultry industry was gangster-ridden, its practices corrupt in the extreme. The word "racket" is said to have originated in this industry. The code attempted to clean up the industry. Besides the usual provisions governing hours and wages of workmen and prices of products, it contained proscriptions of a variety of practices, including sale of uninspected or diseased meat. It also required "straight killing," which meant that a wholesale customer purchasing at the slaughterhouse could not pick out the best birds one-by-one. He had to take the contents of a coop or half-coop.

Four brothers, Joseph, Alex, Martin, and Aaron Schechter, owned the largest kosher slaughterhouses in Brooklyn, the A.L.A. Schechter Company and the Schechter Live Poultry Market, Inc. They were antiracketeer and had grown throughout the 1920s.

In 1933 they signed up with the blue eagle, hoping to profit from the government's administrative beneficence. But they apparently hoped to profit even more by skirting the regulations. In 1934 they were indicted on sixty counts of violating the code. They were charged with undercutting the wages and hour provisions and with permitting favored customers to choose the best chickens from certain coops. Most seriously, they were accused of selling several tons of tubercular chickens below the market price. These diseased birds passed the illness along to persons who had bought them. One of the purposes of the code was to prevent the dumping of these sick chickens on the New York market (a widespread practice before

1933). The authorities also wanted to prevent this action because the appearance of the sick birds scared many potential purchasers away from buying any chicken and depressed the market.

The Schechters were convicted on nineteen counts. The trial judge dismissed twenty-seven counts, and the jury acquitted them on fourteen others. The Court of Appeals, then the most respected court in the country, reversed the convictions on the counts dealing with infractions of the wages and hour provisions but affirmed the rest. For their crimes, including the peddling of one sick chicken, the Schechters faced three-month jail terms and a $7,000 fine, unless the Supreme Court would reverse. They appealed.

The Court heard arguments on May 2 and 3. Solicitor General Reed (later a Roosevelt appointee to the Court) and National Industrial Recovery Board Chairman Donald Richberg argued the government's case. The Schechter's Brooklyn counsel, Joseph Heller, was joined by Frederick H. Wood, a partner in one of New York's most distinguished corporate law firms, Cravath, de Gersdorff, Swaine, and Wood (now Cravath, Swaine, and Moore). Who financed Wood's participation remains unknown.

The Court was plainly hostile to the government. Justice McReynolds zeroed in on the meaning of "unfair competition," the prevention of which the NIRA left in the president's judgment. Reed answered: "The only standard is what industry considers unfair, plus the judgment of the President as to whether they are fair trade provisions." Heller minimized the seriousness of the charge of purveying diseased birds in two ways. He emphasized that the jury had found that his clients had sold only one sick chicken, and he harped on the seeming pettiness of the code provisions requiring straight killing. Justice McReynolds asked what this meant. Wood responded: "Straight killing means you have got to put your hand in the coop and take out whichever chicken comes to you. You hand the chicken over to the rabbi, who slaughters it." McReynolds seemed incredulous that the Schechters could go to jail for letting their buyers look into the coop and pick out the birds they wanted.

The decision came three weeks later, on May 27, Black Monday. At noon the justices took their seats behind the bench and pronounced three critical verdicts against the New Deal.

First, Justice Brandeis read a unanimous opinion. It stated that a federal law providing for the relief of those whose farms were threatened by mortgage foreclosures was unconstitutional.

Second, Justice Sutherland proceeded to rebuke the president for firing a federal trade commissioner, William E. Humphrey, whose actions on the FTC were inconsistent with administration positions. This, said Sutherland, Roosevelt could not do, for Humphrey had occupied a quasi-judicial office. But in so ruling, the Court neglected to make clear that it was overruling a prior case that had seemed to the president's lawyers to give clear authority for Humphrey's dismissal. "Within the Administration," Justice Robert H. Jackson later wrote, "there was a profound feeling that the opinion of the Court was written with a design to give the impression that the President had flouted the Constitution, rather than that the Court had simply changed its mind within the past ten years. The decision could easily have forestalled this by recognizing the President's reliance on an [earlier] opinion of Chief Justice Taft. But the decision contained no such gracious acknowl-

The Schechter brothers, poultry dealers, with their lawyer (center) after the court ruling which virtually crushed the NRA.

UPI

edgment. What the Court had before declared to be a constitutional duty of the President had become in Mr. Roosevelt a constitutional offense."

Then came the fatal blow. Chief Justice Hughes announced the third unanimous opinion of the day by striking down in *A.L.A. Schechter Poultry Corp.* v. *United States* the entire Title I of the National Industrial Recovery Act. Hughes made two points in a rather wooden opinion. First (the reason that the case has remained famous), he declared that the NIRA was an unconstitutional delegation of legislative authority to the president. Picking up on the Court's decision four months earlier in the Hot Oil case, Hughes said that the power to establish codes of fair competition was given no limitation in the act; "fair competition" was nowhere defined or made subject to any standards. Unlike the power granted to the Federal Trade Commission in 1914 to root out "unfair methods of competition," which had a narrow meaning in law, "fair competition" was not a term that had recognized boundaries. Also, an administrative agency with quasi-judicial procedures set up to determine the term's meaning on a case-by-case basis was undefinable. Instead, the president was simply given the power to do what he thought best.

In a concurring opinion, Justice Cardozo, who had dissented in the Hot Oil case, put the Court's reasons more dramatically and eloquently:

Charles Evans Hughes, Chief Justice.

The delegated power of legislation which has found expression in this code is not canalized within banks that keep it from overflowing. It is unconfined and vagrant. . . . Here, in the case before us, is an attempted delegation not confined to any single act nor to any class or group of acts identified or described by reference to a standard. Here in effect is a roving commission to inquire into evils and upon discovery correct them. . . .

A code is not to be restricted to the elimination of business practices that would be characterized by general acceptance as oppressive or unfair. It is to include whatever ordinances may be desirable or helpful for the well-being or prosperity of the industry affected. In that view, the function of its adoption is not merely negative, but positive; the planning of improvements as well as the extirpation of abuses. What is fair, as thus conceived, is not something to be contrasted with what is unfair or fraudulent or tricky. The extension becomes as wide as the field of industrial regulation. If that conception shall prevail, anything that Congress may do within the limits of the commerce clause for the betterment of business may be done by the President upon the recommendation of a trade association by calling it a code. This is delegation running riot.

Like Taney in the *Dred Scott* case, Hughes could have stopped at the point of declaring the act to have delegated too much power without standards. But he went on to consider an entirely separate and unrelated point: that the act was also unconstitutional because the practices the code aimed at were beyond the scope of Congressional power under the Commerce Clause. This was devastating because it promised to gut all kinds of federal laws, existing and yet to be proposed, aimed at curbing commercial abuses and restoring economic vitality. His central point was that the code aimed at practices contained entirely within a single state. Whatever effect on commerce between the states the outlawed practices had, they were clearly "indirect."

Earlier Supreme Court decisions had said that Congress could regulate the "current" or "flow" of commerce, but this principle was inapplicable because "the poultry had come to a permanent rest within the State."

A second set of decisions had permitted Congress to regulate transactions that directly "affect" interstate commerce. The year before, in 1934, the same Court had upheld the antitrust prosecution of a number of people in the very same poultry industry against the contention that what they had done had not affected interstate commerce. Now the Court distinguished that case, saying that part of the conspiracy charged in the earlier case was interference with the shipment and transportation of the chickens in order to monopolize a market that was interstate.

But this was not any part of the offenses for which the Schechters were convicted. What they did was merely to violate rules against practices that had their principal impact within each separate retail market. To rule otherwise, to construe the Commerce Clause "to reach all enterprises and transactions which could be said to have an indirect effect upon interstate commerce, the federal authority would embrace practically all the activities of the people and the authority of the State over its domestic concerns would exist only by sufferance of the Federal government."

With this point, Justice Cardozo (and Justice Stone with him) partially disagreed. The Second Circuit had voided the wages and hours provisions of the code on the ground that this was not within the commerce power, and with this conclusion Cardozo concurred. Because these provisions were inextricably intertwined with the code as a whole, Cardozo saw no way of saving it. But he did not buy the direct-indirect distinction. "The law is not indifferent to considerations of degree," he wrote. He meant that an indirect effect in Hughes's terms could have a sizable enough impact on interstate commerce to permit Congress to regulate it. But that was scarcely enough to save the *Schechter* case. NIRA had fallen.

Hatching a New Plan

Four days later at his press conference, President Roosevelt confronted the problem of how to approach economic regulation in the future. "We are the only nation in the world that has not solved

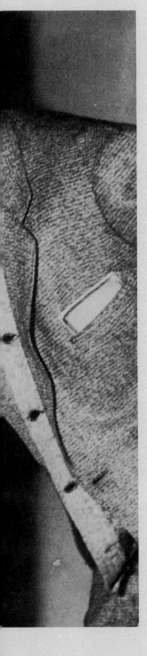

The "Blue Eagle" goes into limbo. The emblem is removed from a door in the Commerce Department building.

UPI

that problem," he said. "We thought we were solving it, and now it has been thrown right straight in our faces and we have been relegated to the horse-and-buggy definition of interstate commerce." There was reason to be worried. The future of securities regulation, agricultural production regulation, labor legislation, trade practices including health matters, stood in jeopardy.

Yet unlike that of *Dred Scott*, the denouement of this case was peaceful. Black Monday was the beginning of an onslaught of anti-New Deal cases that ultimately led to Roosevelt's famous "Court-packing plan" in 1937. Roosevelt's move in turn seemed to cause a switch of two critical votes and transformed the liberal minority into a majority. Cases that seemed headed for certain government defeat now were rescued, and they were solidified soon after when key retirements gave the president the chance at last to name his own men to the bench.

What Edward S. Corwin has called "Constitutional Revolution, Ltd." was thus accomplished only two years after Black Monday. A number of provisions in the NIRA, including the National Labor Relations Act, were enacted separately, and ultimately upheld. By 1941 the Court had completely repudiated the interstate commerce doctrine, when it upheld a law that prohibited farmers from growing certain crops even if they were intended to be consumed entirely on their own farms.

As for the doctrine of excessive delegation of legislative power, the Supreme Court has never since found a single act of Congress to have been lacking constitutional standards, even though several laws have laid down as standards that an administrative agency act "in the public interest." The delegation doctrine, though not manufactured for *Schechter* and probably correctly applied, seems to have become a historical relic.

Though there was talk of reviving bits and pieces of the NRA through a hodge-podge of voluntary codes, the idea was quickly discarded. The one concrete thing the case accomplished, besides goading Roosevelt into attacking the Court, was the disappearance of a general national economic policy of business-government partnership. "Whatever else the Court had done in the Schechter case," Arthur Schlesinger has written in his Roosevelt trilogy, "it had seemed to close the door on the sort of structural change which was the heart of the First New Deal. Roosevelt could go no further along these lines; and, however far he had gone before Black Monday, it was not far enough. What remained was a relinquishment of the organic conception of the economy; a retreat from central planning."

In the late 1930s, Roosevelt brought Thurman Arnold into the administration as his antitrust chief, and he quickly set about revitalizing the competitive policies of the Sherman and Clayton Acts that the government had never entirely foresworn.

At most, the Sick Chicken case was a temporary setback for the president and the country. In the end, only the Schechters themselves were consumed by it. The code gone, their business was quickly demolished, and they were even squeezed out of their homes. Joe Schechter blamed the racketeers for their plight. Like Dred Scott, in a pathetic sort of way, they too were used. "The Liberty Leaguers sent us a lot of letters saying they appreciated what we had done," Aaron Schechter told Drew Pearson, "but they didn't put any money in the letters."

10/ CONGRESS AND
THE GENERAL WELFARE:
THE SOCIAL SECURITY ACT

T he central meaning of the Great Depression was unemployment. For many years during the 1930s, more than ten million people were out of work; at its depths, some sixteen million were jobless, about 25 percent of the entire labor force. By comparison, as this is written, the recession of 1974-75, bad as it has been, has not topped 9 percent. By comparison, too, the effect of the current recession on people's lives, though hardly pleasant, has born little resemblance to the utterly debilitating conditions that faced the masses of unemployed in the bleak days of 1932. That it did not is attributable primarily to a series of New Deal reforms, particularly those embodied in the Social Security Act of 1935.

The States Attack the Problem

In 1932 the Democratic party platform expressed approval of unemployment compensation and old-age benefits through state, not federal, law. In that same year Wisconsin enacted the first unemployment plan, under which companies were required to set aside funds to be used as compensation for those laid off. Companies with the highest unemployment rates had to pay the highest tax (this was called "merit rating"). The plan formed the nucleus of a bill introduced in Congress in February 1934. The bill was designed to encourage states to accept responsibility for unemployment compensation by providing a special employer payroll tax. Any payments made into a state-mandated reserve fund could be deducted from this tax.

In 1932 also, a bill was introduced in Congress to provide federal support for state old-age pension laws, which ten states passed the following year. Although the idea of unemployment compensation was new, state-supported pensions for the elderly had been in existence since 1912 in the United States.

Federal Plans

In late 1933 the Townsend movement began to sweep the country. This was a curious but potent force that built up considerable momentum in 1934 and 1935 and put additional pressure on the administration to produce a comprehensive social security package.

A *"Soup Kitchen"*.

U.S. Information Agency

Spearhead of the movement was Dr. Francis E. Townsend, sixty-six, an unemployed municipal assistant health officer from Long Beach, California. As a clinic physician he saw the hopelessness of his patients' economic conditions. He proposed federal pensions of $150 a month, later $200, for anyone over sixty years of age.

To such hovels were the elderly often shuffled.

U.S. Information Agency

Coming for handouts in the dismal thirties.

H. Armstrong Roberts

A former associate of his, Robert Earl Clements, a real estate broker, promoted the plan. This he did splendidly, starting Townsend clubs that spread quickly throughout the West. The clubs had the mood of a religious revival. If Townsend did not proclaim himself to be the Messiah, many supposed nevertheless that he was. He said that his followers were "the instruments through whom the Divine Will proposes to establish on earth the universal brotherhood of man." By early 1935 he began publishing the *Townsend National Weekly.* Its circulation eventually climbed to more than 200,000.

The object of all this agitation was to circulate petitions and build pressure for a government old-age pension plan that would become the vehicle for restoring national prosperity. The idea was that if all people over sixty would quit working, receive a $200 monthly pension, and spend it before the next monthly pension check was mailed, money would again flow through the economy. Then, as we would say today, demand would pick up, and capital investment could not fail to follow. Ultimately there would be jobs for those under sixty and out of work. In January 1935, the Townsend Plan—to be financed by a complex value-added tax such as is now employed in England—was introduced as a bill in Congress.

The Compromise

There were numerous difficulties with the Townsend Plan, not the least of which was its inordinate cost. Financial experts thought the plan would cost $24 billion a year to start, which was twice as much money as all governments—federal, state, and local—took in as tax revenues, Even Townsend, more conservative in his estimates, supposed that it would cost more than $19 billion.

Against this background the administration's own Social Security bill made its way through Congress. It was not initially a reaction to the Townsend Plan. Roosevelt clearly had contemplated some sort of social security plan long before anyone, including Townsend himself, had ever heard of the Townsend Plan. Frances Perkins, Roosevelt's first secretary of labor, first suggested the idea to the president-elect in late 1932, when he told her that he wanted to appoint her to the job. She was encouraged to pursue it, among many other proposals.

In June 1934, with two independent bills already moving through Congress, Roosevelt sent a formal message to the Hill, accepting Social Security in principle but asking for a delay so that alternatives could be studied. Among the objectives of recovery, he said, must be "security against the hazards and vicissitudes of life." Later that same month he appointed the Committee on Economic Security, chaired by Secretary Perkins, to prepare a workable program. Its deadline was December 1934.

From the outset, the debate centered on the method of administering the unemployment insurance plan. Should it be administered by the states or from the federal government? The president favored the former approach, which ultimately was adopted. There was far less debate over the question of old-age pensions. A consensus that such a plan should be adopted on a national basis through the federal government was reached quickly.

The problem was how such a plan was to be funded. Though some proposed that the annuities be paid for out of the general federal tax receipts, there was never any serious doubt that the system would be contributory and self-supporting. As with unemployment compensation, the employer would be taxed on his payroll. Unlike unemployment compensation, the employee would be taxed as well—a separate and additional income tax. The money would be raised by and paid to the federal government, which would act as the disbursing agent for all Social Security pensions.

A further question was presented. How should pensions for the middle-aged and elderly be financed? These could not be handled entirely according to the plan for a person just entering the labor market following school. The middle-aged had fewer years to pay in to the system, and in the case of those who already were retired, there would be no contributions at all.

The Committee on Economic Security first suggested that these pensions be financed out of general tax revenues. This approach meant, however, that future generations would be paying the bill. Roosevelt opposed the idea. "It is almost dishonest," Schlesinger has quoted him as saying, "to build up an accumulated deficit for the Congress of the United States to meet in 1980. We can't do that. We can't sell the United States short in 1980 any more than in 1935."

The alternative, therefore, was to increase the amount employees would have to contribute. Thus, each generation would be responsible for the pensions of its elderly. This put a bigger burden on younger workers than on others, for they would be contributing longer at higher rates than would have been necessary if the government contributed from general tax revenues (collected from a wider group of people). But this alternative had one irresistible feature. Congress could not very easily in future years abolish Social Security or reduce pensions if the people themselves had contributed part of their annual wages to a fund established for the purpose.

So, as the Social Security plan moved toward final passage in Congress, it had the following features, the core of which it retains to this day.

First, regarding unemployment, employers of eight or more people were required to pay a special excise tax to the federal treasury. This tax was based on a percentage of the total wages that the employees earned. Not all employees were included, however. Agricultural workers and domestic servants were excluded, for example. The employer could receive a credit against his tax liability if he made contributions to a state unemployment fund. For an employer to qualify for the credit (which could be used to reduce up to 90 percent of the federal tax owed), the state unemployment insurance plan had to conform to certain federal standards. This provision was included to insure that the money from state unemployment programs was used to combat unemployment and that eligibility to receive unemployment benefits would not be used to hamper union activity. The funds collected by the states were required to be turned over to the secretary of the treasury, who was to hold the monies in a special fund and to pay them back to the cooperating states as requested. The federal law also authorized Congress to appropriate money to help the states administer their programs.

In essence, therefore, the unemployment provisions of the law were a gigantic inducement to states to adopt unemployment compensation plans quickly. The statistics show how successful this inducement was. Before the Social Security Act only five states had such plans. Within two years after its passage, all forty-eight states had them.

Second, regarding old-age pensions, employers were subject to another excise tax, also based on a percentage of the payroll. Unlike the unemployment provisions, employees also paid a tax, one percent of all earnings below $3,000 annually, (By contrast, today the first $15,000 of earnings is taxed, and by 1977 it is estimated this figure will increase to at least $17,000 and probably more. In 1935 the maximum individual social security tax was $30; today it is $824.85.)

The Old-Age Reserve Account was created within the U.S.

Treasury. Congress was authorized to appropriate money from general revenues (which were to include the Social Security taxes) and pay it into the special Old-Age Reserve Account. The payments would be made according to a formula that permitted the payment of a pension that was not to exceed $85 per month.

The Challenge in the Courts

As familiar as these provisions may seem to us today, in the spring of 1935 they were considered by many to be positively revolutionary. And for the United States, they were. "By destroying initiative, discouraging thrift, and stifling individual responsibility," the law would subvert the American way of life, declaimed James L. Donnelly of the Illinois Manufacturers' Association. New York Republican Congressman James W. Wadsworth made an equally dire pronouncement: "This bill opens the door and invites the entrance into the political field of a power so vast, so powerful as to threaten the integrity of our institutions and to pull the pillars of the temple down upon the heads of our descendants."

This impassioned exaggeration did not affect Congress, which was more concerned about the Townsend alternative that was being pressed forcefully. Several members of Congress were active supporters of Townsend, though few believed in either the actuarial soundness or the economic or administrative efficacy of the doctor's scheme. But it was easier to be against it than to vote against it. In the end, the House of Representatives arranged an anonymous but decent burial: 200 congressmen were missing from the House floor when the vote came, and no roll call was taken. By a voice vote, the House rejected Townsend, and made the administration's plan inevitable. On April 19, 1935, the House approved the Social Security Act by a huge majority, 371 to 33. The Senate followed, after a longer debate, on June 19, by a 76 to 6 vote.

At the end, the House made one administrative change from the draft bill. It created the Social Security Board as an agency independent of the Labor Department, to which it was originally destined. This change stuck. (Today the Social Security Administration is part of the Department of Health, Education, and Welfare.) Finally, on August 14, 1935, the president signed the Social Security Act into law.

There remained the political opposition—businessmen and others who were unreconciled to the act's principles and adamant against paying the tax. In 1935, when the act was passed, there

seemed to be a fair chance that the opposition would prevail in what was increasingly becoming the court of last resort against unwelcomed legislation, the Supreme Court. Between the start of the New Deal in 1933 and 1937, when Roosevelt began his second term, the Court had knocked out many important props of the administration's program for recovery. These included the National Industrial Recovery Act, as we have seen, the Railway Pension Act, the Agricultural Adjustment Act, the Bituminous Coal Act, the Municipal Bankruptcy Act, and a New York state law prescribing a minimum wage for women. The Court, it is true, had upheld some New Deal laws, including the Gold Clause acts, one aspect of the Tennessee Valley Authority Act, the Minnesota mortgage moratorium, and New York milk price support laws. But the laws the Court upheld came in cases that generally were heard early in the New Deal. The Court became increasingly intractable as the years passed.

Opposite page:

Franklin Delano Roosevelt puts his signature on another broad economic act.

U.S. Information Agency

Packing the Courts

By 1937 there was a reasonable basis, therefore, to fear that a number of crucial laws would also be overturned. These included the National Labor Relations Act, the Public Utility Holding Company Act, and the entire TVA Act, as well as various provisions in the Social Security Act. Roosevelt did not believe the fate of these laws should be left to the whims of a Court, the average age of whose justices was the oldest in history.

So on February 5, 1937, he proposed a change in the Court's composition that came to be known as the "Court-packing plan." The basic idea was for Congress to create an additional seat on every federal court for each judge or justice who was over the retirement age but continued to sit on the court. The maximum number of seats on the Supreme Court under the plan was fifteen. Additionally, the privilege of retirement—and thus the privilege of receiving the full salary after leaving the bench—was to be extended to Supreme Court Justices for the first time. Under existing law, only lower court judges could retire with pay, a situation that obviously tended to keep Supreme Court justices on active duty.

Unfortunately for Roosevelt and perhaps fortunately for the Court, the stated rationale for this plan, at least as it affected the Supreme Court, skirted the real reason. The gist of his charge in a special message to Congress was that the burdens of justiceship were heavy and the Supreme Court needed new blood to help. This was a fatal error. Justice Jackson, in his book on the New Deal Court, described the problem as follows:

Perhaps the most serious consequence of the form of the proposal was its alienation of those Justices who had been critical of the Court themselves —such as Brandeis, Stone, Cardozo, and to some extent the Chief Justice. It would have been wise to capitalize their dissents in support of the plan. Instead of accusing some Justices of being stubborn and wrongly reactionary, which the other Justices could hardly deny, the message in effect charged the Justices collectively with inefficiency and inadequate discharge of duty. The charge alienated Brandeis, oldest of the Justices, and, in a sense, the original New Dealer. He joined with the Chief Justice in a letter hotly denying the whole thesis of the message so far as the Supreme Court was concerned. They were, of course, silent as to any defense of the Court's course of decision against which both had at times protested. Had the attack been on the Court's doctrine, there would have been no excuse and, of course, no basis for their counterattack.

Roosevelt made an attack on the Court's erroneous decisions four days later, on March 9, in a national radio address. But the damage had already been done in provoking Brandeis and Hughes. Their letter was critical, swaying enough senators against the plan that it was eventually killed. In its place, along with certain procedural reforms that are not relevant to this discussion, Congress passed a retirement act for the Supreme Court. At the close of the Court's 1937 term, Justice Van Devanter took advantage of this new right to retire. So Roosevelt got his first opportunity to appoint a member of the Court (Hugo Black).

But this legislation, as it turned out, was not the critical factor in reversing the Court's pronounced tendency to rule against New Deal laws. The Court-packing threat itself was. For between March 29 and April 12, the Court made it clear in a number of cases that it was reading the Constitution in a new light. On March 29—White Monday, Justice Jackson later called it—the Court reversed a decision it had announced only nine months before. It upheld a Washington State statute that provided a state minimum wage law for women; it upheld the National Firearms Act; and it approved the Railway Labor Act, which in a slightly altered form it had invalidated a short while before. It also approved an amended law easing the plight of farmers who could not meet their mortgage payments. And on April 12, the Court upheld the National Labor Relations Act, a sweeping law that thrust the federal government into the nooks and crevices of labor practices throughout the nation. The Court-backing plan, it appeared, was not only odious; it was unnecessary.

This was shown to be true for the Social Security Act as well. In two principal decisions the Court upheld its various provisions on May 24, 1937.

The Test

The first case tested the unemployment provision. Steward Machine Company, an Alabama corporation, paid $46.14 due under the act and sued for a refund. It claimed that the act was beyond Congressional power. The lower courts ruled in favor of the government, but the Court of Appeals in Boston in a separate case had gone the other way. Several arguments were advanced against the law, but the principal point was that the purpose of the tax "was not revenue, but an unlawful invasion of the reserved powers of the states; and that the states in submitting to it have yielded to coercion and have abandoned governmental functions which they are not permitted to surrender."

The difficulty with this line of reasoning, Justice Cardozo declared for a bare majority of five, was that it ignored the nature of the problem that Congress was attempting to solve. The problem of unemployment was widespread, but that very fact complicated the ability of any one state to solve it. If one state enacted a relief law while others did not, companies that had to pay the tax would be at a competitive disadvantage. "Two consequences ensued. One was that the freedom of a state to contribute its fair share to the solution of a national problem was paralyzed by fear. The other was that insofar as there was failure by the states to contribute relief according to the measure of their capacity, a disproportionate burden, and a mountainous one, was laid upon the resources of the Government of the nation."

Moreover, said Cardozo, no one is in fact coerced by the federal law. "Not the taxpayer [that is, the corporation]. He pays in fulfillment of the mandate of the local legislature. Not the state. Even now she does not offer a suggestion that in passing the unemployment law she was affected by duress. . . . The difficulty with [the company's] contention is that it confuses motive with coercion." It is true that the motive underlying the Social Security Act was to induce states to enact unemployment laws and that the rebate of up to 90 percent of the federal tax if the employer paid into a state fund was aimed at encouraging such laws. But this was not a gun at the states' heads. The state legislatures were not required to pass such laws, and they themselves lost nothing if they did not do so.

This does not mean, however, Cardozo said, "that a tax is valid, when imposed by act of Congress, if it is laid upon the condition that a state may escape its operation through the adoption of a statute unrelated in subject matter to activities fairly within the scope of national policy and power." Congress could not raise a national tax against employers but rebate it if the states passed a law permitting eighteen-year-olds to vote. Until the ratification of the Twenty-Sixth Amendment in 1971, Congress had no power to regulate the age of voters within the states in connection with state elections. A federal tax had to be related to a power that Congress may exercise, independent of the conditions that the law may impose on the states.

What was this federal power, then? It did not seem to stem

from the power to regulate interstate commerce because unemployment insurance is not a regulation of trade or commerce. It is a measure for the relief of individual citizens. No, the source of the Congressional power was something else altogether.

It was to be found in the clause in the Constitution that grants Congress the power "to lay and collect taxes, duties, imposts, and excises, to pay the debts and provide for the common defence and general welfare of the United States." In the second case, on May 24, testing the validity of the old-age provisions of the Social Security Act, the Court laid down the fundamental principle. By virtue of this clause Congress has an independent power to provide for the general welfare, whether the tax program supports another power or not, such as the power to regulate commerce or to raise an army.

The Court had actually announced the doctrine the year before, but it was set down in a rather backhand way. The decision in which the doctrine was originally declared was one that invalidated the Agricultural Adjustment Act. In that case, the Court conceded the power of Congress to tax for the general welfare. But the Court limited the scope of this doctrine by ruling that if the law providing for the expenditure of the tax money amounted to a regulation, then Congress had to have an independent power in the Constitution to rest it on. Otherwise the law would be unconstitutional.

As a practical matter this emasculated the general welfare power because every tax and every expenditure by the federal government has some regulatory effect. And if the particular regulation interfered with local agriculture or local land policy or local relief measures, there was no federal power that would justify such interference, according to the 1936 majority. Indeed, under conventional interpretation there was not. The old-age provisions could stand only if the General Welfare Clause itself could be construed to permit the federal government to act.

This was precisely what Justice Cardozo ruled, this time for a majority of seven. A shareholder of the Edison Electric Illuminating Company in Boston filed suit against the corporation, seeking to enjoin it from paying the taxes mandated by the Social Security Act. The corporation itself said it was prepared to pay the tax and would do so unless enjoined by the court. The trial court upheld the government, but the Court of Appeals reversed the lower court's ruling. Its decision threw old-age pension provisions into doubt. This was the vehicle for testing these major sections of the law brought before the Court.

On its own terms, the case was peculiar. The corporation, the entity required to pay the tax under the law, was not resisting it. Only a dissident shareholder was. Clearly this was a test case resting on shallow grounds. Four justices (Cardozo, Brandeis, Stone, and Roberts) thought the case should be dismissed because the shareholder was not entitled to the relief he was seeking and that therefore the constitutional issues were not before the Court. But five justices thought otherwise, and so did the government, which was anxious to have the Court clear the air immediately.

So the issue was before the Court. Did Congress have the power to tax employers based on their payrolls and use the proceeds of the tax to pay pensions to employees subject to the tax? This time the Court was unequivocal. The power to spend money in aid of the general welfare is committed to Congress, and "unless the choice is clearly wrong, a display of arbitrary power, not an exercise of judgment," Congress would be upheld. And clearly the decision to tax in order to provide for unemployment benefits was well within the concept of the general welfare. "The concept of the general welfare [is not] static," Cardozo said. "Needs that were narrow or parochial a century ago may be interwoven in our day with the well-being of the Nation. What is critical or urgent changes with the times."

What was critical and urgent during the 1930s was the spread of unemployment, a disease that affected the entire nation. And, Cardozo declared, it mattered little what the cause of the unemployment was to justify the act. "[T]he ill is all one, or at least not greatly different, whether men are thrown out of work because there is no longer work to do or because the disabilities of age make them incapable of doing it. Rescue becomes necessary irrespective of the cause. The hope behind this statute is to save men and women from the rigors of the poor house as well as from the haunting fear that such a lot awaits them when journey's end is near."

Cardozo cited an impressive array of statistics gleaned from industrial surveys that showed how poorly the elderly had fared during the Depression. Even those in their forties were at a great disadvantage compared to those who were younger, and "in practice few were hired if they were over 50 years of age. With the loss of savings inevitable in periods of idleness, the fate of workers over 65, when thrown out of work, is little less than desperate."

To remedy this widespread problem a national solution was necessary. Many states lacked the resources to provide for the aged.

But apart from this, "states and local governments are at times reluctant to increase so heavily the burden of taxation to be borne by their residents for fear of placing themselves in a position of economic disadvantage as compared with neighbors or competitors . . . The existence of [an old-age pension] system is a bait to the needy and dependent elsewhere, encouraging them to migrate and seek a haven of repose. Only a power that is national can serve the interests of all."

So the act was upheld in its entirety, and the power of the federal government was strengthened against constitutional attack. Henceforth Congress would have virtually plenary power to tax and spend for the general welfare of all the peoples of the Unites States.

11/ THE LAW THAT
DEPENDS ON THE FORUM:
ERIE RAILROAD v. TOMPKINS

On April 25, 1938, the Supreme Court announced a constitutional ruling that cut back the scope of federal power. But no great outcry greeted this decision. No one charged the Court with trying to stifle the will of the people, as expressed by their elected representatives.

To the contrary, the case almost escaped notice. But that was because the power the Court curbed was its own power, not Congress's or the president's. For that very reason, the case was a bombshell in legal circles. It reversed a line of precedents stretching back ninety-six years that governed the power of the federal courts to resolve disputes among citizens of different states. The case remains unknown to the public to this day, but it was clearly fraught with the most pregnant consequences for our federal system. It stands out as one of the most important decisions the Court has ever handed down.

The Case of Harry Tompkins

The case began innocently enough; the facts were quite mundane. Harry Tompkins was sauntering along a "much used" footpath that overlapped the right-of-way by the side of the Erie Railroad's main tracks in Hughestown, Pennsylvania. He saw the lights and heard the whistle of a train coming toward him. But he continued on his course because he had often walked thus without harm.

This time it was different. The night was dark. Tompkins did not see a door somehow swing open from the passing freight train, and he was severely injured when the door clapped against him. He subsequently filed suit to recover his damages.

Although there was some dispute, it seemed that the law of Pennsylvania was against Tompkins. The railroad contended, at any rate, that the Pennsylvania supreme court had previously ruled that persons walking on a railroad right-of-way are trespassers. By the principles of the common law, trespassers are not owed a very high degree of care. Unless the railroad deliberately tried to injure Tompkins, which it obviously had not, he was not entitled to recover.

Court Jumping

Tompkins—or his lawyer—avoided this awkward Pennsylvania law by suing in a federal district court in New York. The Erie Railroad was chartered in New York, and Tompkins was a Pennsylvania citizen. By virtue of the original Judiciary Act of 1789, still in effect, the constitutional power to try suits between citizens of different states was vested in the federal court in the state in which the defendant resides. (Although corporations cannot claim to be citizens for such purposes as voting in public elections, they can claim citizenship to take advantage of the federal courts' "diversity jurisdiction," as it is called.)

But what was to be gained by filing the lawsuit in the federal court? A string of precedents dating back to 1842 gave the federal courts the right to decide the law for themselves. According to these rulings the federal court could reject the law of the state unless there was a state statute concerning the specific circumstances of an accident. There were certain exceptions to this rule, but the trial judge in Tompkin's case ruled that they were not applicable. The jury awarded him $30,000.

The Troublesome Doctrine: the Federal Common Law

The railroad appealed to the Circuit Court of Appeals, which affirmed the verdict. That court said that "upon questions of general law the federal courts are free, in the absence of a local statute, to exercise their independent judgment as to what the law is; and it is well settled that the question of the responsibility of a railroad for injuries caused by its servants is one of general law. . . . Where the public has made open and notorious use of a railroad right of way for a long period of time and without objection, the company owes to persons on such permissive pathway a duty of care in the operation of its trains. . . . It is likewise generally recognized law that a jury may find that negligence exists toward a pedestrian using a permissive path on the railroad right of way if he is hit by some object projecting from the side of the train."

At first blush, this seems a strange doctrine. Why should the federal courts be able to apply their own law to assess claims such as Tompkins's, even when the rule they apply clearly contradicts the state law? How can there be two separate and independent rules that govern the same accident but reach opposite results, so that a litigant need only pick the right forum to win his case? Is this a necessary consequence of a federal system? For the answer we must go back to 1789 and the drafting of the Judiciary Act.

As we have already noted, the Constitution grants power to the federal courts to hear cases and controversies between citizens of different states. This was thought to be necessary in an age when there were fierce feelings of independence and sovereignty within each state. The courts of one state might discriminate against "foreigners" from other states. Federal courts were created to act as unbiased forums for the determination of such cases.

None of the grants of judicial power was taken to be self-executing, however. Congress, it was assumed, had to confer jurisdiction on the courts before they could hear any cases. This was done to a limited extent in the Judiciary Act of 1789. The federal courts were not given the general jurisdiction they exercise today over cases arising under the Constitution, laws, or treaties of the United States. These cases, it was believed, could be adequately dealt with in the state courts. And, of course, parties in a case had an ultimate right of appeal to the U. S. Supreme Court. But the federal courts were given the "diversity jurisdiction"—the power to hear cases when the citizenship of the parties was different.

What law, then, was a federal court to apply when it took a case involving a dispute between citizens of different states? "The Federal Court was to secure to a non-citizen the application of the same law which a State Court would give to its own citizens, and to see that within a State there should be no discrimination against non-citizens in the application of justice," Charles Warren wrote in his classic 1923 article on the subject. "The idea that a Federal Court in a State was to administer any other than the law of the State or were to discriminate *in favor of a non-citizen,* and *against a citizen,* or to administer law as an entirely free and independent tribunal, never appears to have entered the mind of any one."

The reasoning: To insure that result, Section Thirty-four was added to the 1789 Act, and its language has endured to this day. It says: "The laws of the several States, except where the Constitution, treaties, or statutes of the United States shall otherwise require or provide, shall be regarded as rules of decision in trials at common law in the Courts of the United States in cases where they apply." For fifty-three years, this somewhat obscure language was interpreted to mean that the federal court had to apply the state law. The federal courts were neither assumed nor held to have the power to apply some different law. If it were otherwise, the danger of conflicts between the courts would be obvious. "The injustice," Justice Bushrod Washington said in circuit court in 1814, "as well as the absurdity of the [federal courts] deciding by one rule, and the [state courts] by another, would be too monstrous to find a place in any system of government."

On more than one occasion, the Supreme Court concurred with this view. In *United States* v. *Hudson and Goodwin* the Court ruled in 1812 that there was no federal common law of crimes. The federal courts could not apply the criminal law even of the nation unless Congress first enacted the appropriate criminal statutes.

This case did not involve the civil law of the states. It can be explained as a reaction to the fear of judicial tyranny that had existed in England, where the courts felt free to declare acts crimes in the absence of any Parliamentary declaration. Thus, the people were at the whim of prosecutors and judges. They had no sure way of knowing what conduct the law permitted or prohibited. Still, the case was an indication that the Court did not believe there was a law of the United States that was not created by Congress.

This view was solidified twenty-two years later, in *Wheaton* v. *Peters*. This famous case concerned the copyright of volumes of the Court's decisions. The dispute was between Peters, the Court's current reporter of decisions and Wheaton, one of its former reporters. Peters had reprinted an abridgement of Wheaton's reports without permission. Wheaton had not obtained copyright under the federal Copyright Act but claimed that he had rights under the federal common law. The Court denied Wheaton's claim:

It is clear, there can be no common law of the United States. The federal government is composed of twenty-four sovereign and independent states; each of which may have its local usages, customs and common law. There is no principle which pervades the Union and has the authority of law, that is not embodied in the Constitution or laws of the Union. The common law could be made a part of our federal system, only by legislative adoption. When, therefore, a common-law right is asserted, we must look to the state in which the controversy originated.

The history of the doctrine: So it appeared clear that, quite aside from Section Thirty-four of the Judiciary Act (the so-called "rules of decision" act), the federal courts could only apply state law in diversity cases. But this was reckoning without the profundity and will of Justice Joseph Story.

In 1842 a case titled *Swift* v. *Tyson* came before the Court. This case raised the question whether the payment of a negotiable bill in return for a promise to cancel a preexisting debt constituted a valid contract. In New York, where the case arose, the law was uncertain. The state courts' decisions did not set forth a clear pattern.

For purposes of the case, Justice Story assumed that the New York courts would rule that there was no contract. "It remains to be considered," he then said, "whether it is obligatory upon this court, if it differs from the principles established in the general commercial law." Here was a new concept: "the general commercial law"—a law that was not of a particular state but existed nationally. His argument rested on the unassailable fact that the case would not, in any event, be governed by a New York statute (a law enacted by the legislature): "It is observable that the courts of New York do not found their decisions upon this point upon any local statute, or positive, fixed, or ancient local usage: but they deduce the doctrine from the general principles of commercial law."

This was the crucial point. Section Thirty-four said that the federal courts must apply the "laws of the several states," and in Story's opinion, laws did not include court decisions that did not rest on statutes. Thus, Story declared:

In the ordinary use of language it will hardly be contended that the decisions of courts constitute laws. They are, at most, only evidence of what the laws are, and are not of themselves laws. They are often reexamined, reversed, and qualified by the courts themselves, whenever they are found to be either defective or ill-founded, or otherwise incorrect. The laws of a State are more usually understood to mean the rules and enactments promulgated by the legislative authority thereof, or long established local customs having the force of laws. . . . [Section Thirty-four applies only] to State laws strictly local, that is to say, to the positive statutes of the State, and the construction thereof adopted by the local tribunals, and to rights and titles to things having a permanent locality, such as the rights and titles to real estate, and other matters immovable and intraterritorial in their nature and character. It never has been supposed by us, that the section did apply, or was designed to apply, to questions of a more general nature, . . . as, for example, to the construction of ordinary contracts or other written instruments, and especially to questions of general commercial law, where the State tribunals are called upon to perform the like functions as ourselves, that is, to ascertain upon general reasoning and legal analogies, what is the true exposition of the contract or instrument, or what is the just rule furnished by the principles of commercial law to govern the case.

With these words, the Court adopted the theory that there could be two separate laws governing the same case. The application of law depended on which court the suit was brought in. Why did Story reach such a result, and how could he persuade the Court to his views? Many explanations have been given.

First, the jurisprudence of the times held, as Story said, that courts did not make law; they found it. If that were so, the state courts might err in announcing what the law of a particular case was. In other words, if a state court's decision was merely evidence of the law, it might not be the correct interpretation of the law. The federal courts could reject that evidence. They could discern the true law and thus apply the law of the state consistent with Section Thirty-four of the Judiciary Act.

Story's Desire to Judge: This philosophy of law came under increasing attack in the early twentieth century. In 1917 Justice Oliver Wendell Holmes denounced it in a famous dissent: "the law is not a brooding omnipresence in the sky," he wrote, meaning that the law is what the courts say it is. The newer theory, called legal realism, ultimately overthrew the philosophical basis for Story's decision.

But there were factors other than philosophy that contributed to *Swift* v. *Tyson*. One was that Story was then embarked on writing a treatise on negotiable instruments. As a recognized jurist of world renown, he was anxious to pronounce as judge, rather than as a mere commentator, on commercial questions.

Perhaps most important of all, as Robert Jackson pointed out in an address given exactly two months after the *Erie* decision, federal judges until 1875 suffered from the fact that Congress had not given them jurisdiction over cases arising under the Constitution, Congressional enactments, or federal treaties. With the bulk of federal cases based on diversity of citizenship, "there was obviously little opportunity for a Federal judge to exercise the legal talents which he might possess unless he was free to do more than echo the 'last breath' of a state judge." *Swift* v. *Tyson* thus freed the judges to exercise their creative talents.

The century-long course of the doctrine that there existed a general national common law, undeclared by state legislatures or

Justice Oliver Wendell Holmes with Justice Louis D. Brandeis.

Congress, created enormous difficulties. Story had hoped to avoid conflicts between the federal courts. Citing Cicero to the effect that the law could not be one thing in Rome and another in Athens, he concluded that the law could not be one thing in Boston and something else in New York. If it had not been for Story's decision in *Swift* v. *Tyson*, Section Thirty-four would have required the Supreme Court to give one rule for a case governed by Massachusetts law and another, perhaps contrary, rule for a case presenting the same facts arising out of New York. This seemed intolerable.

But Story's remedy simply created a new conflict of laws: that between the federal court in a state and the state's own courts. The decision in any case depended, thereafter, on what court the litigants could get into or out of, since there were provisions in the Judiciary Act that permitted litigants under certain circumstances to remove a case begun in a state court to an appropriate federal court.

Gradually, the Supreme Court expanded the boundaries of the general common law far beyond the contours of private and commercial law. In the course of all this, intolerable contradictions arose. The most famous series of cases began in 1864, when the Court was called on to determine the validity of municipal bonds issued by cities and counties of Iowa. The bonds had been sold to raise funds for the purchase of railroad stock. There was considerable question under the Iowa constitution whether the bonds could be issued for this purpose. After first upholding the bonds' constitutionality, the state supreme court unanimously overruled its own previous decisions. It held that the bonds could not constitutionally be issued. This meant that the bondholders could not collect principal or interest from the Iowa municipalities. Bondholders from other states then brought suit in federal court to collect their money. On appeal the Supreme Court held that, in spite of the Iowa ruling, the creditors were entitled to their cash. The practical effect of these decisions was that out-of-state bondholders, who could sue in federal court under the diversity jurisdiction, could recover but that Iowa citizens could not.

Yet this was not the sum and substance of the conflict. Iowa courts sought to circumvent the Supreme Court's ruling by enjoining municipal authorities from taxing its citizens to pay for the bonds. A federal suit was promptly commenced to force the local authorities to assess the tax. The Supreme Court affirmed the suit.

LAWYERS PORTRAY LEGAL MILESTONES

The following pages present original art work done by members of the legal profession, including law school students. The works reproduced were among the winners in the National Lawyers' Art Competition sponsored by West Publishing Company to commemorate its own 100th anniversary and the nation's Bicentennial. The theme: Milestones of U.S. Law.

FIRST PRIZE

Judith L. Irle, Chicago, IL
Student, DePaul University
College of Law

SECOND PRIZE

Curtis G. McCormick,
Des Moines, IA
Attorney

MERIT AWARD

Mary Zimmer McNulty,
Canton, OH
Attorney

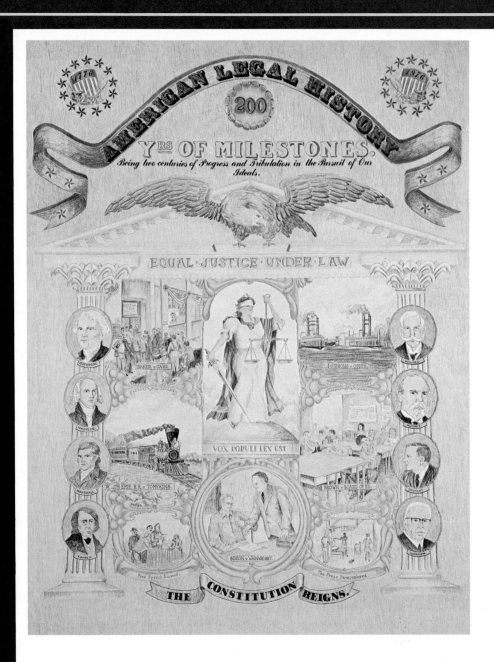

MERIT AWARD
Robert M. Wright,
San Pedro, CA
Attorney

MERIT AWARD
Gregg R. Narber,
Des Moines, IA
Attorney

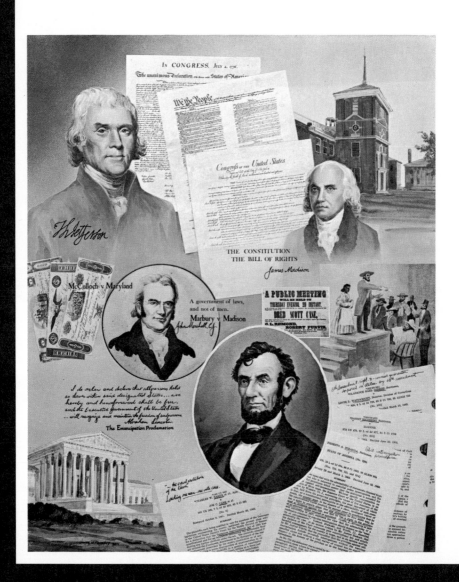

MERIT AWARD

James M. Haughey, Billings, MT

The result was that local authorities had to disregard the state injunction, despite the fact that they would have to exceed the annual tax limit established by Iowa law. As the result of these decisions, municipal bond cases crowded the federal dockets. The Supreme Court itself heard more than three hundred such cases in a thirty-year period.

This same multiplicity of rules quickly developed in ordinary negligence cases. Federal courts claimed the power, as they did in Harry Tompkins's case against the Erie, to decide the common law of torts for themselves. This could mean, for example, that two people receiving identical injuries in the same accident could receive very different treatment. One, being from out of state, might recover his damages under a federal rule. But the other, being a resident of the same state as the person who caused the accident, might recover nothing because the state law was unfavorable to him.

Reversing the Doctrine

In 1923 Charles Warren located original Senate documents from 1789, long thought to be lost. He made a startling discovery. The original draft of Section Thirty-four of the Judiciary Act said this:

[T]he Statute law of the several States in force for the time being and their unwritten or common law now in use, whether by adoption from the common law of England, the ancient statutes of the same or otherwise, except where the constitution, Treaties, or Statutes of the United States shall otherwise require or provide, shall be regarded as rules of decision in the trials at common law in the courts of the United States in cases where they apply.

The section as enacted does not contain the words "statute law" or the clause dealing with the common law. What happened, Warren concluded, was that the final words "laws of the several states" was a more concise version of the original language. Had it been intended to omit the common law only from the laws that the federal courts were required to follow, the word "statute" would not have been dropped also, Warren argued.

This argument was at first rejected. In the much criticized case *Black & White Taxicab Co.* v. *Brown & Yellow Taxicab Co.*, the Court went to some lengths to uphold the *Swift* v. *Tyson* doctrine, over the strong objection of Holmes. Justice Brandeis summarized that case as follows:

Brown and Yellow, a Kentucky corporation owned by Kentuckians, and the Louisville and Nashville Railroad, also a Kentucky corporation, wished that the former should have the exclusive privilege of soliciting passenger and baggage transportation at the Bowling Green, Kentucky, railroad station; and that the Black and White, a competing Kentucky corporation, should be prevented from interfering with that privilege. Knowing that such a contract would be void under the common law of Kentucky, it was arranged that the Brown and Yellow reincorporate under the law of Tennessee, and that the contract with the railroad should be executed there. The suit was then brought by the Tennessee corporation in the federal court for Western Kentucky to enjoin competition by the Black and White; an injunction issued by the District Court was sustained by the Court of Appeals; and this Court, citing many decisions in which the doctrine of Swift v. Tyson *had been applied, affirmed the decree.*

Justice Brandeis

This was the law up to the time the Erie Railroad filed its appeal with the Supreme Court. The company did not take issue with the doctrine. It asked instead that the jury verdict be reversed because the lower courts had erroneously refused to apply the "local usage" exception to the *Swift* doctrine. It was with something of a shock, therefore, that Justice Brandeis' opening words in deciding the case were received. He said:

The question for decision is whether the oft-challenged doctrine of Swift *v.* Tyson *shall now be disapproved.*

For a majority of six, the answer was its final overturning. The benefits expected to flow from the rule did not accrue. Persistence of state courts in their own opinions on questions of common law prevented uniformity; and the impossibility of discovering a satisfactory line of demarcation between the province of general law and that of local law developed a new well of uncertainties.

Since 1842 there had been more than a thousand decisions on the question of the distinction between general and local law. Moreover, the doctrine was "mischievous" in discriminating *against* citizens of the state rather than beneficial in protecting those from out of state. "The doctrine rendered impossible equal protection of the law. In attempting to promote uniformity of law throughout the United States, the doctrine had prevented uniformity in the administration of the law of the State."

But Brandeis did not rely on the discovery that Warren had made fifteen years before, as Justice Reed urged in his concurring opinion. The answer was not simply to reinterpret the "rules of decision" act to include court decisions within the term "laws of the several states." A fundamental question of constitutionality was involved. Brandeis concluded:

Except in matters governed by the Federal Constitution or by Acts of Congress, the law to be applied in any case is the law of the State. And whether the law of the State shall be declared by its Legislature in a statute or by its highest court in a decision is not a matter of federal concern. There is no federal general common law. Congress has no power to declare substantive rules of common law applicable in a State whether they be local in their nature or "general," be they commercial law or a part of the law of torts. And no clause in the Constitution purports to confer such a power upon the federal courts.

Harry Tompkins's verdict was thus thrown out of court. The case was returned to the lower courts to inquire into the law of Pennsylvania. On July 12, ten weeks after the Supreme Court's momentous decision, the Court of Appeals in New York in a brief opinion tossed out Tompkins's claim. Canvassing state court decisions to determine the relevant law, the appellate court ruled that Pennsylvania required the railroad to be especially careful toward those walking on its right-of-way only at well-traveled paths crossing the tracks. No matter how often used, footpaths that parallel the tracks are not the responsibility of oncoming trains. So Harry Tompkins lost his $30,000 verdict because the Court raised a constitutional point that no one had questioned and of which Tompkins and the public were completely unaware.

No Final Solutions

About two weeks after the decision, a letter appeared in the *New York Times,* responding in part to two columns that Arthur Krock had belatedly written on the case. Signing himself only as "L.L.B.," the correspondent wrote: "Heaven knows how much time, energy, and money have been dissipated in controversy as to whether a particular case should be tried in the State or Federal courts, and as to which of two conflicting sets of decisions should govern after it had been decided which tribunal was to hear the case. Happily, that is all over. We need not weep for the yards and yards of learned books on the shelves of law libraries which have been rendered obsolete."

However, the prediction was not fulfilled. The confession of nearly a century of error has not made life particularly simple for federal courts hearing diversity cases. And it has not obliterated federal common law altogether. Instead, still outside the public eye, the *Erie* doctrine has forced a radical change in the way the federal courts go about choosing the proper law for a case. The focus of the inquiry is different, but the necessity of some inquiry remains. And these changes have sometimes resulted in cases seemingly as bizarre as some of those under the regime of *Swift* v. *Tyson*.

Consider, for example, the situation in which a California motorist collides with a Massachusetts driver in Kansas on their way to opposite ends of the country. The California victim, let us suppose, sues the Massachusetts driver in federal court in Massachusetts.

What law must the court apply? Under the *Erie* case, the answer is clearly, "Massachusetts law." But what is that law? The accident, after all, did not happen in Massachusetts; it happened in Kansas. Massachusetts law may require the choice of Kansas law, leaving the federal court to choose between Massachusetts interpretations of Kansas court decisions or Kansas interpretations directly. And suppose further that the previous rulings of the state courts have not been clear on the question at issue, or even that the state courts have never ruled on the question before at all. Must a federal court wait until a state court has spoken, or is the federal court free to guess?

Still another problem: the rules of decision act requires federal courts to apply the law of the states "in cases where they apply." The *Erie* ruling, though on a constitutional plane, does not seem to alter the long-standing tradition that state laws governing the *procedural* rules of courts need not apply to the federal courts when they exercise diversity jurisdiction. In other words, if by state law the defendant has thirty days to answer the plaintiff's complaint, this does not mean that he has the same right in federal court, where the rule is that the defendant has only twenty days. But the line between procedure and substance is elusive, and questions such as these have sparked large amounts of litigation.

As to the federal common law, the era of *Swift* v. *Tyson* knew little federal statutory law. Today Congressional law bulks large. Interpreting these laws and filling in gaps where they are murky or fail to deal with problems that the legislators overlooked is obviously a task for federal courts, applying their own principles. Since a federal statute is superior to any state law with which it conflicts, federal courts will find themselves deciding cases on the basis of a new kind of federal common law in areas that might otherwise be left to the states.

But this is not the place to enter upon a discussion of the complex legal problems that *Erie* created. As sound as the decision was in restoring a proper federal-state balance, it has not simplified the task of the federal lawyer. The complexities that are left are, however, the complexities inherent in a federal system. *Erie* did solve at least one major problem, though: in cases like Harry Tompkins's, the law no longer hinges on which court the litigant manages to get to.

ONE PERSON ONE VOTE

PART V:
REDEEMING THE
AMERICAN PROMISE

12/ EARL WARREN AND THE WARREN COURT

The Supreme Court's dramatic reversal in economic thinking that began in 1937 was a judicial revolution, not a transient phenomenon. For more than forty years the Court had exercised a critical influence in both national and state economic policy by a peculiar reading of the due process clauses and by a narrow reading of the power of Congress under the Commerce Clause. During the next two decades the Court undid its predecessors' handiwork. It restored the paramount place of the legislature in the economic process by rejuvenating the rule of *Munn* v. *Illinois*.

The Fourteenth Amendment

Although the Court's repute did not sink to anything like the low it hit during the post-Civil War period, the Court had been strongly condemned during the early 1930s. Its credibility had been seriously questioned. Determined not to repeat the mistakes that provoked Roosevelt's attack and the seeming threat to its institutional integrity, the Court retrenched along a wide front during the 1940s, much as it was forced to during the 1860s.

But discarding the substantive due process doctrine did not end the Court's involvement with the Fourteenth Amendment. Exactly the opposite happened. Questions that had been long suppressed or avoided now came bubbling to the surface. If there was no longer an economic due process, there was still a Due Process Clause. And large problems of procedural fairness in connection with criminal trials increasingly engaged the attention of the courts.

The federal courts had acted as umpires for the national government since well back into the nineteenth century. Procedural due process was a well-known concept in the federal courts. But the cases had not depended on the language of the Due Process Clause in the Fifth Amendment. The other articles of the Bill of Rights in effect constituted a code of fair dealing for the federal government in its treatment of suspects and criminals. The *Slaughterhouse*

Cases, however, had held that the Privileges and Immunities Clause of the Fourteenth Amendment in the Bill of Rights did not apply to the states.

This was contradictory. A person can be injured just as severely by a heavy-handed state government as by a federal prosecutor or other officer bent on violating the Bill of Rights. With the growth of sophisticated technology and the massive migration from farms to urban centers, serious tensions were created in criminal law because of this contradiction. It was inevitable that the Court would be forced to consider whether the protections in the Bill of Rights applied to the states by virtue of some other constitutional language, like the Due Process Clause of the Fourteenth Amendment.

There was still another problem. Another, potentially very powerful, constitutional clause had lain relatively inactive. That was the Equal Protection Clause, the third and final clause in the great second sentence of the Fourteenth Amendment. As we will explore in the next chapter, this clause, which was supposed to have been written to protect the former slaves, was converted instead into a shield for corporations. Within a generation after the Civil War, the slaves' descendants were virtually precluded from the benefits of the Fourteenth Amendment. Their status was only one notch above the servility of their forebears. The suppression and oppression of the blacks and other minorities could not go on forever, especially in a country that fought a war against ethnic bigotry in its most vicious form.

The particulars of the revival of the Equal Protection Clause will be left to the next chapter, but it will be useful to summarize briefly here the former problem, the application of the Bill of Rights to the states.

Until 1925 only Justice John Marshall Harlan, who sat on the Court from 1877 to 1911, believed that the various provisions of the Bill of Rights were incorporated in the Due Process Clause of the Fourteenth Amendment and thus were applicable to the states. He was the lone dissenter in three important cases in which the Court decisively rejected his views.

In the first decision, in 1884, the Court ruled that the Constitution does not require a state to secure a grand jury indictment of a defendant before he can be tried for committing criminal acts. In the second one, in 1900, the Court held that a state may use a jury of eight rather than twelve members if it chose to do so.

Due process, the Court held, does not mandate a twelve-person jury. And third, in 1908, the Court ruled that a judge may instruct the jury that it may consider the fact that a defendant did not take the stand as possible evidence of guilt (against the claim that such an instruction violated the right against self-incrimination).

This did not mean, of course, that the states consistently violated the Bill of Rights. The constitutions of most states contained some of the same provisions. It did mean, however, that the federal courts would not stop the states if they chose to abolish those rights.

So matters stood until 1923, when for the first time the Court reversed a criminal conviction in a state prosecution because under the circumstances the procedures used in securing it offended the defendants' rights to due process. The case came up from Arkansas, where five black men had been condemned to death under extremely inflammatory conditions for the killing of a white man. The blacks were part of a church congregation meeting to discuss grievances against white landlords; the church was fired upon by whites. In the ensuing disturbance, one white was killed. This sparked a night of insane violence, in which whites sought out and shot blacks; in the midst of the carnage, one white man was killed. For this murder, the five blacks were tried in an atmosphere of extreme prejudice. A lawyer who arrived to consult in the defense barely escaped being mobbed and was actually arrested himself and charged with murder and held for thirty-one days and finally allowed to leave secretly, the charges dropped.

According to affidavits submitted on appeal to the Supreme Court, the defendants, as Justice Holmes summarized, "were brought into court, informed that a certain lawyer was appointed their counsel, and were placed on trial before a white jury, — blacks being systemically excluded from both grand and petit juries. The court and neighborhood were thronged with an adverse crowd that threatened the most dangerous consequences to anyone interfering with the desired result. The counsel did not venture to demand delay or a change of venue, to challenge a juryman, or to ask for separate trials. He had had no preliminary consultation with the accused, called no witnesses for the defense, although they could have been produced, and did not put the defendants on the stand. The trial lasted about three quarters of an hour, and in less than five minutes the jury brought in a verdict of guilty of murder in the first degree." Black witnesses for the prosecution were "whipped and tortured until they would say what was wanted."

The supreme court of the state affirmed the convictions, and the defendants filed a writ of habeas corpus in the federal district court. That court refused the writ on the ground that it had no power to examine into the facts, the state courts having rejected or not considered them. The Supreme Court reversed and ordered the federal district court to hold a hearing, saying: "It does not seem to us sufficient to allow a judge of the United States to escape the duty of examining the facts for himself, when, if true, as alleged, they make the trial absolutely void."

The Court did not relate the procedural defects to specific provisions in the Bill of Rights. Such a relation first occurred two years later, in 1925, when as an aside in a case involving a conviction under the New York Criminal Anarchy Act, the Supreme Court said: "For present purposes, we may and do assume that freedom of speech and of the press—which are now protected by the First Amendment from abridgment by Congress—are among the fundamental personal rights and "liberties" protected by the due process clause of the Fourteenth Amendment from impairment by the States." The defendant lost his case and was packed off to jail anyway. The Court ruled that the state law did not violate the substance of the First Amendment. But it was clear from that point that the Fourteenth Amendment could be found to contain proscriptions against many activities condemned by other articles of the Bill of Rights.

A New Stage

Seven years later, in 1932, the Court moved the Due Process Clause into the procedural rights arena in a famous case, *Powell* v. *Alabama*. The case arose out of the conviction of seven poor black juveniles convicted after a one-day trial of the rape of two white girls riding on a train to Scottsboro, Alabama. The Court reversed the convictions stating that under the circumstances (it was a capital case) the denial of counsel and the defendants' inability to retain counsel was constitutionally unfair. It was not, said Justice Sutherland for a majority of seven, that the Due Process Clause automatically embraces the Sixth Amendment, which condemns the denial of counsel in a federal trial but that "the necessity of counsel was so vital and imperative that the failure of the trial court to make an effective appointment of counsel was . . . a denial of due process of law within the meaning of the Fourteenth Amendment."

Then, in 1937, Justice Cardozo announced the doctrine of "selective incorporation." In *Palko* v. *Connecticut,* the Court grappled with the question of double jeopardy. Was it unconstitutional for a state to retry a man who had been acquitted of first-degree murder but convicted of second-degree murder? The Fifth Amendment ban on twice trying a person for the same offense—the prohibition against double jeopardy—would clearly compel the Court to strike down the first-degree murder conviction the second time around if it had been reached in a federal court.

But did the double jeopardy provision apply to the states? In certain situations, Cardozo wrote, "immunities that are valid as against the federal government by force of the specific pledges of particular amendments have been found to be implicit in the concept of ordered liberty, and thus, through the Fourteenth Amendment, become valid as against the states." But it must be left to the Court to determine in each case "those fundamental principles of liberty and justice which lie at the base of all our civil and political institutions." And, it seemed to Justice Cardozo and seven other members of the Court, that double jeopardy was not among them. It was like the right to trial by jury and to a pretrial grand jury indictment. These rights "may have value and importance. Even so, they are not of the very essence of a scheme of ordered liberty. To abolish them is not to violate a 'principle of justice so rooted in the traditions and conscience of our people as to be ranked as fundamental.' "

Palko's conviction of first-degree murder at his second trial was affirmed, and he was subsequently executed. (In 1969, the *Palko* case was expressly overruled, and the prohibition against double jeopardy was finally incorporated as part of due process.)

Justice Benjamin Nathan Cardozo.

Expanding Due Process

Eleven years later, in 1948, Justice Black announced a new doctrine, though he was in the minority. The case concerned an old question that the Court had ruled on in 1908. Could a prosecutor and judge comment in front of the jury that the defendant had not taken the stand in his own defense? The Court adhered, five to four, to its previous ruling. Such comments (allowed in only a few states) were permissible as far as the federal constitution was concerned.

Black disagreed, and he penned a remarkable dissent in which he argued that the framers of the Fourteenth Amendment intended

Justice Hugo Black.

that the Bill of Rights would be incorporated completely by its addition to the Constitution. Said Black:

My study of the historical events that culminated in the Fourteenth Amendment, and the expressions of those who opposed its submission and passage, persuades me that one of the chief objects that the provisions of the Amendment's first section, separately, and as a whole, were intended to accomplish was to make the Bill of Rights applicable to the states. With full knowledge of the Barron *decision the framers and backers of the Fourteenth Amendment proclaimed its purpose to be to overturn the constitutional rule that case had announced. This historical purpose has never received full consideration or expression in any opinion of this Court interpreting the Amendment.*

And he concluded: "I believe [that] the original purpose of the Fourteenth Amendment [was] to extend to all the people of the nation the complete protection of the Bill of Rights. To hold that this Court can determine what, if any, provisions of the Bill of Rights will be enforced, and if so to what degree, is to frustrate the great design of a written Constitution."

Although certain justices have concurred with Justice Black's reasoning (most consistently, Justice Douglas), the position that the Bill of Rights is totally incorporated by the Fourteenth Amendment Due Process Clause has never been accepted. A majority of the Court since Cardozo's opinion in *Palko* has accepted the selective incorporation approach, even as individual justices have often disagreed about whether a particular provision should be incorporated or not.

The whole process of "incorporating" was anathema to Justice Felix Frankfurter, who preferred an approach he called "absorption." By this he meant that in a particular case the police or prosecutors or trial judge may have done something that "shocks the conscience." In one instance the police pumped a person's stomach (after first beating it severely) to induce him to vomit up morphine capsules that he had just swallowed. In a case such as this, Frankfurter was prepared to rule that the conduct violated the due process owed to any person. "States in their prosecution [must] respect certain decencies of civilized conduct."

To Black and Douglas the difficulty with this approach was its vagueness. There is no defined standard other than the judge's searching of his own conscience to determine when a particular act is impermissible. This smacks too closely of the very vice that the

Court had indulged in during the heyday of substantive due process: substituting personal preference or personal reaction for specific proscriptions. Frankfurter, who was a stern foe of the early New Deal Court's philosophy, admitted this. "Due process of law, as a historic and generative principle, precludes defining, and thereby confining, those standards of conduct more precisely than to say that convictions cannot be brought about by methods that offend a "sense of justice."

Thus by 1952, when Justice Frankfurter announced his "shocks the conscience" test, the main lines of the debate had been drawn. But the Court had taken few concrete steps toward incorporating particular provisions in the Bill of Rights or absorbing certain decencies of civilized conduct into the Fourteenth Amendment.

The Court might have remained content to continue this leisurely attitude toward the fairness that state governments should display if it had not been for the elevation of a Republican politician to the chief justiceship in 1953. It soon became apparent that, for Warren, the most important question to ask of advocates was, "but is it fair?"

Back in the Spotlight

Like his great predecessor, John Marshall, Earl Warren was destined to bring the Court back to the center of searing controversy and to stamp his name indelibly on that period of the Court's history—from 1953 to 1969—when great and enduring constitutional principles were forcefully enunciated. During these years, the Court struck down school segregation and other laws that turned on racial distinctions; remade voting districts across the country in conformity with the "one man, one vote" doctrine; applied most of the Bill of Rights to the states; greatly liberalized the meaning of the freedoms of speech, press, and association; overturned a variety of security laws enacted during the days of Communist fear; took prayers out of public schools; extended the right to counsel in criminal cases; and broke new ground in dozens of other areas.

It was not all Warren's doing. Accidents of retirement and deaths and the temperaments of new appointees were what constituted the new majority. But it is unlikely that the revolution would have come about as quickly or as decisively without the profound instinct Warren had for bringing people together to agree

about the essentials.

Earl Warren was born in Los Angeles on March 19, 1891. His father was a railroad worker who in later years moved away from his family and in 1938 was found murdered. The culprit was never caught. Warren grew up in Bakersfield, working at odd jobs. He received his bachelor's degree from the University of California in 1912 and his law degree from the same university in 1914. He left private practice to serve in World War I as a first lieutenant in the infantry.

In 1920 he began his public life—one that would stretch unbroken for fifty years—by becoming deputy city attorney in Oakland, California. Shortly thereafter he switched to the criminal side of municipal law. He served as deputy district attorney of Alameda County. In 1925 he succeeded to the job of district attorney, and for thirteen years he ran a tight office. His reputation grew as a tough prosecutor. He never lost a conviction on appeal, but he was not a private zealot. He once remarked that "although I fought vigorously in the cases I prosecuted, I invariably felt nauseated when the jury brought in a verdict of guilty."

In 1934 he became state chairman of the Republican party and, in 1936, a national committeeman. Two years later he was elected state attorney general, having won nominations as Republican, Democratic, and Progressive candidate for the office. He served four years and won the governorship in an upset victory in 1942.

Until this point in his career, he had been a fairly conventional politician with pronounced conservative views. He had declared himself in favor of flag salute laws and of outlawing the Communist party. As governor, he vigorously supported the federal incarceration of Japanese-Americans in West Coast camps. But in 1945 he came out for a compulsory state health insurance plan. Other Republicans denounced it as socialistic, and he failed to get the bill through the legislature. His espousal of state health insurance was no ideological switch. Anthony Lewis has written that Warren "had advocated health insurance not because of some philosophical conversion but because he had fallen ill and suddenly realized how catastrophic serious illness would be for the man without resources."

In 1946 he won renomination as the Republican candidate for governor and also captured the Democratic nomination. His reelection was a foregone conclusion. He was the Republican candidate for vice-president in 1948. In 1950 he won an unprecedented third term as governor. Two years later at the Republican National

Opposite page:

Chief Justice Earl Warren.

National Gallery of Art

Convention, he supported General Eisenhower.

On September 3, 1953, less than nine months after Eisenhower had taken office, Chief Justice Fred M. Vinson died. On September 30 Eisenhower announced Warren's appointment during the Congressional recess. Sworn in on October 5, 1953, the Senate ultimately confirmed the nomination the following March over some vocal right-wing opposition. Eisenhower was later to call this appointment "the biggest damn-fool mistake I ever made."

Though some of his early opinions were relatively conservative, at least when compared to later ones, his earliest big opinion was the school desegregation case, rendered less than three months after his confirmation. Warren himself considered this the second most important case on which he sat—legislative reapportionment he considered the most momentous—and his fate with conservatives was sealed.

As his views continued to shift toward a more liberal position, he was pilloried by right-wingers. "Impeach Earl Warren" signs began to appear, but they never appeared to ruffle him. Years later he said that "it was kind of an honor to be accused by the John Birch Society. It was a little rough on my wife, but it never bothered me." As to his shift in views, he said, "No man can sit on the Court over 16 years and remain parochial, for he must look out over all the United States."

As chief justice he was known as a crisp and efficient administrator who put in long hours and mastered the details of every case the Court considered. This was a carry-over from his earliest habits in the district attorney's office, where he was known as a thorough and tireless worker. On the bench he removed himself from most of his old associations. He never became active in bar circles as many jurists do. Only once, in 1963-64, following President Kennedy's assassination, did he take on an extrajudicial assignment—and then unhappily and only at the express wish of President Johnson.

The end of the Warren Court came abruptly. Never an admirer of Richard Nixon, Warren offered his resignation to President Johnson in June 1968, three months after Johnson had announced his withdrawal from the coming presidential race. It was widely believed that he timed his retirement to give Johnson the opportunity to appoint his successor. But Johnson's nomination of Justice Abe Fortas ran into trouble and was withdrawn. Warren then said he would step down the following June. Fortas himself resigned

Such signs did not appear to disturb Chief Justice Warren.

amid scandal shortly before Warren, thus hastening the exit of a Warren Court Justice who might have been expected to serve much longer. With the deaths of Justices Black and Harlan in 1971, President Nixon had the opportunity to remake the Court fairly soon after Warren's own departure. Warren lived in Washington for five years and died on July 9, 1974, at the age of eighty-three.

Earl Warren was a symbol for much that was loved and hated in America. He was a spokesman for freedom from arbitrary government, and he was at the same time condemned by those who saw freedom as anarchy and feared the release of those whom their philosophy had so long held in check. He was hated viciously by the shallow-minded, who saw him destroying the world they imagined they lived in. He was revered by millions as the perfect symbol of the essential meaning of America: that right will be done quietly, peacefully, thoughtfully, that reason will out. And he was faulted by many thoughtful people who saw in his opinions a kind of romanticism that overreached the purposes of the tribunal that he headed.

Criticism of the Warren Court

The role of the Court seemed to shift, in the eyes of critical and informed observers, from one of strict textual exegesis to a result-oriented jurisprudence—just what Roosevelt had condemned a generation before. Precedents were overturned: the Warren Court upset forty-five previous Supreme Court rulings, all in a comparatively short space of time, often without sympathetic expressions of bereavement and the proper explanations of logical necessity. Old cases were overruled, not perhaps because they were wrong but because a new majority didn't like them. The painstaking craftsmanship of a Brandeis or Cardozo was absent; Warren was not a scholar. In place of closely reasoned analysis were sweeping declarations, almost homespun. There was a tendency to reach results immediately, as if the country couldn't wait. So, many critics have said. Because Warren was the visible Chief and because he seemed to have the Marshallian knack of bring his learned and independent and self-assured brethren together to forge a new majority for change, on him has been placed the mantle of responsibility.

Of course he did not write all of the opinions. But he wrote most of the major ones. And it is clear that his jurisprudence was not one of arid technicalities, elegant historical citations, or hair-splitting distinctions. He wrote on a large easel and put his answers to the questions suitors propounded in a warm, real, easily comprehensible way. He was writing for the American citizen more than for lawyers eager for intricate detail. His opinions, like Marshall's, were full of majestic, sweeping vision, even if they had to sweep past mundane, troublesome, or ugly visions that a different man might have troubled to stop and inspect. Like Marshall, he expounded a Constitution.

His answer to the criticism that the Court moved too fast was that, in historical terms, the Court and other institutions had moved much too slowly. His generation had to pay for the sins of its ancestors, for the failure of the Court to rule forthrightly and well during the past fifty or even one hundred years. Had the race question not taken its disastrous turn in 1896, had the states not been permitted to malapportion their legislative districts, had state courts subjected municipal police to some kind of restraints years earlier, the Supreme Court would not need to have become involved in these issues. At least it might not have reached such sweeping conclusions, and the changes in customs and practices would not need to have been nearly so great.

If the Court erred, it erred in trying too hard to be guardian of our liberties—a criticism that can only be a puzzling paradox in the land of liberty. Yet paradox it is, for those who most applauded Barry Goldwater's celebrated dictum in 1964 that "extremism in the defense of liberty is no vice! . . . moderation in the pursuit of justice is no virtue!" were among Warren's fiercest critics.

The problem, of course, lies in the difficulties of answering "which liberties, and for whom?" In stopping states from segregating public facilities and from cutting prosecutorial corners, the Court was doubtless interfering with the liberty of a majority to shape its beliefs into public policy. But in a land whose foremost tradition is a constitutional restraint on majorities precisely in order to preserve other liberties for minorities—even sometimes minorities of one—these were scarcely questions that relied only on the old answers.

Indeed, they were questions that could be raised only in a court. Otherwise they would forever have received the same old answer. There simply is no other forum but a court in which to raise the question of majority tyranny. Political processes would scarcely alter racial segregation or stop police abuse.

In this respect these questions are closely related to the Court's actions in the reapportionment cases. When the states violated their own laws, no one could ever hope to make the legislative process work. To say "let the people change the system" is all very well when the subject at issue is one on which the people may properly decree whatever they like. But it is no answer at all when the problem is the very system through which the change is supposed to be brought about. A record caught in a rut does not unstick itself. A majority that may with impunity dictate to the powerless is no more likely to stray from its groove.

This may not be a legal explanation. What the Warren Court accomplished may more appropriately be called political. But it did not play partisan politics. It did not follow a mean-spirited policy. And in the final analysis, it is not possible to prove that the quality of human life, or democracy, would be better served by political institutions in which a body like the Warren Court—despite its mistakes—could not exist. Rather, one suspects, the reverse is true.

Members of the Warren Court

Warren served with sixteen justices, four of whom are still on the bench as this book goes to press. It would be impossible in a book of this scope even to summarize the careers of all these men, but a brief highlight of some is in order.

Hugo L. Black: Roosevelt's first appointment, Black went to the Court as a senator from Alabama, a position that he had held for ten years. He was a staunch New Dealer and Roosevelt supporter.

Black was born on February 27, 1886, in Clay County, Alabama. At eighteen he went to law school at the University of Alabama. He skipped college entirely. On graduation he set up practice, and his first client was a black convict who had been forced to labor two weeks beyond his sentence. Black brought a civil suit for money damages and won.

After a time, Black took on an additional part-time assignment: police court judge of Birmingham. Here he presided over the disposition of petty crimes, and he gained a reputation for fairmindedness toward Negro defendants. In 1914 he was appointed county prosecutor and like Warren saw firsthand the problems and difficulties of administering criminal justice. During his three years as prosecutor, Black uncovered the use of systematic torture to obtain confessions from black defendants by the suburban police department of Bessemer. He took his case to the grand jury. Black carried the memory with him when cases involving police methods came before the High Court.

After brief service in World War I he returned to Birmingham and started a successful and lucrative private practice. Here he polished his great skills in public speaking through numerous personal injury jury trials and appellate arguments. By 1925 he decided to enter politics and sought the Democratic nomination for the U.S. Senate against four competitors. Not widely known, he stumped the state as the poor man's candidate and carried it by a wide margin.

In Washington in 1927 he began a remarkable program of self-education. This was no country bumpkin who would please the folks back home with a few well-timed votes and retire for an evening of drinking with the boys. Black began to read widely in history and the classics. He quickly tied himself in with what was then a small liberal bloc. With the coming of the New Deal, Black began to play an increasingly more influential role. He was especially active in labor and public utility legislation. By the mid-thirties, he had a national reputation, enhanced by his effective investigation of business lobbying tactics.

On August 12, 1937, Roosevelt appointed him to the seat that Justice Van DeVanter had vacated that June. As a member of the majority party of the body that was required to pass on his nomination, the confirmation was a foregone conclusion (though sixteen conservatives voted against it).

In September, after confirmation, a furor arose over the appointment when the *Pittsburgh Post Gazette* revealed to the nation a fact known in Alabama, that Black had been a member of the Ku Klux Klan, beginning in 1923. Black returned from a European vacation and addressed the nation by radio, confirming that he had indeed once joined the Klan, as he had joined any number of other fraternal organizations. But he had had little to do with it then and, having resigned two years later, had had no further contact with it whatsoever. The crisis passed.

Black served for thirty-four years, one of the longest periods of active service on record. He was a strict constructionist in the liberal mold. He believed for instance that because the First Amendment said that Congress shall make *no* laws abridging freedom of speech or the press there were no exceptions allowed, not even for alleged obscene material. He believed as an integral part of this philosophy that the Fourteenth Amendment incorporated the Bill of Rights only to the extent of what was written in them. Thus he dissented from Justice Douglas's opinion for a seven to two majority in the 1965 birth control case *Griswold* v. *Connecticut*, which held that the states could not constitutionally prohibit a person from using contraceptives.

The gist of Douglas's majority opinion was that the various rights in the first eight amendments have "penumbras" from which other rights, though not specifically spelled out, could be deduced. Though Black almost invariably voted with Douglas, he felt compelled to dissent, for nothing in the Bill of Rights said anything about the use of contraceptives. (Justice Goldberg argued in a concurring opinion that the Ninth Amendment could be used as a source for grounding an evolving law of privacy.)

In his later years many observers felt that Black was growing conservative, voting as he did on several occasions with less liberal members of the Court in certain sit-in and other cases. But Black himself believed that he was merely being consistent with the philosophy that he had so long espoused. In September 1971 at the age of eighty-five, realizing he was fatally ill, he retired from the Court and died before the month was out.

Felix Frankfurter: One of the most brilliant ebullient spirits ever to sit on the High Court, Felix Frankfurter was a great disappointment to liberals who hailed his nomination by President Roosevelt in 1939. His apparent change in philosophy once on the bench was no less stark than Earl Warren's. But Frankfurter saw it as a change in role, not philosophy. He had detested the Supreme Court's earlier unwise interference in national policy, He would not, as justice, substitute his judgment for the legislature's. Both were subservient to the Constitution.

Justice Felix Frankfurter.

Frankfurter had a passion for action, for people, and also for the life of the mind. In all these he succeeded brilliantly. As a professor of law at Harvard Law School from 1914 to 1939 (interrupted formally only briefly by a stint on President Wilson's Mediation Commission), he lectured students, professors, lawyers, politicians, and the nation. His charismatic and irrepressible personality strongly influenced all who knew him, and he had a wide circle of influential acquaintances. His close personal friend Dean Acheson once said: "I can think of no one in our time remotely comparable to him, though it would not surprise me if in another time Dr. Franklin might have had something of the same personal influence."

That he achieved all this as a Jewish immigrant from his native city of Vienna makes his story all the more remarkable. (Frankfurter was one of only six justices in the history of the Court to be born outside the United States, and three of these were appointed in the earliest years.) He came to New York in 1894 at the age of twelve, did his undergraduate work at the City College of New York, and took his law degree at Harvard in 1906.

In that year he became assistant U.S. attorney in the prestigious Southern District of New York (Manhattan) and began with the then U.S. attorney, Henry L. Stimson, the first of countless friendships with distinguished people in public life. Frankfurter worked for Stimson in his unsuccessful campaign for governor of New York in 1910. He then went with him to Washington as his assistant when Taft appointed Stimson secretary of war. He supported Theodore Roosevelt during the 1912 election and stayed on a year as assistant to Stimson's successor in the Wilson cabinet, Lindley M. Garrison. He then went to Harvard, where he remained for a noisy quarter-century.

Arguments in the Supreme Court, articles in the *New Republic,* the bitter fight over Sacco and Vanzetti were all part of professorial years. During the early period at Harvard he took an extended leave as counsel to the Mediation Commission, appointed to find a solution to difficult labor problems in several important war industries. This experience gave Frankfurter a deep sense of labor's troubles. He wrote a report on the notoriously corrupt *Mooney* case, recommending retrial of the California labor radical who had been convicted of murder. His later defense and report of his investigation in the *New Republic* gained him national attention. In 1932, he turned down a proffered appointment to the Massachusetts supreme court.

Frankfurter first met Franklin D. Roosevelt in 1906 in New York, where they came to know each other in the library of the Association of the Bar of the City of New York. They became friends. Their friendship deepened when Roosevelt came to Washington as assistant secretary of the Navy with an office on the same floor as Frankfurter's in the old State Department building. It was a friendship that would last for life, Frankfurter becoming an intimate FDR adviser. In early 1933 Roosevelt asked him to become solicitor general, saying it was a step toward the Supreme Court, but Frankfurter again turned down an appointment to public office, saying he could better serve the president as an adviser from Cambridge. On January 5, 1939, a few months after Cardozo's death, Roosevelt nominated Frankfurter to the Supreme Court.

He fully shared the beliefs of Justices Black and Douglas that the Court not get itself mixed up in economic controversy. He joined the majority that killed off the doctrine of substantive due process in the realm of economics, but he was suspicious of substantive due process in the political realm as well. He often came out on the conservative side of questions involving civil liberties. Thus he dissented in the famous Flag Salute case, when the majority overturned a decision he had written only three years before upholding the right of a state to compel public school students to salute the flag. He dissented in *Mapp* v. *Ohio* (see Chapter 14) and in *Baker* v. *Carr* (see Chapter 15). Yet, as noted earlier, he was quick to condemn police actions that "shocked" his conscience. He retired when he became ill in 1962. He died in 1965.

William O. Douglas: The most consistently liberal justice ever to serve on the Supreme Court, Douglas served longer than any of the one hundred one justices who have sat on the high bench. He was born in 1898 in Minnesota but moved with his family in 1904 to a small town near Yakima, Washington. The family was poverty-stricken, his father having died when he was six. A few years later he was struck with polio and began a regiment of physical exercise and hiking to restore his legs. It was during this period that his deep, lifelong interest in nature and conservation developed. He spent World War I in the army at the Presidio in San Francisco and graduated in 1920 from Whitman College in Walla Walla, Washington.

In 1922, after two years of high school teaching he took a long trek east, signing on as a member of a freight train crew assigned to guard sheep on a cross-country run. But numerous difficulties ensued, and he wound up riding the rails with hobos, spending time in their camps. He eventually hitchhiked to New York, where he enrolled at Columbia Law School. He graduated three years later, second in his class.

For a brief time he practiced with the Cravath firm in New York, then returned to Yakima to practice for a year. In 1927 he joined the Columbia Law School faculty, but shortly thereafter he took a position at Yale Law School, which he found more congenial. He remained there five years.

In 1934 he signed up with the New Deal. He became a member

of the newly created Securities and Exchange Commission in 1936. He became chairman in 1937. He had a host of New Deal friends, played poker with the president, and began a friendship with Lyndon B. Johnson that lasted a lifetime.

On March 20, 1939, Roosevelt named Douglas as his fourth Supreme Court appointment (after Black, Stanley Reed, and Frankfurter). Douglas was then only forty-one, one of the youngest men to have been appointed since Joseph Story 128 years before.

His influence has been too broad and deep to be traced here. His was a facile pen, and he was criticized for having been too glib, though no one has ever accused him of not having a penetrating intelligence. He seemed entirely at ease with such arcane mysteries as economic rate regulation. He was an apostle of the First Amendment and other individual liberties. During the 1940s and 1950s, many Supreme Court opinions that seemed to operate against individual freedoms bore a notation that became quite familiar: "Mr. Justice Black and Mr. Justice Douglas dissenting."

He had an enormous appetite for work and denounced the call of Chief Justice Burger and others for relief from the crushing burdens of review as the Court's docket has increased to record proportions. He has been a voluminous writer with more than twenty books to his credit as well as innumerable opinions and articles. He could be seen writing opinions on the bench during oral arguments, a stack of law books next to him, assistants sent scurrying off after more. But he seemed to have the ability to pay attention to two things at once. Occasionally he would look up from his writing to ask a disputant a question indicating that he had been following the entire discussion.

He was, not unnaturally, a controversial public figure. His position on the Court did not stop him, for example, from speaking out eloquently for proper environmental measures. His ringing declarations for freedom to publish anything, including obscenity, his frequent articles, and his four marriages led in the early 1970s to a brief move, spearheaded by Congressman Gerald R. Ford, to impeach him. But it died aborning.

In December 1974 he suffered a severe stroke and was out for most of the spring 1975 term and on November 11, 1975 he retired from active service, citing "incessant and demanding pain which depletes my energy to the extent that I have been unable to shoulder my full share of the burden." His record of thirty-six years and seven months on the Court seems unlikely to be broken, at least for a long time to come.

John Marshall Harlan: Namesake and grandson of the great dissenter, Harlan was at the head of the bar when President Eisenhower scurried him along to the Supreme Court. He was born in Chicago in 1899, graduated from Princeton, won a Rhodes Scholarship, and took a law degree in 1924 from the New York Law School, then the leading law school in New York. After a brief period of private practice, he became an assistant to the U.S. attorney from 1925 to 1927 and was a special prosecutor in the state's municipal graft scandal.

Returning to private practice he became a partner in 1931. By 1941 he was a senior partner and one of the city's leading litigators. He took a civilian job with the Air Force during World War II and served with great distinction. Governor Thomas E. Dewey appointed him chief counsel to the New York State Crime Commission in 1951, and he served for two years. Throughout this time he was active in the Association of the Bar of the City of New York. In January 1954 President Eisenhower appointed him to the U.S. Court of Appeals for the Second Circuit in New York. Less than a year later, in November 1954, Eisenhower whisked him upstairs to the Supreme Court. He was confirmed in March 1955.

Harlan was known as a man of great learning and was one of the most painstaking judicial craftsmen on the bench. He was the "lawyer's judge," so comprehensive and useful to the lawyering art were his opinions. He was also known as the "conservative conscience" of the Court. He did not demean the importance of civil liberties, but he believed the Constitution gave the states great leeway to experiment to find the political institutions that best suited them. The requirements laid on the federal government by the Bill of Rights, he believed, were not meant to apply wholesale to the states. He firmly believed, as he said in dissent in *Reynolds* v. *Sims,* the 1964 reapportionment case that first struck down malapportioned state legislative districts, that "the vitality of our political system, on which in the last analysis all else depends, is weakened by reliance on the judiciary for political reform."

Toward the end of his life his eyesight failed and he was nearly blind. But he remained gamely on the bench and his opinions lost nothing in strength or acuity. He resigned at the same time as Justice Black, in September 1971 and died two days before the new year.

Earl Warren served substantial periods of time during his tenure as chief justice with three others—William J. Brennan, Potter Stewart, and Byron R. White—who are still on the bench and likely to remain so for years to come. Brennan and Stewart were both Eisenhower appointees, Brennan (1956) coming from the New

Jersey Supreme Court and Stewart (1958) from the Sixth Circuit Court of Appeals to which Eisenhower had also appointed him. White was deputy attorney general under President Kennedy, who appointed him in 1962 and is the only Kennedy appointee to remain on the bench.

The Warren Court: 1958
Top row, left to right: Justices Whittaker, Harlan, Brennan, Stewart.
Bottom row: Justices Douglas and Black, Chief Justice Warren, Justices Frankfurter and Clark.

13/ EQUALITY REDEEMED:
BROWN v. BOARD OF EDUCATION

If at the midpoint of the twentieth century one were to have tried to reconstruct American constitutional history solely through inspection of Supreme Court opinions, one might well have imagined that the Civil War had been fought chiefly over the question of freedom for the possessors of capital, more tentatively over the liberties of newspaper and periodical proprietors and that of some religious sects to breathing space, and possibly over the rights of certain criminal defendants. Only in some kind of obscure way would the war be understood to have had any bearing on the legal, political, and social capacities of the forcibly expatriated African slaves.

A Legally Administered Overdose

The Thirteenth Amendment, to be sure, did abolish slavery. Though there have been occasional outbreaks of peonage (some petty and some rather widespread and long-sustained) formal legal slavery, in which living human bodies were placed on the auction block and sold, was dead and buried. The Fifteenth Amendment abolished racial discrimination in voting. That is, the Constitution said, as of 1870 when the amendment was ratified, that "the right of citizens of the United States to vote shall not be denied or abridged by the United States or by any State on account of race, color or previous condition of servitude." And Congress was given power to enforce this right against recalcitrant state governments.

Yet by the turn of the century, the Amendment's promise had become worthless. With the Supreme Court's approval, the right of blacks to vote was virtually extinct, and the Fifteenth Amendment right had been undermined by the white primaries and numerous grandfather clauses. Civil rights forces in Congress were held in thrall by the seniority of the one-party establishment that was regularly elected to the Senate and House. The Supreme Court did not finally peel away the most blatant forms of discrimination in voting until the 1940s. But even then, concrete progress in registering blacks and letting them go peacefully to the polls was impossible until the most glaring constitutional perversion was straightened out. When this finally was accomplished, it radically changed the national mood and forced Congress itself to act.

This perversion was the interpretation that the Supreme Court gave to the archstone of the three Reconstruction amendments: the Fourteenth Amendment's Equal Protection Clause. This is the third clause of the all-important second sentence of the Fourteenth Amendment: "nor shall any State . . . deny to any person within its jurisdiction the equal protection of the laws." Originally it had been proposed to overcome any doubts about the constitutionality of Congressional attempts to end discrimination through such laws as the Civil Rights Act of 1866.

In a relatively short period of time it fell into a strange sleep akin to a trance, twitching only occasionally when someone had the money to get close enough to appeal to what, even in its coma, it was capable of radiating.

The narcotic that induced this long sleep was administered in two doses, one in 1883 and the other in 1896. In those years, the Supreme Court handed down decisions that largely nullified political progress made possible by the war. One of the decisions was nearly as insensitive and callous as *Dred Scott* itself. The other appeared to be more logically rooted in the nature of the federal system, but from such logic flowed great historical disaster. It continued the degradation of an immense mass of humanity within a nation that stood from the beginning for the equal rights of all.

Finally, in 1954, having screwed up its courage in a few preliminary cases, the Supreme Court reversed course and awakened the Equal Protection Clause with a judicial kiss. In *Brown* v. *Board of Education,* a case embracing a number of contests over school segregation in the South, the Court announced one of the single most important decisions of the century. To examine this case it is necessary to go back a century, when Congress enacted a significant but constitutionally vexing civil rights law.

The Civil Rights Cases

The Civil Rights Act of 1875 was a reaction to nearly a decade of strife and lawsuits in lower courts. These suits involved the necessity of local governments guarding the individual black's enjoyment of the ordinary amenities of life, such as eating in restaurants, traveling on trains and streetcars, attending the theater, shopping in stores. The laws in the Southern states did not require segregation, as they later would. But in many places there was strong sentiment against the mixing of the races. So individual, private streetcar and railroad companies, theater and restaurant owners, and proprietors of other private establishments catered to the communities in which they operated and in one way or another discriminated against blacks. The practice of segregation was not universal. During the 1870s and even into the 1880s, there were many cities in which black and white could travel, eat, shop, and be entertained side by side.

But the practice of social equality was not widespread enough by the lights of Northern Republicans, who saw that the states were not exactly eager to pass strong protective legislation themselves. Massachusetts Senator Charles Sumner, chief proponent of the act, had written to a convention of blacks in South Carolina in 1871:

You must at all times insist upon your rights, and here I mean not only those already accorded, but others still denied, all of which are contained in equality before the law. Wherever the law supplies a rule, there you must insist upon equal rights. How much remains to be obtained you know too well in the experience of life. Can a respectable colored citizen travel on steamboats or railways, or public conveyances generally, without insult on account of color? Let Lieutenant-Governor Dunn, of Louisiana [a black], describe his journey from New Orleans to Washington. Shut out from proper accommodations in the cars, the doors of the Senate Chamber opened to him, and there he found the equality a railroad conductor had denied him. Let our excellent friend, Frederick Douglass, relate his melancholy experience, when, within sight of the executive mansion, he was thrust back from the dinnertable where his brother commissioners were already seated [he had been appointed secretary of the San Domingo Commission that year]. . . . I might ask the same question with regard to hotels, and even common schools. An hotel is a legal institution, and so is a common school. As such each must be for the equal benefit of all. Now, can there be any exclusion from either on account of color? It is not enough to provide separate accommodations for colored citizens even if in all respects as good as those of other persons. . . . The discrimination is an insult and a hindrance, and a bar, which not only destroys comfort and prevents equality, but weakens all other rights.

The result of such considerations was the 1875 Civil Rights Act. It declared "That all persons within the jurisdiction of the

United States shall be entitled to the full and equal enjoyment of the accommodations, advantages, facilities, and privileges of inns, public conveyances on land or water, theatres, and other places of public amusement; subject only to the conditions and limitations established by law, and applicable alike to citizens of every race and color, regardless of any previous condition of servitude."

Even before its enactment, there were warnings that the law was unconstitutional, as invading the right of private citizens to do as they pleased. The law was quickly put to the test, with scores of criminal prosecutions and appeals throughout the country. Some courts upheld the law and fined its transgressor. Others dismissed the suits as based on an unconstitutional statute. A group of these cases ultimately wound their way up to the Supreme Court. It was a ponderous institution in those days, owing to antiquated procedures and a press of business, and quite apparently reluctant to rule too hastily.

Five of the six cases that appeared on the Court's dockets were criminal prosecutions. One stemmed from the refusal of a Topeka, Kansas, hotelman to serve food to a black. Another concerned the refusal of a Jefferson City, Missouri, innkeeper to accept a black guest. A third resulted from the refusal of a San Francisco theater doorkeeper to let a black sit in the dress circle. Two additional cases concerned railroad accommodations: one a criminal prosecution involving a conductor's refusal to let a black woman sit in the ladies' car on the Nashville, Chattanooga & St. Louis Railroad; the other, a civil suit for harassment on the Memphis & Charleston Railroad on a trip from Grand Junction, Tennessee, to Lynchburg, Virginia.

Ironically, the lead case of these six, which have come to be known collectively as the *Civil Rights Cases*, came from New York City, where Samuel Singleton, the doorkeeper at the Grand Opera House, refused to admit William R. Davis, Jr., and his date, both black. (Davis, like those whose rights had not been honored in the other criminal cases, filed a complaint with the federal authorities, and Singleton was indicted for violating the Civil Rights Act.)

On October 15, 1883, after delays of as long as seven years in some of the cases, the Supreme Court disposed of the entire lot. It ruled that the act was unconstitutional.

In the first place, ruled Justice Joseph Bradley for an eight to one majority, the Thirteenth Amendment does not grant power to Congress to enact an equal public accommodations law. Ownership of a person was one thing, but "it would be running the slavery argument into the ground to make it apply to every act of discrimination which a person may see fit to make as to the guests he will entertain, or as to the people he will take into his coach or cab or car, or admit to his concert or theatre." Because a restaurant owner may exclude someone from his public table does not make the person excluded a slave.

In the second place, said Bradley, there is no such power under the Fourteenth Amendment. The Equal Protection Clause applies only to the states themselves. In these cases the states had not excluded the black citizens; other private citizens had. The Fourteenth Amendment "does not authorize Congress to create a code of municipal law for the regulation of private rights; but to provide modes of redress against the operation of State laws, and the action of State officers, executive or judicial. . . . Until some State law has been passed, or some State action through its officers or agents has been taken, adverse to the rights of citizens sought to be protected by the Fourteenth Amendment, no legislation of the United States . . . nor any proceeding under such legislation, can be called into activity. . . . The wrongful act of an individual, unsupported by any [state] authority, is simply a private wrong, or a crime of that individual." The Negro, Justice Bradley concluded, must descend from his elevated status as "the special favorite of the laws" and assume "the rank of mere citizen."

Only Justice John Marshall Harlan dissented. He did so on several grounds. The facilities that the federal act had prohibited from discriminating against blacks were all licensed by the states and under laws of the individual states were required to serve whites equally. Railroads were "public carriers," and restaurants had an obligation to serve all whites who were not boisterous or improperly dressed or for some other appropriate reason. How then could it be said that blacks might lawfully be excluded? This point he linked to both the Thirteenth and the Fourteenth Amendments. He also criticized the Court's failure to uphold the act insofar as it affected the railroad cases under Congress' original power to regulate interstate commerce. This was a prescient point that the Court would ultimately use to uphold the Civil Rights Act of 1964.

Moreover, Harlan said, Congress certainly had the power to outlaw private discriminatory acts. In 1850 Congress had enacted a draconian Fugitive Slave Law that put those who helped runaway slaves against the interests of their owners in jeopardy of large fines and jail sentences. The Court had upheld this law. "I insist that the National Legislature may . . . do for human liberty . . . what it did . . . for the protection of slavery and the rights of the masters of fugitive slaves," he declared.

Finally, in response to Bradley's complaint that blacks were being singled out for the special protection, the ex-slaveholder said this: "Today it is the colored race which is denied, by corporations and individuals wielding public authority, rights fundamental in their freedom and citizenship. At some future time, it may be that some other race will fall under the ban of race discrimination. If the constitutional amendments be enforced, according to the intent with which, as I conceive, they were adopted, there cannot be in this republic, any class of human beings in practical subjection to another class."

The *Civil Rights Cases* had a powerful effect on American legal and political institutions. In prescribing sharp limits beyond which Congress could not act, it put an end to federal attempts to ameliorate the lot of the former slaves. It also encouraged Southern leaders, once again in control of their state governmental machinery, to appeal to whites against the perceived threat of the black minority. The decision, Alan F. Westin has written, "destroyed the delicate balance of federal guarantee, Negro protest, and private enlightenment which was producing a steadily widening area of peacefully integrated public facilities in the North and South during the 1870's and early 1880's."

As a consequence, the South began transforming the widespread custom of private segregation into binding state law. The Supreme Court had said in the *Civil Rights Cases* that the question of discrimination should be left to the discretion of private individuals. But now even that discretion was to be denied. Blacks could no longer find freedom in the egalitarian spirit of a few whites.

Jim Crow legislation began in the railroads in Florida in 1887. By 1892, eight other states had followed suit (Mississippi in 1888; Texas in 1889; Louisiana the following year; Alabama, Arkansas, Georgia, and Tennessee in 1891; and Kentucky in 1892.) By 1900, Virginia and North and South Carolina also joined in.

Plessy v. Ferguson

In Louisiana in 1891 a group of black citizens determined to put the law to the test. Forming a "Citizens' Committee to Test the Constitutionality of the Separate Car Law," they began soliciting funds to bring a lawsuit. To direct the suit they engaged Albion W. Tourgee of New York, a leading carpetbagger in North Carolina during Reconstruction and author of six novels about his experiences.

In June 1892, an elaborately plotted scenario designed to bring a case on the constitutional question to the Supreme Court, was set in motion. A man who could easily have passed for white, Homer Adolph Plessy, climbed aboard the East Louisiana Railroad in New Orleans and sat down in the white-only coach. By pre-arrangement a conductor requested that he move back to the colored car. When Plessy refused to do so, a train detective arrested him. At his arraignment, he pleaded that the law was unconstitutional. Tourgee asked the Supreme Court for an order prohibiting the criminal court judge, John H. Ferguson, from proceeding with the trial. By the end of the year the Louisiana supreme court had upheld the law. This allowed the case of *Plessy* v. *Ferguson* to proceed to the Supreme Court.

The basis for the state court's ruling was that the law could segregate the races in public accommodations if the accommodations assigned to persons of one race were equal to those assigned to the other. Plessy, who was specially chosen for his appearance, was seven-eighths white (one of his eight great-grandparents had been black). If there had been a way to force the justices to concentrate on the way the law classified people as black or white, Plessy might at least have prevailed on the singular facts in his case. (The South was scarcely worried about people who were to all outward appearances white and who were known to be partly black only by their own affidavits.)

Could a law be valid constitutionally if it defined a person of one-eighth African blood as "colored" but did not also define a person with one-eighth Caucasian blood as white? In view of the court's due process decisions that struck down laws burdening property as unreasonable, how could such a law ever be defended as reasonable? "The question is not as to the equality of the privileges enjoyed, but the right of the State to label one citizen as white and another as colored in the common enjoyment" of a host of daily activities, Tourgee said in his brief.

In other words, the Louisiana law—and others like it—were unconstitutional because they made a distinction between black and white. This law, Tourgee argued, violates the policy of equal protection of the laws that the Fourteenth Amendment charges the states to carry out. If the Court had concentrated on this point, it is at least possible that the question might have been kept alive for later cases, in which the manifest absurdity of trying to define what people may or may not do on the basis of their genes would have been shown.

But this is a relatively subtle point, even today, and judges who sat during an era that unquestioningly accepted the genetic superiority of whites were, at best, unwilling to grapple with it. The emphasis of the Court was not on what made a person legally definable as black. Instead they concentrated on what the law might legitimately do with the distinction between white and black, however it was drawn.

Tourgee pointed to the Thirteenth Amendment. He said that slavery was not merely ownership but "a caste, a legal condition of subjection to the dominant class." As for the Fourteenth Amendment, the issue seemed quite clear. A significant feature of the law, Tourgee pointed out, was that "nurses atending the children of the other race" could sit in the forbidden cars (how many white nurses attended black children on railroad trips or anywhere else?) "The exemption of nurses," he said, "shows that the real evil lies not in the color of the skin but in the relation the colored person sustains to the white. If he is a dependent, it may be endured: if he is not, his presence is insufferable, Instead of being intended to promote the *general* comfort and moral well-being, this act is plainly and evidently intended to promote the happiness of one class by asserting its supremacy and the inferiority of another class. Justice is pictured blind and her daughter, the Law, ought at least to be color-blind."

The Court would have none of it. On May 18, 1896, three years after the case was originally docketed in Washington, the Supreme Court upheld the separate car law in all particulars. By today's standards, the decision in *Plessy* v. *Ferguson* was shot through with fallacies, but it was enough to carry the day for fifty-eight years.

Recognizing that here, unlike in the Civil Rights cases, the discrimination complained of resulted from an act of the state, Justice Henry B. Brown ruled for a seven to one majority (Justice David Brewer did not participate) nevertheless that it did not amount to the type of discrimination that the Fourteenth Amendment prohibits. The Equal Protection Clause does not prevent a state legislature from drawing lines or making classifications. All laws do that to some degree or other by the very fact that they permit some activity and prohibit others. To pass the constitutional test, Brown wrote, legislative classifications cannot be arbitrary or unreasonable. What was reasonable depends, said Justice Brown, on the "established usages, customs, and traditions of the people, and with a view to the promotion of their comfort, and the preservation of the public peace and good order."

This was, of course, a prescription for letting the people do just as they pleased, for "the people" will never deviate from their own usages, customs, and traditions. Whatever these are, then, when enacted into law, must be permissible under the Fourteenth Amendment. A separate-but-equal law surely did not go against established usages, customs, or traditions. Indeed in preserving the state's customs, it promoted the racial peace that was necessary for the good order of the state. Despite historical evidence, much of it contemporary to these very judges, "those who drafted the Fourteenth Amendment," Justice Brown concluded, "could not have intended to abolish distinctions based upon color."

But wasn't a distinction made purely on racial lines an unlawful discrimination because it said that some people were inferior to others? In an oft-quoted passage, Justice Brown said the Court considered

the underlying fallacy of [Plessy's] argument to consist in the assumption that the enforced separation of the two races stamps the colored race with the badge of inferiority. If this be so, it is not by reason of anything found in the act, but solely because the colored race chooses to put that construction upon it. . . . Legislation is powerless to eradicate racial instincts or to abolish distinctions based upon physical differences, and the attempt to do so can only result in accentuating the difficulties of the present situation. If the civil and political rights of both races be equal, one cannot be inferior to the other civilly or politically. If one race be inferior to the other socially, the constitution of the United States cannot put them upon the same plane.

To all this, Justice Harlan replied in one of the great dissents in American constitutional history. The purpose of the law was not to provide equal facilities for blacks but to discriminate against them. Their intention, he said, was to put flesh on the idea of supremacy that the white class feels. But, he declared,

in view of the constitution, in the eye of the law, there is in this country no superior, dominant, ruling class of citizens. There is no caste here. Our constitution is color-blind, and neither knows nor tolerates classes among citizens. In respect of civil rights, all citizens are equal before the law. The humblest is the peer of the most powerful. The law regards man as man, and takes no account of his surroundings, or of his color when his civil rights as guaranteed by the supreme law of the land are involved. . . . We boast of the freedom enjoyed by our people above all other peoples. But it is difficult to reconcile that boast with a state of law which, practically, puts the brand of servitude and degradation upon a large class of our fellow citizens—our equals before the law. The thin disguise of "equal accommodations" for passengers in railroad coaches will not mislead any one, nor atone for the wrong this day done. . . . In my opinion, the judgment this day rendered will, in time, prove to be quite as pernicious as the decision made by this tribunal in the Dred Scott case.

No matter how powerful his pen, however, the Great Dissenter could not stem the onrush of law designed to put the blacks in their place. From railroad cars the Jim Crow laws traveled up and down the South and in and out of every nook and cranny where the races might be expected to meet. So powerful was this force and so deep were its foundations that even Harlan himself implied three years later that the Constitution did not forbid racial segregation in the schools.

Starting Back up the Hill

Separate school laws were already on the books of about thirty states (including California and New York) at the time *Plessy* v. *Ferguson* was decided. Their existence and the fact that they had withstood attacks in many state courts was one of the pieces of evidence that Justice Brown cited in *Plessy* to buttress his conclusions. In 1927, the Court reaffirmed the *Plessy* doctrine by implication, this time in connection with the school question.

But the Court had not been entirely insensitive to the means by which the inferior position of blacks was maintained—only mostly so. In a 1917 case, the Court struck down a state law that prohibited blacks from moving into a residential area in which a majority of homes or families was white, and vice versa. The Court voided the law because it interfered with the disposition of property. This in itself may say something about the Court's scale of values at the time, but it does not detract from the correctness of the decision. Similarly, in a case shortly before the housing case, the Court ruled that a state could not provide dining cars for whites on railroads but deny them to blacks on the ground that the numbers of blacks traveling by train did not make it economical to do so.

The distinction between these cases and the school segregation

Opposite page:

These were the involved.

H. Armstrong Roberts

cases rests in the way in which the equality of treatment was perceived. In the school and other segregation cases, it was assumed that the black complainants were receiving benefits or services equal to those the whites were getting. But in the property cases no such assumption could be made. The fact that whites could not move onto black blocks did not prove that black and white blocks were equal.

The fact that whites were entitled to dining cars and blacks were not is on its face an unequal distinction. And in 1927, when Chief Justice Taft upheld school segregation, the Court struck down a Texas statute that made it unlawful for blacks to vote in state primaries on the ground that the law violated the Equal Protection Clause. It was becoming apparent, though slowly, that race was a permissible dividing line in state laws only where some appeal could be made to the separate-but-equal argument.

In time this argument, too, began to erode. By the 1930s the National Association for the Advancement of Colored People (NAACP) began to pursue a course of legal action aimed at ending segregation wherever it could. Formed in 1909, the NAACP developed into a political group with some clout. In 1930, for example, it successfully lobbied the Senate to reject President Hoover's nomination of Judge John J. Parker to the Supreme Court.

In 1938 the NAACP won its first big desegregation case. By a seven to two vote, the Supreme Court ruled that a Missouri law prohibiting blacks from attending the University of Missouri Law School was unconstitutional because there was no other public law school for blacks in the state and because the alternative—a state scholarship to study at a nearby school of the student's choosing outside the state—simply could not be construed as an equal facility. The other law schools would not have taught Missouri law and the student would suffer from great handicaps in trying to practice law in his own state.

Measured by need, the case was a relatively small advance. Still it was a step forward because it straddled two doctrines. Looking like a separate-but-equal case, none of which had ever been struck down before, it managed to latch on to the property and voting cases, in which the Court had been willing to declare the absence of an acceptable, equal alternative. Missouri's response was to set up a separate law school at an existing black institution, Lincoln University.

Turning the Court Around: The Second Mr. Marshall

The following year, in 1939, the NAACP formed a separate unit, the Legal Defense and Education Fund (still active today). It appointed Thurgood Marshall as its general counsel. Marshall had studied law at Howard University under that school's dean, Charles Houston, the guiding spirit of the NAACP's earlier legal efforts. Now the fund began a series of specific, well-planned assaults on a variety of discriminatory laws—in voting, property, transportation, and education.

During the 1940s there was a slow but perceptible change in attitude by the federal government toward the plight of the black. Though by any modern standard, President Roosevelt's actions toward blacks were exceedingly modest, he did not shy away from appointing blacks to a wide variety of lower echelon federal posts, and he abolished racial segregation in federal offices in Washington. During the war years, black migration to major Northern cities that had begun in the depths of the Depression stepped up, as war production jobs in factories beckoned. The blacks would increasingly become a political force to be reckoned with. World War II itself, moreover, forced a change in attitude on the part of many. How could the United States fight a war against fanatic racists and continue on its own peculiar, racist course?

Ten years after the Missouri school case, the careful planning of Marshall and his staff paid off handsomely in one of the most adroit Supreme Court opinions ever devised. In *Shelley* v. *Kraemer*, the Court felled with a single blow the widespread custom of placing racial covenants on land so that blacks could not buy or rent property and houses so encumbered. The opinion was adroit because it did not declare the racial covenant itself void. A covenant, after all, was a private act and by the *Civil Rights Cases* could not be touched. But if a seller violated the covenant and actually sold to a black, then angry neighbors would have to take the greedy and uncaring white homeowner to court to enforce the covenant. Otherwise they could not keep the black family out of their neighborhood. Then a *court* would have to enforce the covenant. If it did so, it would be acting as an agent of the state to prevent a black from buying what a white could buy. And this *was* a discrimination that the Fourteenth Amendment touched—and voided.

You could enter into a private covenant thereafter. You just couldn't enforce it. For a unanimous Court (though three justices did not participate), Chief Justice Vinson in response to the argument that the law was valid because the state courts would equally enforce any covenant excluding whites, said significantly: "The rights established [by the Fourteenth Amendment] are personal rights. It is, therefore, no answer to these [black] petitioners to say that the courts may also be induced to deny white persons' rights of ownership and occupancy on grounds of race or color. Equal protection of the laws is not achieved through indiscriminate imposition of inequalities."

Now the stage was set for a direct assault against the notion of separate-but-equal. Adopting the strategy that in seeking to destroy the edifice of segregation, it was best to weaken it in strategic places rather than try to blast through it at once, the NAACP Fund chose to concentrate on the lack of equality in professional education. A case based on this theory had already been won. Moreover, the states were more likely to bow to Supreme court reversals of separate-but-equal in professional education than in other schools.

Two years later, in 1950, Marshall succeeded in visibly cracking the separate-but-equal facade. A black Houston mail carrier sought entrance to the University of Texas law school. His lawsuit in the state courts resulted in an order to the state to conjure up a law school for blacks. This, of course, was unacceptable because the school was hopelessly inadequate. Marshall paraded a stimulating array of eminent witnesses who testified to the poverty of the curriculum, faculty, and educational atmosphere of the new, black school. But the Texas Supreme Court, citing the evidence Marshall amassed as irrelevant, denied admission to his client. The case went up to the Supreme Court, which reversed the Texas courts and ordered the black admitted to the all-white law school.

Pointing to those "qualities which are incapable of objective measurement but which make for greatness in a law school," Chief Justice Fred Vinson derided the state's position that the two schools were equal. How could the "reputation of the faculty, experience of the administration, position and influence of the alumni, standing in the community, tradition and prestige" of the new school ever hope to compare to that of the established University? "The law school to which Texas is willing to admit [the plaintiff Sweatt]," Vinson wrote, "excludes from its student body members of the racial groups which number 85 percent of the population of the State and include most of the lawyers, witnesses, jurors, judges, and other officials with whom [he] will inevitably be dealing when he becomes a member of the Texas Bar. With such a substantial and significant segment of society excluded, we cannot conclude that the education offered [Sweatt] is substantially equal to that which he would receive if admitted to the University of Texas Law School."

On that same say, the court ruled that if a state chose not to establish a substantially equal school for blacks, it could not segregate them within the white school. The School of Education at the University of Oklahoma roped off its only black student from the white student body in class, in the library, in the dining room, and other places. The Court declared that here, too, there was no equality.

These cases said nothing about the lot of the ordinary black school child, but they were the catalysts for cases that would. Beyond their importance in foreshadowing the sentiment of the Supreme Court, they served to spur a change in strategy in cases that were pending or would soon be pending in a number of public school districts in the South.

The Direct Approach

In 1948 the parents of several black school children, including Harry Briggs, Jr., filed suit in Clarendon County, South Carolina, to obtain school buses, which were generally available to whites. The suit was brought before U.S. District Judge J. Waties Waring, a former white supremacist whose eyes were opened after President Roosevelt appointed him to the bench in 1942. Two rulings favoring blacks in an equal-pay-for-teachers case and a voting rights case made the parents think that they might succeed. Two years later, they sought to broaden their suit. They demanded that the per capita expenditure of funds be proportionately equal for blacks and whites. (With three-quarters of the student population in the county, the blacks received only 41 percent of the funds.)

When the Supreme Court announced its decisions, in June 1950, Marshall's Legal Defense Fund began to think out a broader strategy than they had theretofore been following. In September the NAACP held a national conference in New York to plan its next moves, and decided to push a series of carefully chosen lawsuits in different parts of the country up to the Supreme Court. This time the argument would be that segregation in the public schools—any public schools—was unconstitutional on its face.

Marshall himself was representing the plaintiffs in the *Briggs* case in South Carolina. And now he added another suit to the one for equalization of public expenditures. The new suit contended that there could be no separate schools. This course had been urged by Judge Waring.

This was in November 1950. Marshall's move led the governor-elect, James F. Byrnes, to prepare a legislative program to meet the challenge. A former member of the Supreme Court (for sixteen months in 1941-42), Byrnes called at his inaugural in January for a crash building program of superior schools for blacks to remedy "a hundred years of neglect," and he urged the legislature to act before the courts "take matters out of the state's hands." Byrnes was an ardent segregationist, and he was determined to meet the constitutional argument as he understood it. The schools must be made equal—that much was clearly mandated by *Plessy* v. *Ferguson* and its progeny. And if they could be made equal, they could stand separately.

In June of 1951, a three-judge federal district court, convened to test the constitutionality of the Clarendon County school system, ruled that the facilities were indeed unequal. But, said Circuit Judge John J. Parker (whose nomination to the Supreme Court the NAACP had helped defeat twenty-one years before), the system of racial segregation of itself was not unlawful. The schools were given a reasonable time to make progress toward equalization. Judge Waring dissented, stating passionately his belief that the time had come to strike down the pernicious doctrine of separate-but-equal. Marshall appealed to the Supreme Court.

Clarendon school officials rushed to catch up. To be sure that the doctrine would withstand the constitutional test, Byrnes traveled to New York to retain John W. Davis, one of Wall Street's most eminent lawyers. Davis was regarded by some, Byrnes among them, as the most able constitutional lawyer of the day. A Southerner and a believer in segregation, Davis had had a distinguished career at the bar and in public life. He had been a congressman, solicitor general, ambassador to the Court of St. James, Democratic presidential candidate in 1924, and an advocate who "made more oral arguments in the Supreme Court than any lawyer since the age of Daniel Webster" (140 cases between 1913 and 1954).

Nine months after first talking to Byrnes, Davis argued his greatest case. He succeeded in convincing the Supreme Court that President Truman had unlawfully seized the mills of the major steel companies. That case came up suddenly, following the steelworkers' strike in the spring of 1952. In the meantime, Davis studied the lower court decisions, and he was convinced that he would win the *Briggs* case. There simply could be no question. The precedents were on all fours and had never been shaken.

The other cases were also making their way through the judicial process. In Prince Edward County, Virginia, the NAACP sued in the name of black high school children. The three-judge federal court decided against them on the same grounds as the South

Opposite page:

The children themselves: Sometimes the least disturbed by the passions of the time.

H. Armstrong Roberts

Carolina court. However, it did order the schools to proceed with an equalization program.

In New Castle County, Delaware, suits were filed on behalf of both elementary and high school children. Unlike the other cases, the Delaware courts held for the plaintiffs. They declared the segregation illegal and ordered the immediate placement of all black children in the regular schools. In the District of Columbia (chosen because it is not a state but governed by Congress), the federal district court dismissed the complaint.

And in Topeka, Kansas, a suit filed on behalf of Oliver Brown and others sought to enjoin enforcement of a state law that permitted, but did not require, cities of 15,000 residents or more to maintain separate schools. Topeka elected to segregate its elementary schools only. The three-judge federal court there ruled that although segregation harmed the black elementary school children, it could grant no relief because the "buildings, transportation, curricula, and educational qualifications of teachers" were all substantially equal.

On December 9, 1952, the Supreme Court heard oral argument on all five cases. Though this was clearly to be Marshall's and Davis's show, the first lawyer to argue was Robert L. Carter for the Topeka schoolchildren. Paul E. Wilson, assistant attorney general of Kansas, who had gone over the cases with Davis and other attorneys, followed up for the defense. Then Marshall arose to argue the *Briggs* case. He hammered away at the central point: segregation caused "actual injury" to the school children and was condemned by the Fourteenth Amendment. Davis followed, mocking

the sociological brief that the NAACP had submitted. To Marshall's plea that segregation hurt, Davis essentially replied that nevertheless it was not forbidden by the federal constitution for states to ordain it. The contention that maintaining segregation would work a vast injustice was thus met by the fervently held proposition that upsetting a national policy of a century's standing would be no less unjust.

One of the major points in the argument was that Congress at the very time the Fourteenth Amendment was drafted took no

Below:

Lined up outside the Supreme Court in session in Washington during the case challenging segregation in public schools. Only 50 could be seated.

UPI

steps to integrate the District of Columbia schools (since 1896 this point had been brought up repeatedly). If the framers themselves saw no inconsistency between the amendment and school segregation, it should not be discovered by the Court more than three-quarters of a century later. At the justices' conference a few days following the arguments, Chief Justice Vinson reviewed this fact in his discussion on the case. At that time, five justices, a majority, were inclined to uphold segregation. But a few months later, one or two justices changed their minds, and the question then was whether still others could be persuaded to do likewise.

The Court thereupon called for a reargument. The justices asked the litigants to focus on five questions. First, what historical evidence was there that the amendments' framers "contemplated or did not contemplate, understood or did not understand, that it would abolish segregation in public schools?" Second, if there was no evidence either way, was it possible to conclude that the framers

Some 2,000 white high school students in Baltimore, Maryland march against racial integration.

UPI

intended to give power to Congress to abolish segregation in the future? Or, third, did they intend to give that power to courts in the future? Fourth, in the absence of evidence bearing on these questions, were the courts nevertheless vested with the power "to abolish segregation in the public schools?" Fifth, if the courts did have such power and chose to exercise it, were they required to abolish segregation instantaneously or could they permit the change gradually?

The various litigants now got busy. Several members of Davis's law firm were assigned to do historical research on the drafting of the amendment. They concluded that the evidence was sufficient to show that the framers had not intended to use the amendment to abolish segregation in the schools.

At first the NAACP researchers also came up with this conclusion. Marshall called a conference of leading academicians—lawyers and historians—who were assigned to a variety of task forces to search the records. The evidence initially seemed against them. The Civil Rights Act of 1866, which had sparked the Fourteenth Amendment, had been specifically amended in Congress to permit segregation in the schools. The first drafts of the task force on this question put the matter in general terms. But Marshall rejected it. "I gotta argue these cases," he is quoted as saying, "and if I try this approach those fellows will shoot me down in flames." They would have to meet the questions squarely and present at least a plausible explanation for believing the historical evidence did not destroy their case. They did not have to win the argument, but they could not lose it by default. "A nothin' to nothin' score means we win the ball game," he said.

The argument eventually boiled down to one proposition. While it was impossible to tell what was in the minds of all those who actually voted for the Fourteenth Amendment, it was clear that the purpose of those who drew it up was to make the Negro a citizen in every sense of the word.

This conclusion was buttressed by the government's brief, prepared under the direction of Attorney General Herbert Brownell. It said that no enlightenment could be found in the historical debates or records in 1868 as to the specific intent of the framers on the precise question at issue. "But," said the brief, "the framers in Congress did understand that the Amendment established the broad constitutional principle of full and complete equality of all persons under the law, and that it forbade all legal distinctions based on race or color."

During the NAACP's first strategy sessions, Chief Justice Vinson suddenly died. Within weeks, Earl Warren was the new chief justice.

On December 7, 1953, the reargument got underway. Marshall and Davis were again the stars, although many attorneys participated in the five hours of debate spread over three days' time. The question was not one of states' rights, Marshall said. The real question was whether a white majority would persuade the Court that "the people who were formerly in slavery . . . shall be kept as near that stage as possible. Now is the time . . . that this court should make it clear that that is not what our Constitution stands for."

Davis laced into the NAACP brief with scorn and derision. The question at issue was not what sociologists thought. The question was what the law was, and there simply could be no doubt of the historical record. The principle of *Plessy* was reasonable when rendered and reasonable still, even if the Court was not bound by its precedent, which, Davis thought, it was. "Somewhere, sometime," he said, "to every principle comes a moment of repose when it has been so often announced, so confidently relied upon, so long continued, that it passes the limits of judicial discretion and disturbance."

Presenting the United States argument as *amicus curiae,* Solicitor General J. Lee Rankin was asked whether the Court could decide the case "either way." Rankin responded that the Court "properly could find only one answer."

The Ticking Clock

Then Marshall, Davis, segregated school systems, the South, and the nation waited. The Court was silent from December to mid-May. Behind closed doors, however, there were numerous discussions as to the best means of presenting the opinion voiding segregation in schools. By now the Court's answer was inevitable, as it had been since the previous spring.

The remaining question was how many would join it, and how it would be phrased. Warren was determined that the Court's decision be unanimous if at all possible. To achieve that end, he drafted a short opinion, discarding the historical argument, largely eschewing legal analysis, and most importantly, not committing the Court to any particular form or timing on the all-important question of relief. Five days before the decision was announced, on May 17,

1954, Justice Frankfurter, the last to resist, announced his concurrence. According to an entry Justice Harold H. Burton made in his diary, the unanimous opinion was a "major accomplishment for [Warren's] leadership."

In contrast to the lengthy opinions, concurrences, and dissents that usually attend major doctrinal changes, Chief Justice Warren's ten-page opinion was short and stark and stood alone. No one concurred separately and no one dissented. He dismissed the historical argument as "at best . . . inconclusive." This was, he said, not due merely to the difficulty of knowing what congressmen and state legislators had in mind in 1868. It was due also to "the status of public education at that time." Public education did not play the role a century ago simply because there were so few public schools in the South. Thus the issue of segregation of schools was largely ignored in the debates over the amendment.

Warren reviewed the cases involving school segregation. In a matter-of-fact style he noted that in none of them had the question of the validity of separate-but-equal education been directly presented. It had been assumed in some, but not argued. Now, however, it had been presented. The findings in some of the lower courts that the separate school systems were equal or were being equalized meant that, instead, the Court had to consider the tangible effect of segregation itself on public education.

In approaching this problem, we cannot turn the clock back to 1868 when the Amendment was adopted, or even to 1896 when Plessy v. Ferguson was written. We must consider public education in the light of its full development and its present place in American life throughout the Nation. Only in this way can it be determined if segregation in public schools deprives these plaintiffs of the equal protection of the laws.

Today, education is perhaps the most important function of state and local governments. Compulsory school attendance laws and the great expenditures for education both demonstrate our recognition of the importance of education to our democratic society. It is required in the performance of our most basic public responsibilities, even service in the armed forces. It is the very foundation of good citizenship. Today it is a principal instrument in awakening the child to cultural values, in preparing him for later professional training, and in helping him to adjust normally to his environment. In these days, it is doubtful that any child may reasonably be expected to succeed in life if he is denied the opportunity of an education. Such an opportunity, where the state has undertaken to provide it, is a right which must be made available to all on equal terms.

These paragraphs set forth the essential premise on which the

Court's conclusion is based. They are also a fair sample of the style of the opinion: simple, straightforward, unemotional, and free of legal citation.

Then, in three comparatively brief paragraphs, Warren came to the point: "We conclude," he wrote, "that in the field of public education the doctrine of 'separate but equal' has no place. Separate educational facilities are inherently unequal." Why? Because "to separate [elementary and high school children] from others of similar age and qualifications solely because of their race generates a feeling of inferiority as to their status in the community that may affect their hearts and minds in a way unlikely ever to be undone. . . . Whatever may have been the extent of psychological knowledge at the time of *Plessy* v. *Ferguson,* this finding is amply supported by modern authority."

At this point, the chief justice cited a series of contemporary studies on the psychological effects of discrimination. This passage led James Reston to report in the *New York Times* the next day: "The court's opinion read more like an expert paper on sociology than a Supreme Court opinion. It sustained the argument of experts in education, sociology, psychology, psychiatry and anthropology."

The discussion of psychological and other evidence led to an uproar that has not quieted in some circles to this day. But the argument that the Court overstepped its writ misses the mark. The Court was seeking a way of showing concretely the appalling tragedy that the spurious separate-but-equal doctrine had created. It need not have leaned so hard on this evidence—the degree of its reliance seems great only in light of the virtual absence of other authority cited in the opinion—for it could, from an analytic point of view, have rested its entire case on the proposition that the first Justice Harlan had announced fifty-eight years before: the Constitution is color-blind. In and of itself separating blacks and whites is a denial of equal protection entirely apart from the harm that it may be thought to cause.

Warren concluded with the brief announcement—the heart of the compromise—that "because of the wide applicability of this decision, and because of the great variety of local conditions, the formulation of decrees in these cases presents problems of considerable complexity." There would need to be further argument on the scope of the relief that the Court would grant to the affected schoolchildren. It was done.

In a companion case decided the same day, the Court ruled that the conclusion that segregation in schools was unconstitutional applied as well to the District of Columbia even though as a federal territory it was not governed by the Equal Protection Clause, which applies only to the states. The Court, again through Warren, said that the discrimination in this case was barred by the Fifth Amendment Due Process Clause. "Liberty under law extends to the full range of conduct which the individual is free to pursue, and it cannot be restricted except for a proper governmental objective," and segregation in public schools was not such an objective. "In view of our decision that the Constitution prohibits the states from maintaining racially segregated public schools, it would be unthinkable that the same Constitution would impose a lesser duty on the Federal Government."

But if the legal conclusion was final, the real problem had only begun. The day after the decision was announced, the New York

Thurgood Marshall, special counsel for the N.A.A.C.P., flanked by attorneys George E. C. Hays and James Nabrit, Jr., following the Supreme Court's ruling in their favor in Brown v. Board of Education.

UPI

Times printed a survey of educational leaders:

They did not believe there would be great difficulty in putting the ruling into effect. They did not think that the threats to abandon the public school system would be carried out. Several Southern educators, however, foresaw some difficulty in an immediate application of the antisegregation policy. They felt that time would be needed to bring about the historic change from all-white to mixed public schools. But they did not believe that the long-range program could be thwarted for any considerable period. . . . No one expected any violence nor any real crisis to develop.

Rarely has a prediction of social change been less prescient, proving only that educators are not experts when it comes to politics. The warnings were sounded soon after the Court recessed for the day. Mississippi Senator James O. Eastland said the South "will not abide by nor obey this legislative decision by a political court." Georgia Attorney General Eugene Cook said he would refuse to participate in the Court proceedings the coming year that would decide on the timetable for integration. To do so, he said, would "morally obligate" the state to comply with whatever order was issued. His boss, Governor Herman Talmadge, wasn't ready to concede Cook's point, but he was sure that "the only thing that remains for [the Supreme Court justices] to determine is whether to cut off our heads with a sharp knife or a dull one."

Another warning of things to come was Alabama state representative Sam Engelhardt's declaration that "we are going to keep every brick in our segregation wall intact." Alabama Superintendent of Schools W. J. Terry pointedly noted that Alabama had not been involved in any of the suits involved in the *Brown* decision and that the state would not begin to act until a court told it to do so.

The major domestic problem of the second half of the twentieth century had just begun. The educators who saw few real problems with compliance did not sense what the politicians knew instinctively. This was only the beginning of the effort that would cause racial barriers to tumble in every aspect of life. This would be too radical a change for the South to accept meekly, without protest.

In a brief opinion the following year, the Court announced its delphic remedy. The lower courts must come up with plans that will carry out the admission of the parties to public schools "on a racially nondiscriminatory basis with all deliberate speed." This set the stage for an enormous outpouring of litigation that continues to this day. For a time the uproar even brought talk of "nullification" that had not been heard since 1860.

Brown v. *Board of Education* was the beginning of a struggle for a multiracial democratic society. It ultimately would involve every branch of government, federal and state, to cope with its implications. As more and more racial barriers fell, through the rulings in additional Supreme Court cases, Congress felt the heat and took increasingly tougher positions in the Civil Rights Acts of 1957, 1960, 1964, and 1968, and the Voting Rights Act of 1965. Decisions upholding these acts gradually overturned all the old post-Civil War cases, including, largely in substance (though not in theory) the *Civil Rights Cases* of 1883.

The president, too, became increasingly involved and committed to the civil rights struggle, especially as one administration succeeded the next. Massive resistance, closing of schools, state support for private, segregated academies, and numerous other delaying tactics finally resulted in a Supreme Court repudiation of the "all deliberate speed" requirement: "The obligation of every school district is to terminate dual school systems at once." A generation later, the struggle continues.

For Davis, however, the fight was over. He "was so shattered by what he considered to be the sociological cast of the opinion that one of his partners was later to say that the decision had killed him. . . . Three days passed before he felt up to dictating a letter. Yet, in a sheer act of will, he congratulated Marshall over the telephone on the afternoon of the ruling." Davis died in 1955.

Several of the NAACP lawyers moved on to other posts. Spottswood W. Robinson III and Constance Baker Motley have become federal judges. For Thurgood Marshall, the victorious strategist of the black constitutional revolution and architect of *Brown* v. *Board of Education,* there was to be a special reward. He was appointed to the U.S. Court of Appeals in New York by President Kennedy in 1961 and, three years later, was named solicitor general, the United States' chief attorney before the Supreme Court. He was the first black to hold that position. In 1967, President Johnson decided to integrate the Supreme Court itself, and Thurgood Marshall, who had been refused admission to the University of Maryland Law School in 1929, became the ninety-sixth justice of the Supreme Court, on which he still sits.

14/ THE PRIVACY OF ONE'S HOME: MAPP v. OHIO

Around one-thirty on the afternoon of May 23, 1957, three policemen in squad cars pulled up in front of a house in a residential section of Cleveland bordering Shaker Heights. This was the home of twenty-eight-year-old Dollree Mapp. They knocked on the door and demanded that Mapp, who talked to them from the second-floor window, let them in. They said they wished to question her. But they refused to be more specific. Mapp replied that she would have to consult her attorney, whom she had retained earlier in connection with an unrelated matter. He was in court at that very moment, so she talked instead to his younger associate, Walter L. Greene, who told her not to let the police in without a search warrant.

In giving this advice, he was following common sense rather than any personal knowledge of this branch of the law. "If I had known the way the law worked," Greene later recalled with a chuckle, "I might have told her that she might as well open up the door." The law, as it stood then, entitled the police to seize any evidence of a crime they might have found. They could use this evidence at a later trial even if they broke in without a search warrant. They could use that evidence against her even if they just wanted to talk to her and found it by accident. If Greene had known this, he might have advised her to let the police quietly go about their business. And if Mapp had agreed, there would have been no questions raised about search warrants and unlawful entry, and the course of constitutional history might have been different.

At any rate, Mapp told the policemen that she would not open up the door unless they showed her a proper search warrant. The police temporarily desisted, though they maintained a watch in front of her home. For two and one-half hours they waited, and a crowd of neighbors began to gather, watching with them. Finally, about four o'clock, at least four more policemen arrived, and a few minutes later Greene, too.

One of the policemen claimed that he now had a proper warrant, but he refused to show it to Greene. Instead, the police went around the back of the house and tried to kick in the door. Failing to budge it, one of the officers broke the glass and reached inside to open it.

The house was a two-family dwelling, and Mapp lived on the second floor in a two-bedroom apartment with her daughter. Racing in, the police found her on the stairway. Greene tried to follow, but one of the men yelled "keep that man out," and his way was barred. Racing in to the hallway, the police found Mapp on the stairway. She demanded to see the search warrant, and one of the policemen held up a piece of paper, which he claimed was the document she requested. She grabbed it and stuffed it into her dress. There was a scuffle, and Greene distinctly heard Mapp call out, "get your hand out of my dress."

Having liberated the alleged warrant, the police now handcuffed Mapp to one of the officers. She was forced to sit on her bed with him, while the other officers proceeded to ransack the house. They searched through her dresser, a chest of drawers, a closet, some suitcases in her own room, and through the rest of the rooms in the apartment she lived in. Then they searched the rest of the house and found a large trunk in the basement. During the course of the search, the police came across "four little pamphlets, a couple of photographs, and a little pencil doodle," which no one denied were "lewd and lascivious" under Ohio law. For possession of these materials, Mapp was convicted under a statute making knowing possession of pornography a criminal offense. She was given an indeterminate sentence of up to seven years at the Ohio Reformatory for Women.

The "Issue"

These remarkable goings-on were not inspired by any smut crusade. The police were not zealously swooping down on pornographic dens throughout the city of Cleveland. They went to Mapp's home, they said at her trial, because they had information that "a person [was] hiding out in the home, who was wanted for questioning in connection with a recent bombing." They also said there was information that "there was a large amount of policy paraphernalia being hidden in the home." It was simply a lucky accident that they happened on to evidence of an entirely different crime.

Whether the police really did have such information is impossible to say, though the police produced nothing at the trial to justify their claims. Still, it was barely possible that they did at least have a reason for believing that Mapp was harboring a fugitive. She was known to be friendly with a racketeer who was indeed suspected of having participated in the bombing of a home. (Several years later the fugitive was himself blown up in another bombing.)

On the other hand, Mapp's associations may have provided the police with a motive for wanting to harass her. She had recently pleaded the Fifth Amendment in official proceedings connected with an investigation into her friend's activities, and the bombing incident may simply have given the police an excuse to get back at her. In any event, there was no fugitive in Mapp's home that spring day, and the police did not find any "policy paraphernalia" whatsoever.

On appeal before the Ohio Supreme Court, Mapp pleaded two defenses. The most important one, it seemed, was a claim that the Ohio obscenity law was unconstitutional. At the trial she had offered evidence, not contradicted by the police, that the books and pictures belonged to a former boarder in her home, a man who left suddenly without packing. Deciding to take over his room for herself, she said she packed up his belongings and discovered the books and pictures at that time. These she put into a cardboard box that she placed in the basement and into a suitcase that she stored in her room. The only conflict relating to these events at the trial was the location in which the police found the contraband; their testimony was to the effect that some of the material was found in her dresser, not in the box in the basement.

This conflict seemed to have some importance, because the Ohio obscenity law made it a crime for anyone to have "knowingly . . . in his possession or under his control an obscene, lewd, or lascivious book . . . print, [or] picture." Mapp sought to show that the pictures and books were not really hers, that she did not look again and had no intention of ever looking at them again. She was "merely keeping them pending instructions for their disposition from their owner."

Under a strict interpretation of the law, however, even if all this were true she would still be guilty. When she was cleaning up after her boarder and came across the forbidden articles, she "necessarily learned of their lewd and lascivious character." From that instant in time she had "in" her "possession" and "under" her "control" pictures and books that she knew to be obscene. This was all that the law required.

But if the law could punish her for such a "possession," when she clearly had no intention of selling or exhibiting the pictures, then it must be unconstitutional. Otherwise it would be a serious infringement on the First Amendment rights of Ohio residents. If a person could be put in jail for up to seven years because he had on his library shelf or in his bookstore a book that a jury or judge might someday declare to be obscene, then the law "may discourage law abiding people from even looking at books and pictures and thus interfere with the freedom of speech and press" guaranteed by the First Amendment.

Interestingly, a majority of the judges of the Ohio Supreme Court agreed that the law did have this meaning and that it was therefore unconstitutional. But they did not reverse her conviction because under a peculiar provision in the Ohio Constitution, a state law cannot be held unconstitutional unless all the judges but one (in this case six of seven) agree that it is. But Mapp was able to persuade only four of the seven judges. So her conviction stood.

Sleeper

The other ground on which Mapp's attorneys argued for her freedom was the illegality of the search. She seemed to be on strong factual ground. There was little reason to believe that the police had ever procured a search warrant. As the Ohio Supreme Court put it, "No warrant was offered in evidence, there was no testimony as to who issued any warrant or as to what any warrant contained, and the absence from evidence of any such warrant is not explained or otherwise accounted for in the record. There is nothing in the record tending to prove or from which an inference may be drawn, and no one has even suggested [,] that any warrant that we may assume that there may have been described anything other than policy paraphernalia as things to be searched for." In other words, there probably was no search warrant, and even if there was, it said nothing about obscene materials.

Now under the constitution and laws of Ohio, the police are forbidden from searching through a home in a case such as this without first following prescribed procedures to obtain a warrant "particularly describing the place to be searched . . . and things to be seized." These procedures were not followed, so the state supreme court ruled, the search of Mapp's home and the seizure of the books and pictures were unlawful.

But that was not enough to reverse Mapp's conviction. Notwithstanding the constitutional requirement, said the court, there was nothing to prevent the unlawfully seized evidence from being introduced at trial. The result was that the police were entitled to break the law. Nothing could be done about it. The constitutional provision that was supposed to protect people in the privacy of their homes was a dead letter, even though the United States Supreme Court had ruled in 1949 that police conduct such as occurred in Mapp's case violated the federal constitution as well.

Mapp, through her attorneys, now appealed to that Court. They did not expect to prevail on the question of the search warrant, because in the 1949 case, the Supreme Court itself refused to rule out unlawfully seized evidence. Her attorneys hoped, instead, to persuade at least a majority of the justices (who, of course, were not bound by the quirk in the Ohio Constitution concerning the number of justices necessary to void a statute) to reverse her conviction on the ground that the obscenity law violated the First Amendment.

But the Court never reached that issue. In 1961, it tackled the search-warrant question directly. It overruled its prior decision and, for the first time, extended the so-called "exclusionary rule" (long applicable in federal courts) to govern state trials as well. This

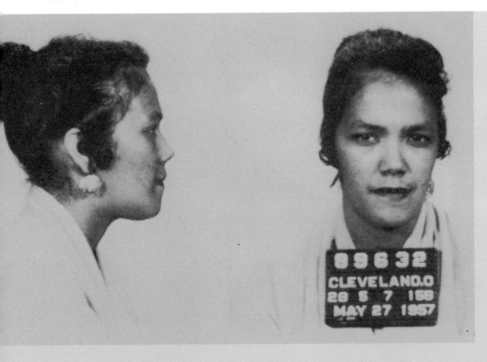

Dollree Mapp.

Wide World Photos

was the beginning of the "due process revolution" in criminal cases that by the end of the decade and the close of the Warren Court swept most of the Bill of Rights, through the Fourteenth Amendment, into the states.

The Decision in Perspective

To understand the significance of the decision, it is necessary to back up to 1914. In that year the Supreme Court decided a case concerning the federal crime of mailing lottery tickets. A United States marshal, without a search warrant, had seized papers from the home of a man named Weeks. He turned these papers over to the prosecutor, who used them in the trial that ended in Weeks's conviction. The Court reversed the conviction on the ground that a warrantless search violates the Fourth Amendment, which reads as follows:

The right of the people to be secure in their persons, houses, papers, and effects, against unreasonable searches and seizures, shall not be violated, and no Warrants shall issue, but upon probable cause, supported by Oath or affirmation, and particularly describing the place to be searched, and the person or things to be seized.

In *Weeks* v. *United States*, the Court said:

If letters and private documents can thus be seized and held and used in evidence against the citizen accused of an offense, the protection of the Fourth Amendment, declaring his right to be secure against such searches and seizures, is of no value, and, so far as those thus placed are concerned, might as well be stricken from the Constitution. The efforts of the courts and their officials to bring the guilty to punishment, praiseworthy as they are, are not to be aided by the sacrifice of those great principles established by years of endeavor and suffering which have resulted in their embodiment in the fundamental law of the land. The United States marshal could only have invaded the house of the accused when armed with a warrant issued as required by the Constitution, upon sworn information, and describing with reasonable particularity the thing for which the search was to be made. Instead, he acted without sanction of law, doubtless prompted by the desire to bring further proof to the aid of the government, and under color of his office undertook to make a seizure of private papers in direct violation of the Constitutional prohibition against such action. Under such circumstances, without sworn information and particular description, not even an order of court would have justified such procedure; much less was it within the authority of the United States marshal to thus invade the house and privacy of the accused.

This was not a mere ruling on the law of evidence that

Congress could reverse if it chose to do so. The Court was not declaring that federal courts should not use tainted evidence because it thought this was bad judicial policy. It was saying that it had no choice under the Constitution. But this ruling did not apply to evidence unlawfully seized by state officials, not even if they proceeded to turn it over to federal authorities (as actually happened in Weeks's case).

State courts could, of course, construe their own constitutions in the same way. Ohio and many other states had the equivalent of the Fourth Amendment (and sometimes an exact copy of it) in their constitutions. But state courts generally refused to do so. They held, with Justice Cardozo, when he was chief judge of the New York Court of Appeals, that the exclusionary doctrine means "the criminal is to go free because the constable has blundered."

In 1949, the Supreme Court took another look at the issue. A Colorado physician named Wolf had been convicted of conspiracy to commit abortions. The conviction rested on the strength of evidence seized by state officials who did not comply with Fourth Amendment requirements. The Court ruled that "the security of one's privacy against arbitrary intrusion by the police" is the "core of the Fourth Amendment," and that a failure of state officials to follow the same rules required of federal officials was a violation of the Constitution.

The Court refused, however, to apply the federal exclusionary rule. Evidence unlawfully seized by state authorities could continue to be used in state trials. Noting that nearly two-thirds of the states opposed the exclusionary rule, the Court said it could not "brush aside the experience of States which deem the incidence of such conduct by the police too slight to call for a deterrent remedy."

Twelve years later, in 1961, the Court was ready to reassess this conclusion. It noted first that two-thirds of the states were no longer opposed to the exclusionary rule. More than half of the states which considered the matter in the interval had adopted the *Weeks* rule. It also noted that other means of preventing unlawful police conduct "have been worthless and futile." Less than half the states had any laws imposing criminal penalties on police or other officials who acted as those in Mapp's case had. Moreover, in all states it was particularly difficult and in many impossible to bring a civil suit against state authorities for violations of privacy.

A Problem of "Shortcuts"

In the years since 1949, the Court had made several inroads on abuses relating to the exclusionary rule. In many instances federal officials dodged the exclusionary rule. If they had evidence that could not be used in federal courts, they would turn it over where appropriate to state prosecutors. And state police who unlawfully seized evidence would hand it over, in turn, to federal prosecutors, who felt no compunctions about using it. In 1956 and 1960 the Court blocked these shortcuts around the Fourth Amendment. The purpose of the exclusionary rule, the Court stated, "is to deter—to compel respect for the constitutional guaranty in the only effectively available way—by removing the incentive to disregard it." To do other than prevent the states from putting such evidence to use "is to grant the right but in reality to withhold its privilege and enjoyment."

Referring to the possibility that some criminals would go free as a result, the Court agreed that "in some cases this will undoubtedly be the result. . . . The criminal goes free, if he must, but it is the law that sets him free. Nothing can destroy a government more quickly than its failure to observe its own laws, or worse, its disregard of the charter of its own existence." And the Court referred to the prescient dissent of Justice Brandeis in a 1928 case. The Court held that the Fourth Amendment does not prevent the government from wiretapping even in the absence of a warrant (a case since overruled). Brandeis said: "In a government of laws, the existence of the government will be imperilled if it fails to observe the law scrupulously. Our government is the potent, the omnipresent, teacher. For good or ill, it teaches the whole people by its example. Crime is contagious. If the government becomes a lawbreaker, it breeds contempt for law; it invites every man to become a law unto himself; it invites anarchy."

In a concurring opinion, Justice Black announced that he had changed his own views concerning the application of the Fourth Amendment exclusionary rule to the states. His original understanding he said, was that the rule was merely a judicial rule. It applied to federal courts, but Congress could negate it. This followed, he said, from the absence of any language in the Fourth Amendment calling for exclusion of evidence discovered by means that violated the amendment's command. But, he continued, considering the "close interrelationship" between the Fourth Amendment and the Fifth Amendment's proscription against self-incrimination, unlawfully seized evidence should be excluded. He concluded in agreement with the words of an earlier Court that declared itself "unable to perceive that the seizure of a man's private books and papers to be used in evidence against him is substantially different from compelling him to be a witness against himself."

Justices Harlan, Frankfurter, and Whittaker dissented (and Justice Stewart concurred only because he thought the obscenity conviction violated the First Amendment). In the dissent, penned by Justice Harlan, the controversy over the due process revolution began. Harlan accused the majority of simply reaching out to overrule the *Wolf* case and of overlooking entirely the major thrust of the case before the Ohio courts, in the briefs and in the argument before the Supreme Court itself—namely, the First Amendment issue. Indeed, Mapp's attorneys did not even cite the *Wolf* case in their brief, and no one supposed beforehand that *Mapp* v. *Ohio* would become a great Fourth Amendment case (any more than anyone could have predicted *Erie Railroad* v. *Tompkins* would have overturned the century-old *Swift* v. *Tyson*). Harlan would have preferred to answer the First Amendment question, "both simpler and less far-reaching than the question which the Court decided today" (indicating, of course, that a larger majority would have struck down the Ohio obscenity law).

Since a bare majority saw fit to overrule *Wolf*, however, Harlan vigorously disagreed at great length. His major premise is that the Due Process Clause of the Fourteenth Amendment does not automatically incorporate the Fourth Amendment in all its particulars. It requires, instead, that the courts inquire in any given case whether the police conduct was so raw as to violate norms of fundamental fairness. He did not say whether he thought the police had done so in Mapp's case, since he was intent on denying the validity of a rule that requires all evidence that violates federal standards to be barred from use in state trials.

He pointed to a great inconsistency that resulted from a ruling intended to overcome inconsistencies: the Court had only recently ruled that the self-incrimination provisions of the Fifth Amendment did not apply to the states. How, then, could Justice Black maintain that the result was constitutionally compelled by reading the Fourth and Fifth Amendments together?

Justice Harlan was correct, of course. There was a great inconsistency. But it could be removed by applying the Fifth Amendment to the states as well. The decision to do so, and the ensuing ramifications, reached five years after *Mapp*, would be the high-water mark of the due process revolution.

Mapp v. *Ohio*, along with the other cases to come, has been severely criticized as imposing burdensome and unfruitful handicaps on the police. The thrust of the criticism is not that the police should be permitted to get away with what they did in Cleveland in May 1957. Under *Mapp's* all-embracing rule, even the slightest technical violations of the extremely tricky and complicated rules governing the obtaining of search warrants would be enough to throw a case out of court against an obvious criminal.

Moreover, when the Court declares that official conduct intended to deter crime is unconstitutional, more than merely the individual defendant is affected. Society is bound to feel that it is being shorn of protection from the lawless and violent. This ruling differs from other kinds of cases in which the Court rules that a state law is unconstitutional (for instance, that it violates the First Amendment). Nor did the *Mapp* decision say that the defendant cannot be prosecuted for an act. When the Court throws out a law prohibiting the improper display of the flag because it violates the First Amendment, it is saying that that act is not a crime. But when the Court throws out a conviction for a narcotics offense because the police merely guessed that there were drugs in a person's apartment, it is not saying that there can be no prosecution of narcotics offenses. Technical niceties should not prevent society from acting effectively against crime.

These are forceful criticisms, but the answer to them is not necessarily a return to the pre-*Mapp* law. The answer is to rationalize the search and seizure rules. A discussion of the problems encountered in doing so is beyond the scope of this book. All that can be said here is that while the criticism has not died down, the *Mapp* case does not seem likely to be overruled, though some members of the present Supreme Court would like to see effective remedies against police abuse so that it can be. And there are signs that the Court may limit the application of the exclusionary rule to the more obvious cases only.

In spite of the criticisms, there is a more important point that should not be lost sight of. The Supreme Court cannot sit as a perpetual board of overseers of police conduct. Justice Harlan's rule, the majority concluded with considerable justification, would mean that the nine justices would have to hear all sorts of cases from lower courts. They would have to root out insensitivities to the requirements of fundamental fairness, as defined by the philosopher-kings who sit on the High Bench. This is an unworkable burden, both because of the number of cases that would be presented and because of the uncertainty in the law that such a "shock-the-conscience" test would create.

In view of the impossibility of hearing all putative, unreasonable search cases the police might be content simply to play the odds. Some of their convictions might be reversed, but most would stand up simply because the Supreme Court has other things to do than to monitor the methods of thousands of police departments and tens of thousands of convictions annually. A flat rule, while not eliminating controversy or even uncertainty, at least minimizes it.

The Court eventually got around to the other problem in Mapp's case as well. In 1969, it ruled that the private possession of books or pictures cannot be the basis of a criminal prosecution.

As for Dollree Mapp, the future was not so rosy. Around 1968 she moved from Cleveland to New York and appeared to continue her questionable conduct. In 1970 she was arrested by police in Queens County, Long Island, who, armed this time with a search warrant, said they found 50,000 envelopes of heroin valued at more than $150,000 and another $100,000 of stolen property. Charged as an operator of a major drug ring, she was eventually convicted of criminal possession of 18 ounces of heroin and in 1971 was sentenced to a term of from twenty years to life.

15/ ENDING ROTTEN BOROUGHS: BAKER v. CARR

I n his sixteen terms on the Supreme Court, Earl Warren participated in thousands of decisions. But of all these he singled out *Baker* v. *Carr* as the most important decided during during his tenure as Chief Justice. This was the initial legislative reapportionment case.

At first blush this must seem a curious claim, for it decided no substantive rights, ordered no legislatures to reapportion themselves, gave no ringing declaration of the right to vote. Its holding was simply that voters have the right to come to court to complain about malapportionment and that the courts cannot refuse to hear their case. Yet this concept, simple enough to state, required a fifty-page majority opinion and more than one hundred additional pages of concurrences and dissents. But its logic contained the seeds of the most remarkable and rapid restructuring of the nation's legislative bodies in history. It signaled the full arrival of urban America.

The problem had been building up for decades. Beginning late in the nineteenth century, massive waves of immigrants flooded into the cities. They joined the steady stream of farmers who were deserting the heartlands in search of industrial employment. The migration from farms to cities accelerated with the depressed economic conditions of the farms that began in the 1920s.

Beginning with World War II, the stream became a roaring flood. In 1939, there were some 31 million farmers, about one-quarter of all Americans. By war's end in 1945, the number of farmers had declined to 24.4 million or 17.5 percent of the total population. By 1959, when *Baker* v. *Carr* was filed in the United States District Court for the Middle District of Tennessee, rural population had declined still further to 16.5 million, which was then about 9 percent of the population. And in 1962, when the Supreme Court decided the case, farmers were down to 14 million, or some 7.7 percent of the American people.

The effect of this mass migration was to concentrate tens of millions of people into urban centers. Huge cities stood where before there had been only good-sized ones. Mere towns became cities. But there was no corresponding shift of voting districts. In most states, the geographic boundaries of a state assemblyman's or state senator's district had been fixed around the turn of the century. The lines made sense then. They were roughly drawn to put an approximately equal number of voters in each district, and if they were not entirely equal, the disparities were not nearly as great as they were after the migration began.

Voters as the Disenfranchised

The constitutions of many states required their legislatures to reapportion themselves after every decennial census. This was the case in Tennessee, whose constitutional provision dates back to 1870. It required the taking of a census by the state (the federal census results were substituted in 1901). There was to be an apportionment every ten years, starting in 1871. The procedure to be used was as follows:

Apportionment of representatives. *The number of Representatives shall, at the several periods of making the enumeration, be apportioned among the several counties or districts, according to the number of qualified voters in each . . . .*
Apportionment of senators. *The number of Senators shall . . . be apportioned among the several counties or districts according to the number of qualified electors in each.*

Though these provisions remained in effect at the time *Baker v. Carr* was filed, the last apportionment of either the state house or senate was in 1901. Even in that year, it was charged, the legislature failed to live up to the constitutional mandate. The district lines remained frozen for sixty years as the population shifted mightily to Nashville, Memphis, Knoxville, and Chattanooga. During that time the state's population grew from 2 million to 3.5 million and its voter rolls swelled from 487,000 to more than 2 million. By the mid-fifties, 37 percent of the voters could elect twenty of the thirty-three senators, and 40 percent could elect sixty-three of the ninety-nine members of the house. These minorities were rural, and the practical effect of the malapportioned legislature was that laws and policies deemed detrimental to rural interests could not be enacted, though they might greatly benefit the urban majority.

A similar situation prevailed in all the states, though the predominance of rural interests was most felt and resented in the large industrial states where the largest urban centers lay. Some of the disparities among the populations contained in the various districts within a given state were astonishing. Colebrook, Connecticut, for instance, had a population of 592 persons, who sent two members to the state assembly—the same number as Hartford, Connecticut, with a population in the late 1950s of more than 175,000. In New Jersey one district had 35,000 people; another had more than 900,000. Similar disparities existed between Congressional districts within a single state. Georgia's largest district had some 825,000 people, and its smallest had less than 275,000. Illinois had one district that numbered 914,000 while another had only 112,000.

The Consequences of the Problem

Within the states, this inequality had important consequences, especially with regard to the state budgets. The rural minorities had decisive power, and they were not afraid to use it because they could not be dislodged by a majority of voters. In 1952-53, for example, the legislature in Tennessee allocated $97.99 per pupil from state tax revenues for all school districts outside the four major urban centers, which received only $63.67 per student. Ten years later the disparity was even greater. In the extreme southwestern corner of the state, Shelby County, which included Memphis, contained more than 600,000 people. It got $95.00 per pupil in school aid. Pickett County, in the north central part of the state, received $226.00 per pupil for its population of 4,000. By the late 1950s, the twelve largest counties contributed about 65 percent of the state taxes, though they had only 37 percent of the representatives in the legislature.

Again, such disparities were by no means confined to Tennessee. In Florida, for example, state racetrack revenues were parceled out to each county on an equal basis. Thus rural counties received sixty-one dollars per person, while Miami received twenty cents per person.

By the mid-1940s, the growing need for municipal services in the cities was rapidly outstripping their ability to cope. In no small measure this was due to the tortured mathematical calculations emanating from the state capitals. One of the most starved cities was Chicago. Underrepresented both in Springfield, the state capital, and in Washington, it could not make its voice heard.

Determined to test the validity of the apportionment of the Congressional district in which he lived, Kenneth W. Colegrove, a professor at Northwestern University, filed suit in federal court against Governor Dwight H. Green, seeking a redistricting. In 1946, the Supreme Court, in a three-way split, dismissed the suit.

"We are of opinion," said Justice Frankfurter (speaking for himself and Justices Reed and Burton), "that the petitioners ask of this Court what is beyond its competence to grant. This is one of those demands on judicial power which cannot be met by verbal fencing about 'jurisdiction.' It must be resolved by considerations on the basis of which this Court, from time to time, has refused to intervene in controversies. It has refused to do so because due regard for the effective working of our government revealed this issue to be of a peculiarly political nature and therefore not meet for judicial determination.

"This is not an action to recover for damage because of the discriminatory exclusion of a plaintiff from rights enjoyed by other citizens. The basis for the suit is not a private wrong, but a wrong suffered by Illinois as a polity. . . . In effect this is an appeal to the federal courts to reconstruct the electoral process of Illinois in order that it may be adequately represented in the councils of the Nation. . . .

"Of course no court can affirmatively re-map the Illinois districts so as to bring them more in conformity with the standards of fairness for a representative system. At best we could only declare the existing electoral system invalid. The result would be to leave Illinois undistricted and to bring into operation, if the Illinois legislature chose not to act, the choice of members for the House of Representatives on a state-wide ticket. The last stage may be worse than the first. The upshot of judicial action may defeat the vital principle which led Congress, more than a hundred years ago, to require districting. . . . Nothing is clearer than that this controversy concerns matters that bring courts into immediate and active relations with party contests. From the determination of such issues this Court has traditionally held aloof. It is hostile to a democratic system to involve the judiciary in the politics of the people. And it is not less pernicious if such judicial intervention in an essentially political contest be dressed up in the abstract phrases of the law.

"The petitioners urge with great zeal that the conditions of which they complain are great evils and offend public morality. The Constitution of the United States gives ample power to provide against these evils. But . . . the subject has been committed to the exclusive control of Congress. . . .

"To sustain this action would cut very deep into the very being of Congress. *Courts ought not to enter this political thicket.* The remedy for unfairness in districting is to secure State legislatures that will apportion properly, or to invoke the ample powers of Congress. . . . The Constitution has left the performance of many duties in our governmental scheme to depend on the fidelity of the executive and legislative action and, ultimately, on the vigilance of the people in exercising their political rights."

Getting the Vote In: Baker v. Carr

Until *Baker* v. *Carr,* the *Colegrove* case was cited repeatedly for the proposition that the federal courts simply had no power to consider or resolve the issue of legislative apportionment. But this conclusion was maintained more on the strength of Frankfurter's bold discussion than on the votes in the case. The split among the justices was unusual. Chief Justice Stone died before the decision was issued, and Justice Jackson was overseas at Nuremberg. The seven remaining justices were divided into three camps.

Three, including Justice Frankfurter, thought there was no jurisdiction at all. One, Justice Rutledge, agreed with the conclusion of these three that the case should be dismissed. But he disagreed with their reasoning. He felt that the particular facts of the case presented an issue too delicate to warrant the Court's involvement. This made a four to three majority for dismissal.

But Justice Rutledge clearly agreed that the Court had jurisdiction, which it could choose to exercise. This was also the opinion of the three dissenters (Justices Black, Douglas, and Murphy), who argued that the Court should strike down the Illinois apportionment act under which Congressional districts were devised. Thus, though the case was dismissed by a four to three vote, the various opinions read together demonstrated also that by a four to three vote the justices thought they did indeed have jurisdiction.

Though *Colegrove* v. *Green* seemed to foreclose any further federal judicial attempts to upset the archaic districts, it only applied directly to the legislative districts of the U.S. Congress. Moreover, it said nothing about the power of a state court to order redistricting under the express command of the state constitution.

In 1955 a group of east Tennessee residents, including several attorneys and local businessmen, formed a group called Tennessee Committee for Constitutional Reapportionment. On March 8, they filed a lawsuit in the state's chancery court. This was *Kidd* v. *McCanless*. The plaintiff was Gates Kidd, a Johnson City Ford dealer and finance chairman of the constitutional committee. George F. McCanless was attorney general of Tennessee. Numerous other plaintiffs and defendants were involved. The suit came before thirty-three-year old Chancellor Thomas W. Steele, and by the time the case was ready for argument, more defendants had been added, bringing the total to 220.

The plaintiffs argued that the state constitution required the chancellor to declare the existing districts invalid. Besides technical matters, the defendants raised the issues discussed in *Colegrove* v. *Green*. "There is nothing plainer in Tennessee law," said one of the attorneys for the defense, "than the constitutional language on separation of power between the judiciary, legislative and executive branches of government. For the courts to write a reapportionment bill would be to destroy that power delegated to the legislature."

In November, Chancellor Steele declared that the apportionment act under which the existing legislative districts were drawn had expired by its own terms and that no future election could be lawfully held under it. He refused to order the state legislature to reapportion nor did he draw up a plan for doing so himself. "That [the legislature would not draw up a new plan] is inconceivable to this court," he said.

Five months later, in April 1956, the Tennessee Supreme Court reversed the chancellor's judgment. The principal ground of the decision there was that declaring the apportionment law unconstitutional would mean that the legislators themselves would not constitutionally be entitled to their offices. This, the court ruled, would "deprive us of the present Legislature and the means of electing a new one and ultimately bring about the destruction of the State itself."

This was not compelling logic. Chancellor Steele had dealt with this problem and decided that to strike down the districting law for the coming election did not mean that all previous acts passed by the legislature were invalid or that the legislators could not sit to correct the situation. But the higher court had ruled, and in December 1956 the U.S. Supreme Court declined to review that decision.

The Nationwide Assault on Malapportionment

In the meantime, citizens were stirring in other places. About the time the Tennessee Supreme Court threw out the *Kidd* case, a federal district court in Hawaii (then a territory) actually ruled that the territorial legislature was malapportioned. Activists in Minnesota, reading about the Hawaii case, decided to make apportionment a campaign issue in a race for a state legislative seat. The candidate, Frank Farrell, a Northern Pacific Railroad attorney, lost, but was determined to press the reapportionment issue. With his friend and neighbor, Daniel B. Magraw, serving as plaintiff, Farrell put together an impressive case. He pitted representatives from all the populous districts that were underrepresented in the legislature against selected election officials.

In July 1958, a three-judge federal district court ruled that it had jurisdiction of the case, despite *Colegrove*. But it took no positive action. It put its faith in the new legislature that would convene the following January.

It is not to be presumed that the legislature will refuse to take such action as is necessary to comply with its duty under the state constitution. . . . It seems to us that if there is to be a judicial disruption of the present legislative apportionment or of the method of machinery for electing members of the state legislature, it should not take place unless and until it can be shown that the legislature meeting in January 1959 has advisedly and deliberately failed and refused to perform its constitutional duty to redistrict the state.

The Minnesota legislature heeded the message and began to redistrict itself. The case was ultimately dismissed without a final ruling.

But it stirred up national attention and reawakened interest among the Tennesseans who had lost the battle two years before. In late 1958, David N. Harsh, chairman of the Shelby County (Memphis) Commission, decided the time was right to bring a new suit. He persuaded Walter Chandler, former congressman and former mayor of Nashville, to act as lead counsel. Chandler had refused to involve himself in the *Kidd* case, but now he too decided the time was right. Incensed by the consistent failure of the legislature even to consider reapportionment, Chandler had come to the conclusion that there could be no progress in the state without reapportionment and that there could be no reapportionment without a judicial order. The political route was closed; no legislator would vote himself out of office and no minority would vote to give up its own power.

Regrouping

In early 1959, Chandler reassembled the old team. This included Z. Thomas Osborn, formerly the Nashville city attorney and now in private practice (he had been the moving spirit behind *Kidd*), and Hobart Atkins, a Republican state senator from Knoxville. They decided to model their suit closely on the Minnesota case. It emphasized the discriminatory effects of the ancient apportionment on the urban areas. It also reduced the number of plaintiffs and defendants from the unwieldy group involved in the *Kidd* case. The lead plaintiff was Charles W. Baker, chairman of the Shelby County Quarterly Court, the county's legislative council. This council had fiscal authority over the public affairs of the more than 600,000 inhabitants. The named defendant was Joseph C. Carr, Tennessee secretary of state. Other defendants included Attorney General McCanless and state election board members.

Suit was filed on May 18, 1959. In late December, the three-judge federal district court, citing *Colegrove*, dismissed it. A month before, however, Mayor Ben West of Nashville decided that his city should support the lawsuit, and he formally intervened. This was an important step, for funds to prosecute an appeal were not easy to come by, and Nashville's financial help was necessary. The city council passed a resolution authorizing Mayor West "to take any and all necessary steps in proving the long continued mistreatment of the people of the City of Nashville at the hands of the unlawfully apportioned General Assemblies of Tennessee convened pursuant to the Apportionment Act of 1901." The city spent an estimated $50,000 during the next two years. West did not come into the suit by accident; the year before he had been national president of the American Municipal Association. The problem was uppermost in his mind.

In February 1960, the mayor went to Washington to hire a lawyer to handle the appeal to the Supreme Court. He chose Charles S. Rhyne, in 1957-58 president of the American Bar Association. Rhyne was an expert in municipal law and a close friend of Richard M. Nixon, his Duke Law School classmate. While Rhyne was chosen for his legal proficiency, it had also occurred to the appellants that their Washington counsel's political contacts might help sway the federal government into joining their side of the appeal as *amicus*. Indeed, Rhyne discussed the case with J. Lee Rankin, the solicitor general, who grew interested. But before the Supreme Court announced its intention to consider the case on November 21, 1960, the Republicans lost the federal government to John F. Kennedy.

There were, however, ties with the new administration. A Nashville lawyer, John Jay Hooker, Jr., was a close friend of John Seigenthaler, a Nashville *Tennessean* reporter who assisted Robert Kennedy during the 1960 campaign. Seigenthaler was appointed administrative assistant to the new Attorney General. Hooker had helped Seigenthaler from Washington during the campaign, but afterward returned to Nashville.

Approached in January 1961 by the *Baker* lawyers, Hooker set up an appointment with another co-campaign worker, the new solicitor general, Archibald Cox. The meeting was low-key, but it was clear that Cox was interested, and not merely because President Kennedy had earlier taken a public position against both state and congressional malapportionment. Attorney General Kennedy quickly approved the Justice Department's involvement.

The case was argued twice, on April 19-20 and again on October 9, 1961. The arguments were highly technical. They dealt not with the substantive issue but rather with the threshold question whether the Supreme Court had any business considering the case in the first place. That Tennessee had violated its own constitution was not at issue; the Supreme Court has no power to review state constitutional questions unless there is also posed a violation of the U.S. Constitution. So the question was whether the Court had jurisdiction, whether the parties had standing, and whether the issue was justiciable, when the claim was that the unequal legislative districts violated the equal protection clause of the Fourteenth Amendment.

The Issues and Strategies

Rhyne and Cox hammered away at what they considered the erroneous interpretation of *Colegrove*. It was not, they said, precedent for denying jurisdiction because four of the seven Justices then on the Court had agreed there was. Moreover, they insisted, that was the only question now before the Court. Since the three-judge lower court had dismissed *Baker* v. *Carr* on the ground that there was no jurisdiction, it had not considered the merits of the case. Consequently the underlying issue was not ready for Supreme Court review. "I think all you need hold," Cox said, "is that the case is within the jurisdiction of the federal courts and that the court below must go on and determine whether this complaint states a cause of action; in other words, adjudicate the merits of the claim that there is a violation under the Fourteenth Amendment."

The plaintiffs' lawyers also emphasized a theme that was perhaps not quite relevant to the case at this stage: that without judicial relief, the underrepresentation of cities in state legislatures would simply grow worse. "For the first time in sixty years," Osborn said in rebuttal, "a state legislature in Tennessee agreed to have an enumeration, and then only after this honorable Court noted probable jurisdiction in this case."

Reargument was apparently ordered because of the strong feelings of Justice Frankfurter, who as author of the *Colegrove* opinion, was a bitter opponent of judicial interference with legislative apportionment. At the second argument, Frankfurter came prepared for a fight, and his questioning of both Rhyne and Cox was intense. Though it was not formally a part of the record, it is interesting to note that Baker's attorneys prepared an up-to-date statistical analysis. They used the newly issued 1960 census data and a packet containing it was placed on the bench where each justice sat shortly before the argument commenced. Each justice individually spent some time perusing it during the oral debate.

Despite the intensity of Frankfurter's jibes and questions, Cox managed to turn one of his former professor's arguments around and use it to telling effect against the justice. The term before, the Court had not only taken jurisdiction in a reapportionment case but actually voided the districts created. The facts, however, were special. The town of Tuskegee, Alabama, carved itself up into a twenty-eight-sided blob to zone out black residents entitled to vote in municipal elections. In a unanimous opinion written by Frankfurter himself, the Court declared that the city's actions violated the Equal Protection Clause. Frankfurter argued that this was clearly a different case, for unlike the *Baker* case, there had actually been an affirmative action: a redistricting had taken place. Where, as in *Baker,* the complaint was that no reapportionment was being made, the courts should not intervene, Frankfurter concluded.

Cox disagreed. The distinction did not lie in the power of the courts to hear the cases but in the ultimate remedies they might devise. The Court was not worried about striking down an obvious case of racial discrimination because it could frame a judicial order with some precision based on solid precedent. It might not want to enter the "political thicket" and actually order an apportionment in *Baker*. But that did not mean the Court did not have the power to hear the merits of the complaint and consider the remedy suggested. And the question of remedy, said Cox, the Court did not need to consider to decide the case.

Prying the Lid Open: The Decision

On March 26, 1962, with Justice Whittaker not participating, and over the dissents of Justices Frankfurter and Harlan, the Court ruled that the lower court had jurisdiction to consider the merits. The case was remanded for trial.

In brief compass, the Court made three closely related points.

First, as to jurisdiction, the Court said there could be no doubt that the claim that Baker and his co-plaintiffs were asserting was one that "arises under" the Constitution, because they alleged an injury under the Fourteenth Amendment, and their assertion was plainly not frivolous. In other words, if their interpretation of the law was correct, there could be no doubt of the injury. By Congressional enactment, federal courts are vested with the power to determine any cases or controversies "arising under" the Constitution, federal law, or treaty. In his opinion for the Court, Justice Brennan devoted six pages to showing that prior cases had never denied the power of the federal courts to consider districting questions.

Second, the Court ruled that the particular litigants—Baker and other residents of various counties elegible to vote for state representatives—had standing to sue. The Constitution does not permit

Justice William Brennan.

federal courts to strike out at and void statutes whenever the judges feel a particular one is improper. The judicial power can only be exercised in the context of a particular case, which means that the litigants themselves must have a personal stake, or standing, in the suit. Otherwise anyone could test a law in the abstract simply by cooking up a case and asking the judges for an opinion. The alleged injury in the case, the Court said, was that the legislative districting "disfavors the voters in the counties in which they reside, placing them in a position of constitutionally unjustifiable inequality *vis-à-vis* voters in irrationally favored counties. . . . They are asserting 'a plain, direct and adequate interest in maintaining the effectiveness of their votes.' "

Third, and most importantly, the Court ruled that the issue in *Baker* v. *Carr* was not a "political question" that the Court could not answer. This was the sticky part of the case, and Justice Brennan took twenty-eight pages to overcome the dissenters' contentions.

The "political question" doctrine has had a long and somewhat obscure history in the decisions of the Supreme Court. Its basic premises are that under the Constitution certain questions are given exclusively to other branches of the federal government to answer and that these questions are not of the type to which courts can formulate meaningful answers. Examples of such questions are those dealing with foreign affairs—such as the presidential prerogative in recognizing foreign states or the dates of duration of hostilities. But the fact that the issue at bar deals with political rights does not make it a political question unanswerable by courts. To the contrary, many of the most important rights courts are called upon to vindicate are political in nature, such as the right to vote.

The chief sticking point was the long-standing principle that the Court would not enforce any right claimed under the so-called Guaranty Clause. Article Four, Section Four of the Constitution says that "the United States shall guarantee to every State in this Union a Republican Form of Government, and shall protect each of them against Invasion; and on Application of the Legislature, or of the Executive (when the Legislature cannot be convened) against domestic Violence." The Court has held on a number of occasions that whether a particular state government was "republican" and whether the level of domestic violence required federal intervention were not questions for the Court. They should be decided by the president and Congress.

But the question of equally apportioned legislative districts did not need to hinge on the Guaranty Clause; whether or not equal districts were contained in the notion of a "republican form of government," it also was contained, at least as a claim, in the equal protection clause of the Fourteenth Amendment. Under this clause the courts had ample reason and power to adjudicate.

It was against this last conclusion that Justice Frankfurter wrote his impassioned sixty-six-page dissent. "A hypothetical claim resting on abstract assumptions is now for the first time made the basis for affording illusory relief for a particular evil even though it foreshadows deeper and more pervasive difficulties in conseqence." Because "the Court's authority—possessed of neither the purse nor the sword—ultimately rests on sustained public confidence in its moral sanction," he deeply feared that the decision would seriously damage the Court's image when it eventually had to rule on the merits of a reapportionment case. And it would ultimately have to rule on an apportionment case despite the absence of any "guidelines for formulating specific, definite, wholly unprecedented remedies for the inevitable litigations that today's umbrageous disposition is bound to stimulate in connection with politically motivated reapportionments in so many States."

Justice Frankfurter was at least right about the "inevitable litigations." Within one year of the Court's ruling in *Baker* v. *Carr*, thirty-six states were involved in reapportionment cases. By then the Court had moved into the substantive area. The necessity of actually exercising its jurisdiction was bluntly foreshadowed in Justice Clark's concurring opinion. "Although I find the Tennessee apportionment statute offends the Equal Protection Clause," he said, "I would not consider intervention by this Court into so delicate a field if there were any other relief available to the people of Tennessee. But the majority of the people of Tennessee have no 'practical opportunities for exerting their political weight at the polls' to correct the existing 'invidious discrimination.' Tennessee has no initiative and referendum. I have searched diligently for other 'practical opportunities' present under the law. I find none other than through the federal courts. The majority of the voters have been caught up in a legislative strait jacket. Tennessee has an 'informed, civically militant electorate' and 'an aroused popular conscience,' but it does not sear 'the conscience of the people's representatives.' This is because the legislative policy has riveted the present seats in the Assembly to their respective constituencies, and by the votes of their incumbents a reapportionment of any kind is prevented. The people have been rebuffed at the hands of the Assembly; they have tried the constitutional convention route, but since the call must originate in the Assembly it, too, has been fruitless. They have tried Tennessee courts with the same result, and Governors have fought the tide only to flounder. It is said that there is recourse in Congress and perhaps that may be, but from a practical standpoint this is without substance. To date Congress has never undertaken such a task in any State. We therefore must conclude that the people of Tennessee are stymied and without judicial intervention will be saddled with the present discrimination in the affairs of their state government."

In the first case on the merits to come before it, the Court tossed out the county unit system that Georgia prescribed for voting in state and federal primaries. This was a complicated device to give rural areas control. Noting that the Fifteenth and Nineteenth Amendments prohibit the states from weighting votes on the basis of race or sex, the Court said:

How then can one person be given twice or ten times the voting power of another person in a state-wide election merely because he lives in a rural area or because he lives in the smallest rural county? Once the geographical unit for which a representative is to be chosen is designated, all who participate in the election are to have an equal vote—whatever their race, whatever their sex, whatever their occupation, whatever their income, and wherever their home may be in that geographical unit.

With this conclusion, a new constitutional slogan entered the language: "The concept of political equality from the Declaration of Independence to Lincoln's Gettysburg Address, to the Fifteenth, Seventeenth, and Nineteenth Amendments can mean only one thing—one person, one vote."

One year later, the Court decided a series of cases that sweepingly attacked the existing basis of apportionment of state senate, house, and congressional districts. In February 1964, it held that congressional seats must be reapportioned on the basis of population. Its conclusion was bottomed on the language of Article One, Section Two of the Constitution, which says that representatives "shall be apportioned among the several states . . . according to their respective numbers" and "chosen . . . by the people of the several states."

In June, the Court upset legislative districts in six states in separate cases decided the same day. By the Fourteenth Amendment, state districts were required to be apportioned on a basis of equal population. Not even the time-honored practice of making the upper house the representative body of geographical areas, such as counties, was sustained, where the counties were composed of unequal numbers of people.

The lead case came up from Alabama, where the legislature had hurriedly reapportioned itself following the Court's pronouncement in *Baker* v. *Carr.* Even so, 25.1 percent of the people elected a majority in the state senate and 25.7 percent elected a majority in the state house. Moreover, there were discrepancies as high as 41 to 1 between the populations of senate districts and 16 to 1 in the case of house districts.

Delivering the opinion of the Court, Chief Justice Warren declared in a celebrated passage:

Legislators represent people, not trees or acres. Legislators are elected by voters, not farms or cities or economic interest. As long as ours is a representative form of government, and our legislatures are those instruments of government elected directly by and directly representative of the people, the right to elect legislators in a free and unimpaired fashion is a bedrock of our political system. It could hardly be gainsaid that a constitutional claim had been asserted by an allegation that certain otherwise

qualified voters had been entirely prohibited from voting for members of their state legislature. And, if a State should provide that the votes of citizens in one part of the State should be given two times, or five times, or ten times the weight of votes of citizens in another part of the State, it could hardly be contended that the right to vote of those residing in the disfavored areas had not been effectively diluted. It would appear extra-ordinary to suggest that a State could be constitutionally permitted to enact a law providing that certain of the State's voters could vote two, five or ten times for their legislative representatives, while voters living elsewhere could vote only once. And it is inconceivable that a state law to the effect that, in counting votes for legislators, the votes of citizens in one part of the State would be multiplied by two, five, or ten, while the votes of persons in another area would be counted only at face value, could be constitutionally sustainable. Of course, the effect of state legisla-tive districting schemes which give the same number of representatives to unequal numbers of constituents is identical. Overweighting and over-valuation of the votes of those living here has the certain effect of dilution and undervaluation of the votes of those living there. The resulting dis-crimination against those individual voters living in disfavored areas is easily demonstrable mathematically. Their right to vote is simply not the same right to vote as that of those living in a favored part of the State. Two, five, or ten of them must vote before the effect of their voting is equivalent to that of their favored neighbor. Weighting the votes of citizens differently, by any method or means, merely because of where they happen to reside, hardly seems justifiable. One must be ever aware that the Constitution forbids 'sophisticated as well as simple-minded modes of discrimination.'

The floodgates had opened. By the end of the decade, every state in the Union had either reapportioned or was subject to a court order to do so. And the Court did not stop at the statewide level. In a series of decisions the Court extended its one-man, one-vote principle to all sorts of local governing bodies, such as school boards. But unlike the decision in *Brown* v. *Board of Education,* the Court's reapportionment cases were not greeted by massive re-pudiation.

Though there is still litigation concerning the disparities be-tween districts in certain states, the major principle is conceded. During the mid-sixties, Senator Everett McKinley Dirksen (R.-Ill.) pushed a constitutional amendment in the Senate to permit the up-per house of state legislatures to be apportioned on a basis other than population, but he was unable to overcome the resistance of urban senators, and the movement to amend the Constitution shriv-eled up when Senator Dirksen died in 1969.

But the states did not wait to see whether Dirksen would succeed. They went about redistricting, either on their own or under court order, and the legislative map of America was remade in less than a decade. Justice Frankfurter's fears that the Court's prestige would suffer dissolved with the old district lines.

16/ THE RIGHT TO COUNSEL: GIDEON v. WAINWRIGHT

O f all the constitutional criminal law cases that the Warren Court handed down, the one that seems most likely to stand unrevised or unqualified by future decisions is the celebrated case of *Gideon* v. *Wainwright*. Unlike most of the Court's criminal law decisions, *Gideon* was unanimous (though not every justice agreed with the exact thrust of Justice Black's opinion).

The Historical Context

It established the principle that, in any felony prosecution, the states must provide the accused with a lawyer if he is too poor to retain counsel for himself. The Court read into the injunction of the Sixth Amendment ("in all criminal prosecutions, the accused shall enjoy the right . . . to have the assistance of counsel for his defense") the stern command that no felony trial may go forward anywhere in the United States unless the defendant is represented.

This is a radical notion. Throughout the American colonial period, the English legal system did not permit felony defendants to be represented by counsel (the only exception, enacted by Parliament in 1695, was for treason trials). Against this historical background, the Sixth Amendment might have been taken to mean simply that the courts cannot refuse to let a defendant show up for trial with a lawyer if he chooses to do so.

But the *Gideon* decision went beyond this understanding of the right to counsel. Letting each accused defend himself as his pocketbook permits is a fine rule for those whose pocketbooks are large enough. But it is not a rule of fairness at all for those whose pocketbooks are empty. The *Gideon* ruling recognized this difficulty. It required states to insure the fundamental fairness of a trial by providing every person accused of crime the means to contest the government's charges.

Powell v. Alabama

Judges, not surprisingly, have long recognized the importance of counsel. Indeed, the story of *Gideon* v. *Wainwright* begins with the second case in which the Supreme Court overturned a state prosecution on the grounds that it lacked the fundamental fairness required by the Fourteenth Amendment. That was in 1932, in the case of *Powell* v. *Alabama,* involving the rape prosecution of the Scottsboro boys, nine black youths ranging in age from twelve to nineteen. The incident that gave rise to a long series of trials and appeals began on March 25, 1931, when a fight broke out between the Scottsboro boys and a group of white youths, including two white girls aged seventeen and twenty-one, on a freight train traveling through northeastern Alabama. One of the white boys, thrown from the train, reported the fight to a stationmaster, and a posse soon stopped the train and took the nine black youths in custody. One of the white girls, Ruby Bates, told the sheriff that her companion, Victoria Price, had been raped by each of the nine black teenagers. The youths were held in a small jail in Scottsboro (hence the label that has stuck ever since) and a lynching was prevented only because the Alabama National Guard was called out. Two weeks later, in a trial that was started and finished in a single day eight of the nine were convicted in this small town while some eight to ten thousand waited in the streets outside the courthouse.

Before the trial commenced, the judge engaged in a long colloquy with a Tennessee lawyer, not a member of the local bar, to see whether he would appear as counsel for the defendants. He said he had come "as a friend of the people who are interested and not as paid counsel" and that he was not familiar with Alabama procedure nor had he had a chance to prepare for the case. The following discussion then ensued:

The COURT: Well gentlemen, if Mr. Roddy [the Tennessee lawyer] only appears as assistant that way, I think it is proper that I appoint members of this bar to represent them, I expect that is right. If Mr. Roddy will appear, I wouldn't of course, I would not appoint anybody. I don't see, Mr. Roddy, how I can make a qualified appointment or a limited appointment. Of course, I don't mean to cut off your assistance in any way—Well, gentlemen, I think you understand it.

Mr. MOODY (an Alabama lawyer):   I am willing to go ahead and help Mr. Roddy in anything I can do about it, under the circumstances.

The COURT: All right, all the lawyers that will; of course I would not require a lawyer to appear if—

Mr. MOODY: I am willing to do that for him as a member of the bar; I will go ahead and help do anything I can do.

The COURT: All right.

These instructions were anything but clear. A lawyer who had said he could not appear as counsel but was willing to assist suddenly became the chief counsel. He was assisted by a local lawyer whom the judge apparently drafted into service. Thus the trial began.

The Scottsboro boys with their attorney, Samuel S. Leibowitz.

It is impossible to say whether these two lawyers ever thought they were acting as real lawyers for the defense. Obviously they had not prepared for the trial at all, and so they did not stand in the way of a speedy conviction. They certainly did not bring out what Samuel S. Leibowitz, the appointed counsel in the retrial in the spring of 1933, discovered. He determined that Victoria Price was a well-known prostitute apparently traveling on the train with a customer. She fabricated the rape story to cover up the fact that she was crossing state lines illegally.

The first jury knew none of this (though the second jury thought nothing of it). As Justice Sutherland put it: "The trials immediately proceeded. The defendants, young, ignorant, illiterate, surrounded by hostile sentiment, haled back and forth under guard of soldiers, charged with an atrocious crime regarded with especial horror in the community where they were to be tried, were thus put in peril." The convictions never in doubt, they were sentenced to death, and their appeal ultimately came before the Supreme Court.

By a 7 to 2 vote, the Court reversed. No one could be convicted of crime, Justice Sutherland said for the majority, unless there were first some kind of hearing. This was a basic element of due process. But standing alone, without the assistance of counsel, the hearing would have little meaning or importance:

The right to be heard would be, in many cases, of little avail if it did not comprehend the right to be heard by counsel. Even the intelligent and educated layman has small and sometimes no skill in the science of law. If charged with crime, he is incapable, generally, of determining for himself whether the indictment is good or bad. He is unfamiliar with the rules of evidence. Left without the aid of counsel he may be put on trial without a proper charge, and convicted upon incompetent evidence, or evidence irrelevant to the issue or otherwise inadmissible. He lacks both the skill and knowledge adequately to prepare his defense, even though he have a perfect one. He requires the guiding hand of counsel at every step in the proceedings against him. Without it, though he be not guilty, he faces the danger of conviction because he does not know how to establish his innocence. If that be true of men of intelligence, how much more true is it of the ignorant and illiterate, or those of feeble intellect?

But the decision in *Powell* v. *Alabama* was specifically limited to the particular facts of the case. And the most important fact was that it was a capital case. When death is a possible sentence, the Court said, "where the defendant is unable to employ counsel, and is incapable adequately of making his own defense because of ignorance, feeblemindedness, illiteracy, or the like, it is the duty of the court, whether requested or not, to assign counsel for him as a necessary requisite of due process of law." The question of whether a defendant had a constitutional right to counsel in non-capital case or not was left hanging.

One Step Forward, Two Back

In 1938, by a bare majority of five, Justice Black delivered an opinion in a case that extended the holding in *Powell* to all *federal* prosecutions. This did not pose any special constitutional dilemmas. The case was a straightforward interpretation of the Sixth Amendment, which of course applies directly to the federal government and prosecutions conducted under its authority.

In 1942, the Court abruptly changed the course on which it seemed to be heading. In a case titled *Betts* v. *Brady*, the Court was presented with the robbery conviction of a Maryland farmhand. Smith Betts had asked the trial judge to appoint a lawyer for him because, he said, he was too poor to pay for legal representation. The judge denied his request. He pointed out that it was the practice in rural Carroll County to appoint lawyers to represent indigent defendants only in murder and rape cases. Betts thereupon represented himself, calling witnesses, examining these and cross-examining the state's witnesses. The judge, sitting without a jury, found him guilty and sentenced him to eight years in prison. On appeal to the Supreme Court, Betts lost.

The question, Justice Roberts said for a six to three majority, was whether representation in a courtroom and in the preparation for a trial is "so fundamental and essential to a fair trial, and so to due process of law, that it is made obligatory upon the states by the Fourteenth Amendment." Examining the practice of each of the states, Roberts found a disparity of rules. But only a few states required appointment of counsel in all criminal cases. Roberts concluded from this review that right to counsel was not a fundamental right. A defendant's right to counsel depended on the circumstances in each particular case. "Exceptional" circumstances might warrant such appointment (these included a defendant's mental illness, youth, or lack of education).

The Court summarized this rule in 1948: "Where the gravity of the crime and other factors—such as the age and education of the defendant, the conduct of the court or prosecuting officials, and the complicated nature of the offense charged, and the possible defenses thereto—render criminal proceedings without counsel so apt to result in injustice as to be fundamentally unfair . . . , the accused must have legal assistance."

But like all high-sounding rules, this one left much obscured. What was the requisite degree of education? What kind of conduct on the part of officials would require a lawyer, and how could this be determined before the trial? How complicated did the offense have to be? Or the defense?

After all, what appears obvious to a Supreme Court justice might bewilder even highly educated persons who are not legally trained. Rules dealing with conspiracy, the hearsay evidence rule, and rules governing criminal intent defy rational explanation in many of their applications. Even the reasonably educated may not know of defenses that would be perfectly apparent to the ordinary lawyer. Besides the layman is not entitled to represent criminal defendants. Only members of the bar, licensed by a state board following a course of legal training, are legally permitted to appear in court. If this is so, why should nonlawyer defendants be assumed capable of handling their own defenses?

Establishing Right to Counsel

During the next several years, the Court heard a number of right-to-counsel cases. After 1950 it consistently reversed the convictions on finding that "exceptional" circumstances in fact appeared in the case. And an increasing number of justices were calling for the flat overruling of *Betts* v. *Brady*.

The events that led to the Court's doing so began on June 3, 1961, when someone broke into the Bay Harbor Poolroom in Panama City, Florida. The thief made off with some beer, wine, and petty change from a cigarette machine and juke box. Police arrested Clarence Earl Gideon, a fifty-one-year-old drifter. He had four convictions for felonies, including burglary.

At the beginning of his trial, on August 4, occurred the following conversation between Gideon and Judge Robert L. McCrary.

The COURT:	The next case on the docket is the case of the state of Florida, Plaintiff, versus Clarence Earl Gideon, Defendant. What says the state, are you ready to go to trial in this case?
Mr. HARRIS:	The state is ready, your Honor.
The COURT:	What says the Defendant? Are you ready to go to trial?

The DEFENDANT: I am not ready, your Honor.

The COURT: Did you plead not guilty to this charge by reason of insanity?

The DEFENDANT: No sir.

The COURT: Why aren't you ready?

The DEFENDANT: I have no counsel.

The COURT: Why do you not have counsel? Did you not know that your case was set for trial today?

The DEFENDANT: Yes sir, I knew that it was set for trial today.

The COURT: Why, then, did you not secure counsel and be prepared to go to trial?

[There was difficulty in hearing Gideon's answer, and he was asked to repeat it.]

The DEFENDANT: Your Honor, I said: I request this court to appoint counsel to represent me in this trial.

The COURT: Mr. Gideon, I am sorry, but I cannot appoint counsel to represent you in this case. Under the laws of the state of Florida, the only time the court can appoint counsel to represent a defendant is when that person is charged with a capital offense. I am sorry, but I will have to deny your request to appoint counsel to defend you in this case.

The DEFENDANT: The United States Supreme Court says I am entitled to be represented by counsel.

The COURT: Let the record show that the defendant has asked the court to appoint counsel to represent him in this trial and the court denied the request and informed the defendant that the only time the court could appoint counsel to represent a defendant was in cases where the defendant was charged with a capital offense. The defendant stated to the court that the United States Supreme Court said he was entitled to it.

Gideon's trial then followed. It was a brief one. Two witnesses testified for the prosecution. One, a man named Henry Cook, said he saw Gideon inside the poolroom at five-thirty on the morning of the robbery. He said that he watched Gideon leave with a bottle of wine and that Gideon then made a telephone call in a public booth and left in a taxi that shortly thereafter pulled up to the phone booth. Cook then said he went into the poolroom and "saw it had been broken into." Next, the poolroom's owner, Ira Strickland, Jr., testified that he had locked the place up at midnight that night. When he returned about eight o'clock the following morning, he saw a smashed window and clear signs that the cigarette machine and juke box had been looted and some wine and beer taken.

Gideon's case was less than compelling. He did not bring out the fact that he occasionally worked in the poolroom. He did not dig deeply into Henry Cook's background or the reason that he was outside the poolroom so early in the morning. He did not explain why he was carrying so much change on his person. The jury did not take long to bring back a guilty verdict.

Here, then, was the perfect case to test whether *Betts* v. *Brady* was a good law. In Gideon's case, as in Betts's, the crime was straightforward, the facts apparently simple. Gideon was not unintelligent, even if not highly educated. He was white. He was middle-aged. He was known in the community. There did not appear to be any of the special circumstances that *Betts* called for.

Gideon was, if anything, more than average. He was not content to ride out the injustice he believed had been done to him. He personally applied to the Florida supreme court for a writ of habeas corpus. That was denied. He then petitioned the United States Supreme Court for review on the ground that he had been denied counsel.

Gideon's petition was filed in early January 1962. It took three months for the papers to be processed and for the state of Florida to respond. Then, two months later, in early June, the Court agreed to take the case. It specifically noted that counsel should prepare to discuss whether the *Betts* case should be reconsidered. Later that month, the Court appointed Abe Fortas, then in private practice in Washington, to represent Gideon.

The very fact that the Court asked for argument on the *Betts* case indicated the direction of legal thought. As Fortas and his associates threw themselves into researching Gideon's case, so much became clear. Most telling, however, was a development, unsolicited by Fortas, Gideon, or the Court: the decision by twenty-three states to file briefs as *amicus curiae* on behalf of Gideon.

The original idea came from Bruce R. Jacob, then the assistant attorney general of Florida, who thought it would be useful to have the participation of other states. Obviously he wished for that participation on his side. So he sent letters to the attorneys general of the other states. But the response was tepid, not surprisingly, in view of the fact that thirty-seven states then had rules making appointment of counsel mandatory in felony cases. In an exchange of correspondence, Walter F. Mondale, then attorney general of Minnesota (now U. S. senator) wrote that he would welcome the overruling of *Betts*. This correspondence was passed along to the attorney general of Massachusetts, Edward J. McCormack, Jr., who gave the go-ahead to the chief of one of his divisions who wished to submit a brief on behalf of Gideon. McCormack and Mondale then rallied the attorneys general in twenty-one other states to sign on. It was an impressive showing. By contrast, only two states—Alabama and North Carolina—submitted a brief in favor of Florida's position.

Betts v. *Brady* was a case very much concerned about the nature and limits of federalism. A federal court should not intrude into the affairs of the states, unless there is some constitutional command or prohibition requiring it to do so. The majority in *Betts* did not wish to impose its views on what was fair in the absence of special circumstances that made proceeding without an attorney manifestly unfair.

But in the oral argument before the Court in Gideon's case, in mid-January 1963, Abe Fortas neatly turned this proposition around. "I believe in federalism," he said in answer to a remark of Justice Harlan, whose opinions always showed a scrupulous regard for the delicate task of drawing constitutional lines between federal and state authority. Fortas continued: "It is a fundamental principle for which I personally have the highest regard and concern, and which I feel must be reconciled with the result I advocate. But I believe that Betts against Brady does not incorporate a proper regard for federalism. It requires a case-by-case supervision by this Court of state criminal proceedings, and that cannot be wholesome."

Like the situation confronting the Court in *Mapp* and in many other constitutional criminal law cases, a flat rule is often less disrupting to state procedures, once accommodation is made to the rule, than repeated exercise of the Court's power to review. In right-to-counsel cases, the state courts might suppose they were following the *Betts* rule by deciding that there were no special circumstances warranting appointed counsel but discover a few years later that the Supreme Court thought otherwise. Such a turn of events would require a retrial, which would mean extra expense and running the risk of losing the case due to the deaths of witnesses and the decay of memories over time.

A flat rule, also, would relieve the Court of the duty of reviewing countless cases to ensure that justice was done. This was an impossible task that only undermined the notion of justice because the Court would never have time to review all of these cases. Moreover, the *Betts* rule was, in Fortas's words, "administratively unworkable." In answer to Justice Stewart's query, Fortas asked rhetorically: "How can a judge, when a man is arraigned, look at him and say there are special circumstances? Does the judge say, 'You look stupid,' or 'Your case involves complicated facts'?"

The only point which seemed to worry some of the justices—how far the Court would have to go if it decided that *Betts* should be overruled—Fortas agreed need not be settled then and there. In this he followed one of the oldest traditions of the Court—that it is prudent and responsible for the Court to answer only the most immediate question before it. That the logic of the decision might compel attorneys to be appointed to represent indigent defendants in misdemeanor cases (a conclusion the Court reached in 1971) or in traffic court or even in civil cases could be put off.

On March 18, 1963, the Court handed down its decision, unanimously reversing Gideon's conviction and overruling *Betts* v. *Brady*. Of the *Betts* case, Justice Black said that the Court's decision that " 'appointment of counsel is not a fundamental right, essential to a fair trial' . . . made an abrupt break with its own well-considered precedents. In returning to these old precedents, sounder we believe than the new, we but restore constitutional principles established to achieve a fair system of justice." Moreover, he continued,

in our adversary system of criminal justice, any person haled into court, who is too poor to hire a lawyer, cannot be assured a fair trial unless counsel is provided for him. This seems to us to be an obvious truth. Governments, both state and federal, quite properly spend vast sums of money to establish machinery to try defendants accused of crime. Lawyers to prosecute are everywhere deemed essential to protect the public's interest in an orderly society. Similarly, there are few defendants charged with crime, few indeed, who fail to hire the best lawyers they can get to prepare and present their defenses. That government hires lawyers to prosecute and defendants who have the money hire lawyers to defend are the strongest indications of the widespread belief that lawyers in criminal courts are necessities, not luxuries. The right of one charged with crime to counsel may not be deemed fundamental and essential to fair trials in some countries, but it is in ours.

While Justice Harlan concurred, he took issue with Justice Black's characterization of *Betts* as having limited the reach of the Court's prior right-to-counsel holdings. But he agreed that *Betts* required overruling because "[t]he Court has come to recognize . . . that the mere existence of a serious criminal charge constituted in itself special circumstances requiring the services of counsel at trial." In other words, in view of the Court's studious findings in case after case that special circumstances existed that warranted the appointment of counsel, *Betts* had become a ghost whose exorcism had finally become an obvious necessity.

This was a decision that the states could not usefully fight. Unlike the desegregation cases, where the states could delay in countless ways, or the *Mapp* case, where police could always claim that the defendant suddenly dropped the evidence right before their very eyes (thus eliminating the need for a warrant,) there was no way of getting around the plain holding of *Gideon*. If there was no lawyer, there would be no conviction—or an automatic reversal if a judge had the temerity to move ahead with the trial anyway. The holdout states began to move quickly to implement the decision. Today some form of public defender service exists in all states.

As for Clarence Earl Gideon, the case had a personal significance that overshadowed in his mind its historic meaning. Florida was permitted to retry him, and the new trial began on August 5. This time Gideon had a lawyer, a local man named W. Fred Turner. And this time the outcome was different. Turner knew Henry Cook, the damaging witness at the first trial, and Cook did not have as easy a time in Turner's hands as he did in Gideon's. Turner cleverly demonstrated the high probability that the thief had been Cook, not Gideon. The jury promptly announced what Gideon—who had persevered enough to push the Supreme Court into changing our constitutional law—knew all along but could not prove without a lawyer: not guilty.

17/ THE RIGHTS OF SUSPECTS: MIRANDA v. ARIZONA

On March 3, 1963, an eighteen-year-old woman employed by a Phoenix, Arizona, theater was kidnapped and driven into the desert, where she was raped. Ten days later, police arrested Ernesto Miranda, an indigent twenty-three-year old who had not completed the ninth grade. The year before he had been arrested for the robbery of eight dollars from a Phoenix bank employee. Placing him in a lineup, the police watched the victim identify Miranda as her assailant. He was taken directly to a separate room for questioning. At first he denied guilt, but within two hours, his two police interrogators persuaded him to confess. After giving them complete details of the crime, he wrote his statement down in longhand. There was no indication then or later that the police had used physical force, had threatened him, or had promised leniency in return for the confession.

Victims of Circumstance

It looked like a straightforward case. Normally it would have been, but Miranda and the policemen were in a vortex of history that had been sucking more and more confession cases from trial courts around the country to the Supreme Court in Washington. Unbeknownst to the Phoenix police, they omitted to do one thing that five justices would later declare to be of paramount importance in all station houses. They did not advise the suspect of his rights and provide him with counsel prior to interrogation if he so requests.

No case at the Supreme Court is isolated from its time, and it is rare that a decision cannot be guided by some precedent or be discerned from a steady judicial development. *Miranda* v. *Arizona,* though it could hardly be guessed at the time, represented the culmination of the Court's efforts to bring the Fourteenth Amendment into the workings of police routine on every beat and in every precinct in the country. It was also destined, as a result, to plunge the Court into an ocean of abuse and to make the Court one of the leading issues of the 1968 presidential campaign. The Court became a target of those who attributed the mounting wave of crime to the softness of judges and to their seemingly irrational predilection to shackle the police rather than the criminals. So much and worse was said.

To get at the meaning of *Miranda*, it is necessary to step back and try to see the due process revolution as a whole. Before the theory of incorporation took hold, the Court would not interfere with the criminal process in the states. The only exceptions involved some procedural aspect of a case that was so unfair that it deprived the defendant of his life, liberty, or property without due process of law. This was an exceedingly flexible formula. The Due Process Clause simply meant that the Supreme Court could reverse a conviction whenever, on examination of the specific facts in the case, it saw that the decision had been arrived at unfairly.

The Court first acted on this premise in 1923 in *Moore v. Dempsey,* when it declared that a hurried trial conducted under the white-hot glare of a lynch mob could not pass constitutional muster. From that time until the 1960s, the Court heard and decided several hundred state criminal cases alleging the lack of procedural due process. But these were only a small fraction of the total number of petitions for review. And they were a still smaller fraction of the total number of prosecutions that the Court overturned.

It is obviously impossible, as has been remarked, for the Court to sit as a police review board. It cannot screen all prosecutions that smack of high-handed tactics. So in the early 1960s, as we have seen, the Court began to incorporate particular provisions of the Bill of Rights into the Due Process Clause of the Fourteenth Amendment—the Fourth Amendment's ban against warrantless searches and seizures and the Sixth Amendment's right to counsel. In other words, a comprehensive, seemingly well-defined rule was substituted for the case-by-case approach that had woefully failed to educate state police and judges in the requisites of procedural fairness.

But no matter how sweepingly a particular provision of the Bill of Rights was incorporated, litigation would continue. As long as the meaning of the provision could be interpreted and reinterpreted or as long as some other procedurally unfair device lurked in the shadows or in the open so as to defeat it, lower court decisions would be tested. Thus exporting federal standards to the states for obtaining search warrants clearly meant that a search without any warrant at all could not be tolerated—any state judge, and the police as well, could be expected to understand that. But the *Mapp* rule did not of itself say anything about whether a particular search warrant was valid under the circumstances of a particular case. Similarly, after *Gideon,* a felony conviction obtained in a trial at which an indigent defendant was not provided with counsel would surely have to be reversed, but what good was a lawyer at a trial if the police had already used some unfair means to snatch evidence or secure a confession?

The Next Logical Step

The problem was that once the Court started down the road of incorporation, it became impossible to avoid bringing along all the provisions of the Bill of Rights. And as the Court attempted to call a halt to what it perceived as official abuses, it was compelled by its very course to lay down firmer, sharper, more comprehensive rules so that there could be no argument about what fairness required. But every rule has a loophole, a way to avoid its sting. Litigation thus breeds litigation, and instead of ending the questions the Court must remain open to ever more of them, though each question would be more refined and focused than the last.

Following *Gideon,* the Court began to face this problem in the one major provision of the Bill of Rights still unincorporated: the Fifth Amendment's right against self-incrimination. This right has an ancient lineage. The abuse of prisoners, who were flogged by agents of the Star Chamber for refusal to answer questions, led by the end of the seventeenth century to the general principle in the common law that a person could not be compelled to incriminate himself. This principle was well understood when it was written into the Fifth Amendment in 1789 and ratified in 1791. But what does the privilege encompass?

It surely encompasses the right of an accused to be free of physical abuse for remaining silent in the face of his accuser's questions. The use of torture to extract confessions is so old and obvious an evil that the Court had little difficulty in forbidding the states from indulging in it in the first state confession case to come before it—surprisingly not until 1936. In that case, Mississippi police had beaten confessions out of two blacks with the aid of belts with metal studs. No one doubts that the "third degree" is beyond the constitutional pale.

More subtle questions are presented when a suspect is not physically assaulted but is subjected to a grueling routine that may involve physical suffering. For instance, nonstop relay questioning that may last for days, during which time the suspect may not get adequate sleep or food, is physical abuse. But physical suffering is not the only means by which an accused may be thought to be coerced into confessing. Adroit psychological techniques, employed specifically to break down a person's will, may yield a statement that leads to a conviction. For instance, an interrogator might falsely state that the suspect's wife would be brought in to the police station to undergo rigorous questioning.

The vice in all these techniques is twofold. Coercion is not guaranteed to yield the truth; to the contrary, it is more likely to produce falsity, simply to put an end to the coercion. But coercion also offends the democratic sense. It smacks of methods used by totalitarian regimes that care little about human dignity. As Justice Frankfurter put it in 1961, conviction obtained after admitting into evidence an involuntary confession "cannot stand. This is so not because such confessions are unlikely to be true but because the methods used to extract them offend an underlying principle in the enforcement of our criminal law: that ours is an accusatorial and not an inquisitorial system—a system in which the State must establish guilt by evidence independently and freely secured and may not by coercion prove its charge against an accused out of his own mouth."

Most states have long had their own constitutional prohibitions against self-incrimination; by the 1960s, every state did. But as in the case of search warrants and apportionment statutes many states did not follow their own law. Here, as in other areas of the criminal legal process, the Court found itself becoming drawn more and more into devoting valuable time to deciding whether a confession obtained under a particular set of circumstances was voluntary or not.

One of the most intractable problems was that of continuous interrogation or interrogation over a considerable period of time. The Supreme Court found a way of imposing at least partial restraints on federal authorities. In two cases (one in 1943, the other in 1957) it ruled that confessions obtained in violation of a federal law requiring prompt arraignment before a magistrate cannot be used in federal trials. These cases provoked considerable criticism—a foreshadowing of what was to come—because they seemed to exclude even voluntary confessions. But the exclusion of the confessions at trial, as in *Mapp,* was designed to prevent violation of federal law by the law officers themselves.

The First Steps

In 1964, the Supreme Court took two large steps toward the federalization of the law of confessions. First, it incorporated outright the Fifth Amendment's prohibition against being compelled to be a witness against oneself into the Fourteenth Amendment. The case involved a man sentenced to jail for contempt by a Connecticut court when he "pleaded the Fifth" during a state investigation of gambling activities. This provision of the Fifth Amendment thus joined the First, Fourth, Sixth, and Eighth Amendments in their governance of state officials' conduct.

Second, in 1964 the Court made a bridge between the Fifth and Sixth Amendments. In two cases it ruled that confessions or admissions from the accused's own mouth could not be used at trial when, under the circumstances in each case, the accused had been without counsel.

In the first case, a merchant seaman named Massiah and certain others, including Colson, were arrested and indicted for unlawful possession of narcotics aboard a United States vessel and for a variety of related offenses under the conspiracy laws. Before trial the defendants were released on bail, and Colson decided to cooperate with the federal authorities. Colson's car was wired to record conversations, and a federal agent subsequently picked up incriminating statements made by Massiah when driving with Colson. The agent summarized these conversations at Massiah's subsequent trial, and Massiah was convicted.

The Supreme Court reversed the conviction. It held that the Sixth Amendment was violated "when there was used against [Massiah] at his trial evidence of his own incriminating words, which federal agents had deliberately elicited from him after he had been indicted and in the absence of his counsel." Justice White, for himself and Justices Clark and Harlan, dissented, saying that "this is nothing more than a thinly disguised constitutional policy of minimizing or entirely prohibiting the use in evidence of voluntary out-of-court admissions and confessions made by the accused."

Escobedo v. Illinois

Massiah was a federal case, decided without reference to any concern over incorporation by the Fourteenth Amendment. But before the term of Court was completed, a bare five-man majority moved beyond it and attached an even tougher rule to state proceedings. This was the famous case of *Escobedo* v. *Illinois*.

On January 19, 1960, the husband of Danny Escobedo's sister was shot and killed. Escobedo was taken in for questioning and released after his lawyer interceded. Eleven days later, a man in police custody implicated Escobedo in the murder. Escobedo and his sister were arrested and again taken to police headquarters. Questioning began as soon as the two were put in the police car. He was told that a witness had named him the killer and that the case against him was tight. He was encouraged to confess, but Escobedo said, "I am sorry, but I would like to have advice from my lawyer."

Daniel A. Escobedo (right) whose name is a short-form reference to a Supreme Court landmark decision, is shown with his attorney in court in Chicago.

Wide World Photos

Shortly after Escobedo arrived at the police station, his lawyer appeared at the police station and asked to speak to his client. He was told that he could not. Though he repeatedly made the same request to a variety of officers, including those in the homicide bureau where Escobedo had been transferred, his efforts were unavailing, despite the fact that an Illinois statute purported to guarantee an attorney the right to see his client. During the three hours that his lawyer sought unsuccessfully to see him, Escobedo himself continued to ask for counsel. He was told, as the police later confirmed, that his lawyer "didn't want to see him." After a course of interrogation that involved a mild degree of trickery, Escobedo made some incriminating statements that led to his conviction.

Unlike Massiah's case, Escobedo had not been formally indicted at the time of police interrogation. Yet (also unlike the facts in *Massiah*), Escobedo had explicitly requested that he be permitted to speak with his lawyer. The Court reversed the conviction. For the majority, Justice Goldberg wrote:

We hold, therefore, that where, as here, the investigation is no longer a general inquiry into an unsolved crime but has begun to focus on a particular suspect, the suspect has been taken into police custody, the police carry out a process of interrogations that lends itself to eliciting incriminating statements, the suspect has requested and been denied an opportunity to consult with his lawyer, and the police have not effectively warned him of his absolute constitutional right to remain silent, the accused has been denied "the Assistance of Counsel" in violation of the Sixth Amendment to the Constitution as "made obligatory upon the States by the Fourteenth Amendment." . . . and that no statement elicited by the police during the interrogation may be used against him at a criminal trial.

This case set off an uproar in law enforcement circles, for it seemed to deny to the police the time-honored practice of questioning suspects at all. In his dissent Justice Harlan argued that "the rule announced today is most ill-conceived and that it seriously and unjustifiably fetters perfectly legitimate methods of criminal law enforcement."

Justice White, in a dissent joined by Justices Clark and Stewart, said that "the right to counsel now not only entitles the accused to counsel's advice and aid in preparing for trial but stands as an impenetrable barrier to any interrogation once the accused has become a suspect."

And in noting that Escobedo's confession was voluntary by any previously announced tests, Justice Stewart wrote: "I cannot escape the logic of my Brother White's conclusions as to the extraordinary implications which emanate from the Court's opinion in the case, and I share their views as to the untold and highly unfortunate impact today's decision may have upon the fair administration of criminal justice. I can only hope we have completely misunderstood what the Court has said." Time was to show that the four dissenters were only too correct in what they foresaw.

Yet the Escobedo holding itself was narrow, or so the passage from Justice Goldberg's majority opinion clearly indicates. Taken on the specific facts in the case, there really was far less to quarrel about than the dissenters, who were looking ahead to implications, thought. As Professor Arthur E. Sutherland wrote a year after *Escobedo*, and several months before *Miranda*, the holding was "a fairly obvious proposition to anyone who recognizes that Escobedo's only significant "trial" was being conducted in secret by the police, who were barring from the accused the lawyer he had retained, for whom he was asking. Escobedo's lawyer was the only person who would have told Escobedo what the state and federal constitutions both guaranteed to him—the privilege of remaining silent, a privilege about which his police interrogators told him nothing at all." The link between the right to counsel and the right against self-incrimination had been constitutionally forged. It remained to be seen how long the chain that could be constructed from it would be.

Forging the Final Link

A few months after the Supreme Court announced its decision in the *Escobedo* case, a sensational series of events involving two shocking murders began to unfold in New York. In the autumn of 1964, a young black man named George Whitmore, Jr., confessed to the police that he had raped and killed Janice Wylie and Emily Hoffert, two socially prominent young women, in their eastside Manhattan apartment. Thus a case that had been a source of acute embarrassment for the New York City police, who had not come up with any clues in the months since the crime had been committed, apparently was solved. Now at last, as the chief of detectives said, "We got the right guy. No question about it."

More than that, the Whitmore confession was heralded as the most telling answer imaginable to the Supreme Court's unwonted interference in the process of police investigation. A high level assistant in the Manhattan district attorney's office used the

Whitmore case to illustrate the folly of the Supreme Court's attempts, as he perceived it, to handcuff the police. He said:

Let me give you the perfect example of the importance of confessions to law enforcement. This, more than anything else, will prove how unrealistic and naive the Court is. Whitmore! The Whitmore case. Do you know that we had every top detective on the Wylie-Hoffert murders and they couldn't find a clue. Not a clue. I tell you, that if that kid hadn't confessed, we never would have caught the killer.

But Whitmore was innocent, it turned out some time later, when someone else owned up to the crimes. Whitmore's confession was a product of police overbearing, of a technique of interrogation applied against a person of weak intellect who could not withstand the onslaught. A prosecutor tried to explain: "Call it what you want—brain-washing, hypnosis, fright. They made him give an untrue confession. The only thing I don't believe is that Whitmore was beaten." The naivete was that of the prosecutors, after all, not the Supreme Court.

The *Whitmore* case and others that soon came to light had considerable influence on the Court's deliberations a year later, when four convictions resulting from confessions obtained during interrogation of the accused while in police custody came up on appeal. One was the conviction of Ernesto Miranda. Another was that of Michael Vignera, who was picked up by New York police for questioning about a dress shop robbery on October 11, 1960.

A third involved Carl Calvin Westover, arrested by the Kansas City police on March 20, 1963, for commission of two local robberies. Fourteen hours later, after lengthy interrogation in which he denied any knowledge of the crime, he was turned over to agents of the FBI, who wanted to question him about an unrelated robbery in California. Within three hours, they had his confession. (The FBI had advised him of his rights; the Kansas police had not.)

The fourth case concerned Roy Allen Stewart, arrested in Los Angeles on suspicion of having perpetrated a series of purse-snatching robberies. In the course of one of them a victim was injured and later died. Stewart let the police search his home, and they discovered objects taken from each of the victims. During eight interrogation sessions on the next five days, Stewart refused to confess. Finally during the ninth session, he admitted robbing the deceased, and for the first time was brought before a magistrate for arraignment.

Rules to Arrest By

On June 13, 1966, in a decision labeled *Miranda* v. *Arizona*, the Supreme Court upset the convictions of Miranda, Vignera, and Westover and affirmed the California supreme court's reversal of Stewart's conviction. The cases were decided together because they all shared "salient features—incommunicado interrogation of individuals in a police-dominated atmosphere, resulting in self-incriminating statements without full warnings of constitutional rights." In his opinion for a bare majority of five, Chief Justice Warren stated a new multipart constitutional rule, so detailed as to amount to a code of police conduct, and worth repeating here in full:

The prosecution may not use statements, whether exculpatory or inculpatory, stemming from custodial interrogation of the defendant unless it demonstrates the use of procedural safeguards effective to secure the privilege against self-incrimination. By custodial interrogation, we mean questioning initiated by law enforcement officers after a person has been taken into custody or otherwise deprived of his freedom of action in any significant way. As for the procedural safeguards to be employed, unless other fully effective means are devised to inform accused persons of their right of silence and to assure a continuous opportunity to exercise it, the following measures are required. Prior to any questioning, the person must be warned that he has a right to remain silent, that any statement he does make may be used as evidence against him, and that he has a right to the presence of an attorney, either retained or appointed. The defendant may waive effectuation of these rights, provided the waiver is made voluntarily, knowingly and intelligently. If, however, he indicates in any manner and at any stage of the process that he wishes to consult with an attorney before speaking there can be no questioning. Likewise, if the individual is alone and indicates in any manner that he does not wish to be interrogated, the police may not question him. The mere fact that he may have answered some questions or volunteered some statements on his own does not deprive him of the right to refrain from answering any further inquiries until he has consulted with an attorney and thereafter consents to be questioned.

Beginning with a review of methods by which the police induce suspects to confess, the chief justice noted that third-degree techniques were still employed. He cited a New York case in the 1960s in which "the police brutally beat, kicked, and placed lighted cigarette butts on the back of a potential witness under interrogation for the purpose of securing a statement incriminating a third party."

Outright physical abuse, Chief Justice Warren said, is undoubtedly the exception, but it is "sufficiently widespread to be the object of concern. Unless a proper limitation upon custodial interrogation is achieved—such as these decisions advance—there can be no assurance that practices of this nature will be eradicated in the foreseeable future." But there was no evidence of physical abuse in any of the four cases reviewed in *Miranda.*

Instead, the vice in each was psychological coercion. Warren devoted considerable attention to police manuals outlining the most efficient means of securing confessions. The manuals all recommended isolating the suspect and persisting despite initial denials or refusals to talk. One manual put it this way:

Where emotional appeals and tricks are employed to no avail, [the interrogator] must interrogate steadily and without relent, leaving the subject no prospect of surcease. He must dominate his subject and overwhelm him with his inexorable will to obtain the truth. He should interrogate for a spell of several hours, pausing only for the subject's necessities in acknowledgment of the need to avoid a charge of duress that can be technically substantiated. In a serious case, the interrogation may continue for days, with the required intervals for food and sleep, but with no respite from the atmosphere of domination.

The writer concluded this passage with the observation that "it is possible in this way to induce the subject to talk without resorting to duress or coercion."

It is precisely this conclusion that Warren denied, finding instead that the very practices described amount to unlawful coercion: "The very fact of custodial interrogation exacts a heavy toll of individual liberty," the chief justice said, "and trades on the weakness of individuals."

In reviewing the cases before the Court, Warren conceded that "we might not find the defendants' statements to have been involuntary in traditional terms. . . . The fact remains that in none of these cases did the officers undertake to afford appropriate safeguards at the outset of the interrogation to insure that the statements were truly the product of free choice."

In announcing the rules that were quickly to become known as *Miranda* warnings (illustrated nowadays on all television detective programs), the Court was determined to avoid having to consider this issue on a case-by-case basis. In a homogeneous culture of high literacy and education, it might be taken for granted that everyone would know his rights. Not so in the real world, where the Fifth Amendment is meant to protect the ignorant as well as the knowledgeable:

The Fifth Amendment privilege is so fundamental to our system of constitutional rule and the expedient of giving an adequate warning as to the availability of the privilege so simple, we will not pause to inquire in individual cases whether the defendant was aware of his rights without a warning being given. Assessments of the knowledge the defendant possessed, based on information as to his age, education, intelligence, or prior contact with authorities, can never be more that speculation; a warning is a clear-cut fact. More important, whatever the background of the person interrogated, a warning at the time of the interrogation is indispensable to overcome its pressures and to insure that the individual knows he is free to exercise the privilege at that point in time.

The other warnings that *Miranda* made compulsory on the police—that whatever the suspect says may be used against him, that he has the right to counsel, and that if he cannot afford a lawyer one will be appointed for him—followed, the chief justice said, from similar considerations. Unless suspects are effectively advised of these rights and unless the rights themselves are effectively implemented, the Fifth and Sixth Amendments could become empty formalities. They would be grand gestures at a later trial, the outcome of which would be foregone. And since these rights are always available to any person, the mere fact that a suspect says at the outset of interrogation that he does not wish to remain silent or does not wish to consult with a lawyer or to have counsel present does not operate to waive his right to do so later. In all these rules, the Court was striving to eliminate any possibility of trickery and to limit the capacity of the government to act in a lawless manner.

Obstacles Real and Imagined

The outburst that greeted this decision was entirely predictable. Police issued dire warnings that the new rules would cripple law enforcement. There can be no doubt, however, that the police anguish was a considerable overstatement. Unless a person walks into a police station and gives himself up, he can never be arrested unless there is some reason, other than a confession, to believe that he committed the crime. In the very cases at hand, the chief justice pointed out, there was considerable evidence to prove the defendants' guilt. The FBI, moreover, had long been in the habit of advising suspects of their rights substantially as the Court was now requiring local police to do. There had been no showing that this practice hindered the FBI's efforts or federal prosecutors' later ability to succeed in winning convictions.

As to the person who surprises the police by confessing without being asked, the Court found no objection to the use of his statement at the trial. The object of the *Miranda* warnings is not to do away with confessions altogether but to provide safeguards to insure that people confess only when they really desire to do so. The purpose of the Fifth Amendment, as the majority saw it, can have no other meaning. Constitutional prohibitions against an overbearing government can scarcely be violated in order to obtain a result in a particular case where it is "known" that the suspect is in fact guilty, for that is the very question at issue.

The dissenters viewed the decision differently. Justice White put it this way:

The Court largely ignores . . . that its rules impair, if they will not eventually serve wholly to frustrate, an instrument of law enforcement that has long and quite reasonably been thought worth the price paid for it. There can be little doubt that the Court's new code would markedly decrease the number of confessions. . . . How much harm this decision will inflict on law enforcement cannot fairly be predicted with accuracy. . . . We do know that some crimes cannot be solved without confessions, that ample expert testimony attests to their importance in crime control, and that the Court is taking a real risk with society's welfare in imposing its new regime on the country. The social costs of crime are too great to call the new rules anything but a hazardous experimentation. . . . The Court portrays the evils of normal police questioning in terms which I think are exaggerated. Albeit stringently confined by the due process standards interrogation is no doubt often inconvenient and unpleasant for the suspect. However, it is no less so for a man to be arrested and jailed, to have his house searched, or to stand trial in court, yet all this may properly happen to the most innocent given probable cause, a warrant, or an indictment. Society has always paid a stiff price for law and order, and peaceful interrogation is not one of the dark moments of the law.

Much of the trouble with the Court's new rule is that it will operate indiscriminately in all criminal cases, regardless of the severity of the crime or the circumstances involved. It applies to every defendant, whether the professional criminal or one committing a crime of momentary passion who is not part and parcel of organized crime. It will slow down the investigation and the apprehension of confederates in those cases where time is of the essence, such as kidnapping . . . those involving the national security . . . and some of those involving organized crime. In the latter context the lawyer who arrives may also be the lawyer for the defendant's colleagues and can be relied upon to insure that no breach of the organiza-

tion's security takes place even though the accused may feel that the best thing he can do is to cooperate.

Moreover, Justice White predicted, the rule of *Miranda,* could not be expected to bring certainty into a confused area. "Today's decision," he said, "leaves open such questions as whether the accused was in custody, whether his statements were spontaneous or the product of interrogation, whether the accused has effectively waived his rights, and whether nontestimonial evidence introduced at trial is the fruit of statements made during a prohibited interrogation, all of which are certain to prove productive of uncertainty during prosecution."

After Miranda

Like *Baker* v. *Carr,* the decision in *Miranda* v. *Arizona* may be understood in historical terms as the reaction of the Court to what it perceived as governmental overreaching and lawlessness. Unlike *Baker* v. *Carr,* however, the overreaching was explainable at least in part as a reaction to a specific social evil. The great increase in urban crime had caused a worried public to applaud whatever efforts a hard-pressed and overworked police force could muster to defeat it. This put the Court in an untenable position: facing both a rise in crime and an increase in official lawlessness, the Court was forced to choose between the two. But the only weapon at its disposal was that which acted against official lawlessness, not against street crime. The Court's choice, as the majority saw it, was either to crack down on the government's own violation of the law or to leave the government alone. As the guardian of constitutional liberties, the Court majority thought its choice must clearly be the former course.

In the long run, the majority thought, *Miranda* would restore to the police a large measure of public confidence that it felt sorely lacking at the time of the decision. Public confidence is itself a critical ingredient in the performance of police duties. A public that refuses to become "involved" will thwart the police in their efforts to solve many crimes.

But the public that might be reassured by police adherence to the *Miranda* rules was counterbalanced by a vast and influential segment of the public that already had confidence in the police as long as the men in blue could continue unshackled by judicial pronouncements. To this increasingly vocal segment of the public, *Miranda* did not restore public confidence. It shattered it. Two years later, Richard Nixon would play on the fears of this part of the public in calling for a new Supreme Court that he promised to appoint, given the chance. He was, and he did.

Eight years after the decision, how does *Miranda* hold up? As a practical matter, the fears that it would destroy police effectiveness have vanished. Numerous studies have shown that while the confession rate has dropped in many cities, the conviction rate has not changed appreciably. In some, in fact, it has even gone up, the *Miranda* rules apparently giving the police incentive to be more thorough in locating hard evidence to make their cases.

It has also turned out that confessions continue to be obtained and used. In part this may be because those who are guilty are willing to talk and may be encouraged by officers who advise them in sincerity that they need not. Law that respects the accused may give the accused a reason to respect the law and the people who represent it. Confidence that the law is even-handed and not coercive may induce confessions that previously would not have been forthcoming. In part the continued willingness of suspects to confess may stem from the ease with which *Miranda* warnings can be circumvented (one New York detective was quoted as advising a suspect as follows: "You mungble bruup stend lawyer"). In the end it is a policeman's word against that of the defendant, and a jury may well choose to trust the policeman every time.

As a legal matter, the continued viability of *Miranda* is equivocal, but a full discussion is beyond the scope of this book. In any event, it is unnecessary since other books have treated the problem in great detail. Still a few observations may here be made.

In 1968, angered at *Miranda,* Congress enacted the Omnibus Crime Control Act. The purpose of this act was to overrule the case altogether. It provided that in any federal prosecution, no confession can be excluded if the trial judge concludes from all the circumstances that the defendant in fact confessed voluntarily. If the Court in *Miranda* had merely been announcing a rule in exercise of its power to supervise the lower federal courts, Congress doubtless could have overturned it and substituted its own. But, though there was language in the opinion permitting police and prosecutors to devise methods of obtaining confessions, *Miranda* was a constitutional ruling. The gist of that warning was that under the Fifth Amendment a confession could not be voluntary unless preceded by the proper warnings. Thus the constitutionality of the Crime Control Act is open to some question, though the Burger Court has not yet ruled definitively on it.

If the Warren Court were still sitting, there could be no doubt about the outcome of a case squarely presenting the issue. But the Burger Court has an undisguised antipathy toward *Miranda,* and it went out of its way in 1971 to undercut that case seriously.

The opportunity to do so came in *Harris* v. *New York.* The police failed to warn Harris, who had been arrested on a narcotics charge, of his rights, though he asked to have counsel present. During the interrogation Harris made incriminating statements. This occurred after *Escobedo* but before *Miranda.*

At the trial, Harris took the stand and contradicted a statement he earlier had made to police. The prosecution introduced the prior incriminating statement, even though it was apparently false. Their purpose was not to convince the jury that he had done what he had confessed (since they knew that the statement was false) but to impeach his character. Of course, the very fact that he had made such incriminating statements to the police could not fail to suggest guilt to the jury.

By a five to four vote, the Court ruled that the use of such statements did not violate the Fifth Amendment. As a practical matter, this means that the police now have a large incentive to continue their old practice of interrogating without advising the suspect of his rights. If they secure a confession in violation of *Miranda,* they cannot use it unless the defendant takes the stand. As a practical matter, therefore, *Harris* may act as a deterrent to a defendant's decision to testify in his own behalf.

This may become significant, in light of the Court's announcement, as this is written, to hear arguments concerning "whether an accused who asserts his right to silence following his arrest properly subjects himself: (a) to questions as to why he did not protest his innocence at the point of arrest, at the preliminary hearing, or at some time earlier than at the trial; (b) to the prosecutor's argument to the jury that an unfavorable inference could be drawn against the accused as a consequence of his having exercised these constitutional rights." This augurs a reopening of the question, considered settled in 1965, that a prosecutor who comments on the defendant's failure to take the stand in his own defense violates the self-incrimination clause of the Fifth Amendment.

If this rule is limited or overruled, the implications are obvious. If police may coerce a confession that may then be used if the defendant takes the stand, the defendant will not take the stand. If he does not, the prosecutor may argue that his failure to do so is an indication of guilt. For a broad class of cases, *Miranda* will thus have been indirectly but effectively overruled.

Chief Justice Burger has been accused of making a "shocking distortion" of the facts in the *Harris* case in saying that Harris had never claimed his statement to be coerced, when in fact Harris had claimed so all along. This makes the holding in the case somewhat obscure legally. By its own terms it did not deal with a situation in which the confession, aside from the lack of *Miranda* warnings, was in fact involuntary.

Whether the Court will in the future close its eyes to allegations of coercion is open to question. If it does, *Miranda* will have been seriously undercut, if not destroyed. Prosecutors argue that at least here it should be undercut so that defendants will be prevented from taking the stand and shamelessly lying about their complicity in a crime. Whether one agrees or not depends on one's views about whether police interrogation is inherently coercive, about the value of the Fifth Amendment protection against compulsory self-incrimination, and about the morality of a government that seeks to circumvent it.

Miranda is still law, but it does not stand strong. As the constitutional scholar Leonard W. Levy has summed it up: "*Harris* did not overrule *Miranda*. *Harris* throttled *Miranda*, circumvented it, excepted it, and invited law-enforcement agencies to do the same." At this writing the controversy over *Miranda* continues unabated, and it doubtless will continue to dominate discussions about crime and the criminal process for years to come.

As for Ernesto Miranda himself, the 1966 decision did not materially aid him. On February 24, 1967, less than a year after the Court reversed his original conviction, a jury again found him guilty of the crimes of rape and kidnapping. His confession, of course, was excluded. But during his confinement in jail, he had been visited by his former common-law wife. He told her that he had indeed committed the crimes with which he was charged. At the trial she took the stand and told the jury what Miranda had told her. The jury deliberated less than one hour before returning its verdict. He was sentenced to prison for a term of from twenty to thirty years. In 1971 he was reconvicted on the earlier robbery charge. On December 12, 1972, Miranda was paroled.

Three years later, on January 31, 1976, he was stabbed to death in a skid-row bar in Phoenix during a quarrel over a card game. In his pockets were two "Miranda cards". The police have used such cards on which *Miranda* warnings are printed, since 1966. Ernesto Miranda was said to have been printing and selling them near the Maricopa County Superior Court for $2 each. The Phoenix police read from a card he had been carrying to advise one of the suspected murderers of his rights.

In photo at left, Ernesto Miranda (right) with his attorney, John Flynn, was convicted for a second time on kidnap-rape charges. His first conviction was overturned by the Supreme Court.
UPI

18/ THE RIGHTS OF JUVENILES: IN RE GAULT

The Due Process Clause of the Fourteenth Amendment places its protective mantle over "persons." This word has an expansive meaning, as we have seen. It includes corporations as well as real people. Nevertheless, it has limits. For instance, a human fetus is not a person within the meaning of the Fourteenth Amendment, as we will see in Chapter 19. And until 1967 the word also excluded about one-third of the total living human population of the country: children. In that year the Supreme Court ruled for the first time that many of the various procedural protections it was steadily extending to adults charged with crimes must be available to juveniles as well.

The Crime of Gerald Gault

The events that led up to this decision began on June 8, 1964 in Gila County, Arizona, where the county sheriff picked up 15-year-old Gerald Francis Gault and his friend Ronald Lewis. A neighbor, Mrs. Cook, told police that the boys had made an obscene telephone call to her. The boys were taken to Children's Detention Home, where Gault was held for several days.

No notice was sent to Gerald's home, so that when his mother came home from work (his father being out of town at work), she had to make inquiries before finally tracking down her son. When she located him at the detention home, she was told there would be a hearing the following day. These proceedings were not entirely foreign to her. Gerald was still on probation as the result of having been in the company of another boy who had stolen a wallet from a lady's purse several months earlier.

There is considerable confusion as to what transpired at the hearing on June 9 as well as at a further hearing on June 15, because there is no record of what was said. Mrs. Gault later said her son admitted dialing the phone but his friend actually made the remarks to Mrs. Cook. The deputy probation officer recalled that

Gerald had owned up to making a lewd statement. After the June 9 hearing, Gerald was kept at the detention home until June 11 or 12, when he was released. The authorities never explained why he was held or why he was released.

On the day of his release his mother received a note stating that another hearing had been scheduled for June 15 in connection with his "delinquency." At this hearing, attended by both his parents, recollections again differed. Mr. and Mrs. Gault said later that Gerald once again denied making the remarks, and time, the deputy probation officer agreed with their recollection. But the juvenile judge later recalled that Gerald did admit making one of the remarks.

At neither of the hearings was Mrs. Cook present. At no time did the judge contact her or attempt to verify the complaint she had made. And Gerald never had the opportunity to confront her.

Following the June 15 hearing, a "referral report" was made up. It was not shown to the Gaults. It listed the offense as making "lewd phone calls" (in the plural). Immediately after the hearing Gerald was committed to the Juvenile Industrial School, a state home for juvenile delinquents. His term was to last until his twenty-first birthday or in other words, six years. Had he been an adult, the maximum sentence for making a lewd telephone call would have been a fifty dollar fine, two months imprisonment, or both.

Arizona law did not permit an appeal from an order of the juvenile judge. So two months later the Gaults filed a petition with the state supreme court for a writ of habeas corpus to free their son. At the hearing the juvenile judge was asked under what law he had sentenced Gerald. He answered as follows: "Well, there is— I think it amounts to disturbing the peace. I can't give you the section, but I can tell you the law, that when one person uses lewd language in the presence of another person, that it can amount to— and I consider that when a person makes it over the phone, that it is considered in the presence. I might be wrong, that is one section. The other section upon which I consider the boy delinquent is Section 8-201, Subsection (d), habitually involved in immoral matters."

The basis for his conclusion that the youth was "habitually involved in immoral matters," the judge said, was threefold. First there was the probation that still hung over Gerald's head (for being in the company of a purse snatcher). Second, he had been accused of stealing a baseball glove from another boy. This accusation

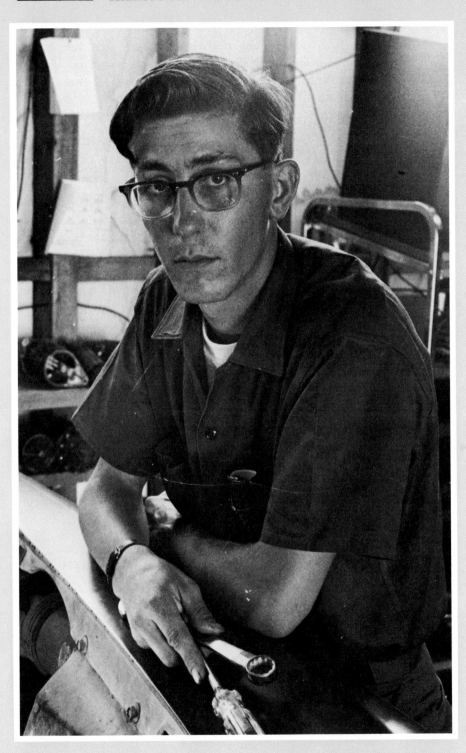

Gerald Gault.

Wide World Photos

had come to the judge's attention two years before, though there was never any hearing or even a formal accusation, "because of lack of material foundation." Third, Gerald had admitted making nuisance calls in the past (only the judge remembered these statements). The Arizona supreme court denied the writ, leaving the youth to his six-year term.

The American Juvenile System

These extraordinary proceedings have been a commonplace feature of juvenile justice throughout the United States since the turn of the century. The first juvenile court law was enacted in Illinois in 1899. By 1917 forty-five states had created such court systems. The idea behind the juvenile reform movement was that adult prisons were harmful in the extreme and that the state ought to try to rehabilitate the wayward youngster rather than punish him. The emphasis was on saving the child from the life of adult crime: "They are born to it," said a penologist in 1880, "brought up for it. They must be saved."

But the dream was far beyond the ability of reformers to achieve. The process of determining whether to send a child to a reform school was supposed to be a civil, not a criminal, proceeding.

A typical scene from a training school for boys where juveniles were kept under harsh and bleak conditions.

Minnesota Historical Society

The outcome was supposed to be a decision to treat a problem, not to produce a verdict. The reformatories were rehabilitation centers, not prisons.

Unfortunately, the philanthropists and philosophers who decided that such a system would be better for the child were not those called upon to staff the courts and the schools.

A description of one such place, the St. Charles School, in Illinois in the late 1920s indicates what a dismal failure reform had been. According to an investigation undertaken by the Illinois Crime Commission: "During the early months of Major Butler's regime, all whippings were administered by a disciplinary officer who, in company with the military officer of the day, went to each cottage each evening after supper and whipped any boys who had been reported earlier by the house father, or for whom the house father requested punishment at the time." Other punishments for infractions of the school's military rules included being locked up for periods of up to thirty-two days in a "hole," which contained no mattress and where the boys were permitted no shoes. Wooden boards were nailed to concrete floors for sleeping, and some boys were even "handcuffed to iron pipes and kept manacled day and night."

By the 1960s, there were some well-run juvenile institutions. But the majority of the hundreds that existed throughout the United States were overcrowded, dreary, even brutal places run by at best indifferent, and at worst, sadistic, staffs. And because there were almost no judicial safeguards surrounding the "admissions" procedure, a child's fate was often determined casually, with little thought for his best welfare.

The Gault Decision and Its Importance

That indeed seemed to be the attitude that prevailed in the proceedings that sent Gerald Gault to a reformatory for six years. The laxness of procedure was supposedly to be made up for by careful scrutiny of all the circumstances of his case. Yet the very lack of standards encouraged the judge to take no pains at all. The simplified process turned out to be no process. The judge did not inquire into the quality of Gault's home life or the likelihood that his parents could exercise control over his conduct in the future. And he did not undertake to discover whether what Gault had done was anything more than the prank of a high-spirited youth.

Despite this, the Arizona supreme court approved the reformatory sentence. Because Gault was still on probation, "the Judge could have committed Gerald without any further showing of delinquency if he decided Gerald's welfare and the interests of the state so required," the court said. It added that it was not necessary for the juvenile judge to make a specific finding that the parents were unfit to retain custody of their child.

The state justified its failure to require the procedures necessary in the trial of adult crimes by claiming that the child benefits by the informality of the proceedings. For instance, under the juvenile court law, the child is not classified as a criminal but as a delinquent. The state also noted that under the juvenile system the wayward youth is protected from disclosure of his conduct "to hide youthful errors from the full gaze of the public and bury them in the graveyard of the forgotten past."

But, as Justice Fortas pointed out, these benefits were more theoretical than real. The status of being a delinquent is scarcely a comforting one by which to be known. At that time the police had full access to a delinquent's record, subject only to completely standardless discretion of the courts. Moreover, justifying the withdrawal of procedural safeguards by pointing to such benefits is a non sequitur. There is nothing about procedural safeguards that would prevent the state from continuing to classify youths as delinquent rather than as criminals or from sealing the records of juvenile proceedings.

These considerations led the Supreme Court in 1967 (by an eight to one vote) to void Gault's sentence. "Under our Constitution, the condition of being a boy does not justify a kangaroo court," Justice Fortas wrote in the majority opinion. For the first time the Court held that four basic procedures required by due process in adult trials are also required in juvenile delinquency proceedings.

The first is the right to timely notice of the charges. Mrs. Gault did not know why her son was being held until she went to the detention center on the night her son was taken into custody. Two or three days after the first hearing she was given a short note to the effect that "further hearings on Gerald's delinquency" were set for a few days hence. The formal petition required by state law to be filed with the court was never served on the Gaults. The petition itself did not set forth any facts from which anyone could draw the conclusion that the boy might be a delinquent. Not until the first hearing itself was it explained that Gerald could be sent away for being habitually involved in "immoral matters."

These procedures, said the Court, were constitutionally defective. "Notice to comply with due process requirements, must be given sufficiently in advance of scheduled court proceedings so that reasonable opportunity to prepare will be afforded, and it must 'set forth the alleged misconduct with particularity.' "

Second, the Court laid down a right-to-counsel requirement. The Arizona state supreme court had rather fatuously said that "the parent and the probation officer may be relied upon to protect the infant's interests." This proposition was not a part of this case, but it is instructive to examine how dangerous an unqualified acceptance of this proposition can be.

One of the most lawless examples of the juvenile court system was in El Paso, Texas, where even after the *Gault* decision, juveniles were regularly denied counsel. In many instances, they were not even afforded a hearing. Indeed, from 1966 until 1971, when publicity caught up with him, one El Paso juvenile judge summarily committed 375 children to juvenile homes without holding any sort of hearing at all.

Frequently this occurred with the connivance of parents, who for their own reasons, simply wished to dump their children on the state. In testimony before the Senate Subcommittee to Investigate Juvenile Delinquency in 1971, Bill Payne, an *El Paso Times* reporter who first broke the scandal, told about one such incident:

Despite the fact that the practice of "baby-sitting" juveniles in the County Juvenile Detention Home at parental request without formally charging them was exposed as illegal in the Times as far back as Oct. 29, 1970, in February and March of this year [1971] a 16-year-old girl was locked up for more than a month in the Detention Home at her mother's request. The mother simply said the girl was "incorrigible," and during the girl's confinement by obliging juvenile authorities, the mother actually went on a two-week vacation with her paramour. When the mother returned to town, the little girl was released, never having seen a lawyer, never having been formally charged, never having been produced "forthwith" before the judge as required by Texas law and certainly never having been convicted of anything.

There was no indication of a conflict between the Gaults and their son, but the Court observed numerous reasons to suppose that the probation officer could not be relied on to protect the "infant's" interest. "Probation officers, in the Arizona scheme, are also arresting officers," Justice Fortas noted. "They initiate proceedings and file petitions which they verify, as here, alleging the delinquency of the child; and they testify, as here, against the child. And here the probation officer was also superintendent of the Detention

Home. The probation officer cannot act as counsel for the child. His role in the adjudicatory hearing, by statute and fact, is as arresting officer and witness against the child."

The Court held that the rule of *Gideon* v. *Wainwright* is fully applicable in juvenile proceedings and that the court must specifically advise the child and parents of the availability of court-appointed counsel if they are indigent.

Third, the Court incorporated the full constitutional privilege against self-incrimination in juvenile proceedings. Neither the arresting officer nor the juvenile judge advised Gerald of any right to remain silent or that statements he might make could be the basis for an order sending him to the juvenile home for six years.

The state supreme court did not feel that such a warning was necessary. "We think," that court said, "the necessary flexibility for individualized treatment will be enhanced by a rule which does not require the judge to advise the infant of a privilege against self-incrimination." It added that to require such a warning would mean that the number of confessions would be reduced. This would be a bad result, the state court thought. It believed that confession is good therapy for the child.

The Supreme Court disagreed. It cited studies that showed that "where children are induced to confess by 'paternal' urgings on the part of officials and the confession is then followed by disciplinary action, the child's reaction is likely to be hostile and adverse—the child may well feel that he has been led or tricked into confession and that despite his confession, he is being punished." And, more to the point of the constitutional question, it examined several current instances in which juvenile confessions were shown to be completely untrustworthy, for reasons similar to those discussed in *Miranda* v. *Arizona*.

Fourth, the Court ruled that any youth subjected to proceedings such as those that occurred in Gault's case is entitled to hear sworn testimony of the complainant and to confront all the witnesses by cross-examination. In neither of Gault's hearings did the complaining witness, Mrs. Cook, show up. At no time did the judge see or talk with her. The only evidence that Gault committed the unlawful act charged was the hearsay testimony of the arresting officer and the disputed incriminating statement by Gault himself. State law required sworn testimony "of all witnesses including police officers, probation officers and others who are part of or officially related to the juvenile court structure." The Court held that this is not enough. There was no rational reason for omitting the sworn testimony of other witnesses and figures in the case.

As important as the *Gault* case was in bringing to juvenile courts at least the rudiments of fairness, it has not obliterated the juvenile courts. The juvenile court system exists substantially as it was, especially because in 1971 the Supreme Court refused to extend the right of jury trials to juvenile proceedings. Thus the finding of delinquency was left in the hands of the juvenile judges.

Similarly the *Gault* decision has not led all lawyers to fight vigorously on behalf of child clients. A study of the Chicago public defender published two years after *Gault* concluded that the decision has led to a conflict between the lawyer's role as an "officer of the court" and an advocate for the child. "The public defender resolves this dilemma," the study stated,

by doing "what is best for a kid." If he considers his client a "good kid," he will do everything to have the charge dismissed or will plead guilty in return for a warning or light sentence, such as probation. "Bad kids" are given up on. The public defender assumes, along with all juvenile court functionaries, that little can be done to "help" these clients..He pleads them guilty and cooperates to process them into reformatories. They have long records, they are charged with "serious" offenses, and they are likely to antagonize judges with their poor school record. The public defender does not waste his time or credit on "bad kids" because a serious effort on their behalf would only jeopardize his chances with more "worthy" defendants. . . . Juvenile clients are regarded even by their lawyers as subordinates and "nonpersons" who have little competence to appreciate their own behavior or determine where their best interests lie. The Gault *decision will not in itself enhance the bargaining power or autonomy of young offenders. The participation of lawyers in juvenile court is likely to make the system more efficient and orderly, but not substantially more fair or benevolent.*

This is, of course, more a criticism of the continued existence of the traditional juvenile justice system than it is of *Gault*, which sought to introduce standards into a totally chaotic field of quasi-criminal prosecution. The larger problem cannot be solved by the Court—it did not pretend that it could or that it wanted to do so. But it is a problem growing more critical daily. The fastest growing element of the criminal population is the juvenile, and it is in a shocking disproportion to the total population. Juveniles between ten and seventeen make up some 16 percent of all Americans, but they account for nearly one-half of all arrests for violent crimes and thefts. In light of statistics such as these, one can conclude that *Gault* was a vindication of fairness in a system becoming increasingly outmoded.

19/ THE PRIVACY OF ONE'S BODY: ROE v. WADE

With the retirement of Earl Warren in 1969, the resignation of Justice Fortas, the inauguration of Richard Nixon in that same year, the sudden retirements and deaths of Justices Black and Harlan in 1971, the Warren Court came to a relatively quick end as an institution. Retrenchments from the main lines of many of the Warren Court's most important cases were foreordained. One of the central campaign issues, after all, had been to restore strict constructionism to the High Bench.

To replace Earl Warren, President Nixon nominated Warren Earl Burger, then a judge on the U.S. Court of Appeals for the District of Columbia Circuit. The replacement of Justice Fortas prompted a memorable row. The Senate first rejected Circuit Judge Clement F. Haynsworth, Jr., and then rejected Nixon's second nomination, G. Harrold Carswell, also a circuit judge (who subsequently resigned and was defeated in a race for the Senate from Florida).

Nixon's third nominee, Circuit Judge Harry A. Blackmun, finally took the oath of office as associate justice in June 1970. And in January 1972, Lewis F. Powell, Jr., and William H. Rehnquist were sworn in to take the seats vacated by Justices Black and Harlan. In short order it became clear that the pioneering days of extending Bill of Rights protections had ended. The Court had become circumspect.

But a president can never entirely predict what course of action his appointments to the Court will take. Theodore Roosevelt was sorely disappointed in Oliver Wendell Holmes, Felix Frankfurter surprised the entire liberal community, and Earl Warren vexed President Eisenhower. Just so, the strict constructionists whom President Nixon supposed were now a working majority of the Court have not always turned out to be such. In no case has this been more evident than in the 1973 abortion decision *Roe* v. *Wade*.

The Assault on Abortion Laws

The state of Texas had a statute making it a crime to "procure an abortion" or to attempt one, unless the abortion was necessary according to medical judgment to save the life of the mother. This statute was typical of the abortion laws in a majority of the states. In Texas the language of the law dated back to 1857.

In March 1970, a single woman identified only as Jane Roe filed suit in federal court against the Dallas County district attorney for a declaratory judgment that the Texas law violated the Constitution. She also sought an injunction to restrain the district attorney from enforcing the law. Roe said that she was unmarried and pregnant and that she wanted to terminate the pregnancy by an abortion "performed by a competent, licensed physician, under safe, clinical conditions."

She could not afford to travel outside the state for an abortion. And the Texas law kept her from having one because her life was not in danger. She contended that the existence of the criminal statute preventing doctors from performing the operation and her from seeking it violated her right to privacy. These rights were protected under the First, Fourth, Fifth, Ninth, and Fourteenth Amendments. She was suing "on behalf of herself and all other women" similarly situated.

A physician, James Hubert Hallford, intervened in the suit. Two criminal prosecutions for having performed abortions were pending against him. The abortion law, he claimed, was vaguely worded, made it difficult for him to determine when he could properly perform abortions, and that, in any event, the restrictions violated his right to practice medicine and his patients' right to privacy in the doctor-patient relationship.

At the same time, a couple identified pseudonymously as John and Mary Doe filed a similar suit involving different facts. Married, the Does were childless. Mrs. Doe was said to be suffering from a "neural-chemical" disorder. She was under her doctor's order "to avoid pregnancy until such time as her condition has materially improved." She stated that pregnancy would not present "a serious risk" to her life. However, because of her medical condition, she had ceased using birth control pills. She wanted to be able to have an abortion performed, if necessary, without the awkward interference of a law that made it a crime.

A three-judge federal court, convened because the litigants were seeking an injunction against a state law that they claimed

Opposite page:

Chief Justice Warren E. Burger.

violated the federal constitution, ruled that the Does had no standing to sue and dismissed their complaint. But it ruled in favor of both Roe and Dr. Hallford by declaring the act unconstitutional. It refused, however, to grant an injunction against the district attorney. The parties appealed to the Supreme Court.

The Court in the Midst of Social Change

If there ever was a classic case for reversal, here it was. A lower federal court had declared unconstitutional a criminal statute punishing what many believed was murder of the human fetus. Not until very recent years had there even been so much as a whisper that such laws could be considered unconstitutional. Surely the state had the power to outlaw conduct resulting in the cessation of life.

But the Court did not think so. To understand its opinion, we must take a look at the social climate in which the issue was raised. Although abortion is condemned in the Hippocratic Oath, to which physicians still subscribe today, it is reasonably clear that abortion was prevalent in the ancient world. And the Hippocratic Oath did not persuade medieval jurists to condemn abortion outright. Under common law, abortions performed before the so-called *quickening* of the fetus—that is, its first movement, around the fourth month— were entirely lawful.

Abortions performed on the quick fetus may have been considered criminal—the evidence is equivocal—but in any event they were not considered serious. At most they were a misdemeanor. Not until 1803 in England was there an abortion statute. It made abortion of a quick fetus punishable by death. By an 1837 law, all abortions were so punishable. Not until 1929 was an exception made for abortions performed for the purpose of "preserving the life of the mother." (The law was considerably liberalized in 1967.)

In America, the English common law remained generally the law on the subject until after the Civil War. The earliest statutes— Connecticut in 1821, New York in 1828—maintained a distinction between the unquick and the quick fetus. Many states adopted laws based on this distinction. But by the 1870s, state after state began to adopt laws that made all abortions criminal (unless, in most states, performed to save the mother's life).

Why were these laws passed? Three reasons have been advanced. One is protection of the fetus. A second, on which there is much historical evidence, is protection of the mother. Surgical procedures were relatively primitive, of course. There was considerable danger in undergoing any kind of surgery. (There were attempts made in 1828 in New York to prohibit any surgery that was not essential to preserving life, but the bill was defeated because in every type of surgery but abortion, there were sound reasons to rely on the caution of patients.) Only in the case of abortions was it thought that extramedical considerations might sway women into taking unnecessary risks or men into persuading them to do so. A third, double-jointed reason advanced for the enactment of criminal laws banning abortion was to keep women in their place through emphasis on the legal necessity of bearing children and to preserve Victorian sexual mores.

By the late 1950s, two of these reasons were vanishing. Surgery, especially in the early months, was no longer particularly risky. On the contrary, the real risk resulted from the continued outlawing of the surgery, requiring women desperate enough for abortions to seek the operations under black market conditions that often led to serious injury or death. And the notion that women should be remitted to a procreative function only was finally capsizing under a torrent of books and other commentary.

In the 1960s, interest in the abortion problem grew enormously from a confluence of related factors. In 1961-62, the discovery that thalidomide caused serious birth defects caused grave anxiety in thousands of women. The tribulations of one thalidomide user, Mrs. Sherri Finkbine, whose scheduled Arizona abortion was canceled and whose later trip to Sweden to secure an abortion of a fetus that was indeed deformed, received world wide publicity. Her case helped focus public concern on laws that were beginning to be understood as too harsh. The problem of birth defects was further aggravated in the wake of a German measles epidemic in 1964.

By the late 1960s the impact of these prior incidents and the advent of the pill, new sexual mores, fears of a population crisis and the growing respectability of family planning, and, finally, the explosion of long-suppressed social and economic suffragism that quickly became known as "Women's Lib," prompted a reform movement. Legislatively, it began in 1967.

New statutes were passed in California, Colorado, and North Carolina. These added new grounds for having abortions, including in some instances the physical and mental health of the mother, fetal deformity, and conception due to rape. By 1970, one-third of the states had enacted some sort of abortion reform. People were no longer afraid of talking about abortion—or demanding it. Hundreds of suits came before federal and state courts between 1969 and 1972. Some courts were beginning to hold restrictive abortion statutes unconstitutional, as the three-judge federal court did in Jane Roe's case.

The Rising Legal Tide

In legal terms many of the cases were constitutional offspring of a 1965 Supreme Court decision, *Griswold* v. *Connecticut*. In this ruling the Court voided a Connecticut statute prohibiting anyone from giving out birth control information, even to married couples. Justice Douglas, in his opinion for the Court, said that at issue was the right of privacy of the married couple. He set forth a theory that protected this right by means of specific constitutional guarantees—in the First, Third, Fourth, Fifth, and Ninth Amendments.

Although only three other justices subscribed to Justice Douglas's opinion, the decision was concurred in by seven justices. A right of privacy, at least in intimate family affairs, looked to have great constitutional potential.

With all this in the air, the *Roe* case was first argued on De-

Justice William O. Douglas.

Minnesota Historical Society

cember 13, 1971, just before Justices Powell and Rehnquist assumed office. To permit them to join in the decision, reargument was scheduled and held on October 11, 1972. On January 22, 1973, the Court dropped its bombshell. It overturned all state statutes that prohibited abortions during the first three months of pregnancy. Six justices joined in Justice Blackmun's opinion for the Court. Chief Justice Burger and Justices Douglas and Stewart each filed concurring opinions. Only Justices White and Rehnquist dissented.

The threshold question was whether the litigants—Roe, Dr. Hallford, and the Does—had standing to sue. The only reason that Roe could not have had standing was that she could not possibly have remained pregnant from March 1970, when she filed the suit, until December 13, 1971, when the first Supreme Court argument was held. Somewhere along the way, the condition that gave rise to the case must have disappeared one way or the other. In light of this circumstance the district attorney contended that the suit, at least as to her, was moot.

The Court denied this. Because the appellate process takes as long as it does, it would be practically impossible ever to bring a case before the Court while a woman remained pregnant. Here was a case "capable of repetition, yet evading review." The Court refused to let Texas wriggle out of facing the issue as to Jane Roe.

Dr. Hallford, however, was dismissed from the case. Because prosecutions were then pending against him, he was held to have an adequate means of testing the constitutionality of the laws in the state cases. The Does' suit, too, was dismissed. Their claimed injury was simply too tenuous. It rested "on possible future contraceptive failure, possible future pregnancy, possible future unpreparedness for parenthood, and possible future impairment of health. . . . In the Does' estimation, these possibilities might have some real or imagined impact upon their marital happiness. But we are not prepared to say that the bare allegation of so indirect an injury is sufficient to present an actual case or controversy." But these dismissals hardly mattered, for the determination of Jane Roe's case determined theirs.

What, then, of Jane Roe's claimed right to choose to terminate her pregnancy, said to be embodied in the "liberty" of the Fourteenth Amendment's Due Process Clause and "in the personal, marital, familial, and sexual privacy said to be protected by the Bill of Rights or its penumbras"?

Justice Blackmun reviewed the history of abortion law and

practice from ancient times. He considered the position of the American Medical Association. For more than a century the AMA had condemned abortion on the ground that it was the taking of human life. But in 1970 it made a dramatic change of policy favoring abortions based on "sound clinical judgment" and "informed patient consent." He noted the position of the American Public Health Association, which also in 1970 adopted standards for abortions. And he referred to the American Bar Association's approval of the Uniform Abortion Act, drafted and approved in August 1971 by the Conference of Commissioners on Uniform State Laws. None of these groups' opinions amounted to constitutional justification of voiding the statute, of course, but they indicated a trend of popular and professional feeling.

In discussing the reasons advanced for restrictive abortion laws, Blackmun dismissed any argument based on Victorian sexual mores. He noted that the state's interest in providing safe surgical environment was valid, but implied that this did not extend to prohibiting surgery altogether. This was especially true since the medical evidence indicated

that abortion in early pregnancy . . . prior to the end of the first trimester, although not without its risk, is now relatively safe. Mortality rates for women undergoing early abortions, where the procedure is legal, appear to be as low as or lower than the rates for normal childbirth. Consequently, any interest of the State in protecting the woman from an inherently hazardous procedure, except when it would be equally dangerous for her to forego it, has largely disappeared.

But the critical question that the Court was required to decide was the balance between the woman's right to the privacy of her body and the state's interest in protecting at least the *potential* life of the fetus. Here, in remarkably murky passages, the Court managed to compromise. It gave each side a little of what it asked (though the antiabortion forces quite reasonably viewed the Court's ultimate disposition with the same horror as the unprepared woman who is informed she is a "little bit pregnant").

Privacy, said Justice Blackmun, is contained within the personal liberty guaranteed by due process. This concept

is broad enough to encompass a woman's decision whether or not to terminate her pregnancy. The detriment that the State would impose upon the pregnant women by denying this choice altogether is apparent. Specific and direct harm medically diagnosable even in early pregnancy may be involved. Maternity, or additional offspring, may force upon the woman a distressful life and future. Psychological harm may be imminent. Mental and physical health may be taxed by child care. There is also the distress, for all concerned, associated with the unwanted child, and there is the problem of bringing a child into a family already unable, psychologically and otherwise, to care for it. In other cases, as in this one, the additional difficulties and continuing stigma of unwed motherhood may be involved. All these are factors the woman and her responsible physician necessarily will consider in consultation.

But these considerations are not enough to permit a woman the absolute right to terminate pregnancy. "A State may properly assert important interests in safe-guarding health, in maintaining medical standards, and in protecting potential life. At some point in pregnancy, these respective interests become sufficiently compelling to sustain regulation of the factors that govern the abortion decision."

Justice Blackmun disclaimed any desire or ability to determine when life begins: "When those trained in the respective disciplines of medicine, philosophy, and theology are unable to arrive at any consensus, the judiciary, at this point in the development of man's knowledge, is not in a position to speculate as to the answer."

Justice Harry A. Blackmun.

If a fetus were held to be a human life at the instant of conception, and thus a "person," the state would have a perfect right to prohibit abortion. The prenatal "person" would have a right under the Fourteenth Amendment not to be deprived of life. But no reference in the Constitution and none in the cases, Justice Blackmun said, can be found to hold that a fetus is a "person." So the state cannot rest its justification of the law on the Fourteenth Amendment.

At some point, however, the fetus does become at least potential human life. And that point, the Court concluded, comes at "viability," that is, the point at which "the fetus then presumably has the capability of meaningful life outside the mother's womb." Viability is generally recognized to come at or near the end of the second trimester.

Linking together its chain of reasoning, the Court came up with a threefold "rule":

First, up to the end of the first trimester, "the abortion decision and its effectuation must be left to the medical judgment of the pregnant women's attending physician."

Second, thereafter, "the State, in promoting its interest in the health of the mother, may, if it chooses, regulate the abortion procedure in ways that are reasonably related to maternal health."

Third, in the last trimester, or "the stage subsequent to viability, the State in promoting its interest in the potentiality of human life may, if it chooses, regulate, and even proscribe, abortion except where it is necessary, in appropriate medical judgment, for the preservation of the life or health of the mother."

The Problems with Roe: A Partial Answer

This threefold rule bristles with difficulties. The state may obviously prohibit any but licensed physicians from performing abortions even during the first trimester. Its interest in promoting the health of the woman is as great during the first three months of pregnancy as it is later. What, then, is the sense of the second rule? Does it mean anything more than that the state may prohibit unsafe abortions at any time?

The Court gave at least a partial answer to these questions in a companion case, *Doe* v. *Bolton*, decided the same day. An indigent, married Georgia woman sued to overturn that state's abortion law. The Georgia law was more liberal than that of Texas, but it did prohibit abortion on demand. It also imposed three procedural hurdles for any woman seeking an abortion. The operation had to be performed in a hospital accredited by the Joint Commission on Accreditation of Hospitals. The procedure had to be approved by the hospital staff abortion committee. And no abortion could be performed until two physicians in addition to the patient's doctor gave their own consent following independent examinations.

Justice Blackmun, writing for the same seven to two majority, struck down all these procedural requirements. They were invalid, he wrote, because at least as to the first trimester, they bore no rational relationship to safeguarding the patient's health. And they did unduly restrict her rights. The state had not shown the necessity of performing an abortion in a hospital rather than a doctor's office. It did not require a hospital committee to pass on other operations, and the woman was protected sufficiently by the requirement that her own doctor attend her. Presumably, however, there might be certain restrictions—such as operating in a hospital—that are medically required for abortions done during the second trimester. Under the second rule in *Roe* v. *Wade*, the state has room to legislate.

There are, however, other difficulties with the three-part rule. Having disclaimed any intention of defining the moment of life, why be even more foolhardy and proceed to define the moment of *poten-*

tial life? A fertilized ovum is potentially human in the first second of its existence. What legal ground is there for thus distinguishing between the previable and viable fetus? If a woman's body is her own and she is free to terminate unwanted pregnancies, what real difference can it make to the state that she does so in the seventh month rather than in the second?

And why, if the question is one of privacy, must the abortion decision be committed to the judgment of the attending physician? (As a practical matter, of course, few physicians will refuse to perform abortions sought for no other reason than because the woman requests one.)

Answers to these questions are not given. The opinion remains opaque. The suspicion seems warranted, therefore, that the Court was persuaded that the time had come for a recognition that social mores had changed sufficiently that some means of permissive abortions had to be allowed. Too many dangerous unlawful abortions were being performed for anyone to believe reasonably that they could ever be prevented. But the Court was not ready to believe that the recognition should be perfectly frank. So it recognized a nonabsolute, though spacious, realm of privacy. Having liberated this realm from its close confinement, the Court chose to leave to the political process any further expansion of its borders.

The Irrepressible Issue

This is not a tidy judicial solution. It certainly is not "strict construction." But it is not outside the Constitution, and the major objection, once the Court's premise about privacy is accepted, can only be over the limitations imposed on the breathing space the Court provided.

Not everyone, of course, has accepted the Court's major premise. In his dissent, Justice Rehnquist observed that

the fact that a majority of the States reflecting, after all, the majority sentiment in those States, have had restrictions on abortions for at least a century is a strong indication, it seems to me, that the asserted right to an abortion is not "so rooted in the traditions and conscience of our people as to be ranked as fundamental." . . . Even today, when society's views on abortion are changing, the very existence of the debate is evidence that the "right" to an abortion is not so universally accepted as [Roe] would have us believe.

But even this statement is a curiously mild rejoinder, for it clearly implies that the day might come when the debate will be settled and there no longer will be any doubt. In this sense, Justice

Rehnquist appears to be quarreling mainly about the timing of the decision.

Constitutionally, he appears to be on stronger ground in questioning the Court's overturning of the abortion statute on due process grounds. "The test traditionally applied [for voiding a statute] in the area of social and economic legislation is whether or not a law such as that challenged has a rational relation to a valid state objective," he said, identifying the test that emerged after the New Deal Court had finally repudiated the doctrine of substantive due process. Since the Court assumes that states do indeed have a valid objective in protecting potential human life, it is difficult to understand why it is not rational for the state to believe it is doing so by prohibiting abortion altogether (except for a provision permitting abortion to save the mother's life). The Court seems to have tried to slice the "rational" into halves. That, perhaps, is an operation too delicate to be performed.

The tension in the case will not go away. *Roe* v. *Wade* can never be reconciled with earlier Court decisions unless it is modified by recognizing the irrationality of preventing abortions at any time prior to birth, or unless it is overruled. Given the very debate to which Justice Rehnquist alluded, neither alternative is likely in the near future. The tension doubtless will remain with us for some time to come.

Indeed, the first fallout from *Roe* v. *Wade* has reached the Supreme Court as this book went to press. On October 6, 1975, the Court agreed to review the Missouri abortion statute, which was enacted in response to its ruling in *Roe* v. *Wade*. Among other things, the law requires consent in certain cases, either of parent or spouse, before the abortion can be performed. It prohibits the use of a medical technique called "saline amniocentesis" after the twelfth week. Challengers of the law say it effectively bars abortions during the second trimester. It requires doctors, on penalty of manslaughter charges, to attempt to preserve the life of the fetus, in the same way they would attempt to preserve a fetus born prematurely.

A case-by-case adjudication of particular state statutes is not the only legal burden the Court will soon face. Congressional attempts to prohibit health insurance benefits from being used for abortions and similar state restrictions will probably come before the Court in the next few years.

So, too, will suits over private restrictions that hospitals themselves impose on abortions necessarily come before the Court. A national study conducted by the Alan Guttmacher Institute of the Planned Parenthood Federation of America revealed that hospitals were performing even fewer abortions after *Roe* than before. Some 85 percent of public hospitals had performed no abortions during the first quarter of 1974. Since the poor often cannot afford abortions in private clinics, where the bulk of this surgery is being performed, sooner or later the Court must grapple with demands that the right to privacy means also the right to secure abortions cheaply. Thus the controversy will rage for years to come.

Supreme Court

PART VI:
THE ENDURANCE
OF CONSTITUTIONAL
GOVERNMENT

20/ THE PRESIDENT IS UNDER THE LAW: UNITED STATES v. NIXON

On July 23, 1974, a Tuesday, a long line began to form on the spacious steps of the Supreme Court building. The sight was unusual even to the Washingtonian hardened to the interminable tourist queues that spring up all over town during the hot summer months. Rarely do so many people mass in front of the Court. A line this long could be explained only by some momentous happening. Never in the twentieth century had the Court sat so late in the summer, its traditional vacation period.

A Sense of History

The fact that nothing of note occurred that day made the line even more impressive. These people had come an entire day early and waited all night to secure a place in the limited public seating space available inside. Space for the press, which normally has no difficulty getting seats, was strictly rationed. Reporters who were accustomed to sitting close to the bench reckoned themselves lucky to be seated behind marble columns where, though they could see little, they could hear all.

What the hopeful spectators anticipated was clearly worth waiting for: the most important political case in recent memory. The Court would pronounce judgment in a case directly involving no less important a personage than the president of the United States. No one could be unaware, least of all the eight justices who participated in the case, that the decision rendered on July 24, 1974, might well cost the president his very office. Here was a moment of drama rare in the history of the country.

The events that had brought the world's attention to the Court's doorstep that day had, of course, been building up for some time. But this buildup had a double nature. The incredible series of events that collectively became known as Watergate were the immediate reason for the litigation, but they must be set against a larger background of continual accretion of presidential prerequisites and powers during the present century.

The Presidency: Past and Present

A brief review will show how great the prerequisites of the office have become. In 1825 President John Quincy Adams spent $61 of federal money to purchase billiard equipment for the White House. Congressional critics denounced him for turning the executive mansion into a "gaming establishment." Adams paid the government back out of his own pocket. Not until the time of Calvin Coolidge, one hundred years later, did Congress appropriate federal funds to pay for state dinners. Thomas Jefferson reflected that he had to tap his own purse for more than $10,000 just to pay for wine during his eight years as president.

We are not so parsimonious today. The cost of running the White House and all other presidential operations has been estimated at close to $100 million a year. Unlike the chief executives of many other nations, the president of the United States does not pay for domestic help out of his government salary. Taxpayers provide him with seventy-five maids, butlers, cooks, and technicians. Taxpayers also provide a sumptuous fleet of cars, planes, and boats: President Nixon enjoyed five Boeing 707 jetliners, sixteen helicopters, and eleven Lockheed Jetstars to carry mail and staff. He also apparently enjoyed the benefits of several million dollars' worth of renovations at his Florida and California homes.

Mr. Nixon's Legal Prerogatives

These and other luxuries did more than go to his head. They seemed to make him think that he occupied an office whose powers knew no limits, or at least none capable of being pronounced by anyone other than himself. Thus he once expressed the opinion, in an open letter to a U. S. senator, that the Senate had no business rejecting his nominees to the Supreme Court. He believed, he said, that this followed from the fact that the Constitution gave him the sole power of appointment.

This was merely one, and far from the most important, of his constitutional gaffes. The Constitution explicitly gives the Senate the power to reject presidential nominees, and the Senate displayed no eagerness to adopt Mr. Nixon's peculiar theory on that point, rejecting, as they did, two of his nominees in a row.

Another of his constitutional theses provoked a much larger stir. He claimed that as president he had the power to withhold at his sole discretion all White House documents and to preserve, again at his sole discretion, the confidentiality of all conversations between his top advisers and himself. At one point, speaking through his attorney general, Richard G. Kleindienst, he made a sweeping claim on behalf of this so-called "executive privilege." No federal employee, it was said, would be permitted to testify before Congress. The principles of separation of powers and confidentiality of presidential communications were invoked to justify this claim.

The president soon softened his stand. Kleindienst's broadest extension of executive privilege was obviously absurd: postal workers were, as a body, scarcely privy to policy-making at the White House, and if Congress could not call postmen to testify about conditions in post offices, then the result would be not separation of powers but lack of any power in Congress itself. Richard Nixon had something like that in mind.

Damming Up Watergate

Events made even more limited claims difficult to maintain. As the Senate Watergate Committee began to dominate the front-page headlines and a Washington grand jury began to call new witnesses, the administration retreated from the flat position that Kleindienst had earlier enunciated.

On April 30, 1972, H. R. Haldeman, John Ehrlichman, John Dean, and Richard Kleindienst were forced to resign. To replace

Part of the text of the subpoena signed by a Los Angeles Superior Court judge ordering President Nixon to appear and testify at the trial of his former aides.

UPI

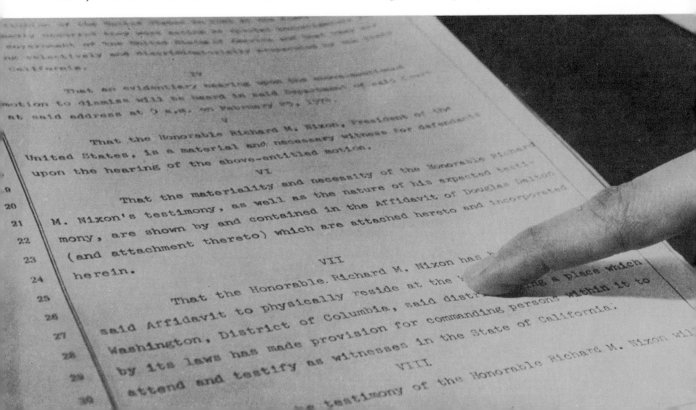

Copy of subpoena issued for former President Richard Nixon to appear as a witness in the Watergate cover-up trial of his former aide, John D. Ehrlichman.

UPI

Kleindienst as attorney general, the president announced his intention to move Elliott L. Richardson from his post as secretary of defense. On May 1, the Senate by voice vote passed a resolution calling on the president to appoint a special prosecutor. On May 3, the White House issued a set of guidelines dealing with testimony and papers of executive department officials. Among other things, it required that

past and present members of the President's staff questioned by the FBI, the Ervin Committee, or a Grand Jury should invoke the privilege only in connection with conversations with the President, conversations among themselves (involving communications with the President) and as to Presidential papers. Presidential papers are all documents produced or received by the President or any member of the White House staff in connection with his official duties.

Enter the Special Prosecutor

Several days later, Richardson pledged in his Senate confirmation hearings to appoint a special prosecutor and to give him broad authority to conduct an independent investigation. The Senate Judiciary Committee informed him that it could not confirm him unless he announced his choice in advance and spelled out the authority the prosecutor would have. In response Richardson announced on May 18 that he would name the former solicitor general and his former professor at Harvard Law School, Archibald Cox.

The day before, the Senate Watergate Committee had begun to hear its first witness. One day later, May 19, Richardson unveiled the rules by which Cox would be guided in performing his duties as the Watergate special prosecutor. These guidelines stated, in part, that

There will be appointed by the attorney general, within the Department of Justice, a special prosecutor to whom the attorney general shall delegate the authorities and provide the staff and other resources described below.

The special prosecutor shall have full authority for investigating and prosecuting offenses against the United States arising out of the unauthorized entry into Democratic National Committee headquarters at the Watergate, all offenses arising out of the 1972 presidential election for which the special prosecutor deems it necessary and appropriate to assume responsibility, allegations involving the President, members of the White House staff, or presidential appointees, and any other matters which he consents to have assigned to him by the attorney general.

In particular, the special prosecutor shall have full authority with respect to the above matters for:

—Conducting proceedings before grand juries and any other investigations he deems necessary.

—Reviewing all documentary evidence available from any source, as to which he shall have full access.

—Determining whether or not to contest the assertion of "executive privilege" or any other testimonial privilege.

On May 21, in speaking of Richardson's authority over him before the Senate, Cox said: "The only authority he's retained is the authority to give me hell if I don't do the job." And Cox said he would follow the trail even if it should lead to the oval office of the White House. The committee accepted the guidelines and Cox's and Richardson's understanding of them as providing sufficient independence. Cox could only be fired for "extraordinary improprieties."

The following day, May 22, the president significantly reduced still further his commitment to claim executive privilege on behalf of his assistants. Admitting for the first time that there had indeed been a cover-up, Nixon wrote in a four-thousand-word statement released to the press:

Considering the number of persons involved in this case whose testimony might be subject to a claim of Executive privilege, I recognize that a clear definition of that claim has become central to the effort to arrive at the truth. Accordingly, Executive privilege will not be invoked as to any testimony concerning possible criminal conduct or discussions of possible criminal conduct, in the matters presently under investigation, including the Watergate affair and the alleged cover-up.

Significantly, he did not release any White House documents from the shield of executive privilege. The next day Richardson was confirmed. Cox was officially appointed on May 25.

On one matter Nixon held firm. The president himself would not provide any information to the Senate committee or the grand jury. He would neither testify nor hand over any written papers. To do so, he said, would be a clear violation of the "separation of powers." On July 6, he set forth his position in a letter to Senator Ervin. "No President could function," Nixon wrote,

if the private papers of his office, prepared by his personal staff, were open to public scrutiny. Formulation of sound public policy requires that the President and his personal staff be able to communicate among themselves in complete candor, and that their tentative judgments, their exploration of alternatives, and their frank comments on issues and personalities at home and abroad remain confidential. . . . I have concluded that if I were to testify before the Committee irreparable damage would be done to the Constitutional principle of separation of powers.

Citing a letter that Harry Truman had written to the House Un-American Activities Committee in 1953, declining to answer its subpoena after his term of office, Nixon concurred in Truman's endorsement of an 1879 opinion of the House Judiciary Committee: "The Executive is as independent of either house of Congress as either house of Congress is independent of him, and they cannot call for the records of his actions, or the action of his officers against his consent, any more than he can call for any of the journals or records of the House or Senate."

A Whiff of Smoke

Ten days later, on July 16, a single witness before the Watergate Committee moved the argument onto a new plane.

Alexander P. Butterfield, formerly an aide to Haldeman, testified that the White House had been taping most of the President's office and telephone conversations and that the tapes had been stored away. Though memories might have faded, now, miraculously, there was a way to substantiate or disprove any presidential involvement in the Watergate break-in or the subsequent cover-up.

That very day, in the wake of Butterfield's disclosures, the president directed George P. Schultz, who as secretary of the treasury was responsible for the Secret Service (which was in charge of the taping system), not to let any secret service officer or agent "give testimony to Congressional committees concerning matters observed or learned while performing protective functions for the President or in their duties at the White House."

The next day Alfred C. Wong, deputy assistant director of the Secret Service, appeared before Senators Ervin and Howard H. Baker Jr., the committee's vice chairman. He refused to talk as the result of the presidential invocation of executive privilege. The May 22 statement was apparently "inoperative."

While the Senate Watergate Committee struggled to find a way to obtain the tapes, a more serious threat arose from Watergate Special Prosecutor Cox. He, too, was determined to obtain certain tapes believed to contain significant evidence of the various crimes he was investigating. On July 18, he wrote to J. Fred Buzhardt, the president's special counsel, requesting tapes of eight carefully delineated conversations between the president and various of his advisers.

On July 23, responding on behalf of Buzhardt, Charles Alan Wright, professor of law at the University of Texas and special legal consultant to the White House, declined to make any of the tapes available. Wright wrote that as a member of the executive branch, Cox was required to abide by the decision of the president as to what papers would be released. Moreover, said Wright, because Cox intended to use the tapes in possible trials, a significant separation-of-powers problem was presented:

It is for the President, and only for the President, to weigh whether the incremental advantage that these tapes would give you in criminal proceedings justifies the serious and lasting hurt that disclosure of them would do to the confidentiality that is imperative to the effective functioning of the President. In this instance the President has concluded that it would not serve the public interest to make the tapes available.

Throwing Down the Gauntlet

All hope of voluntary cooperation had vanished. Both the committee and Cox responded with subpoenas—five altogether—to the president himself. These were the first subpoenas to be served on a president since Thomas Jefferson received one in the Aaron Burr treason trial 166 years earlier. In resisting the subpoenas, the president chose to contest in court the prosecutor's right to the information he was seeking. Thus the judicial branch of government was brought into Watergate at the highest possible level.

In his official reply to Cox's subpoenas (the litigation over the Watergate committee's subpoenas will not concern us here), his lawyers spoke darkly of the inevitable consequence "of an order to disclose recordings or notes." Such an order would mean

that no longer could a President speak in confidence with his close advisers on any subject. The threat of potential disclosure of any and all conversations would make it virtually impossible for President Nixon or his successors in that great office to function. Beyond that, a holding that the President is personally subject to the orders of a court would effectively destroy the status of the executive branch as an equal and coordinate element of government. . . . In the exercise of his discretion to claim executive privilege the President is answerable to the nation but not to the courts. The courts, a co-equal but not a superior branch of government, are not free to probe the mental processes and the private confidences of the President and his advisers. To do so would be a clear violation of the constitutional separation of powers. Under that doctrine the judicial branch lacks power to compel the President to produce information that he has determined it is not in the public interest to disclose.

The issue here is starkly simple: will the presidency be allowed to continue to function?

To this apocalyptic warning, Cox argued in more measured, less emotional language. The separation of powers, he reasoned, must be confined to its proper meaning. It is true that the

President cannot be limited by judicial intrusion into the exercise of his constitutional powers under Article II. Here, however, the grand jury is not seeking to control the President in the exercise of his constitutional power to withhold the evidence sought by the subpoena merely by his own declaration of the public interest. The grand jury is seeking evidence of criminal conduct that the respondent happens to have in his custody— largely by his personal choice. All the Court is asked to do is hold that the President is bound by legal duties in appropriate cases just as other citizens—in this case, by the duty to supply documentary evidence of crime. In the language of the authoritative precedents, this is a "ministerial duty."

Cox denied that an order to produce the particular conversations would put a cloud over every future discussion in the oval office. The court may always decide after its own *in camera* inspection to uphold the president's request to keep the documents secret. Moreover, what Cox sought was not merely a presidential conversation. There was good reason to believe that the tapes contained evidence of a criminal conspiracy. "There will be few occasions upon which a grand jury will have similar cause to believe

Archibald Cox.
Wide World Photos

there may be material evidence of the criminality of high officials in the papers and documents in the Executive Office of the President."

Finally, Cox contended, even if the president had a legitimate claim, he had waived it. Many of his highest officials had testified extensively following his May 22 declaration that executive privilege would not be invoked.

In a televised address on August 15, the president repeated his fundamental concern: "The Presidency is not the only office that requires confidentiality. A member of Congress must be able to talk in confidence with his assistants. Judges must be able to confer in confidence with their law clerks and with each other. For very good reasons, no branch of Government has ever compelled disclosure of confidential conversations between officers of other branches of Government and their advisers about government business."

The Historical Context

As a matter of historical record, the president's assertion was much too sweeping. As early as *Marbury v. Madison*, the claim of absolute executive privilege was rejected. When Attorney General Levi Lincoln asserted the right to refuse to testify concerning missing commissions, Chief Justice Marshall gave him a night to think over his position. Lincoln returned the next day and substantially complied with the Court's order to answer its questions.

At the Aaron Burr treason trial, conducted in 1807 in a circuit court over which Marshall himself presided, President Jefferson was subpoened to provide certain letters that were thought to bear on Burr's complicity in the matters charged. During the course of the proceedings, Marshall struck a compromise between the president's claim to sole discretionary power to make public official papers and the assertion that the defense always has the right to compel the production of any relevant document.

Following Burr's acquittal on the charge of treason, but before his subsequent trial on a misdemeanor count, Marshall said this: "That the president of the United States may be subpoenaed and examined as a witness, and required to produce any paper in his possession, is not controverted. I cannot, however, on this point, go the whole length for which counsel have contended. The President, though subject to the general rules which apply to others, may have sufficient motives for declining to produce a particular paper, and those motives may be such as to restrain the court from enforcing its production."

Whether the Court would order production would depend on the circumstances in the given case. The procedure to be used was a secret inspection by the court. In the *Burr* case, Jefferson entrusted his counsel with the responsibility of withholding from the defense all portions of a particular letter that were "not material for the purposes of justice." Jefferson's counsel, in turn, was prepared to verify the truth of his statement concerning portions to be excised by submitting the original letter to the court, for its own inspection.

President Nixon refused to accede to this procedure. At the oral argument before Judge John J. Sirica, Charles Alan Wright said that a court lacks power "to compel the President to produce the evidence so long as he remains President. I cannot concede that a court has power to issue compulsory process to an incumbent President of the United States." The nub of Richard Nixon's claim, throughout the nearly twelve months of litigation, was simply that he, alone of all persons in the United States, was outside the judicial system.

More History and A Strategic Retreat

The difficulty with the president's position was equally simple. The precedents were against him. Of course, as a practical matter, it will be a rare occasion when a court finds it necessary to extend an order directly to the president. In most previous instances in which the courts were asked to determine the limits of presidential power (there have been some eight hundred cases altogether, of which less than 10 percent held against the president), the lawsuit was framed in such a way that the remedy would not directly interfere with the president personally. In one earlier incident President Nixon claimed the inherent power to conduct "national security" wiretapping without conforming to the requirements of the Fourth Amendment. The Supreme Court struck down the claim. But the decision resulted in the reversal of a defendant's conviction, not in an order to the president to cease such wiretapping in the future.

In the famous *Steel Seizure Case,* however, the Supreme Court affirmed an injunction that ran in everything but name directly to the president. In April 1952, the steel unions were about to call a national strike. President Truman believed that the strike would cripple the national security, in view of the hot war in Korea. Accordingly, he directed Charles Sawyer, secretary of commerce, to "seize" the steel mills and operate them as government property.

The government claimed the power to negotiate new contracts with the unions. The companies went to court to force Secretary Sawyer to return the mills to their private owners.

In less than two months (from April 9, when the companies first went to court, to June 2, when the Supreme Court delivered its decision), the companies had their mills back again. The Supreme Court, by a six to three vote, ruled that the president had no inherent executive power under Article Two of the Constitution to seize private property.

In form the injunction was directed against the secretary of commerce because he had been delegated the job of seizing the mills. But there was no indication in the Court's opinion that the decision would have come out differently had the president seized the mills directly. If the *Steel Seizure Case* "still stands," said the U. S. Court of Appeals in Washington, reviewing Judge Sirica's order that the president submit the tape recordings to the court for inspection,

it must stand for the case where the President has himself taken posses-sion and control of the property unconstitutionally seized, and the injunc-tion would be framed accordingly. The practice of judicial review would be rendered capricious—and very likely impotent—if jurisdiction vanished whenever the President personally denoted an Executive action or omission as his own. . . . Here, unfortunately, the court's order must run directly to the President, because he has taken the unusual step of assuming personal custody of the Government property sought by the subpoena.

All that said, it was no less true, as a purely factual matter, that the Supreme Court had never in its history ruled on this matter. The issue of the constitutionality of a federal court's order to the president of the United States to produce evidence that was arguably necessary for the prosecution of a criminal case and that he had in his possession had never arisen. In that sense alone, there was no authoritative precedent for what Archibald Cox sought to do.

During the course of the *Steel Seizure* argument before U. S. District Judge David A. Pine, Assistant Attorney General Holmes Baldridge was asked whether the government felt that the presi-dent has unlimited power in time of an emergency? "He has the power to take such action as is necessary to meet the emer-gency," Baldridge replied. "If the emergency is great, it is un-limited, is it not?" Judge Pine pressed him. Baldridge answered: "I suppose if you carry it to its logical conclusion, that is true. But I do want to point out that there are two limitations on the

Executive power. One is the ballot box and the other is impeachment."

The President's New Clothes

Stated in a variety of ways, this was the essence of Nixon's position as well. The president cannot be questioned in the courts. The Constitution grants him plenary power to act, and he may be challenged directly in two ways only: by the voters once every four years or by Congress pursuant to impeachment proceedings. In short, what Nixon asserted was the prerogative of the elected king: You may depose me, but until you do, I must be left to my own devices.

In light of the American Revolution and the two hundred years of legal history that followed, this was an audacious claim. The only thing that saved it from being branded as preposterous was that the president of the United States asserted it with a straight face. He hired eminent counsel to argue it with equally straight faces before the courts. But it could scarcely be an argument that would prevail.

Judge John Sirica
Wide World Photos

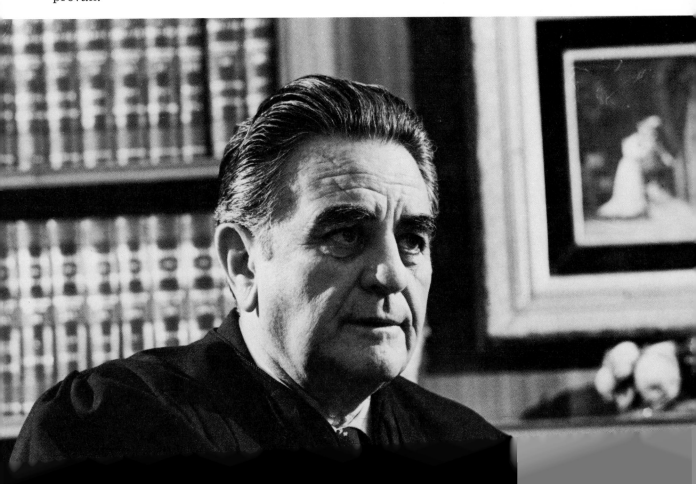

On August 29, Judge Sirica ruled that the president was not absolutely privileged and must submit the tapes for the Court's *in camera* inspection to determine the relevance of the conversations. By a five to two vote, the Court of Appeals upheld Judge Sirica's decision on October 12. Apparently afraid of a Supreme Court ruling that would be politically impossible to resist, Nixon let the five-day period for appeal to the High Court lapse.

The Saturday Night "Massacre"

The president had other ideas, however, on how to avoid compliance with the subpoena. He proposed a "compromise," by which he would supply edited transcripts of the tapes, to be verified by Senator John Stennis of Mississippi. He also directed that the special prosecutor refrain in the future from going to court to seek evidence that he, the president, held.

Opposite page:

Leon Jaworski.

Wide World Photos

Cox refused to accept this deal. So on the evening of October 20, Cox was discharged by Solicitor General Robert H. Bork, who only minutes before had become acting attorney general in the wake of the resignation of Attorney General Richardson and the firing of Deputy Attorney General William Ruckelshaus, both of whom refused the president's order to fire Cox.

The "firestorm" that resulted from the "Saturday night massacre" led the president to perform an abrupt about-face on October 23. Wright announced that Nixon would comply with the subpoena. However, subsequent revelations that two of the conversations were not recorded and that the sound of a third had inexplicably been obliterated for a crucial eighteen and one-half minutes did nothing to instill confidence that the president really was at last determined to abide by judicial rulings.

Full-Scale Retreat

The uproar had one other enormously important consequence. A new special prosecutor, Leon Jaworski of Houston, was appointed, and he was given explicit guarantees of independence from presidential supervision. He not only received "full authority for investigating and prosecuting offenses" arising out of Watergate and related matters, but he also was delegated full authority to review "all documentary evidence available from any source, as to which he shall have full access" and to determine "whether or not to contest the assertion of 'Executive Privilege' or any other testimonial privilege."

Finally, he could not be removed except for "extraordinary improprieties." Even then the president first had to consult with and obtain a consensus from a number of senior congressional leaders. This last provision was added specifically to buttress Jaworski's foregoing powers and rights, all of which, as quoted, were identical with those delegated to Cox. (A federal district court later ruled that Cox had been unlawfully discharged, since he had committed no "extraordinary improprieties.")

Jaworski's appointment was effective on November 2. Following through on the investigation that Cox had begun, the Watergate grand jury, upon hearing evidence presented to it by Jaworski, on March 1, 1974, indicted seven high-ranking presidential assistants on a variety of charges, including conspiracy to defraud the United States and to obstruct justice.

The Inexorable Process Grinds On

At the same time, the grand jury named Richard Nixon as an "unindicted co-conspirator." They apparently did not believe that an incumbent president could be indicted prior to impeachment. And they believed that the attempt to do so, being legally uncertain, would jeopardize the trials of the other seven. The significance of naming the president (and others) lies in the fact that statements made by the president and relevant to the case could, it was expected, be used in evidence against those formally indicted for conspiracy.

On April 16, Jaworski asked Judge Sirica to issue a subpoena to the president for the production of sixty-four tape recordings that he asserted were relevant to the case against the seven alleged conspirators. Two days later, Judge Sirica did so, directing that the tapes be turned over by May 2. On April 30, President Nixon went on national television to announce that he was turning over to the House Judiciary Committee, by then in the middle of its impeachment proceedings, 1216 pages of edited transcripts of forty-three conversations. These transcripts included parts of twenty of the sixty-four conversations that Jaworski had subpoenaed. On the following day, the president's lawyers went to court to quash the subpoena.

The Final Stand

Judge Sirica denied the president's motion on May 20, in the first round of *United States* v. *Nixon*. The lines were thus drawn for the ultimate Supreme Court test. Sirica rejected the president's arguments that "courts are without authority to rule on the scope or applicability of executive privilege when asserted by the President." He also rejected the claim that the case was not justiciable because the entire matter was merely an "intrabranch dispute" within the executive that the president alone was constitutionally empowered to settle. He ruled further that the president's objections to the issuance of the subpoena under the Federal Rules of Civil Procedure were without merit. He allowed the president four days in which to appeal and stayed the order should the president do so.

The president now had new counsel, Boston attorney James D. St. Clair. (Wright withdrew from active management of the president's legal concerns following the debacle of the tapes the preceding October.) St. Clair filed a notice of appeal to the Court of Appeals. Jaworski short-circuited this move, however, and sought direct review of Judge Sirica's decision by the Supreme Court. This procedure is invoked only in the rarest of instances. It was used in the *Steel Seizure Case.* The Supreme Court agreed to hear argument on an expedited basis, over St. Clair's objections.

The Case before the Supreme Court

At breakneck speed, Jaworski and St. Clair prepared massive, exhaustive briefs, analyzing every possible aspect of the president's privileges and the power of the courts. The special prosecutor's brief was written with a consciousness of the gravity of the case, but it lacked the special fire of St. Clair's. He argued that the very life of the nation as it has been for two hundred years hung in the balance and would be saved or destroyed by what the Court decided. "In a very real sense," he said,

every case that comes before this Court is unique, but few in the Nation's history have cut so close to the heart of the basic constitutional system in which our liberties are rooted. . . . The stakes are enormously high, from a constitutional standpoint. . . . At its core, this is a case that turns on the separation of powers.

All other considerations are secondary, because preserving the integrity of the separation of powers is vital to the preservation of our Constitution as a living body of fundamental law. If the arguments of the Special Prosecutor were to prevail, the constitutional balance would be altered in ways that no one alive today could predict or measure.

The one new question raised in the briefs was that of the president's vulnerability to being named by a grand jury as an unindicted co-conspirator. The question had not been raised earlier because the grand jury had kept its action secret—even from Judge Sirica. The president's "status" became known only in May when Jaworski cited the grand jury's finding to support his argument for the subpoena.

This argument, like all of those in the briefs too long and complex to detail here, produced one moment of supreme irony. St. Clair argued that the president was entitled to see the evidence that the grand jury had examined before it named him as an unindicted co-conspirator. He condemned Jaworski for pointing out that he, St. Clair, had failed to cite any case "in which *any* person" so named was permitted to do so. St. Clair then said: "Yet the Special Prosecutor, in spearheading numerous attempts to overturn the doctrine of executive privilege, has failed to cite any precedent which authorizes the grand jury's action in naming the President as an unindicted co-conspirator. The reason for his failure to offer any support for the unauthorized, impermissible action of the grand jury is starkly simple. There is no such authority in the annals of American jurisprudence." Of course not! And not surprisingly: never was there, either, a president quite like Richard Nixon.

Despite the lengthy argument, the Supreme Court ultimately failed to address this question. It also failed to address another problem that particularly irked St. Clair: the fact that the grand jury had voted to send its evidence, sealed, to the House Judiciary Committee. St. Clair argued that, in so doing, the House was impermissibly using the grand jury as a means through which evidence could be discovered against the president. Though he pressed the point during oral argument, he failed to persuade the justices that they should forebear from acting against the president because it in effect would convert the Court into a tool of the House impeachment inquiry.

In the entire debate, perhaps one point above all showed with crystal-clarity St. Clair's difficulty. In his reply brief, St. Clair argued that the mere fact that Jaworski had been delegated authority to prosecute did not make him independent enough of the executive to transform an intrabranch dispute into a controversy that a court could hear and decide. One of the reasons he advanced to prove this conclusion was as follows: "The Judiciary has never had jurisdiction to review or determine what evidence the executive branch shall or shall not use in the furtherance of its own case in a criminal proceeding."

In the normal case, this is of course undisputed. An assistant United States attorney cannot sue his boss if the assistant's desire to use a particular piece of evidence is overruled.

But this was scarcely the normal case. The evidence was not in the hands of the prosecutor but in those of someone who described himself as the prosecutor's boss. The person who had the evidence and the person who just might turn out to be criminally involved were one and the same. Does anyone suppose that, if the U. S. attorney himself were indicted, he could continue to make decisions about what evidence he would request from himself? Can a person be a judge of his own case?

This reasoning can be true only if the person is somehow above the law. That such a thing cannot be admitted in a constitutional system is the very reason, politically, that the attorney general was required in the first place to appoint an independent prosecutor.

Oral argument began before a packed Court at 10:02 A.M., Monday, July 8. Because time for preparation had been exceedingly short, perhaps because of the personalities of the litigants, and because the justices constantly interrupted, the arguments were not particularly eloquent. At some points, the logic seemed opaque. St. Clair, for example, argued that Jaworski had never been delegated the authority "to order the President to give up confidential communications." Of course, Jaworski had never claimed that any such authority had been given. This was a spurious point, as one justice finally brought out:

Mr. ST. CLAIR: That [right to order the President to give up confidential communications] was not delegated.

QUESTION: Not the unfettered right to get it, but the right to go to court and ask a court to decide whether or not he is entitled to it.

Mr. ST. CLAIR: Right. And the President, under no circumstances, gave up any of his defense with respect to that.

QUESTION: And you are making those defenses right here and now.

Mr. ST. CLAIR: Making them right now.

QUESTION: No question about that.

Jaworski had no power himself, as special prosecutor, to order the president to hand over confidential documents and tapes, but that had nothing whatsoever to do with the Court's power to do so.

At another point, Justice Powell asked St. Clair whether he was asserting an absolute privilege on the part of the president to withhold the tapes if it had been established that they contained conversations showing a criminal conspiracy. St. Clair answered in the affirmative. Powell then asked: "What public interest is there in preserving secrecy with respect to a criminal conspiracy?" To which St. Clair replied in a memorable line: "The answer, sir, is that a criminal conspiracy is criminal only after it's proven to be criminal."

A few minutes later, following up this point, one justice asked what St. Clair's position would be if the evidence the president was keeping confidential might show that the president had accepted a bribe to appoint a person to the bench. St. Clair stuck to his guns.

Mr. ST. CLAIR:	If the President did appoint such an individual, the remedy is clear, the remedy is he would be impeached....
JUSTICE MARSHALL:	How are you going to impeach him if you don't know about it?
Mr. ST. CLAIR:	Well, if you know about it, then you can state the case. If you don't know about it, you don't have it.
JUSTICE MARSHALL:	So there you are. You're on the prongs of a dilemma, huh?
Mr. ST. CLAIR:	No, I don't think so.
JUSTICE MARSHALL:	If you know the President is doing something wrong, you can impeach him, but the only way you can find out is this way; you can't impeach him, so you don't impeach him. You lose me some place along there. [Laughter].

For his part, Jaworski conceded early in his argument that the grand jury's naming of the president as an unindicted co-conspirator was not essential to the subpoena. Even if the grand jury had not done so, Jaworski admitted, the special prosecutor would still be standing before the Court and making the same arguments. The issue seemed to drop out of the case at that point.

Only at one point did the fatefulness of the proceeding seem to come alive—when Jaworski neatly turned upside down St. Clair's argument that the future of the country depended on continued recognition of the absolute inviolability of presidential communication.

Simply, but effectively, Jaworski said this:

Now, the President may be right in how he reads the Constitution. But he may also be wrong. And if he is wrong, who is there to tell him so? And if there is no one, then the President, of course, is free to pursue his course of erroneous interpretations. What then becomes of our constitutional form of government?

So when counsel for the President in his brief states that this case goes to the heart of our basic constitutional system, we agree. Because in our view, this nation's constitutional form of government is in serious jeopardy if the President, any President, is to say that the Constitution means what he says it does, and that there is no one, not even the Supreme Court, to tell him otherwise.

To which St. Clair replied, at the very end of the argument: "The President is not above the law. Nor does he contend that he is. What he does contend is that as President the law can be applied to him in only one way, and that is by impeachment, not by naming him as a co-conspirator in a grand jury indictment, not by indictment or in any other way."

The Decision: Still a Nation of Laws

At 1:04 p.m., three hours and two minutes after it had begun, the question in the *United States* v. *Nixon* was out of the hands of the lawyers, the prosecutors, and the president. It was in the hands of those who would ultimately have the last say, eight justices. (Because he has served in the Office of Legal Counsel of the Department of Justice—the "president's lawyer's lawyer" President Nixon has called him when he announced his appointment to the Court—Justice Rehnquist did not participate in the case.)

And so, at last, on July 24, sixteen days after the argument, in a courtroom bursting with spectators, the justices convened again to listen to the chief justice read their unanimous opinion. In prose devoid of passion or rhetoric, Chief Justice Burger set what turned out to be the seal on the president's doom.

Rights Divine and Mortal

The Court decided these points (among others):

First, the dispute was not merely an "intrabranch" argument. Special Prosecutor Jaworski had been delegated the authority to seek the presidential subpoena. Though the president, through the attorney general, had at least the theoretical right to "amend or revoke the regulation defining the Special Prosecutor's authority, . . . he has not done so. So long as this regulation remains in force the Executive Branch is bound by it, and indeed the United States as the sovereign composed of the three branches is bound to respect and enforce it." And the particular dispute concerned "the kind of controversy courts traditionally resolve." Evidence for a pending criminal case "is sought by one official of the Government within the scope of his express authority; it is resisted by the Chief Executive on the ground of his duty to preserve the confidentiality of the communications of the President."

Second, the subpoena met the various procedural requirements of the federal rules. The special prosecutor was required to show that the evidence sought was relevant, admissible, and specific. In reviewing Judge Sirica's determination that Jaworski had met his burden of demonstrating each of these factors was present, the Court under its own prior holdings was required only to conclude that Judge Sirica had not abused his discretion in making such a determination.

Third, and critically, the Supreme Court ruled for the first time in the nation's history that there is no absolute executive privilege in a criminal case.

Neither the doctrine of separation of powers, nor the need for confidentiality of high level communications, without more, can sustain an absolute, unqualified presidential privilege of immunity from judicial process under all circumstances. The President's need for complete candor and objectivity calls for great deference from the courts. However, when the privilege depends solely on the broad, undifferentiated claim of public interest in the confidentiality of such conversations, a confrontation with other values arises. Absent a claim of need to protect military, diplomatic or sensitive national security secrets, we find it difficult to accept the argument that even the very important interest in confidentiality of presidential communications is significantly diminished by production of such material for in camera *inspection with all the protection that a district court will be obliged to provide.*

If there is no absolute privilege, is there one in this case? The Court also held for the first time that the claim of executive privilege is "fundamental to the operation of government and inextricably rooted in the separation of powers under the Constitution." But, Chief Justice Burger said,

this presumptive privilege must be considered in light of our historic commitment to the rule of law. This is nowhere more profoundly manifest than in our view that "the twofold aim [of criminal justice] is that guilt shall not escape or innocence suffer." We have elected to employ an adversary system of criminal justice in which the parties contest all issues before a court of law. The need to develop all relevant facts in the adversary system is both fundamental and comprehensive. The ends of criminal justice would be defeated if judgments were to be founded on a partial or speculative presentation of the facts. The very integrity of the judicial system and public confidence in the system depend on full disclosure of all the facts, within the framework of the rules of evidence. To ensure that justice is done, it is imperative to the function of courts that compulsory process be available for the production of evidence needed either by the prosecution or by the defense.

In this case we must weigh the importance of the general privilege of confidentiality of presidential communications in performance of his responsibilities against the inroads of such a privilege on the fair administration of criminal justice. The interest in preserving confidentiality is weighty indeed and entitled to great respect. However we cannot conclude that advisers will be moved to temper the candor of their remarks by the infrequent occasions of disclosure because of the possibility that such conversations will be called for in the context of a criminal prosecution.

On the other hand, the allowance of the privilege to withhold evidence that is demonstrably relevant in a criminal trial would cut deeply into the guarantee of due process of law and gravely impair the basic function of the courts. A President's acknowledged need for confidentiality in the communications of his office is general in nature, whereas the constitutional need for production of relevant evident in a criminal proceeding is specific and central to the fair adjudication of a particular criminal case in the administration of justice. Without access to specific facts a criminal case may be totally frustrated. The President's broad interest in confidentiality of communications will not be vitiated by disclosure of a limited number of conversations preliminarily shown to have some bearing on the pending criminal cases. . . . The generalized assertion of privilege must yield to the demonstrated, specific need for evidence in a pending criminal trial.

Finally, the Court laid down some rules that Judge Sirica had to follow when examining and releasing the evidence to the prosecution and defense. Any conversations found to be neither relevant nor admissible had to be excised. "We have no doubt," the chief justice concluded, "that the District Judge [Sirica] will at all times accord to presidential records that high degree of deference suggested in *United States* v. *Burr* . . . and will discharge his responsibility to see to it that until released to the Special Prosecutor no *in camera* material is revealed to anyone."

In the end, President Nixon obviated the need for care on three particular tapes by releasing transcripts that showed his obvious participation in the two-year-long cover-up. The "smoking gun" was at last produced, proving conclusively that the very claim of executive privilege in this particular case was part of the general cover-up strategem.

The decision to release the transcripts was not made willingly, however. It was forced on the president. The previous fall, before the decision in *Nixon* v. *Sirica,* the president had suggested he might refuse to obey a judicial decision that was less than definitive. Now, stunned by the definitiveness of this unanimous decision (written by his choice as chief justice and joined in by two of his three other appointments), the president hesitated about eight hours before announcing that he would comply, finally persuaded that if he did not his own lawyers would quit his cause and his impeachment and conviction would then be a certainty. This must have seemed a Hobson's choice to the only man in the White House who knew on July 24 what was really in the subpoenaed tapes. Release was sure to trigger an equally intense reaction and, of course, it did.

Tally sheet shows the 27 to 11 vote by which the House Judiciary Committee recommended to impeach President Nixon for obstruction of justice.

UPI

Ordered by Judge Sirica to listen to the tapes and to speed up delivery of the transcripts, St. Clair (and a few others who also finally heard them) realized what their client had for so long hidden. They persuaded the president that he must release the tapes and take his chances. Sixteen days after the Court announced its decision, Richard Nixon became the first president in American history to resign his office.

It cannot fairly be claimed that the Court was responsible for the president's resignation. Without the impeachment proceedings in the House, without an already outraged public opinion, the decision might only have provoked a brief storm that would have blown over. But the Court's decision was unquestionably the trigger. The president understood that to disobey the plain command of these nine men, who without an army, were powerless to enforce the order of Judge Sirica, would have stripped him of his last shred of honor.

That Richard Nixon did bow demonstrates that the rule of law —the spirit of constitutionalism—retains the respect of the people and remains the fundamental principle of American government.

In no other nation would the sovereign power of the state proceed in a court of law against the nation's own chief executive, who remained in office, who actively maneuvered in his own interests, who yet would be unable to deter his eventual defeat.

In no other nation is it even conceivable that there would be a lawsuit entitled The Nation v. Its Leader. No guns were fired, no blood was shed.

"Here, the people rule."

White House Attorney James St. Clair, left, and a Secret Service agent deliver the first 20 White House tapes to U.S. District Judge Sirica.

UPI

Notes

Because this is not a scholarly treatise, no attempt has been made to give page references to every quotation from cases cited throughout the text. These notes are not intended to be a comprehensive summary of the pertinent literature; references appear herein only as necessary to identify a particular quotation or series of facts in the text.

Author's Preface

Page xiii — "Principal obstacle to justice": Christian Bay, review of Richard E. Flathman's *The Practice of Political Obligation, The Annals of Political and Social Science* (January 1974), p. 225.

xvii — First general history: Lawrence M. Friedman, *A History of American Law* (1974), p. 9.

xvii — Phelps, quoted in Henry S. Commager, *The American Mind* (1959), p. 370.

Chapter 1: The Declaration of Independence

6 — "Brooding omnipresence in the sky": Justice Holmes dissenting in *Southern Pacific Co.* v. *Jensen*, 224 U.S. 205 (1917).

8 — Lord Coke in Friedman, *A History of American Law*, pp. 20-21.

8 — Colonial enactments: *Id.* pp. 78ff.

9 — Daniel J. Boorstin, *The Mysterious Science of the Law*, 1941, p. 3.

9 — Virginia company charter: Quoted in Samuel E. Morison, *The Oxford History of the American People* (1964), p. 49.

10 — 1629 Massachusetts charter: Quoted in Friedman, *A History of American Law*, p. 33.

10 — Privy Council: *Id.*, p. 44.

10 — Stamp Act, provoking outcry: Dumas Malone, *The Declaration of Independence* (1954), p. 11.

10 — Declaratory Act: *Id.*, p. 17.

10 — "Rally in support of Boston": *Id.*, p. 30.

14 — Acts "exaggerated": Morison, *The Oxford History of the American People*, p. 223.

15 — Paine, quoted: Friedman, *A History of American Law*, p. 94, from Philip S. Foner, ed., *Complete Writings of Thomas Paine, Vol. 2*, (1945), p. 1003.

15 — Jefferson, quoted: Bernard Schwartz, *The Law in America*, (1975), p. 11; "common toast": *Id.*

16 — Henry Clay: Friedman, *A History of American Law*, pp. 95-99.

16 — Continental Congress: Quoted in Friedman, *A History of American Law*, p. 95, from Elizabeth Gaspar Brown, *British*

Statutes in American Law, 1776-1836, (1964), p. 21.

Page 16 — French codes: See Schwartz, *The Law in America,* pp. 12f. Virginia reception statute: Quoted in Friedman, *A History of American Law,* p. 127.

17 — *Seeley* v. *Peters,* 10 Ill. 130 (1848).

18 — *Grigsby* v. *Reib,* 105 Tex. 597 (1913). Declaration moved to National Archives: Malone, *The Declaration of Independence,* p. 264; see the discussion pp. 248-64.

22 — Anastaplo case: *In re Anastaplo,* 366 U.S. 82 (1961). Ten years after this case, the Supreme Court in effect conceded its error, when it ruled that bar committees may not constitutionally probe the memberships and beliefs of lawyers-to-be. See *Baird* v. *State Bar of Arizona,* 401 U.S. 1 (1971); *In re Stolar,* 401 U.S. 23 (1971).

Chapter Two: The Constitution of the United States

25 — Madison: Quoted in Catherine Drinker Bowen, *Miracle at Philadelphia,* (1966), p. 14.

26 — Correction of Confederation's defects: Max Farrand, *The Framing of the Constitution,* (1913), pp. 202-3.

26 — Same document in other nations: Indeed, the Indian Constitution, patterned in part after the American one, lasted just barely longer than the quarter-century that some of the dispirited delegates had given their just-completed work in 1787.

28 — "Congress of states": Farrand, *The Framing of the Constitution,* p. 3.

28 — Madison: Quoted in Morison, *The Oxford History of the American People,* p. 280.

29 — Madison, on problems of trade: Quoted in Farrand, *The Framing of the Constitution,* p. 7.

29 — Adams' proposal: Morison, *The Oxford History of the American People,* p. 303.

31 — Hopkinson letter to Jefferson: Quoted in Bowen, *Miracle at Philadelphia,* p. 31.

31 — Wilson: Quoted in *Id.,* p. 85.

32 — Morris: Quoted in Farrand, *The Framing of the Constitution,* p. 94.

33 — "Practically nothing in the Constitution": Farrand, *The Framing of the Constitution,* p. 202.

33 — *Federalist Papers,* No. 40.

33 — "Accounted for in American experience": Farrand, *The Framing of the Constitution,* p. 204.

33 — Seven-thousand-word document: This includes the twenty-six amendments.

34 — Constitution too well-known: See, e.g., Edward S. Corwin, *The Constitution and What It Means Today,* (1974), rev. ed. by Harold W. Chase and Craig R. Ducat.

35 — Franklin: Quoted in Bowen, *Miracle at Philadelphia,* p. 60.

Page 37 — Procedure for electing the president changed on three occasions: The Twelfth Amendment in 1804, the Twentieth Amendment in 1933, and the Twenty-Fifth Amendment in 1967.

39 — 1869 case: *Ex parte McCardle,* 7 Wall. 506 (1869).

40 — "Not a treaty, nor an agreement": Farrand, *The Framing of the Constitution,* p. 209.

41 — Four meanings of privileges and immunities: See Corwin, *The Constitution and What It Means Today,* pp. 208-10.

41 — Religious test for state office: Torasco v. Watkins, 367 U.S. 488 (1961).

42 — Washington: Quoted in Bowen, *Miracle at Philadelphia,* p. 305.

43 — Hamilton, Webster, Sherman: Quoted in *Id.,* pp. 245-46.

45 — New York quoted on ratification: in Broadus Mitchell and Louise Mitchell, *A Biography of the Constitution,* (1964), p. 185.

46 — Massachusetts ratification of Bill of Rights: *Id.,* p. 204.

46 — Second Amendment: See Corwin, *The Constitution and What It Means Today,* p. 299.

47 — Fourth Amendment: This capsule description is necessarily loose. The police need not obtain warrants for every arrest or for every search. In the past fifteen years there has been an enormous volume of litigation over the precise limits of this amendment. *Cf.,* Corwin, *The Constitution and What It Means Today,* pp. 301ff.

Chapter Three: John Marshall and the Marshall Court

54 — *Calder* v. *Bull,* 3 Dall. 386 (1798).

55 — Deportations of communists: See *Harisiades* v. *Shaughnessy,* 342 U.S. 589 (1952). See also Fleming v. Nestor, 363 U.S. 603 (1960), permitting revocation of Social Security benefits of an ex-Party member.

55 — "Small and undignified chamber": Charles Warren, *The Supreme Court in United States History,* (1926), Vol. 1, p. 171. For discussion of the Court's peregrinations to present, see "When the Supreme Court Was in the Capitol," 61 *American Bar Association Journal* 949 (1975).

55 — Jay letter to Adams: Quoted in Warren, *The Supreme Court in United States History,* Vol. 1, p. 173.

56 — Marshall recounts moment of his appointment: Quoted in Herbert Alan Johnson, "John Marshall," in Leon Friedman and Fred L. Israel, eds., *The Justices of the Supreme Court of the United States,* (1970), p. 285.

56 — Virginia party leader on Marshall: Quoted in Warren, *The Supreme Court in United States History,* Vol. 1, p. 179.

57 — Marshall's becoming political boss: See Johnson, "John Marshall," in Friedman and Israel, *The Justices of the Supreme Court of the United States,* p. 287.

Page 59 — Statements about Marshall's abilities as a lawyer: Quoted in Warren, *The Supreme Court in United States History*, Vol. 1, p. 180.

59 — Jefferson on Marshall: Quoted in *Id.*, p. 182.

60 — Frankfurter on Marshall: Felix Frankfurter, "John Marshall and the Judicial Function," 69 *Harv. L. Rev.* 217, 220-21 (1955).

61 — *Gibbons* v. *Ogden:* It is curious that *American Bar Association Journal* readers answering the survey that led to the contents of this volume neglected the case of *Gibbons* v. *Ogden*, 9 Wheat. 1 (1824), the Court's first interpretation of the Commerce Clause and one of the seminal constitutional cases. In briefest compass, it concerned New York State's exclusive grant in 1800 to Robert R. Livingston and Robert Fulton of the right to operate a steamboat on the state waterways.

A number of lawsuits over the years failed to dislodge the monopoly; New York even passed a law permitting seizure of any unauthorized steam vessel on the state's navigable waters. Connecticut, New Jersey, and Ohio enacted laws in retaliation prohibiting the Livingston-Fulton ships from sailing across their boundaries. Feelings rose to fever pitch by the early 1820s.

In 1819, Aaron Ogden, former governor of New Jersey who had built a competing company for trips between the states, brought a test case. He had earlier been enjoined by the Livingston-Fulton monopoly from operating in New York and was forced to take a license from the monopoly. When his ex-partner, Thomas Gibbons of Georgia, started his own business and began steamship runs between New Jersey and New York, Ogden sued to stop him.

In 1822 the case reached the Court, but it was not argued until February 4, 1824. The principal attorney was Daniel Webster, who argued long and eloquently that the Constitution granted the power to Congress to regulate commerce between the states and that the states could not interfere with such commerce in the absence of Congressional regulation.

Accepting Webster's argument completely, Chief Justice Marshall defined commerce in an expansive manner and struck down the monopoly on March 2.

61 — Cardozo on Marshall: Benjamin N. Cardozo, *Law and Literature* (1931), p. 10.

61 — Marshall's constitutional dissent: *Ogden* v. *Saunders*, 12 Wheat. 213 (1827). The Court ruled that the states could constitutionally enact bankruptcy legislation that would affect debts entered into after the time of the enactment. *Cf. Sturges* v. *Crowninshield.*

62 — Marshall and Story entering theater: Quoted in Leonard

Baker, *John Marshall, A Life in Law*, (1974), p. 762.

Page 62 — "One of the great jurists": Gerald T. Dunne, "Joseph Story," in Friedman and Israel, *The Justices of the Supreme Court of the United States*, p. 435.

63 — "An outburst virtually unrivalled": *Id.*, pp. 43-44.

63 — Jackson on Story: Quoted in *Id.*, p. 445.

63 — *United States* v. *Hudson and Goodwin*, 7 Cranch 32 (1812).

64 — Story's eulogy of Washington: Quoted in Albert P. Blaustein and Roy M. Mersky, "Bushrod Washington," in Friedman and Israel, *The Justices of the Supreme Court of the United States*, p. 257.

65 — Johnson to Jefferson: Quoted in Donald Morgan, "William Johnson," in Friedman and Israel, *The Justices of the Supreme Court of the United States*, p. 367.

Chapter Four: The Supreme Court Has the Last Word—Almost

67 — Jackson epigram: *Brown* v. *Allen*, 344 U.S. 443, 540 (1953) (concurring opinion).

70 — Jay on health: Quoted in Warren, *The Supreme Court in United States History*, Vol. 1, p. 173.

70 — Leading Republican newspaper on Judiciary Act: Quoted in *Id.*, p. 187.

70 — Constituent to Breckenridge: Quoted in *Id.*, p. 189.

71 — Republican congressman on the commissions: *Id.*, p. 201.

73 — Marshall letter to brother: Quoted in Baker, p. 394.

73 — Jefferson later recounted: Quoted in *Id.*, p. 413.

73 — "This outrage on decency": Quoted in Warren, *The Supreme Court in United States History*, Vol. 1, p. 201.

74 — Breckenridge to Monroe: Quoted in *Id.*, p. 204.

81 — Lower federal courts: In fact, of course, Congress had created two types of lower courts: the district courts, with original jurisdiction only, and circuit courts, which initially had both original and appellate jurisdiction.

83 — "An attempt in subversion": Quoted in Warren, *The Supreme Court in United States History*, Vol. 1, p. 244.

83 — "America's original contribution," Albert J. Beveridge, *The Life of John Marshall*, Vol. 3 (1917), p. 142.

83 — Court had no jurisdiction: Quoted in Warren, *The Supreme Court in United States History*, Vol. 1, p. 250.

84 — Elbridge Gerry: Quoted in Max Farrand, *The Records of the Federal Convention*, Vol. 1 (1911), p. 109.

85 — "At no period in American history: Warren, *The Supreme Court in United States History*, Vol. 1, pp. 256-57.

87 — "I do not think the United States would come to an end": Oliver Wendell Holmes, "Law and Literature." in *Collected Legal Papers* (1921), pp. 295-6.

87 — For discussion of congressional restrictions on the Court's

jurisdiction, see Walter F. Murphy, *Congress and the Court,* 1962.

Page 88 — Court reversed by constitutional amendment: *Chisholm* v. *Georgia,* 2 Dall. 419 (1793) (Eleventh Amendment); *Dred Scott* v. *Sandford,* 19 How. 393 (1857) (Fourteenth Amendment) (see Chapter 6 *supra*); *Pollock* v. *Farmers' Loan & Trust Co.,* 158 U.S. 601 (1895) (Sixteenth Amendment); *Oregon* v. *Mitchell,* 400 U.S. 112 (1970) (Twenty-Sixth Amendment).

89 — Circuit courts have no power to issue mandamus against government: *McIntire* v. *Wood,* 7 Cranch 504 (1813); but Washington, D.C. circuit court does: *Kendall* v. *United States,* 12 Pet. 524 (1838); see discussion in Henry M. Hart, Jr., and Herbert Wechsler, *The Federal Court and the Federal System,* 2d ed., Paul M. Bator, Paul J. Mishkin, David L. Shapiro, and Herbert Wechsler, eds., (1973), pp. 98ff.

Chapter Five: The Sanctity of Contracts

93 — *Fletcher* v. *Peck,* 6 Cranch 87 (1810).

93 — Fascinating diatribe: Gustavus Myers, *History of the Supreme Court of the United States* (1912), p. 263; on Wilson: pp. 155ff.

94 — "Nothing could more certainly bring the Court": Warren, *The Supreme Court in United States History,* Vol. 1, p. 398.

94 — Indian case: *New Jersey* v. *Wilson,* 7 Cranch 164 (1812).

95 — 1815 cases: *Terrett* v. *Taylor,* 9 Cranch 43 (1815); *Town of Pawlet* v. *Clark,* 9 Cranch 292 (1815).

95 — Smith on reasons for incorporation: Quoted in Jere R. Daniel, II, "Eleazar Wheelock and the Dartmouth College Charter," unnumbered, undated, published by Dartmouth College.

96 — Charter quoted: *Id.*

97 — Morin: Richard W. Morin, "Will to Resist: The Dartmouth College Case," reprinted from April 1969 *Dartmouth Alumni Magazine,* unnumbered.

100 — Jefferson to Plumer: Quoted in Warren, *The Supreme Court in United States History,* Vol. 1, pp. 484-85.

102 — Dartmouth College state decision: 1 N.H. 111 (1817).

103 — Webster to Brown: Quoted in Morin, "Will to Resist."

104 — Goodrich on Webster: Quoted in Baker *John Marshall, A Life in Law,* p. 660.

105 — Webster preoration: Quoted in *Id.,* p. 662; 1830 account, *Id.*

110 — *Sturges* v. *Crowninshield,* 4 Wheat. 122 (1819).

110 — Story to Kent: Quoted in Warren, *The Supreme Court in United States History,* Vol. 1, p. 490.

111 — General incorporation statutes: Any group of investors may incorporate by following a general plan, rather than having

to apply specifically to the legislature for a charter, as had been the procedure earlier in the century.

Page 111 — *Charles River Bridge* v. *Warren Bridge,* 11 Pet. 420 (1837).

111 — Kent and Story quoted in Warren, *The Supreme Court in United States History,* Vol. 2, pp. 28-29.

112 — "Police power" cases: Series began with *Boston Beer Co.* v. *Massachusetts,* 97 U.S. 25 (1877); *Stone* v. *Mississippi,* 101 U.S. 814 (1879).

112 — Mortgage Moratorium Case: *Home Building & Loan Assn.* v. *Blaisdell,* 290 U.S. 398 (1934).

114 — Federal chartering: For a recent, detailed discussion of how federal law might restructure corporations, and reasons for doing so, see Christopher D. Stone, *Where the Law Ends, Toward Social Control of Corporate Behavior,* (1975).

114 — "The clause is of negligible importance": Corwin, *The Constitution and What It Means Today,* (1958), 12th ed., p. 85; see note of revisers that "recent decisions by lower courts make the issuance of the clause's death certificate premature," p. 105.

114 — Florida federal court ruling: *Aerojet-General Corp.* v. *Askew,* 366 F.Supp. 901 (N.D. Fla. 1973). Other cases, including state court decisions, are collected in Corwin, *The Constitution and What It Means Today,* pp. 556, 613.

115 — New York municipal crisis: See *New York Times,* October 30, 1975, p. 48.

Chapter Six: The Power and Supremacy of the Federal Government

119 — Hamilton argument: Quoted in Mitchell and Mitchell, *A Biography of the Constitution,* p. 256.

119 — Jefferson letter: Quoted in Warren, *The Supreme Court in United States History,* Vol. 1, p. 501.

122 — Story on Pinkney: Quoted in *Id.,* pp. 507-8.

122 — "Justice hides her face": Quoted in Mitchell and Mitchell, *A Biography of the Constitution,* p. 260.

122 — 1805 Marshall decision: *United States* v. *Fisher,* 2 Cranch 358 (1805).

122 — "It was highly unfortunate": Warren, *The Supreme Court in United States History,* Vol. 1, p. 503.

129 — Court's response to Governor of Arkansas: *Cooper* v. *Aaron,* 358 U.S. 1 (1958).

130 — Ohio newspaper quoted in Warren, *The Supreme Court in United States History,* Vol. 1, p. 532.

130 — Governor Allen quoted in *Id.,* p. 533.

130 — *Osborn* v. *Bank of the United States,* 9 Wheat. 738 (1824).

Chapter Seven: People as Property

137-8 — Morison on Compromise: Morison, *Oxford History of the American People,* p. 405; Adams in diary: quoted in *Id.*

Page 138 — For language of the various proposals, see Wallace Mendelsohn, "Dred Scott's Case—Reconsidered," 38 *Minn. L. Rev.* 16 (1953); reprinted in Stanley I. Kutler, *The Dred Scott Decision: Law or Politics?* (1967), pp. 152ff.

139 — South's last chance: Herbert Agar, *The Price of Union*, (1966), p. 329.

139 — Clay quoted in *Id.*, pp. 154, 155.

140 — *Prigg* v. *Pennsylvania*, 16 Pet. 539 (1842).

141 — Section 14, Kansas-Nebraska Act: 10 Stat. 227 (1854); quoted in Mendelsohn, "Dred Scott's Case," p. 158.

141 — Zenith of popular esteem: Warren, *The Supreme Court in United States History*, Vol. 2, p. 207.

142 — *Booth Cases*, 21 How. 506 (1859).

146 — On Mrs. Emerson's peregrinations, see Vincent C. Hopkins, *Dred Scott's Case*, (1971), p. 23.

148 — Justice Curtis letter to brother: Quoted in Warren, *The Supreme Court in United States History*, Vol. 2, pp. 290-91.

148 — *Strader* v. *Graham*, 10 How. 82 (1851).

149 — Catron to Buchanan: Quoted in Warren, *The Supreme Court in United States History*, Vol. 2, pp. 294-95.

150 — Charles Warren has exculpated Grier to a degree by pointing out that many justices confided "to an intimate friend or relative the probable outcome of a pending case," and he cites some examples. *Id.* Still, none of those to whom the confidences had in the past been made was a president-elect.

150 — Grier to Buchanan: Quoted in *Id.*, pp. 296-97; italics in original.

152 — Taney vilified: In many accounts at the time and in many historical accounts thereafter, Taney and the Court were accused of uttering *obiter dicta*, gratuitous comments unnecessary to the disposition of the case. Having determined the Court had no jurisdiction, after all, how could the Court then go on to discuss the constitutionality of the Missouri Compromise? There is only a mild degree of fairness in the accusation; what Taney was really doing was discussing alternative reasons for the lack of jurisdiction: if his first reason be thought wrong, his second was ready. Moreover, he was writing the opinion in response to the pressure to reply to the dissenters, who, he and the others felt, forced his hand. For a discussion of the propriety of considering the Missouri Compromise question, see Edward S. Corwin, "The Dred Scott Decision in the Light of Contemporary Legal Doctrines," *The American Historical Review* XVII (October 1911): 52-69; reprinted in Kutler, *The Dred Scott Decision*, pp. 123-38.

160 — Lincoln on Dred Scott: Speech of June 17, 1858, quoted in Kutler, *The Dred Scott Decision*, p. 70.

160 — Booth cases: *Ableman* v. *Booth; United States* v. *Booth*, 21 How. 506 (1859).

Page 160 — Wisconsin nullification: Wisconsin finally bowed, after the Civil War had begun. *Arnold* v. *Booth,* 14 Wis. 180 (1861) ; see Warren, *The Supreme Court in United States History,* Vol. 2, pp. 342-43.

161 — "Gross abuse of trust": Corwin in Kutler, *The Dred Scott Decision,* p. 138; Taney elected Lincoln: Warren, *The Supreme Court in United States History,* Vol. 2, p. 347.

Chapter Eight: Between Then and Now

164 — For works dealing with the drafting and implementation of the Fourteenth Amendment, see: Henry J. Abraham, *Freedom and the Court, Civil Rights and Civil Liberties in the United States,* (2nd ed., 1972) ; C. Peter Magrath, "The Case of the Unscrupulous Warehouseman," in John A. Garraty, ed., *Quarrels That Have Shaped the Constitution* (1964), pp. 109-27; Robert G. McCloskey, *The American Supreme Court,* (1960), Chapters 5 and 6; Howard N. Meyer, *The Amendment That Refused to Die,* (1973) ; Schwartz, *The Law in America,* Chapter 4; Warren, *The Supreme Court in United States History,* Vol. 2, Chapters 32 and 33.

164 — Sumner quoted in Schwartz, *The Law in America,* p. 91.

167 — Howard quoted in Abraham, *Freedom and the Court,* p. 41.

167 — "No genuine doubt": *Id.,* pp. 41-42.

167 — *Slaughterhouse Cases,* 16 Wall. 36 (1873).

167 — "More than ordinarily corrupt": Alexander Bickel, *The Morality of Consent,* (1975), p. 42.

168 — Campbell quoted in Charles Fairman, *Reconstruction and Reunion 1864-1888,* (1971), p. 1345.

170 — Case permitting repeal of slaughterhouse monopoly: *Butcher's Union Slaughter-House* v. *Crescent City Live-Stock Landing Co.,* 111 U.S. 746 (1884).

172 — New York state case: *Wynehamer* v. *People,* 13 N.Y. 378 (1856).

172 — Granger cases: *Munn* v. *Illinois,* 94 U.S. 113 (1877).

173 — Earlier cases dealing with states' power to act: See, e.g., *Cooley* v. *Board of Wardens of the Port of Philadelphia,* 12 How. 299 (1851).

174 — 1934 case: *Nebbia* v. *New York,* 291 U.S. 502 (1934).

174 — Chicago Tribune: March 10, 1877, quoted in Warren, *The Supreme Court in United States History,* Vol. 2, p. 587.

174 — St. Paul Pioneer Press: March 29, 1877; quoted in *Id.,* pp. 588-89.

175 — *Santa Clara County* v. *Southern Pacific Railroad,* 118 U.S. 394 (1886). The principle that a corporation is a person was upheld in *Pembina Mining Co.* v. *Pennsylvania,* 125 U.S. 181 (1890).

175 — Later historians: See Graham, "The 'Conspiracy Theory' of the Fourteenth Amendment," 4 *Yale L. J.* 371 (1938).

175 — *Stone* v. *Farmers Loan and Trust Co.,* 116 U.S. 307 (1886).

Page 176 — "Exchange value": John R. Commons, *Legal Foundations of Capitalism*, (1924), Chapter 2.

176 — "The term . . . drops out of the clause": Corwin, *The Constitution and What It Means Today*, p. 327; see *Chicago, Milwaukee & St. Paul R.R.* v. *Minnesota*, 134 U.S. 418 (1890).

176 — Cigar case: *Matter of Application of Jacobs*, 98 N.Y. 98 (1885).

176 — Louisiana insurance case: *Allgeyer* v. *Louisiana*, 105 U.S. 578 (1897).

176 — *Lochner* v. *New York*, 198 U.S. 45 (1905).

178 — Justice Miller: *Davidson* v. *New Orleans*, 96 U.S. 97 (1878).

Chapter Nine: The Uncertain Cackle of the Sick Chicken

183 — "History will probably record": Quoted in Arthur M. Schlesinger, Jr., *The Coming of the New Deal*, (1958), p. 102; "implications are much more important": Schlesinger, *The Politics of Upheaval*, (1960), p. 285.

185 — "If a retailer": Frank Freidel, "The Sick Chicken Case," in Garraty, *Quarrels That Have Shaped the Constitution*, p. 197.

186 — "In the course of its short life": Louis L. Jaffe and Nathaniel Nathanson, *Administrative Law*, (2nd ed.), 1961, p. 60.

186 — "Mopstick, corn-cob pipe": Freidel, "The Sick Chicken Case," p. 197.

187 — Sugar Trust Case: *United States* v. *E. C. Knight Co.*, 156 U.S. 1 (1895); Court reversed itself: *Swift & Co.* v. *United States*, 196 U.S. 375 (1905); child labor case: *Hammer* v. *Dagenhart*, 247 U.S. 251 (1918); women's minimum wage law case: *Adkins* v. *Children's Hospital*, 261 U.S. 525 (1923); Gold Clause cases: *Norman* v. *Baltimore & Ohio R.R.*, 294 U.S. 240 (1935).

187 — Hot Oil case: *Panama Refining Co.* v. *Ryan*, 293 U.S. 389 (1935).

190 — Reed decides not to appeal: See Schlesinger, *The Coming of the New Deal*, p. 276; "people in general": *Id.*, p. 277.

192 — Heller quoted in Freidel, "The Sick Chicken Case," p. 203.

192 — Farm mortgage relief case: *Louisville Bank* v. *Radford*, 295 U.S. 555 (1935).

193 — Jackson: Robert H. Jackson, *The Struggle for Judicial Supremacy*, (1941), p. 109; the case dealing with the president's removal powers was *Humphrey's Executor* v. *United States*, 295 U.S. 602 (1935).

198 — 1942 farm case: *Wickard* v. *Filburn*, 317 U.S. 111 (1942).

198 — "Whatever else the Court had done": Schlesinger, *The Coming of the New Deal*, p. 291.

199 — "Schechter told Pearson": Quoted in Freidel, "The Sick Chicken Case," p. 209.

Chapter Ten: Congress and the General Welfare

Page 204 — Townsend quoted in Schlesinger, *The Politics of Upheaval*, p. 34.

205 — FDR quoted in *Id.*, pp. 309-310.

207 — Donnelly, Wadsworth, quoted in *Id.*, pp. 311, 312.

210 — Jackson, *The Struggle for Judicial Supremacy*, p. 190.

211 — Steward Machine Company case: *Steward Machine Co.* v. *Davis,* 301 U.S. 548 (1937).

213 — Agricultural Adjustment Act case: *United States* v. *Butler,* 297 U.S. 1 (1936).

213 — Second social security case: *Helvering* v. *Davis,* 301 U.S. 619 (1937).

Chapter Eleven: The Law that Depends on the Forum

219 — Warren's classic article: Charles Warren, "New Light on this History of the Federal Judiciary Act of 1789," 37 *Harv. L. Rev.* 49 (1923).

220 — Washington quoted in Robert H. Jackson, "The Rise and Fall of *Swift* v. *Tyson*," 24 *American Bar Assn. Journal* 609, 610 (1938).

220 — *United States* v. *Hudson and Goodwin,* 7 Cranch 32 (1812).

220 — Copyright case: *Wheaton* v. *Peters,* 8 Pet. 591 (1834).

221 — *Swift* v. *Tyson,* 16 Pet. 1 (1842).

222 — "Brooding omnipresence": *Southern Pacific Co.* v. *Jensen,* 244 U.S. 205 (1917).

222 — Jackson address quoted: Jackson, "The Rise and Fall of Swift v. Tyson," pp. 610-11.

224 — Iowa bond cases: *Gelpcke* v. *Dubuque,* 1 Wall. 175 (1864); *Riggs* v. *Johnson County,* 6 Wall. 166 (1868).

225 — Original draft of Section 34: Quoted in Warren, "New Light on the History of the Federal Judiciary Act of 1789," p. 87; italics added.

225 — *Black & White Taxicab Co.* v. *Brown & Yellow Taxicab Co.,* 276 U.S. 518 (1928).

227 — Tompkins' case on remand: *Tompkins* v. *Erie Railroad Co.,* 98 F.2d 49 (2nd Cir. 1938).

227 — Correspondent to the Times: *New York Times,* May 7, 1938, p. 14.

229 — For the later ramifications of *Erie Railroad*, the intrepid reader may consult Hart & Wechsler, passim.; Note, "The Federal Common Law," 82 *Harv. L. Rev.* 1512 (1969); Note, "*Swift* v. *Tyson* Exhumed," 79 *Yale L. J.* 284 (1969); Henry J. Friendly, "In Praise of *Erie*—and of the New Federal Common Law," 39 *N.Y.U. L. Rev.* 383 (1964).

Chapter Twelve: Earl Warren and the Warren Court

234 — Three important cases: *Hurtado* v. *California,* 110 U.S. 516 (1884); *Maxwell* v. *Dow,* 176 U.S. 581 (1900); *Twining* v. *New Jersey,* 211 U.S. 78 (1908).

Page 235 — 1923 Arkansas case: *Moore* v. *Dempsey*, 261 U.S. 86 (1923).

236 — Freedom of speech case: *Gitlow* v. *New York*, 268 U.S. 652 (1925). For later First Amendment cases, see *Fiske* v. *Kansas*, 274 U.S. 380 (1927) ; *Near* v. *Minnesota*, 283 U.S. 697 (1931).

236 — *Powell* v. *Alabama*, 287 U.S. 45 (1932).

237 — *Palko* v. *Connecticut*, 302 U.S. 319 (1937) ; Palko overruled in *Benton* v. *Maryland*, 395 U.S. 784 (1969).

237 — Black's new doctrine: *Adamson* v. *California*, 332 U.S. 46 (1948).

238 — Frankfurter's doctrine: *Rochin* v. *California*, 342 U.S. 165 (1952).

241 — "Felt nauseated": *New York Times*, July 10, 1974, p. 24.

241 — Lewis on Warren: Anthony Lewis, "Earl Warren," in Friedman and Israel, *The Justices of the Supreme Court of the United States*, p. 2728.

242 — "Honor to be accused": *New York Times*, July 10, 1974, p. 24.

246 — For the story of a curious attempt to have Black's appointment declared unconstitutional, see the discussion in J. K. Lieberman, *How the Government Breaks the Law*, (1973), Chapter 5.

247 — *Griswold* v. *Connecticut*, 381 U.S. 479 (1965).

247 — Acheson on Frankfurter: Quoted in Albert M. Sacks, "Felix Frankfurter," in Friedman and Israel, *The Justices of the Supreme Court of the United States*, p. 2402.

249 — Flag salute cases: *Minersville School Dist.* v. *Gobitis*, 310 U.S. 586 (1940) ; *West Virginia State Board of Education* v. *Barnette*, 319 U.S. 624 (1943).

251 — *Reynolds* v. *Sims*, 377 U.S. 533 (1964).

Chapter Thirteen: Equality Redeemed

257 — Sumner to South Carolina convention: Walter L. Fleming, *Documentary History of Reconstruction*, (1966 ed.), Vol. 2, p. 292.

257 — 1875 Civil Rights Act: 18 Stat. 335 (March 1, 1875).

258 — *Civil Rights Cases*, 109 U.S. 3 (1883).

260 — Westin on *Civil Rights Cases:* Alan F. Westin, "The Case of the Prejudiced Doorkeeper," in Garraty, *Quarrels That Have Shaped the Constitution*, p. 143.

261 — Tourgee quoted in C. Van Woodward, "The Case of the Louisiana Traveler," in Garraty, *Quarrels That Have Shaped the Constitution*, p. 153.

261 — *Plessy* v. *Ferguson*, 163 U.S. 537 (1896).

264 — Harlan himself implied: *Cumming* v. *County Board of Education*, 175 U.S. 528 (1899).

264 — Court reaffirmed *Plessy: Gong Lum* v. *Rice*, 275 U.S. 78 (1927).

264 — 1917 case: *Buchanan* v. *Warley*, 245 U.S. 60 (1917).

Page 264 — Dining car case: *McCabe* v. *Atchison, Topeka & Santa Fe R. Co.*, 235 U.S. 151 (1914).

266 — 1927 voting case: *Nixon* v. *Herndon*, 273 U.S. 536 (1927); the Court had not yet decided that a primary was an election and so found itself unable to void the law under the Fifteenth Amendment, a position ultimately reached in *United States* v. *Classic*, 313 U.S. 299 (1941).

266 — Missouri law school case: *Missouri ex rel. Gaines* v. *Canada*, 305 U.S. 337 (1938).

267 — *Shelley* v. *Kraemer*, 334 U.S. 1 (1948).

268 — Texas law school case: *Sweatt* v. *Painter*, 339 U.S. 629 (1950).

268 — Oklahoma graduate school case: *McLaurin* v. *Oklahoma State Regents*, 339 U.S. 637 (1950).

270 — "Made more oral arguments": William H. Harbaugh, *Lawyer's Lawyer, The Life of John W. Davis*, (1974), pp. xv, 531. By comparison, Webster argued some 200 cases, and Walter Jones, who argued on Maryland's behalf in *McCulloch* v. *Maryland*, is said to have argued 317 cases between 1801 and 1835.

275 — Marshall quoted in Alfred H. Kelley, "The School Desegregation Case," in Garraty, *Quarrels That Have Shaped the Constitution*, pp. 263-64.

275 — Government's brief quoted in *Id.*, p. 511.

276 — Marshall and Davis: Quoted in Harbaugh, *Lawyer's Lawyer, The Life of John W. Davis*, pp. 513-14; Rankin quoted in Kelley, "The School Desegregation Case," p. 267.

277 — Justice Burton's diary entry: Quoted in Harbaugh, *Lawyer's Lawyer, The Life of John W. Davis*, p. 517.

278 — Reston: *New York Times*, May 18, 1954, p. 14.

279 — Companion case: *Bolling* v. *Sharpe*, 347 U.S. 497 (1954).

280 — Survey of educators: *New York Times*, May 18, 1954, p. 14.

280 — Eastland: Quoted in *New York Times*, May 18, 1954, p. 19.

280 — Second *Brown* case: *Brown* v. *Board of Education*, 349 U.S. 294 (1955). "Nullification": See *Cooper* v. *Aaron*, 358 U.S. 1 (1958).

281 — *Civil Rights Cases* overturned: See *Heart of Atlanta Motel* v. *United States*, 379 U.S. 241 (1964); *Katzenbach* v. *McClung*, 379 U.S. 294 (1964). Repudiation of "all deliberate speed" as test: *Alexander* v. *Holmes County Board of Education*, 396 U.S. 19 (1969).

281 — Davis calls Marshall: Harbaugh, *Lawyer's Lawyer, The Life of John W. Davis*, p. 518.

Chapter Fourteen: The Privacy of One's Home

283 — Course of constitutional history might have been different: In view of the Court's apparent eagerness to decide the search and seizure issue, however, it is likely that one of the next search cases to reach the Court would have resulted

in the same decision. I am indebted to Walter L. Greene, Esq., for discussing with me the background of this case; telephone interview, October 2, 1975.

Page 284 — "Four little pamphlets": the words are those of Justice Douglas.

286 — Ohio decision: *State* v. *Mapp,* 166 N.E.2d 387 (1960).

288 — *Weeks* v. *United States,* 232 U.S. 383 (1914).

289 — Cardozo quoted: *People* v. *Defore,* 242 N.Y. 13, 150 N.E. 585 (1926).

289 — Colorado case: *Wolf* v. *Colorado,* 338 U.S. 25 (1949).

290 — Purpose of exclusionary rule: *Elkins* v. *United States,* 364 U.S. 206 (1960).

290 — "To grant the right": Justice Clark in *Mapp,* 367 U.S. at 656.

290 — Brandeis quoted: *Olmstead* v. *United States,* 277 U.S. 438 (1928).

291 — Earlier court decision: *Boyd* v. *United States,* 116 U.S. 616 (1886).

292 — Some would like to see *Mapp* overruled: See *Bivens* v. *Six Unknown Federal Narcotics Agents,* 403 U.S. 388 (1971); *Coolidge* v. *New Hampshire,* 403 U.S. 443 (1971). For a thorough discussion of the difficulties into which the Court has put itself as the result of its numerous due process criminal law decisions, see Fred P. Graham, *The Self-Inflicted Wound,* (1970). In 1975, a majority of five justices refused to order suppression of evidence uncovered by U.S. immigration authorities in a "roving border patrol" whose methods the Court had declared unconstitutional (in an unrelated case subsequent to the occurrences that led to the 1975 case). See *Almeida-Sanchez* v. *United States,* 413 U.S. 266 (1974); *United States* v. *Peltier,* 43 L.W. 4918 (U.S. 1975).

293 — Private possession of pornography: *Stanley* v. *Georgia,* 394 U.S. 557 (1969).

293 — Mapp's fate: *New York Times,* April 24, 1971, p. 12; May 27, p. 27.

Chapter Fifteen: Ending Rotten Boroughs

295 — Population statistics source: *Statistical Abstract of the United States* (1968), Table No. 894, p. 594.

296 — Tennessee constitution: Article Two, Sections Five and Six; there are minor qualifications.

298 — 1946 Illinois case: *Colegrove* v. *Green,* 328 U.S. 549 (1946); italics in Justice Frankfurter quotation added.

300 — *Kidd* v. *McCanless,* 292 S.W.2d 40 (Tenn. 1956); *appeal dismissed,* 352 U.S. 920 (1956). Attorney in *Kidd* quoted: Gene S. Graham, *One Man, One Vote: Baker v. Carr and the American Levellers,* (1972), p. 70; many of the facts recited in the text are drawn from Graham's account.

Page 300 — Chancellor Steele quoted in Gene Graham, *One Man, One Vote: Baker v. Carr and the American Levellers*, p. 75.

301 — Minnesota case: *Magraw* v. *Donovan*, 159 F.Supp. 901 (D. Minn. 1958).

302 — Nashville City Council quoted in Gene Graham, *One Man, One Vote: Baker v. Carr and the American Levellers*, pp. 179-80.

302 — Cox quoted in *Id.*, p. 235; Osborn quoted in *Id.*, p. 239.

304 — Tuskegee redistricting case: *Gomillion* v. *Lightfoot*, 364 U.S. 339 (1960).

308 — New constitutional slogan: *Gray* v. *Sanders*, 372 U.S. 368 (1963).

308 — Series of cases: Beginning with *Wesberry* v. *Sanders*, 376 U.S. 1 (1964); lead case from Alabama: *Reynolds* v. *Sims*, 377 U.S. 533 (1964).

310 — For current litigation, see e.g., *Mahan* v. *Howell*, 410 U.S. 315 (1973).

Chapter Sixteen: The Right to Counsel

314 — *Powell* v. *Alabama*, 287 U.S. 45 (1932).

316 — The story of the second Scottsboro trial is told by Don Carter, "A Reasonable Doubt," in *Stories of Great Crimes and Trials*, American Heritage, (1974), pp. 316ff.

317 — 1938 case: *Johnson* v. *Zerbst*, 304 U.S. 458 (1938).

317 — *Betts* v. *Brady*, 316 U.S. 455 (1942).

317 — Rule summed up in 1948; *Uveges* v. *Pennsylvania*, 335 U.S. 437 (1948).

318 — The colloquy is printed in Anthony Lewis, *Gideon's Trumpet*, (1964), pp. 9-10, on which the account in the text is based.

322 — Fortas quoted in *Id.*, pp. 171-72.

Chapter Seventeen: The Right Against Self-Incrimination

327 — Mississippi third degree case: *Brown* v. *Mississippi*, 297 U.S. 278 (1936).

328 — "Falsely stating that suspect's wife": *Rogers* v. *Richmond*, 365 U.S. 534 (1961); Frankfurter quoted from *Id.*

328 — 1943 and 1957 cases: *McNabb* v. *United States*, 318 U.S. 332 (1943); *Mallory* v. *United States*, 354 U.S. 449 (1957).

329 — Incorporation of Fifth Amendment: *Malloy* v. *Hogan*, 378 U.S. 1 (1964).

329 — Massiah's case: *Massiah* v. *United States*, 377 U.S. 201 (1964).

330 — *Escobedo* v. *Illinois*, 378 U.S. 478 (1964).

332 — Sutherland quoted: Arthur E. Sutherland, Jr., "Crime and Confession," 79 *Harv. L. Rev.*, 21, 36 (1965).

333 — High-level Manhattan D.A's assistant quoted: Louis Pollak, *The Constitution and the Supreme Court*, Vol. 2, (1966), pp. 187-88.

Page 333 — Prosecutor tries to explain: *New York Times,* January 28, 1965, p. 28.

334 — New York 1960s brutality case: *People* v. *Portelli,* 15 N.Y. 2d 235, 205 N.E.2d 857, 257 N.Y.S.2d 931 (1965).

335 — Police manual quoted: O'Hara, *Fundamentals of Criminal Investigation,* (1956), p. 112.

339 — New York detective quoted: Fred Graham, *The Self-Inflicted Wound,* p. 279; for surveys, see *Id.,* Chapter 12 *passim.*

339 — Other books: Fred Graham, *The Self-Inflicted Wound;* Leonard W. Levy, *Against the Law, The Nixon Court and Criminal Justice,* (1974).

340 — *Harris* v. *New York,* 401 U.S. 222 (1971).

340 — Court's announcement to hear arguments: *United States* v. *Martinez-Fuerte,* No. 74-1560. The 1965 self-incrimination no-comment case: *Griffin* v. *California,* 380 U.S. 609 (1965).

341 — Chief Justice Burger accused: Levy, *Against the Law: The Nixon Court and Criminal Justice,* p. 151.

341 — Levy quoted: *Id.,* p. 162.

341 — Miranda's fate: *New York Times,* February 25, 1967, p. 13; March 2, p. 40; December 13, 1972, p. 25.

343 — Miranda's death: *New York Times,* February 2, 1976, p. 8.

Chapter Eighteen: The Rights of Juveniles

348 — Penologist quoted: Anthony M. Platt, *The Child Savers, The Invention of Delinquency,* (1969), p. 45.

349 — Illinois Crime Commission: Quoted in *Id.,* p. 150.

350 — Arizona Supreme Court: *Application of Gault,* 99 Ariz. 181, 407 P.2d 760 (1965).

351 — Senate testimony: Hearings before the Senate Subcommittee to Investigate Juvenile Delinquency, Ninety-Second Congress, 1st Sess., 1971, p. 72; portions of this testimony and a fuller discussion appear in J. K. Lieberman, *How the Government Breaks the Law,* (1973), pp. 144-151.

353 — 1971 jury trial case: *McKeiver* v. *Pennsylvania,* 403 U.S. 528 (1971).

353 — Study published two years after: Platt, *The Child Savers,* pp. 168, 175.

353 — Juvenile crime: According to FBI Uniform Crime Reports, quoted by Irving R. Kaufman, *New York Law Journal,* August 22, 1975, p. 1.

Chapter Nineteen: The Privacy of One's Body

358 — Three reasons: Reviewed in Betty Sarvis and Hyman Rodman, *The Abortion Controversy,* (1971), pp. 16-20. *Griswold* v. *Connecticut,* 381 U.S. 479 (1965).

362 — *Potential:* The italics are Justice Blackmun's.

364 — *Doe* v. *Bolton,* 410 U.S. 179 (1973).

366 — Missouri abortion law appeal: *Danforth* v. *Planned Parenthood,* No. 74-1419.

367 — National study: *New York Times,* October 7, 1975, p. 16.

Chapter Twenty : The President Is Under the Law

Page 372 — Perquisites: Dan Cordtz, "The Imperial Life Style of the U.S. President," *Fortune,* October 1973, p. 143.

372 — Facts and quotations not otherwise cited were culled from Congressional Quarterly, *Watergate: Chronology of a Crisis,* Vol. 1, 1973; Leon Friedman, ed., *United States* v. *Nixon, The President Before the Supreme Court,* (1974).

375 — Guidelines: Congressional Quarterly, *Watergate: Chronology of a Crisis,* Vol. 1, p. 47.

375 — Cox quoted in *Id.,* p. 96.

376 — Truman's letter is reprinted in *Id.,* p. 190.

378 — First president since Jefferson: President Monroe received a court-martial subpoena; though he did not personally appear, he did submit answers to written interrogatories; Friedman, *United States* v. *Nixon,* pp. 458-59.

378 — The Watergate committee eventually lost its lawsuit to enforce its subpoena.

380 — *United States* v. *Burr,* 25 Fed. Cas. 187, Case No. 14,694 (Cir. Ct. 1807).

381 — Wright argument: Friedman, *United States* v. *Nixon,* p. 8.

381 — 800 cases: Cited by Alan Westin, in his introduction to Friedman, *United States* v. *Nixon,* p. xviii.

381 — Wiretapping case: *United States* v. *United States District Court,* 407 U.S. 297 (1972).

382 — Steel Seizure Case: *Youngstown Sheet & Tube Co.* v. *Sawyer,* 343 U.S. 579 (1952).

382 — U.S. Court of Appeals quoted: *Nixon* v. *Sirica,* 487 F.2d 700 (D.C. Cir. 1973).

382 — Baldridge quoted in Alan F. Westin, *The Anatomy of a Constitutional Law Case,* (1958), p. 62.

384 — Sirica's ruling: *In re Grand Jury Subpoena Duces Tecum Issued to Richard M. Nixon,* 360 F.Supp. 1 (D.D.C. 1973).

386 — Cox firing unlawful: *Nader* v. *Bork,* 366 F.Supp. 104 (D.D.C. 1973).

386 — The seven were John N. Mitchell, H. R. Haldeman, John D. Ehrlichman, Charles W. Colson, Robert C. Mardian, Kenneth W. Parkinson, and Gordon Strachan. The first five were ultimately convicted and, except for Colson, who pleaded guilty, their appeals are pending as this is written.

387 — "Special fire" of St. Clair brief: Friedman, *United States* v. *Nixon,* p. 327; "no such authority in annals of American jurisprudence": *Id.,* p. 207.

388 — "One point with crystal clarity": *Id.,* p. 476.

389 — St. Clair colloquy: *Id.,* p. 557.

390 — St. Clair/Marshall colloquy: *Id.,* pp. 579-80.

391 — Jaworski quoted in *Id.,* p. 529.

395 — The ruling in *United States* v. *Nixon* by no means settled all the problems surrounding the concept of "executive

privilege." In fact it settled only the one, narrow question raised. The far more vexing problem of the president's right to withhold information from Congress, completely untouched by the Court's decision, and always the more serious of the two general issues, remains. At this writing, the secretary of state has refused to turn over to a House Select Committee on Intelligence documents dealing with the nation's intelligence-gathering capacity. The dispute centers on documents that purportedly detail dissent within the State Department, raising memories of the days of McCarthyism when an irresponsible Senate investigation destroyed careers and seriously undermined the morale and effectiveness of the Department. See, e.g., *New York Times,* October 26, 1975, Section 4, p. 2. The general problem of congressional-executive disputes over confidential information is treated comprehensively in Raoul Berger, *Executive Privilege: A Constitutional Myth,* (1974), criticized in Abraham D. Sofear, Book Review, 88 *Harv. L. Rev.* 281 (1974).

Page 395 — The last line, of course, is from Gerald R. Ford's Inaugural Address on August 9, 1974.

Index

He has obstructed the Administration of Justice, by refusing his Assent

He has made Judges dependent on his Will alone, for the Tenure of th

He has erected a Multitude of new Offices, and sent hither Swarms of C

He has kept among us, in Times of Peace, Standing Armies, without

He has affected to render the Military independent of and superior to th

He has combined with others to subject us to a Jurisdiction foreign to ou pretended Legislation:

For quartering large Bodies of Armed Troops among us:

For protecting them, by a mock Trial, from Punishment for any Mur

For cutting off our Trade with all Parts of the World:

For imposing Taxes on us without our Consent:

For depriving us, in many Cases, of the Benefits of Trial by Jury:

For transporting us beyond Seas to be tried for pretended Offences:

For abolishing the free System of English Laws in a neighbouring Prov

as to render it at once an Example and fit Instrument for introducing the sa

For taking away our Charters, abolishing our most valuable Laws, and

For suspending our own Legislatures, and declaring themselves invested

He has abdicated Government here, by declaring us out of his Protectio

He has plundered our Seas, ravaged our Coasts, burnt our Towns, and

He is, at this Time, transporting large Armies of foreign Mercenaries

cumstances of Cruelty and Perfidy, scarcely paralleled in the most barbarou

He has constrained our fellow Citizens taken Captive on the high Seas to

Brethren, or to fall themselves by their Hands.

He has excited domestic Insurrections amongst us, and has endeavoured

known Rule of Warfare, is an undistinguished Destruction, of all Ages, Sexe

In every stage of these Oppressions we have Petitioned for Redress in

ed Injury. A Prince, whose Character is thus marked by every act which

Nor have we been wanting in Attentions to our British Brethren. We

unwarrantable Jurisdiction over us. We have reminded them of the Circum

Justice and Magnanimity, and we have conjured them by the Ties of our c

Connections and Correspondence. They too have been deaf to the Voice of

denounces our Separation, and hold them, as we hold the rest of Mankind,

We, therefore, the Representatives of the UNITED STAT

pealing to the Supreme Judge of the World for the Rectitude of our Intenti

lemnly Publish and Declare, That these United Colonies are, and of Right

absolved from all Allegiance to the British Crown, and that all political C

solved; and that as Free and Independent States

Commerce, and to do all other Acts and Things which Independe

firm Reliance on the Protection of divine Providence, we mutually pledge to

Signed by ORDER

JOHN

Attest.

CHARLES THOMSON, Secretar

PHILADELPHIA: